PUBLIC RECORDS

IN CLASSIC.

STUDIES IN THE HISTORY OF GREECE AND ROME

P. J. Rhodes and Richard J. A. Talbert, editors

JAMES P. SICKINGER

Public Records and Archives
in Classical Athens

THE UNIVERSITY OF NORTH CAROLINA PRESS

CHAPEL HILL AND LONDON

© 1999 The University of North Carolina Press

All rights reserved

Designed by April Leidig-Higgins

Set in Minion by Keystone Typesetting, Inc.

Manufactured in the United States of America

The paper in this book meets the guidelines for permanence
and durability of the Committee on Production Guidelines for
Book Longevity of the Council on Library Resources.

Library of Congress Cataloging-in-Publication Data

Sickinger, James P. Public records and archives in classical Athens
/ by James P. Sickinger.

p. cm.—(Studies in the history of Greece and Rome)

Includes bibliographical references (p.) and index.

ISBN-13: 978-0-8078-2469-6 (cloth: alk. paper)

ISBN-13: 978-0-8078-5851-6 (pbk. : alk. paper)

1. Archives—Greece—Athens—History—To 500. 2. Paleography,
Greek—Greece—Athens. 3. Public records—Greece—Athens
—History—To 500. 4. Greece—History—To 146 B.C.—Archival
resources. I. Title. II. Series.

CD996.S53 1999   352.3'87'09385—dc21   98-30098 CIP

03 02 01 00 99   5 4 3 2 1

FOR MY WIFE AND PARENTS

CONTENTS

This study of written records and archives in ancient Athens has its origins in a dissertation on the Metroon and fourth-century Athenian archives submitted to the Department of Classics at Brown University in 1992. My interests in Athenian record keeping stemmed from the use of documents by the fourth-century Attic orators and in works such as the *Athēnaiōn Politeia*. But although these issues have been the subject of considerable scholarly debate, a comprehensive study of the Metroon's archives and Athenian record keeping in general has not appeared since that of C. Curtius, *Das Metroon als Staatsarchiv in Athen*, published in 1868. So a new study seemed in order. Chapters that formed part of the dissertation have been completely revised for the present book, and several new chapters have been added that consider the keeping of written records by the Athenian people and their magistrates down to the end of the fifth century. Most writing and revisions were completed in December 1996, and I have incorporated references to only a limited number of works that reached me after that date.

Quotations in Greek have been confined to the notes in the attempt to keep my discussion accessible to Greekless readers, but I have not discovered a wholly satisfactory or consistent method of rendering Greek into English in the text itself. My practice has been to retain latinate or anglicized forms for commonly known Greek authors and terms, but I have generally transliterated less familiar words directly from Greek into English.

Completion of this book would not have been possible without the assistance of numerous institutions and individuals. Financial support from the United States Educational Foundation in Greece and the American School of Classical Studies at Athens allowed me to visit Greece and complete most of my dissertation there. I would like to thank Professor W. D. E. Coulson, former director of the American School, and Dr. Nancy Winter, librarian of the Blegen Library, for allowing me access to the school's facilities and for creating a congenial atmosphere in which to carry out my work. Work on the book itself was largely completed while I held a grant from the National Endowment of the Humanities, whose support I gratefully acknowledge.

Professors C. W. Fornara, K. A. Raaflaub, and W. F. Wyatt Jr. served as readers of the dissertation and offered valuable suggestions on several points of argument and detail. Professor L. J. Samons and Dr. J. Kennelly read through an earlier draft of the book, and their notes and queries have saved me from many errors of both fact and omission. Professor R. S. Stroud read and critiqued a penultimate draft, and his detailed comments caused me to rethink my arguments in several places. I am also grateful to the anonymous readers of the University of North Carolina Press for their comments and criticism on a difficult manuscript, and to Lewis Bateman of the University of North Carolina Press for his patience through numerous delays. My greatest debts are to Professor A. L. Boegehold, who supervised the original dissertation and has since offered encouragement and guidance. His teaching and scholarship have served as models of excellence, which I still strive to emulate.

My deepest thanks go to my parents, Richard and Eileen Sickinger, who have provided unfailing support throughout my education and early career, and to my wife Katherine, who helped with proofreading and put up with much else while this book was in the making.

PUBLIC RECORDS AND ARCHIVES
IN CLASSICAL ATHENS

In the course of a speech delivered before an Athenian lawcourt in 330, the orator and politician Aeschines offered the following praise of written records and their preservation: "A fine thing, my fellow Athenians, a fine thing is the preservation of public records. For records do not change, and they do not shift sides with traitors, but they grant to you, the people, the opportunity to know, whenever you want, which men, once bad, through some transformation now claim to be good."[1] Aeschines made these comments at a trial in a *graphē paranomōn*, a legal procedure used against unconstitutional proposals, that he had brought against his fellow Athenian Ktesiphon. Six years earlier, Ktesiphon had proposed a decree honoring the politician Demosthenes for his services to Athens. Aeschines' indictment claimed that the motion was unconstitutional not only on procedural but also on substantive grounds: the honors proposed for Demosthenes were both illegally moved and undeserved. To prove this second point, Aeschines cites and has read out to the court several official documents illustrating Demosthenes' political career over the preceding twenty years. Because of their preservation, Aeschines claims in this passage, the jurors could judge both the expediency and patriotism of Demosthenes' past public acts.

At the time of Aeschines' speech, many Athenian public records were housed in the Metroon, the sanctuary of the Mother of the Gods, and most scholars believe that that building served in some capacity as a state archives during the fourth century. Beyond that point, however, little agreement exists about the form and nature of its holdings. The Metroon is thought by some scholars to have held copies of every state document; others argue that its holdings were extremely limited, haphazardly arranged, and poorly organized. Even more controversial are questions surrounding the nature of Athenian public records before the Metroon's foundation in the late fifth century. There is some agreement that the laws of Drakon and Solon, the city's earliest written laws, survived into later times, but how and even if public records were routinely made and preserved, even as late as the fifth century, are matters of some debate. One scholarly view holds that the Athenians maintained no archives of state documents, and that the only permanent copies of most texts were those inscribed and publicly displayed on stone stelai. Another popular view maintains that archives of state documents did exist but were scattered around Athens at the offices of different magistrates.

Uncertainty is not a result of a lack of interest, as issues related to Athenian public records have attracted a good deal of attention over the past century.[2] Ancient, narrative accounts of Athenian history during the seventh and sixth centuries first appear in sources of the late fifth and fourth centuries, and their historical reliability depends to some extent on the degree to which their authors had access to authentic materials, including written records of an official nature, dating back to the archaic period. Consequently, scholars have considered in some detail whether early documents, especially texts of laws and decrees, were preserved and accessible to the writers who are our chief sources for the political history of early Athens. Some have argued that authentic, written materials did survive, but others take a more skeptical stance and question whether the Athenians were so careful in their preservation of old written records, pointing out, among other things, that not until the late fifth century did the Athenians establish the Metroon as an archives building, where many important state documents were henceforth housed.

In more recent years, questions surrounding the use of written records in Athens have attracted interest from a different perspective, that of ancient literacy. Many scholars now question the traditional but often tacit assumption that classical Athens was in any sense a literate society, at least before the fourth century. The arguments advanced in favor of this view are many and complex, but the Athenian use of writing and documents in public life has played no small role in the debate. It is now clear that the institutions of Athenian society retained oral practices long after the introduction of writing, and that even in those areas in which literacy made some inroads, written texts were often supplemented by information preserved orally. The foundation of the Metroon as an archives building at the end of the fifth century represents something of a turning point, and over the course of the fourth century documents were used increasingly as their probative value in many areas came to be recognized.

One feature shared by many studies, regardless of their perspective, is that Athenian documents and record keeping are approached only as a secondary concern. That is, scholars have often examined the use of written records by the Athenians not as a question in its own right, but as prelude to discussions of related but broader issues. Thus, historians of Athenian political and constitutional history generally address the preservation of early written records by the Athenians in the context of studies of Athenian political history or the development of Athenian law. This approach is both natural and reasonable, for only by assessing the foundations of later traditions can we determine their value in reconstructing the history of the archaic period, which is so crucial for understanding aspects of the democracy of the fifth and fourth centuries. It is seldom possible to know with absolute certainty whether a particular tradition, such as a reference to a Solonian law, goes back to an authentic document, but it is also at times difficult to determine whether the conclusions of some scholars about the preservation of early written records are informed more by preconceived notions about the nature of archaic Athenian society than ancient evidence for the preservation of Athenian state documents. More important, by focusing primarily on the degree to which official documents informed later accounts of early Athenian history, scholars tend to overlook types of documents that once existed but made no mark on accounts of literary sources.

Studies that treat Athenian documents from the perspective of ancient literacy and orality sometimes exhibit a similar characteristic. Among the most notable advances in classical scholarship over the past decade has been the realization that modern, rationalist attitudes toward literacy do not account for the diversity of uses that writing enjoyed in antiquity: not only were ancient societies less literate than modern ones; they also used writing in very different ways. Written texts served as transmitters of information but also as symbolic objects conveying nontextual messages, and many literate practices can only be understood in the context of societies that still relied primarily on oral modes of communication. This emphasis on the nonliterate, oral background to ancient writing has provided a welcome reaction to the earlier tendency to take ancient, and Athenian, literacy for granted. But by stressing the oral character of Athenian society and the late date of writing's impact in many areas of Athenian life, scholars have sometimes downplayed or ignored evidence for more advanced uses of writing, especially in the realm of written records. The Athenians undoubtedly retained oral practices in their public and private institutions. But they also made, used, and kept written records related to their public business from a very early time, much earlier than some works on literacy and orality imply, and the evidence for these uses deserves fuller airing on its own terms.

The keeping of official, written records of state business at Athens, then, forms the subject of this study. Its aim is not to examine the possibly documentary origin of every tradition about early Athenian history, to determine the authenticity of every Athenian document cited or quoted in an ancient source, or to explore the complex workings of literacy and its functions in Athenian society. It seeks instead to trace the growth in use of written documents for records of a public nature from their earliest appearances down to the establishment of the Metroon, the sanctuary of the Mother of the Gods, as the state archives of Athens at the end of the fifth century B.C. Emphasis will fall on written texts of laws, decrees, and other documents reflecting the activities of the Athenian Boule and Ekklesia. Although other types of documents will be discussed, it has proved impossible to consider fully the record-keeping practices of Athenian boards, magistrates, and subdivisions of the Athenian state, especially because of the volume of evidence in the fifth, fourth, and later centuries. In terms of laws, decrees, and other state documents, the investigation will especially focus not on the more familiar texts of Athenian documents published on stone, but on those texts that were recorded on media such as wooden tablets and papyrus, were kept in archival collections, and have not survived to the present day. These uninscribed records, it is argued, were the principal documents of Athenian society, and their study forms a necessary first step for a proper evaluation of writing and its role in Athenian public life.

This focus on records not inscribed on stone may require a brief discussion. Apart from the Parthenon and other architectural monuments of classical Athens, stone inscriptions constitute perhaps the most tangible remains of the ancient Athenian democracy. The Athenians began to publish some state documents on stone in the late sixth century, but the practice gained widespread currency around the middle of the fifth century, from which time documents ranging from financial accounts to honorary decrees were displayed on stone stelai. Scholarly study of epigraphical texts has done much to enhance modern understanding of many areas of Athenian political, economic, and social history. Inscriptions were also important documents in antiquity. They are referred to with some frequency by ancient writers, especially the Attic orators, and the Athenians recognized that stone inscriptions recorded valid and authoritative documents. The authoritative quality of inscribed texts has led some scholars to believe that documents on stone were the principal documents of Athenian society, on the assumption that if archival texts had existed, their texts and not ones on stone should have been referred to and cited with greater frequency. Most recognize that the Athenians also used documents written on other materials, but because stone documents survive in large numbers and are therefore more accessible, their texts and practices related to their use have served as the basis for many of the broader and often negative conclusions about Athenian record keeping and Athenian attitudes toward written documents.

But documents on stone formed only a small part of the much larger picture of Athenian public records. Not every official document, not even every law and decree, was published on a stone stele in any period. Indeed, the practice of erecting stelai inscribed with state documents seems to have been a relatively late phenomenon: the Athenians had been keeping written records of public decisions and using written documents in the administration of public business long before they started to publish in large numbers some documents on stone in the decades around 450. In addition, the documents that were displayed on stone were often drawn from fuller collections of texts that magistrates created and used while going about their business. Many of the documents not published on stone were destroyed as soon as their immediate usefulness expired, but others were preserved for periods of several years, decades, and even centuries. Unlike documents on stone, these archival texts do not survive. We learn of their existence and their contents from chance references in literary texts, and further information can be extracted from documents that were displayed on stone. Reconstructions based on evidence such as this necessarily involve some degree of speculation, and definitive answers to many questions will remain elusive. Evidence, however, there is, and much of it cannot be adequately explained on the view that inscriptions served as the primary or only permanent documents of Athenian society. However important inscriptions may have been to the Athenians, many features of epigraphical texts are comprehensible only when understood within a broader framework of documents written and kept on other materials.

Use of the terms "archive" and "archives" in this study may also require some explanation. Scholars have sometimes questioned their applicability and warned that their use in connection with ancient collections of documents is potentially anachronistic.[3] According to some modern definitions, documents or records become archival only when they cease to be in current use and are judged to possess long-term or enduring value; the latter step sometimes involves transfer to a centralized, archival agency. Not all modern documents and records possess such enduring value, so all documents and records cannot be labeled archival.[4] Since it is not clear that the Athenians or other ancient peoples recognized a distinction between current and noncurrent records, it may be anachronistic to speak of ancient archives according to this definition. But archival terminology is not entirely uniform, and archives can also refer more generally to documents and records from the time they are created and received by officials or public agencies, even while they remain in current use.[5] It is in this more general sense that the term archives will be used in this study, a usage that seems justified by etymology. The word archives itself derives ultimately from the Greek word *archeion* and denoted a building or place occupied by a city's magistracies (*archai*); later it and its plural *archeia* came to apply not only to particular buildings but also to the objects, including documents, housed within those buildings. The Athenians, in fact, did not use the word *archeia* to describe the documents and records of their magistrates, but these officials did use and keep written records of the official business and transactions they oversaw, and the Athenian people as a whole maintained records of the decisions they themselves made as a community. Exploration of questions related to these archives—the types of documents they included, how they were organized, the ways in which the Athenians made use of them—is the chief aim of this study.

The laws of Drakon and Solon, which were written down in the late seventh and early sixth centuries respectively, are some of the best attested and perhaps the earliest written records of Athenian society. Chapter 1 therefore returns to their work and attempts to assess the extent of their legislation, particularly in light of suggestions that legislation of early Greek lawgivers was more limited in scope than ancient sources for their work suggest. Chapter 2 traces the expanding uses of written documents and records by Athenian officials in the sixth century, and focuses on the appearance of Athenian secretaries and the survival of some records for centuries. The sixth century, it is argued, was pivotal in the development of public uses of writing and laid the groundwork for practices more evident in later periods. Chapter 3 examines Athenian record keeping in the fifth century, focusing especially on the archives of the Boule. The relationship between the archival texts of documents and documents on stone is considered, as is the old view, which has recently regained popularity, that stone inscriptions were the archives of Athens and the only permanent texts of many state documents. In Chapter 4 two developments of the late fifth century are discussed: the revision of the Athenian law code and establishment of the Metroon as a state archives building. It is argued there that both developments responded not to an earlier failure of the Athenians to maintain written records or archives of their public business, but to the vast accumulation of archival texts over the course of the fifth century and the peculiar manner in which written records were preserved and organized in the fifth-century archives of the Boule.

The remaining three chapters focus on the Metroon and several as-

pects of its archives. Since the nature of Metroon as an archival repository is related to the types of documents housed within it, Chapter 5
examines in detail the contents of the Metroon with a view toward
determining how narrow or broad its holdings actually were. Chapter 6
looks at the state officials who administered and worked with these
archives and attempts to reconstruct how some of the Metroon's documents were arranged and organized. Chapter 7 then investigates some of
the contexts and situations in which the Metroon's archives were used
and consulted by Athenian citizens. The Conclusion traces the history of
the Metroon and its holdings in the Hellenistic and later periods, and
offers some final observations on the use and preservation of written
records in the Athenian democracy of the classical period.

CHAPTER ONE

Thesmothetai, Drakon, and Solon

The origins of public record keeping at Athens are obscure. Some Athenians were familiar with the newly created Greek alphabet by the middle of the eighth century, and from that time the number of examples of Attic writing on pottery, stone, and other materials increases markedly. Conspicuously absent, however, from the corpus of early inscriptions are any texts that might be characterized as documentary in character; financial records, official lists, legislative texts are not represented. The earliest Athenian laws or decrees on stone date from the late sixth century and take the form of regulations concerning the Eleusinian Mysteries and a decree of the Athenian *dēmos* concerning settlers on Salamis. But even then the quantity of official texts remains small until around 450, at which time the Athenians began to inscribe decrees, financial records, and other state documents on stone with greater frequency.[1]

In the absence of contemporary epigraphical material we are forced to reconstruct the early development of public writing at Athens from literary sources of later date. These suggest that writing was first introduced into the official life of the city to record laws. Traditions of the classical period spoke of two early lawgivers, Drakon and Solon, who were responsible for Athens' earliest written laws. Drakon lived in the late seventh century, and his laws originally covered many subjects. Later generations knew them for their severity, but only his laws on homicide remained in force into the classical period. Solon was active about a generation after Drakon. He repealed all of Drakon's laws, except for those on homicide, and issued new ones touching on many areas of public and private life. The Athenians often referred to laws of Drakon and Solon, which they believed provided the foundation of the laws still used by them in the fifth and fourth centuries.

Although most modern accounts of early Athens rely in varying degrees on later traditions, especially those surrounding Solon, the same traditions pose numerous problems of interpretation, as scholars have long recognized. The ancient Greeks were fond of attributing significant developments, inventions, and discoveries to individual figures from their past, some of whom were historical, others mythical; stories about the work of Drakon and Solon reflect this tendency. Details about the life of Drakon were scant already in the fifth century, and by the same century Solon had become a legendary figure around whom circulated many stories of dubious historicity. The Athenians of the fourth century ascribed laws and reforms to Drakon and Solon wrongly, and their view that Solon was the author of most or all their laws is demonstrably false. These contradictions illustrate the weaknesses of the literary tradition, and although they do not invalidate it entirely, they serve as strong reminders of the challenges facing any reconstruction based on its contents.[2]

Apart from doubts about the authenticity of individual laws, the false attribution of laws to Drakon and Solon raises broader questions about their preservation and the ability of Athenians of the fifth and fourth centuries to differentiate them from later legislation. Some historians take the failings of the literary accounts about Drakon and Solon as evidence that little authentic information actually survived about them, including texts of their laws. The Athenians could ascribe many measures to their early lawgivers because they had no way of knowing what laws the two had actually issued; their original laws were so confused with subsequent legislation that it was impossible to distinguish Drakontian and Solonian originals from later accretions.[3] Doubts about the authenticity of individual laws have also led to doubts about the scope of their work and the issuance of large-scale law codes in the seventh and sixth centuries more generally. Many scholars now believe that written laws first appeared in the Greek world not in large codes issued by individual lawgivers, but more gradually and anonymously and in response to very specific situations and crises. This is shown not only by the literary traditions about early lawgivers, but also by the inscribed laws surviving from the archaic period, which consist largely of individual measures addressing specific topics, not broad, comprehensive codes. On this view, figures like Drakon and Solon might have played some role in the development of written law, but their contributions were more limited in scope than later traditions suggest.[4]

The earliest written laws of Athens form the subject of this chapter. Its aim, however, is not to reexamine all the evidence for the work of

Drakon and Solon or to reconstruct the background to and content of their legislation in detail; excellent surveys are available elsewhere. But the origins, scope, and preservation of their laws do demand our attention. The laws of Drakon and Solon enjoyed a special status in the minds of later generations of Athenians, and attitudes toward their texts should have some effect on how we assess the Athenians' treatment of their laws, decrees, and public records in general. For if the Athenians were careless and haphazard in the preservation of their earliest written laws, it will not be surprising to find similar practices reflected in attitudes toward state documents of the fifth and fourth centuries. But if the laws of Drakon and Solon were still available in later times, we will have some reason to believe that the Athenians attached some importance to the preservation of public records. The evidence, I shall argue, supports the latter case. This evidence is certainly not unproblematic, and arguments for the survival of early laws are not meant to prove the reliability of all later traditions about Drakon and Solon. But some elements of these traditions are more reliable than others, and working from them we can reach some tentative conclusions about the extent, organization, and later treatment of Athens' earliest written records.

1. Thesmothetai

Before turning to the lawgiving of Drakon and Solon, we must first consider a passage of the *Athēnaiōn Politeia* with possible significance for the development of record keeping and written law at Athens. Aristotle says that thesmothetai were first chosen "so that having written up *ta thesmia* they might preserve them for the judgment of disputes."[5] The thesmothetai of the classical period were judicial magistrates, six in number, with authority over specific types of cases. Aristotle's account suggests that the office was created to write down and keep texts called *thesmia*, which many scholars believe were records of judicial decisions issued in individual cases or the principles underlying those decisions.[6] By Aristotle's reckoning, appointment of the first thesmothetai occurred after the chief archonship had become an annual office, an event dated to 683/2 in Athenian tradition, but before the legislation of Drakon, whose work was traditionally put in 621/0.[7] If the dating and the duties described by Aristotle are correct, some Athenian magistrates were writing down, using, and preserving written documents in the administration of their duties sometime around the middle of the seventh century. More important, this information, if authentic, might also support the view that the earliest written laws of the Greek world appeared not as the result of the work of specially appointed lawgivers, but more gradually and at the hands of regular magistrates carrying out their normal duties.

Can we accept Aristotle's account? Scholarly opinion is divided; some scholars accept it and assume, implicitly or explicitly, that Aristotle drew on authentic material.[8] Others are more skeptical, and with good reason. The duties assigned by Aristotle to the thesmothetai are essentially scribal or secretarial in nature: they are to record and keep *thesmia*. This is odd, because the thesmothetai of the fifth and fourth centuries were judicial officials who presided over certain types of legal proceedings, and apart from this passage there is little reason to suppose that they were ever anything but magistrates with judicial duties. It is also difficult to believe that six annually elected officials were required to exercise the scribal duties described by Aristotle already in the seventh century. In addition, the *thesmia* that the thesmothetai are said to have recorded can hardly have been judicial decisions, as some scholars have believed. Not only would the keeping of an archive of judicial verdicts be unparalleled (we have little evidence for such archives even in later periods), but the meaning "verdicts" or "judgments" is unparalleled.[9] A *thesmion* was a basic rule, institution, or even a law. Such rules or laws might have arisen from judgments issued in individual cases, but *thesmion* is nowhere else used to refer to an actual judgment. Aristotle should be understood to mean that the thesmothetai kept some type of early written legal rules or laws. But this interpretation conflicts with the tradition, attested later in the *Athēnaiōn Politeia* itself (*Ath. Pol.* 41.2), that Drakon was the first to write down laws for the Athenians. Because of difficulties such as these, many scholars have doubted that Aristotle had any authentic details about the function of the first thesmothetai, and it is regularly assumed that he based his description on an inference he drew from the title of their office.[10]

These objections are weighty but not decisive. First, although it is true that Aristotle assigns the original thesmothetai primarily scribal duties, he also says that they recorded and kept *thesmia* for use in settling disputes (*pros tēn krisin amphisboutontōn*); a judicial function seems implicit in these duties. Second, the supposed contradiction with Drakon's role as the first Athenian to issue written laws is not as grave as some have supposed, because that tradition is weak. It surfaces later in the *Athēnaiōn Politeia* (41.2) in a list of historical changes in the Athenian constitution. We read there that "in the time of Drakon they [sc. the Athenians] first wrote down laws."[11] Oddly, it is not Drakon but the Athenians in general who are said to have first recorded laws. This use of the plural may be a careless slip, or it may reflect an ill-considered attempt to reconcile Drakon's role as lawgiver with the earlier statement that the thesmothetai had issued written *thesmia*. But whatever the explanation, reference to Drakon's constitution in this list is problematic for other reasons. Unlike each of the other constitutional changes mentioned in the list, Drakon's constitution is not numbered and the entire sentence is widely regarded as an addition to the text, carelessly inserted there at the same time that the false constitution of Drakon was added at chapter 4 of the *Athēnaiōn Politeia*.[12] If the sentence is indeed a later insertion, the contradiction between the recording of written *thesmia* by the thesmothetai and the alleged priority of the lawgiving of Drakon may not be so serious; at the very least, we ought not dismiss Aristotle's account of the first thesmothetai because of the conflicting testimony of a notoriously problematic passage. Drakon may have been remembered as the oldest Athenian lawgiver, but the tradition making him the first Athenian to use writing to write down laws is too weak to be marshaled against the potentially conflicting testimony about the duties of the first thesmothetai.[13]

Nor are we compelled to accept the view that Aristotle's account of the earliest thesmothetai is based on his etymology for the term *thesmothetai*. Thesmothetai are, literally, officials who make *thesmoi*, not *thesmia*. *Thesmos* was in fact the term used by the Athenians for their oldest laws, and Aristotle's use of a different term to describe the texts recorded by the first thesmothetai may suggest that something other than etymology underlies his account. A later passage in the *Athēnaiōn Politeia* may offer a clue to his sources. Aristotle quotes (*Ath. Pol.* 16.10) what he believed was an old Athenian law (*nomos*) on tyranny outlawing anyone who established or assisted in the establishment of a tyrant. But Aristotle's quotation of the law is preceded by the words "the following are *thesmia* and ancestral practices [*patria*] of the Athenians."[14] These prefatory words are significant in several respects. First, they show that Aristotle equated *nomoi*, the fourth-century term for laws, with *thesmia*; he understood *thesmia* to be some type of general, legal rules. Second, the preface to the tyranny law uses the plural *thesmia*, which could suggest that the provision on tyranny was only one of several measures included in Aristotle's source.[15] Third, the preface reveals that Aristotle's source for this *thesmion* consisted of two, chronologically distinct layers: the old law on tyranny itself and the preface declaring it ancestral. Scholars have usually thought that the preface was added when the old law on tyranny was renewed or republished. Ostwald believed this renewal took place after Hippias, the son of Peisistratos, was expelled as tyrant in the year 511/10, and that the original measure was part of Drakon's legislation.

Gagarin has argued that the old tyranny law was a *thesmion* recorded by the thesmothetai, later incorporated into the laws of Solon. Other contexts are also possible.[16] But at whatever time the preface was appended to the collection of *thesmia*, it is significant that those responsible for making that collection chose to call them *thesmia* and not *thesmoi*, the term regularly applied to the laws of Drakon and Solon; *thesmia* were distinguished from the legislation of the two lawgivers. How this distinction was made is unclear, but it is reasonable to suppose that there was some basis on which to make it.

Aristotle's access to a collection of *thesmia* should caution us not to reject out of hand his account of the thesmothetai's origin and in particular their use of written *thesmia*. He quotes a single provision from what may have been a larger collection; here and elsewhere his sources for early Athenian history were probably more detailed than his brief sketch suggests. But perhaps we may go further. Renewal or republication of older measures will have involved more than a simple statement declaring them ancestral; it might have also included other introductory or explanatory material. When the Athenians reaffirmed some ancestral practices (*patria*) of the Praxiergidai, an Athenian clan with connections with the cult of Athena, around the middle of the fifth century, they did not publish the *patria* without explanation. They prefaced the list of *patria* with a decree responding to a request of the Praxiergidai and prescribing publication of their *patria* on stone. They also published an oracle of Apollo in some way related to these *patria*, though its connection to them is not entirely clear.[17] In the same way, we may guess (and it is only a guess) that a decree or introductory statement preceding the *thesmia* included the tyranny law and explained the reasons for its re-enactment or republication. From this preliminary material Aristotle may have inferred a connection between *thesmia* and thesmothetai, and this served as the basis for his account of the functions of the earliest thesmothetai.[18] Aristotle's source need not have explained the origins of the thesmothetai in precisely same way that he relates them, and his description of their duties may be an inference, but it is far from obvious that his inference was based on etymology alone.

An association of Aristotle's account of the thesmothetai's origins with the collection of *thesmia* that included the law on tyranny cannot of course be proved. But it explains how Aristotle arrived at the original duties of these magistrates, and it provides a source for his account, something that is necessary if we are to put any weight on its details. Once we accept that Aristotle's account relies on more than etymology, we gain possibly valuable information about the origins of written law at

Athens. At some point in the seventh century one or several Athenian thesmothetai wrote down rules or regulations they intended to follow as they adjudicated disputes that came to them; other magistrates may have followed their lead. What circumstances led them to take this step and on what authority they published these rules we do not know. The thesmothetai of the classical period were concerned with disputes that fell outside areas traditionally handled by the archon, *basileus* (the "king" archon), and polemarch (the "war" archon), the original chief magistrates of Athens, and when the thesmothetai were first appointed it may have been thought desirable, by individual thesmothetai or by the Athenians responsible for their appointment, to fix in writing the rules, in terms of procedures or penalties, that these officials were to apply as they decided cases.[19] Thesmothetai may have based these rules on precedents set by earlier cases or they may have drafted them anew in anticipation of conflicts or crises threatening the community. Such rules were called *thesmia*. If Aristotle is correct in his belief that the thesmothetai preserved their *thesmia* for use in judging cases, the texts of *thesmia* may have been handed down from one year's board of thesmothetai to the next. How many *thesmia* existed cannot be determined, but their number was probably never very large, and most aspects of the Athenian legal system during the seventh century remained governed by custom and unwritten practices. Some *thesmia*, however, like the old tyranny law cited by Aristotle, may have survived by being incorporated into later legislation.[20]

Rules promulgated by individual magistrates may not have been laws in the sense of measures ratified by an assembly of citizens or issued by a lawgiver or commission entrusted with the specific task of framing laws. Their authority and the willingness of members of the community to accept them may have depended on little more than the prestige of the individual magistrates who issued them, and we have no way of knowing whether thesmothetai were bound to abide by any *thesmia* left to them by their predecessors. But the significance of these early written rules should not be underestimated. The first official use of writing at Athens was not the work of a great lawgiver, but of individual magistrates who adapted the new technique for practical use in dealing with situations they faced in the course of their duties.

II. Drakon

The possible recording of legal rules or laws by Athenian officials around the middle of the seventh century deprives Drakon of his place as Athens' first lawgiver. But it does not deprive Drakon of any significance in the development of Athenian record keeping, writing, and law. The Athenians remembered Drakon as their earliest lawgiver and the author of the homicide laws they used in the fifth and fourth centuries. They dated his lawgiving to the archonship of Aristaichmos, which fell in 621/0, and believed he had originally issued laws on a number of crimes ranging from homicide and theft to idleness; the penalties provided by these laws were proverbial for their severity. But Solon had repealed the laws of Drakon leaving only those on homicide in force.[21]

Other details about Drakon and his legislation were few in number and vague in content. Sealey points out that the Athenian tradition of two lawgivers is anomalous in the Greek world. Most Greek cities knew only one lawgiver, so Sealey suggests that Drakon was not a historical person but a sacred snake (Drakon means "snake") who lived on the Acropolis and on whose authority early laws were issued. The tradition that Drakon was a real person who had issued many laws, most of which were repealed by Solon, was a product of fourth-century rationalization and arose to account for a real distinction in the Athenian law code between some laws attributed to Drakon and others attributed to Solon.[22] These arguments are weak. The distinction in the Athenian law code was genuine and preceded the fourth century. But we have no evidence that the Athenians ever believed in a sacred origin for their laws, much less that they viewed a sacred snake on the Acropolis as a source of their laws. The anomalous nature of the Athenian tradition of two lawgivers may in fact be an argument in favor of its authenticity. For if other cities regularly credited a single, ancient lawgiver with authorship of their laws, why should the Athenians not have simply attributed all their laws to a single lawgiver as well? The simplest explanation for the two lawgivers of Athenian tradition is that two individuals were the authors of some of the city's oldest laws.

Still, we are left with few details about the historical Drakon. No source reveals the circumstances in which he issued his laws. Many scholars connect his work with the attempt of an Athenian aristocrat named Kylon to make himself tyrant of Athens sometime in the late 630s.[23] This plot failed, but it precipitated a series of blood feuds and vendettas, which the homicide legislation of Drakon sought to mitigate. Traditions in other states attest to similar conditions of civic unrest leading to the appointment of lawgivers, so the causal connection between Kylon's coup and the laws of Drakon is attractive.[24] But we are also nowhere told what position Drakon held when his laws were published. His lawgiving was dated to the archonship of Aristaichmos, which implies that he was not archon at the time. A passing reference to Drakon by Pausanias suggests that Drakon was a *thesmothetēs*. This could suggest that Drakon was a member of the board of thesmothetai in 621/0, and it might allow the suggestion that he compiled a series of written rules that had accumulated over a period of time. But Pausanias is not a strong authority for Athenian constitutional matters, and his words cannot be taken as decisive. In the absence of any better evidence, it is probably preferable to conclude that Drakon held a special appointment when he wrote his laws for the Athenians, just as Solon would some thirty years later.[25]

A collection of laws ascribed to Drakon circulated by the fourth century. Aristotle (*Pol.* 1274b15–16) noted that Drakon was the author of laws (*nomoi*) but not a constitution (*politeia*), and Plutarch (*Sol.* 19.3) later observed that Areopagites, members of the Areopagos Council, were not mentioned in the laws of Drakon. The collections known to Aristotle and Plutarch have not survived, and their authenticity is difficult to ascertain because other authors attribute measures to Drakon that are later in origin or of disputed authorship. The most egregious example of invention is the Drakontian constitution outlined in chapter 4 of the *Athēnaiōn Politeia*; its contents are almost universally regarded to be the product of political propaganda of the late fifth or fourth century.[26] Elsewhere, Aeschines (1.6) ascribed to Drakon laws on the upbringing and education of young men, but Drakontian authorship of the measures is commonly and rightly rejected by modern scholars.[27] Lysias too labeled as Drakontian a law on idleness with a penalty of death for offenders. But other writers attributed the same law to Solon or Peisistratos, and the author of the law, perhaps an ancient one still in force in the 340s, may have been unknown.[28] A well-attested tradition also claimed that Drakon made death the penalty for all crimes, but one reference to a Drakontian law speaks of fines imposed for unspecified offenses.[29] Finally, some orators claimed Athens' laws on homicide had remained unchanged for all times, but this is incorrect; as we shall see, there is good evidence that legislation on homicide was enacted after the date assigned to Drakon.[30]

A more useful starting point for evaluation of Drakon's laws and their preservation is supplied by an inscription dating from the late fifth century (*IG* I[3] 104).[31] It preserves an Athenian decree of 409/8 ordering a board of *anagrapheis*, "recorders," to inscribe on stone the law of Drakon on homicide. The *anagrapheis* are told (lines 1–10) to fetch a copy of the law from the *basileus* and, together with the secretary of the Boule, to inscribe it on a stone stele to be set up in front of the Stoa Basileios, the office of the *basileus*. After some provisions for inscribing costs, the words *Protos Axon*, "First Axon," appear, followed by the text of the law itself (lines 10–56).

The law's text is worn and incomplete, but several features point to its antiquity. The verb *dikazein* is used at line 11 in an archaic sense. In the classical period *dikazein* meant "to judge" and referred to the activity of the dikasts who passed final judgment in lawsuits. In this law, however, it refers to the activity of the presiding magistrates and apparently has the meaning "to state the right."[32] The law also calls itself a *thesmos* (lines 19–20), the term used by Solon to refer to his laws; Athenians of the late fifth century called their laws *nomoi* or *psēphismata*. The inscribed law also mentions border markets (line 27), which were probably obsolete by the time the law was republished in the late fifth century.[33]

More significant are the headings "First Axon," which precedes the text of the law, and "Second Axon," which can be restored at line 56. The headings are similar to source rubrics found in an inscribed calendar of sacrifices dating from the late fifth century, which is also believed to be the work of the *anagrapheis*, and their presence should indicate that the law's text derived ultimately from objects called *axones*.[34] The *axones*, whose physical nature we shall discuss in more detail later, appear to have been wooden beams or planks inscribed on all sides and set within some sort of frame. *Axones* are generally associated with the laws of Solon, but the presence of the headings in this inscription indicates that Drakon too used them to record and preserve his laws, and Stroud has shown that the *axones* of the two lawgivers formed separate monuments.[35] The presence of these rubrics does not prove that the *anagrapheis* consulted the original *axones* on which Drakon's law was originally recorded. It is possible, for example, that they had access only to copies of the law written on papyrus or some other material that were kept and consulted by the *basileus* when he presided over homicide trials.[36] But these source rubrics are evidence that the *anagrapheis* did not simply copy all Athenian homicide laws. They published laws that originally stood on objects called *axones*.

The restoration of the heading "Second Axon" at line 56 is significant in another way, because it reveals that the law published by the *anagrapheis* extended onto a second *axon*. It also enables us to calculate the amount of text an *axon* could hold. The text of the law between the rubrics "First Axon" and "Second Axon" occupies forty-five lines. The entire inscription is inscribed in stoichedon pattern, with fifty letters in each line, yielding a total of 2,250 letters for the law recorded on the first *axon*. We do not know how many *axones* the homicide law attributed to Drakon took up, but even if the number was limited to two, they recorded a document of substantial length.[37]

The law published by the *anagrapheis* is archaic in wording, was derived from ancient objects called *axones*, and is portrayed as the law of Drakon on homicide. But is it an authentic text dating back to the seventh century? Most scholars concede that portions of the inscribed law originated at an early date, but many have doubted whether the entire published text is the work of Drakon himself. The Athenians, they argue, could not or did not differentiate between the original law of Drakon and later legislation; some provisions included in Drakon's law must have become obsolete and were therefore lost or destroyed, while post-Drakontian measures were mixed in with Drakon's laws and were thus indistinguishable from them. What the *anagrapheis* published was not the work of Drakon but a compilation of Drakontian and later measures available to them in the late fifth century.[38] Although these views usually appear in works dealing with Athenian legal or constitutional matters, they also bear directly on the Athenians' treatment of and attitude toward their public records. A failure by the Athenians to maintain Drakon's original law or their inability to distinguish its text from laws of later date also implies some indifference toward or neglect of the city's written laws. Such a view, if correct, could support similar arguments about the nature of Athenian record keeping in the fifth and fourth centuries.

But several features of the text published by the *anagrapheis* argue for its authenticity as a seventh-century law, free of revisions and later additions. First, the decree orders the *anagrapheis* to publish the law of Drakon, not later additions and not all Athenian homicide laws. While it is true that the orators attributed non-Drakontian measures to Drakon, the *anagrapheis* were not orators pleading a case in court. They were state officials entrusted with a specific task, accountable for their actions. As we shall see, there is also evidence that the *anagrapheis* did differentiate between Drakontian and later measures on homicide. Second, the inscribed text of the law derived from objects called *axones*, and *axones* are associated only with Drakon and Solon. Of course, laws of later date could have been added to an original *axon* or *axones* of Drakon. But we have very little evidence for legislative activity in the sixth century, and when evidence starts to appear in the late sixth and early fifth centuries, the Athenians publish public decisions on stone or bronze *stelai*.[39]

Third, Athenian legislative practice often left earlier measures physically intact in spite of later revisions. When the Athenians drafted new laws they regularly framed them in the form of supplements and amendments to existing legislation. A fourth-century law concerning the offering of firstfruits to the Eleusinian goddesses begins by reaffirming an earlier law of Chairemonides on the same subject before introducing several new provisions; the stele carrying Chairemonides' law was not altered by the later provisions.[40] Since this inscription reflects fourth-century practice, it might be objected that its evidence is not relevant for earlier periods. But a quotation from a homicide law found in Demosthenes' speech *Against Aristokrates* indicates that earlier laws were treated in a similar way. Demosthenes cites, in the course of his attack on the legality of a decree proposed by Aristokrates, a series of homicide provisions that he claimed Aristokrates' decree contravened. Among these is one that reads as follows: "It shall be lawful to kill or seize killers in the territory, as it says on the *axon*, but not to mistreat or ransom them, or else he shall owe twice as much for the damage he does. The archons shall introduce cases over which they have jurisdiction for anyone who wishes, and the Heliaia shall adjudicate" (Dem. 23.28). The law is one of several homicide laws cited and read out by Demosthenes, all of which he attributes to Drakon.[41] But the law is not Drakontian, at least not in its entirety. It refers to the Heliaia, a court widely agreed to have been instituted by Solon. The law also allows prosecution by "anyone who wishes" and not simply the injured party; this right also is thought to be a Solonian innovation. We must dismiss Demosthenes' attribution of it to Drakon as an exaggeration or a mistake or both.[42]

But the law may offer a clue to the treatment of Drakon's original law. Its initial clause permits the killing of condemned homicides found in Attica "as it says on the *axon*." The full law cited by Demosthenes apparently was a revision of an older one, the text of which was found on an *axon* and which allowed killing or seizing convicted killers under certain conditions. The material following this opening sentence is presumably a revision of that original measure, but it does not call for the physical destruction of the older law. It simply amends it without tampering with its text.[43] That the *axon* in question is one of Drakon is indicated by the inscribed copy of Drakon's law. Its text (lines 30–31) has room for the opening provision of the law cited by Demosthenes, which allows the killing of a convicted killer found on Attic territory. But the inscription seems not to have space for the provisions setting down penalties against those who maltreat or ransom killers: the traces on the stone are incompatible with the supplementary provisions preserved in Demosthenes' speech.[44] The *anagrapheis* of 409/8 apparently did not rewrite the law of Drakon by inserting later revisions; they published what they took to be his original law.

A peculiarity of Drakon's law, however, one that has long troubled scholars, also requires discussion. The law set up by the *anagrapheis* begins with the phrase *kai eam*, which normally means "and if." The words "and if" seem an unusual way to start a law, and many scholars explain their presence in this position as evidence that Drakon's law originally began with an earlier provision, one that was omitted from the republication of 409/8. This impression is reinforced by the fact that the inscribed law begins not with intentional homicide, as we might expect, but with unintentional homicide. It has seemed natural to conclude that a provision on intentional homicide once preceded the law as it was published in 409/8, and that this provision was superseded by later legislation, became obsolete, and was therefore not included in the text published by the *anagrapheis*. One way to interpret this development is to assume that Drakon had given jurisdiction over intentional homicide to the *ephetai*, who were responsible for trying cases of unintentional homicide in the preserved portions of the law on stone. The *ephetai* later lost this jurisdiction to the Areopagos Council, which is known to have tried cases of intentional homicide in the classical period. At the time of that change, Drakon's original provision on intentional homicide was revised and perhaps erased from its *axon*.[45]

Other explanations, however, of the law's opening words are possible.[46] If an earlier provision on intentional homicide had been repealed and replaced, it is difficult to see why the Athenians would have preserved an initial *kai*, meaning "and." This word presumably too would have been erased when the provision on intentional homicide itself was rescinded. To meet this difficulty, Gagarin has argued that the law's provision on unintentional homicide actually applied to both unintentional and intentional homicide. Following a suggestion of Stroud, he translates the law's first clause not "and if" but "even if a man not intentionally kills another," and he claims that the words "even if" should imply that the procedures and penalties specified by the law for unintentional homicide were also to apply to cases of intentional homicide.[47] This suggestion has its merits, since it would show that the *anagrapheis* published the precise, original text of Drakon's law. But it also removes the distinction between intentional and unintentional homicide; why mention unintentional homicide at all if all killers were to be treated the same, regardless of intent?[48] Stroud also translates the opening words of the law "even if," and argues that interpreted this way the words *kai eam* are not an objectionable beginning for the law. Drakon simply dealt with intentional homicide in a later portion of his law, one that is missing from the inscription.[49] This argument has some weight. Perhaps less than one-third of the inscribed text is now legible, and the stone itself is broken at the bottom; more provisions may have existed on pieces of the stone now missing. Moreover, although to begin a law with provisions for unintentional homicide certainly strikes us as incongruent, modern expectations of the law's inner logic may not conform to the expectations prevailing in seventh-century Athens. The possibility that Drakon's original law addressed intentional homicide after unintentional killing, and that this provision was inscribed elsewhere in the inscription of 409/8, cannot be too lightly dismissed.

Still, a majority of scholars seem to favor the omission of a provision on intentional homicide because that provision was no longer in force in the late fifth century, and the weight of scholarly opinion is formidable. Let us assume for the sake of argument, therefore, that the majority view is correct. What implications would this carry for the state of Drakon's laws and the ability or inability of the Athenians to distinguish his legislation from later amendments to it? We might suppose that the sources for Drakon's law consulted by the *anagrapheis* included Drakon's original measure on intentional homicide. Recognizing this part of the law was no longer valid, they omitted it from the text they published. This would mean that the *anagrapheis* did not publish all of Drakon's law, but only those portions of it still in force in the late fifth century. But it would also show that Athenians who looked closely could differentiate between original laws and later revisions to them. The survival of a measure rescinded by later legislation might seem unusual, especially in light of the later Athenian practice of destroying laws, decrees, and other documents once their contents became invalid. But erasure of obsolete texts was not a universal or automatic practice, and we cannot be certain that an original provision was not changed simply by amendment rather than replacement, as was the case with the homicide law cited by Demosthenes.[50]

A second possibility is that Drakon's original legislation on intentional homicide had been revoked and erased long before 409/8. The sources from which the *anagrapheis* obtained the law of Drakon began with unintentional homicide, and they published precisely what they discovered. In this case, the fidelity of the *anagrapheis* to their task and to their sources deserves recognition. They were not as troubled as modern scholars by a law beginning with the word *kai* and provisions on unintentional homicide. They did not tamper with the text they found by inserting the current provision on intentional homicide in its "proper" place but published precisely what they found in their source. Perhaps this was because they did not set out to publish all homicide legislation, but only the original law of Drakon, to the extent they could recover it.

Another possibility, however, is that the *anagrapheis* published a provision on intentional homicide in a section of the inscription now missing, but that this provision was a revision of Drakon's original measure. The original provision had been erased from the start of Drakon's law when it was rescinded, and the revised provision was appended at the end of the original law but on the *axon* or *axones*. The *anagrapheis* published what they found in their sources, but they were unable or unwilling to recognize the non-Drakontian origin of the later measure. The inscribed version of Drakon's law, on this view, included both Drakontian and non-Drakontian measures and was simply a compilation of Athenian homicide laws enacted at various times.[51] We have already discussed several objections to this view. The *anagrapheis* were ordered to publish Drakon's law and not later revisions of or additions to it. The text now preserved does not contain any measure demonstrably later than Drakon, and it derived from objects called *axones*, which are otherwise identified only with the work of Solon, and his laws stood on a separate set of *axones*. If the *anagrapheis* included later additions in their publication of Drakon's law, we must also assume that Athenians after the time of Drakon and Solon continued to record laws on *axones*. This is a possibility, but one that is not supported by any evidence.

There is evidence, however, that not all ancient writers grouped all Athenian homicide laws under the name of Drakon. Plutarch (*Sol.* 19.2) states in a discussion of the origins of the Areopagos Council that the laws of Drakon mentioned only *ephetai* and not Areopagites in connection with homicide cases. The Areopagos Council had jurisdiction over cases of intentional homicide in the classical period, so Plutarch's collection cannot have been a simple collection of Athenian homicide laws in the fourth century. We do not know where or when Plutarch's collection of Drakon's laws originated, and scholars have reached different conclusions about its reliability. But correspondences between Plutarch's collection of Drakon's laws and the law inscribed in 409/8 are suggestive. Plutarch's collection named only *ephetai*; the inscribed law too names *ephetai*. Plutarch's collection did not mention Areopagites; the inscribed law does not name Areopagites and omits the one provision (on intentional homicide) that might have referred to them. One possible explanation for these correspondences is that Plutarch's collection of Drakontian laws goes back to the same sources as the published text or to the inscription itself.[52] If, however, the inscription and Plutarch's collection belonged to the same tradition, and if Areopagites were not part of that tradition, then the inscription's text will not have mentioned the Areopagos's role in homicide cases, not even in those portions no longer preserved for us. Thus, the *anagrapheis* did not include later additions to Drakon's law in their inscription.[53]

Total certainty is unattainable with evidence of this nature, but neither the preserved parts of the inscribed copy of Drakon's law nor Athenian legislative practice indicates the presence in the inscription of anything but measures originally issued by Drakon. If we accept this hypothesis, more conclusions follow. The survival of the law of Drakon on homicide is itself significant. Not only was the law preserved, but its text was not obscured by later legislation. Although the orators might ascribe all Athenian homicide legislation to Drakon, individuals like the *anagrapheis*, who were willing to look, could draw some distinctions between older and more recent measures. It is possible that one provision (and possibly others) of Drakon's original law had been repealed and then lost, but nothing suggests that revisions became physically part of and indistinct from Drakon's original law. In addition, the publication of Drakon's homicide legislation on two *axones* suggests a text of considerable length and scope. The inscription of 409/8 includes provisions for unintentional homicide, pardon of convicted killers, proclamations against accused killers, and additional provisions that have not survived. Scholars generally see the publication of homicide regulations by Drakon as a response to a crisis brought on by the unsuccessful attempt by Kylon to make himself tyrant. This may be true. But Drakon responded to the crisis not with a few, isolated measures, but with a law on homicide that was broad in scope and sought to cover a wide range of situations arising from homicide cases.

What relationship Drakon's laws on homicide may have had to earlier written rules issued by thesmothetai or other officials cannot be established. If Athenian magistrates were already recording legal rules before Drakon, his laws did not constitute the first use of writing in the Athenian legal system, and he may have incorporated some earlier, written measures into his laws. But we know so little about such rules that it is idle to speculate further on their possible incorporation into Drakon's work. The failure of these early written rules to leave a strong mark in later traditions, however, may be a sign of the greater authority possessed by Drakon's laws, perhaps because his were commissioned by the people or specially approved by them after Drakon issued them. Drakon may have based his laws on earlier practices, written and unwritten, but the homicide law may also contain evidence for innovations on his part. The law grants competence over homicide cases to *basileis*, "kings," and this is not likely to have been a recent innovation; Drakon presumably built on a body of traditional customs and procedures when he included their jurisdiction in his law. But the law of Drakon also includes a clause declaring that those who had killed previously were to be bound by his law's terms. This clause, which immediately follows measures treating pardon of convicted killers, suggests with its retroactive force that prior to the law's enactment procedures governing pardon had not been entirely uniform or universally accepted.[54] In this and perhaps other areas Drakon may have sought to fix practices where customary procedures had been imprecise or simply ignored by some members of the community. Setting these rules down in writing could not ensure compliance by citizens or prevent arbitrary judgments by magistrates, but it could provide fixed controls against which the actions of both magistrates and citizens could henceforth be measured.

III. Solon

When we turn from the legislation of Drakon to that of Solon, our problem is less a paucity of sources than their abundance. The Athenians remembered Solon as a lawgiver, statesman, and poet. He was appointed archon in 594/3 amid severe economic and political distress, and he addressed the crisis by overhauling Athenian political, legal, and social life. Solon did so in part by repealing the laws of Drakon on subjects other than homicide and issuing new ones of wide scope.[55]

Stories about Solon first appear around the middle of the fifth century. By that time details of his life had already passed into the realm of myth and legend. Herodotus knew Solon not only as a lawgiver but also as a sage, who traveled widely sharing his wisdom. Later authors, many of whose views appear in Plutarch's *Life of Solon*, elaborated further on his education, travels, and reforms. A large number of these stories, however, reflect topoi that recur in traditions about other lawgivers of the archaic period, and they must be approached with a great deal of caution. Later generations might have garnered some information about Solon's life from his poetry, and even the surviving fragments of his poems offer occasional commentary on the social and economic conditions of his day. But there can be no question that the traditions concerning Solon available to us contain much that is fictional. The process of invention also affected traditions about Solon's laws. Athenian orators of the fourth century often referred to Solon as the author of the city's laws, even in cases where a law was demonstrably of later date. Andokides

(1.96) cites a law against subversion of the democracy and calls it a law of Solon, but its text, which is found in his speech, shows that it was enacted only a decade earlier. Demosthenes (20.93) made Solon the author of the laws governing *nomothesia* (lawmaking), but scholars today believe that these procedures were instituted only after a reform of the Athenian law code in the late fifth century.[56]

Discrepancies of this sort naturally raise questions about the survival of Solon's laws and the ability of later authors to consult them. Did the Athenians preserve the texts of his laws? Could fourth-century Athenians know what the laws of Solon actually contained? The preservation of Drakon's law on homicide should make the survival of those of Solon more likely, but although some scholars have no trouble believing in their survival into the fourth century, others argue that the laws of Solon, like those of Drakon, did not survive or were hopelessly entangled with later changes to them, thus making it impossible to determine the character of his legislation. The question is usually examined in the context of studies of Athenian constitutional history and whether Solon wrote "constitutional" laws, but it also has obvious consequences for the history of Athenian writing and public records.[57] Confusion of Solonian laws with later legislation might illustrate the haphazard nature of Athenian record keeping. Only measures with practical value were preserved, texts made obsolete by later revisions were discarded, but everything was attributed to Solon. Such confusion might also cast doubt on the extent of Solon's contribution to the development of written law; instead of a large-scale law code, Solon wrote down only a few laws on a limited number of subjects. By attributing more and more laws to him, later generations exaggerated the size and scope of his legislation out of all proportion.[58]

Attributions of individual laws and political innovations to Solon certainly cannot be trusted blindly, and every allegedly Solonian measure must be evaluated separately according to the style and vocabulary of an individual law (when a text is available), its content, and the overall historical probability of its origin in the early sixth century. But the freedom exercised by orators and other ancient authors in their ascription of laws to Solon, even those of demonstrably later date, cannot be taken as evidence against the existence of genuinely Solonian measures in later times. For false attribution is, strictly speaking, evidence only for the practices of individual authors and the genres in which they worked. False attributions remind us that modern principles of historical accuracy did not govern ancient oratory, biography, or historiography. But the survival of Solon's laws is a question of documentary, not literary, practice. There was a strong tradition that the Athenians swore not to change Solon's laws, and an archaic law, possibly Solonian, prescribes severe penalties for any magistrate or private citizen who erases or changes the *thesmos* of which it was a part.[59] The probability that this tradition reflects the actual treatment of Solon's laws is strengthened by detailed references to the physical objects on which the laws were written. Survival of these objects into later times will not prove the authenticity of any law attributed to Solon, but it does suggest that these objects survived, and this provides a possible means for assessing other features of Solon's lawgiving.

Several ancient sources mention objects called *axones* and *kyrbeis* as the media on which Solon's laws were published. Scholars now generally agree that the *axones* (literally, "axles") were squared, wooden boards inscribed on each of their faces. Several *axones* were set within a rectangular frame in such a way that each *axon* could be rotated and the texts on each face read.[60] The physical appearance of the *kyrbeis* and their relationship to the *axones* are more problematic. Many scholars, supported by some ancient testimony, believe that the terms *axones* and *kyrbeis* were simply alternative names for the same set of objects, and that both terms were used indiscriminately for them in the fifth and fourth centuries.[61] By the Hellenistic period, however, the term *axones* had become standard, and the identification of *axones* with *kyrbeis* was forgotten, thereby giving way to debate and speculation about the form of the *kyrbeis* and their relationship with *axones*. Other modern scholars, also supported by ancient testimony, maintain that the terms denote separate and distinct objects. They believe that the *axones* were rotating beams of wood, while the *kyrbeis* were upright pillars or pyramid-shaped objects made of bronze or stone. Solon originally published his laws on *axones*, but at some later time they were also copied onto *kyrbeis*, perhaps to make their texts more accessible and give them greater visibility to the community at large.[62]

The ancient testimonia for the *axones* and *kyrbeis* are confused and often contradictory, and no explanation of their relationship can satisfy all the available evidence. My own view is that the *axones* were the original monuments on which the laws of Solon were recorded. They alone were numbered and they held the "official" text. The *kyrbeis* were a separate publication of Solon's laws on stele-like monuments, perhaps made from bronze, but they may not have preserved a text of all Solonian laws. Several ancient references to the *kyrbeis* suggest that these held primarily sacred laws, and since the contents of the earliest Athenian documents on stone are predominantly sacred in nature, it may be that the Athenians originally reserved publication on bronze or stone for texts with strong religious significance. By the end of the fifth century, confusion had arisen over the relationship between the *axones* and *kyrbeis*, and it was possible to refer to both sets of objects as *kyrbeis*, perhaps because the *kyrbeis* were located in a more public location and were therefore the more visible monuments. Confusion may also have arisen because of a similarity in shape: both *axones* and *kyrbeis* were pillar-like objects, except that *axones* were set horizontally in a frame while *kyrbeis* stood upright within a base.

Whatever the relationship of *axones* and *kyrbeis*, there is strong evidence that they survived well into the fourth century.[63] A fragment of the comic poet Kratinos mentions *kyrbeis* of Drakon and Solon used for roasting barley; the implications of this passage for the physical form of the *kyrbeis* are much debated, but it at least implies that the *kyrbeis* were objects familiar enough to be parodied before a fifth-century audience.[64] Lysias, in the speech *Against Nikomachos*, refers to sacrifices found on *kyrbeis* (30.17, 18, 20), and a fourth-century inscription calls for the purchase of wood for public sacrifices "in accordance with the *kyrbeis*."[65] In both cases, the texts on the *kyrbeis* appear to be Solonian laws. Aristotle himself was the author of a treatise entitled *On the Axones of Solon*, in five books, a work that suits well the collection of laws and other materials undertaken by him and his students.[66] In the third century, Hellenistic scholars debated the form of the *axones* and their relationship with the *kyrbeis*. Although their works survive only in fragments, autopsy is fairly certain in at least one case. Eratosthenes claimed in a work of unknown title that the *axones* and *kyrbeis* were identical and that they were three-sided. Polemon, however, corrected Eratosthenes by noting that the *axones* were actually four-sided but looked three-sided when viewed from a certain angle.[67] The *axones* seem to have fallen into ruins during the Roman period: by Plutarch's day, only a few fragments remained to be seen in the Prytaneion (*Sol.* 25.1).

Hellenistic debates about Solon's *axones* do not prove that the laws inscribed on them were still legible in that period, and the discussions of Hellenistic scholars may have been based on little more than older accounts of their textual contents and a few crumbling pieces preserved at Athens.[68] But some references to *axones* are quite specific, and these imply that the laws on the *axones* were once legible enough for detailed study. Nearly a dozen glosses in ancient lexicographers preserve entries on words or phrases said to have been recorded on the *axones* of Solon.[69] Other references assign individual laws to numbered *axones*. Plutarch mentions Solonian laws that appeared on the first, thirteenth, and sixteenth *axones*, and he describes Solon's amnesty law as the eighth law on the thirteenth *axon*. We hear elsewhere of a fifth and probably twenty-first *axon*.[70] Such references presumably go back to a work that contained a text of the laws taken from the *axones*. Since Aristotle is credited with a work on the *axones*, and since we hear nothing of detailed study of the *axones* before his day, the most reasonable assumption is that the Solonian *axones* survived into the fourth century when Aristotle compiled a collection of their laws from study of the *axones* themselves.[71] His work served as the source of later references to specific words or laws written on these objects.

Preservation of Solon's *axones* to the fourth century does not prove the authenticity of a single statement about Solon found in the orators, nor does it show that every statement about Solon made by Aristotle stems from information recorded on the *axones*.[72] The orators do not refer to specific *axones*, and they probably did not take the time to consult their contents. Their interests in Solon were not scholarly but rhetorical; their goals were to convince mass audiences to support their causes, not to provide obscure information about Solon's legislation. Aristotle's authorship of a work on the *axones*, on the other hand, should lend his opinions on Solonian matters greater authority. Laws, however, possess limited value for historical research, since they seldom explain the circumstances in which they were enacted, and Aristotle was not immune from errors or misinterpretations in his study of laws. Many of the views offered by Aristotle may rest on little more than inferences drawn from Solon's laws, and some of these conclusions, though based on reliable information, were bound to be in error.[73]

The availability of the *axones* to Aristotle, however, does provide a means by which we can reach an estimate of the extent of Solon's original legislation. *Axones* are not associated with lawgivers other than Drakon and Solon, and the Athenian treatment of Drakon's law suggests that later legislation was not written over Drakon's original measures but amended to them, leaving the original text intact. It was also possible to differentiate some Solonian measures from other laws of archaic date, as Ruschenbusch has shown.[74] Although we cannot exclude entirely the possibility that some later measures were added to Solon's original *axones*, no compelling evidence has been produced to demonstrate this, and we may proceed, albeit cautiously, on the assumption that numbered *axones* refer to laws of Solon.[75] A minimum of sixteen Solonian *axones* are attested, and the number may have been as high as twenty-one. A Drakontian *axon* could accommodate 2,250 letters, and if Solon's *axones* were of similar size, this figure yields a minimum, written text for Solon's laws of

36,000 letters. Topics covered by laws attributed to numbered *axones* include restrictions on exports (first *axon*), interference with legally sanctioned seizures (fifth *axon*), an amnesty law (thirteenth *axon*), prices of sacrificial animals (sixteenth *axon*), and requirements for the dissolution of an adoption (twenty-first [?] *axon*). Other references indicate that boundaries, theft, and rape were also treated. In general terms, Solon's laws appear to have addressed economic matters, adoption, inheritance, aspects of criminal law, and a sacrificial calendar.[76]

Further aspects of the written laws issued by Solon also emerge from specific references to the *axones*, although on these matters the difficulty of differentiating precisely between Solonian and non-Solonian laws renders any conclusions less certain. Many of the laws attributed to Solon are framed as instructions to magistrates, and it has been suggested that the laws of Solon were arranged in part according to the magistrates with competence over specific laws. Aristotle mentions a Solonian law on the treasurers, and two laws falling under the jurisdiction of the archon may have stood on the first *axon*, where we might imagine other laws administered by the archon were also located.[77] Athenian laws of the fourth century were grouped into categories partly determined by magistrates, and a similar arrangement by Solon would indicate that he did more than write out a series of unconnected laws. Grouping of laws according to magisterial authority, even in part, shows a conscious effort to impose some order on a large written text, perhaps to make it accessible to the magistrates whose activities the laws governed. Whether the numbering of *axones* and individual laws went back to Solon himself is more difficult to determine. Numbered *axones* appear in the copy of Drakon's law set up by the *anagrapheis* in 409/8, so the practice could have preceded the scholarly study of Solon's laws by Aristotle.[78] The *anagrapheis* themselves, however, could have been responsible for this numbering, so we cannot take the numbering of individual *axones* past the late fifth century. In favor of a Solonian origin, however, it is noteworthy that an East Lokrian law of circa 500 preserves a series of individually numbered provisions. Numerical designations were not out of place by the late archaic period.[79]

We are more poorly informed about the location in which Solon and the Athenians deposited the *axones* and the laws written on them. Ancient sources put the *axones* and *kyrbeis* in no fewer than four distinct places: the Bouleuterion, Prytaneion, Stoa Basileios, and on the Acropolis.[80] The Bouleuterion is the least likely candidate; the existence of a Solonian Boule is open to doubts, and the remains of the building identified as the Bouleuterion of the classical period date only from the late sixth century. Aristotle says that Solon put his laws, written on *kyrbeis*, in the Stoa Basileios (*Ath. Pol.* 7.1), and his authorship of a work on the *axones* lends this comment some weight. But the remains identified with the Stoa Basileios probably date from the late sixth century, so we must assume either that Aristotle is referring to a precursor to the classical stoa or that he is incorrect.[81] That Solon's laws were originally kept in the Prytaneion is a more attractive suggestion. They were certainly located there in the second century A.D., when Plutarch saw a few scraps of them, and already in the early sixth century legal proceedings were being conducted at the Prytaneion. So the placement of laws in or near this building would seem natural.[82] Other evidence, however, may point to a later move of the *axones* to the Prytaneion. A fragment of the fourth-century historian Anaximenes relates that Ephialtes transferred the *axones* and *kyrbeis* from the Acropolis to the Agora and the Bouleuterion.[83] Because the Bouleuterion was located in the Agora, Wilamowitz suggested that Anaximenes meant simply a metaphorical transfer of power from the Areopagos to the Boule, Ekklesia, and lawcourts.[84] A variant of this fragment, however, points to a more literal interpretation. According to Pollux, the *axones* and *kyrbeis* were stored on the Acropolis "long ago" but were transferred to the Prytaneion and Agora to make them more accessible.[85] Since the Stoa Basileios stood at the northwest corner of the Agora, Pollux's reference conforms to the statements of Aristotle and Plutarch about the locations of the *kyrbeis* and *axones*. Anaximenes, however, is not wholly reliable; in another fragment he gave the funeral oration a Solonian origin, an attribution widely regarded as false.[86] But an original location for the *axones* on the Acropolis receives indirect support from another source. In the fourth century, the nine archons swore two oaths before taking office, one at a *lithos* or stone in front of the Stoa Basileios and another on the Acropolis. Will interpreted this double oath as reflecting the shift in location of the *axones*: originally the archons swore their oath on the Acropolis alone, where the laws of Solon first stood; when the laws were transferred to the Stoa Basileios at a later time, the archons began to swear their oath there as well.[87]

Deposition or display of the *axones* on the Acropolis might offer some insight into the original function of Solon's laws and how they were viewed by the Athenians. The placement of early laws within religious sanctuaries is sometimes taken as a sign of their religious or symbolic character. Through publication, it is argued, laws became widely visible and accessible, and all citizens were given the opportunity, at least in theory, to see and know what the "law" was on particular subjects. But publication also gave written laws a monumental form and symbolic meaning transcending their written contents. Written laws possessed a special status and were invested with a higher authority than oral customs, and this symbolic power was reinforced by their location in or near temple buildings, which formed the symbolic center of the community and where the laws themselves fell under divine protection.[88]

The symbolic character of much ancient writing has been a chief concern of many works on ancient literacy over the past decade. But in exploring the symbolic meaning of early Greek laws, we must guard against downplaying or overlooking the basic, practical functions of written documents to fix, preserve, and disseminate the texts contained on them for practical use. Symbolic interpretations of early Greek laws generally cite the publication of laws on individual stone stelai or large walls, like the great Gortynian code. If the *kyrbeis* on which Solon's laws are sometimes said to have been published were bronze or stone pillars, distinct from the *axones* and carrying primarily sacred laws, they might have possessed the symbolic and monumental force detected by scholars in other early Greek laws. But it is hardly clear that the *axones* were analogous in form or function to inscribed walls or stelai. Most reconstructions of the *axones* see them as wooden beams that could be turned and the texts written on their surfaces viewed; these were objects designed for consultation. The most obvious audience for the laws on the *axones* were the magistrates charged with applying them. It is well known that many early Greek laws, including Solon's, were largely procedural in content; they recorded rules and regulations governing the conduct of legal proceedings. When Athenian archons took office each year, they swore to uphold the laws and to dedicate a gold statue if they transgressed any of them; it seems likely, therefore, that magistrates were familiar with their contents, a familiarity that presumably derived from study of the laws themselves.[89] Athenian magistrates were also accountable for their conduct in office, and with the advent of written laws this accountability should have included their proper observance of the procedures embodied in these laws.[90] Many Athenians, unfamiliar with the regular use of written texts, may have seen their published laws as symbolic objects invested with some type of special authority, and I do not wish to deny that written texts carried such meaning. But written laws also provided guidelines by which Athenian magistrates were expected to conduct legal proceedings, and there is no reason to doubt that some Athenians read and used them in precisely this way.

The application of written laws to many activities did not of course entail an immediate abandonment of traditional, orally communicated practices. Written laws were grafted onto an existing body of orally transmitted practices and customs, and unwritten customs and beliefs remained powerful forces in Greek society centuries after the introduction of writing. But what impact did written laws have in those areas on which they did touch? Thomas suggests that writing was first used to record primarily those rules not universally agreed on, especially measures of a procedural or constitutional nature.[91] Thus, fixed practices were instituted where previously there had been conflict and inconsistency. Sealey, who deals more specifically with the Athenian evidence, also stresses the continuity between the first written laws and earlier, unwritten practices. He suggests that Solon may have been the first Athenian to write down laws extensively, but he emphasizes that without a detailed knowledge of the conditions and legal practices in the time before Solon, the innovative nature of his laws cannot be precisely determined. In some instances, Solon may have changed very little and simply confirmed practices already in use.[92]

These are important observations, as they remind us that writing was introduced into societies with preexisting institutions and customs, which continued to function even after the advent of written laws. Writing is an inherently neutral skill; it does not by itself revolutionize a society.[93] Written laws can regulate and confirm earlier customs, modify them slightly, or replace them altogether by the introduction of new practices. How one assesses the impact of Solon's legislation will depend on what one thinks of its contents and earlier conditions in Athens and Attica, and since those conditions are unknown, definitive answers are unattainable. But we ought not on account of our ignorance reduce Solon to a mere compiler of existing rules and practices, whether written or oral, for even a conservative reading of the measures attributed to him suggests that his laws involved both continuity and change. The *seisachtheia* was by most accounts radical and changed patterns of landholding in Attica, and some of the economic measures attributed to Solon, such as restrictions on agricultural exports except for olive oil, may have had dramatic effect on agricultural life. Solon's adoption and inheritance laws, on the other hand, may have confirmed practices already current, and his amnesty law did not apply to all disfranchised persons and so left the previous decisions of some courts intact, although it still affected many individuals and essentially overturned earlier judgments by which some Athenians had lost their civic rights. Solon was also credited with creating the Areopagos Council by many ancient authors, and many modern scholars attribute the Areopagos Council's competence in intentional homicide to him; either change was innovative. The nature and extent of the constitutional reforms ascribed to Solon are hotly disputed among scholars, but here too I see no reason to doubt that Solon set down in writing some new rules governing political life.[94] The effect of some Solonian laws may have taken years to set in, and in some areas their promulgation may have changed very little. But in a conservative society, writing may also have been the only means to effect change or establish order. At the very least, Solon's commitment of so many laws to writing betrays a nascent belief in the power of writing to affect, regulate, and perhaps alter practices in many areas of human activity.

iv. Conclusion

Athenian society developed rapidly during the seventh and early sixth centuries, and new struggles and conflicts undoubtedly arose for which traditional methods of settling disputes no longer proved satisfactory or sufficient. One way in which the Athenians addressed these changing conditions was through the written word. The moment at which the Athenians first recorded written laws is beyond recovery, but Aristotle's report about the duties of the earliest thesmothetai suggests that writing was introduced by these judicial magistrates acting in the course of their duties. How many written rules the thesmothetai or other officials may have issued on their own authority we cannot know, nor can we ascertain when they lost the right to do so. By the end of the seventh century, however, the Athenians appear to have begun to compile larger and more systematic collections of written rules on different subjects, and it was these laws and not the rules of individual magistrates that governed the life of many areas of society.

Many details about these collections of laws, from their contents to the precise conditions instigating their promulgation, remain shadowy, but in terms of the development of writing and public record keeping, several features invite comment. First, laws were preserved. The copy of Drakon's law published in the late fifth century bears the marks of antiquity, and although its opening words raise questions about the loss of an earlier measure, nothing in the preserved text necessitates a post-Drakontian date for its origin. How many other laws Drakon may have issued cannot be determined, but the tradition about other laws cannot be easily dismissed; references to specific Drakontian measures on matters other than homicide are otherwise difficult to account for. Evidence for the survival of Solon's laws is stronger. The *axones* on which these laws were written survived for centuries, and preservation was not limited only to those laws still in force but included measures that had become obsolete. Aristotle (*Ath. Pol.* 8.3) knew of Solonian laws no longer in use, and Solon's amnesty law, which restored rights to some citizens and whose practical significance was lost soon after its enactment, was among the surviving laws. We cannot be certain that every outdated or lapsed Solonian law survived into later times, but many evidently did.

The laws of Drakon and Solon were also extensive. Recent studies of early Greek law have rightly objected to use of the phrase "law code" to describe the collections of early Greek laws. The word "code" carries connotations of a systematic, comprehensive treatment of law not likely to have been found in the earliest times.[95] But rejection of the term "code" should not diminish the fact that Drakon and especially Solon published legislation of some magnitude. The extent of Drakon's original legislation can only be a matter of speculation, but Stroud's discovery of the heading "Second Axon" on the inscribed copy of Drakon's homicide law indicates that the law, if not comprehensive and all-inclusive, aimed at treating a wide range of situations related to homicide. Solon's laws took up at least sixteen *axones* and were evidently far more numerous and detailed; they treated a diverse range of situations. Moreover, these laws may have displayed a rudimentary system of organization according to the magistrates who used and applied them as they administered justice.

Publication of large bodies of laws in the late seventh and early sixth centuries does not mean that all the practices embodied in those collections came into being at the time of publication. Nor does it exclude the further development of Athenian law over succeeding centuries. But the publication and preservation of laws does imply a recognition of the practical role written records could play in the public life of the emerging city-state. It will be useful to keep this in mind as we examine further uses of written documents in the following chapters.

CHAPTER TWO

Documents and Records
in the Sixth Century

Solon's promulgation of a large body of written laws leads naturally to a consideration of what other types of documents Athenian officials were using at the start of the sixth century. But if our sources offer few definitive answers about the nature and contents of Solon's legislation, they have even less to say about other official uses of writing in his day. One example will illustrate the difficulties. According to Diodorus, a historian of the first century B.C., one of Solon's laws was borrowed from an Egyptian law that required individuals to list to the authorities the sources of their income. The verb used by Diodorus to describe this list, *apographesthai*, was the same verb used by the Athenians to describe written lists and inventories drawn up for submission in a variety of legal proceedings in the fifth and fourth centuries. If Diodorus is reproducing the precise wording of a Solonian law, we would have good evidence that Solon's legislation actually required a further use of writing. Herodotus, however, writing centuries before Diodorus and only a century or so after Solon, seems to refer to the same law but uses two different verbs, *apophainein* and *apodeiknynai*, to denote the property statement made by citizens. These verbs mean simply "to show" or "to point out," and neither necessitates a use of writing. Thus, even if we accept that the Solonian law cited by Herodotus and Diodorus is authentic, that law may have required only that citizens declare orally, perhaps in the presence of witnesses, the sources of their livelihood. We certainly cannot exclude the possibility that Solon's laws included provisions encouraging or requiring the use of written documents by Athenian citizens and magistrates. But our sources for his work are too incomplete to pursue the question any further.[1]

As the sixth century develops, however, several sources reveal a growing use of writing in the public sphere. Earlier studies have considered sixth-century Athenian documents in some detail, but their focus has generally fallen less on what documents existed or how they were used than on what documents survived and were available for consultation by historians of the fifth and fourth centuries, when written accounts of sixth-century events first appear.[2] This approach is a reasonable one, given the interests of the scholars who have adopted it. But it also runs the risk of overlooking certain types of documents that once existed but did not survive or other types that did exist but failed to attract the attention of later historians. Evidence for documents of both types survives, and its implications for Athenian record keeping have been only partially explored. Study of this evidence forms the subject of this chapter. Although the written word would hardly displace the spoken word in Athenian public life, the use of documents spread widely, and by the end of the sixth century written texts may have been a familiar, if not necessary, feature of the administration of many state magistrates.

1. Sixth-Century Secretaries

Among the most significant developments in Athenian record keeping during the sixth century is the appearance of officials who serve as *grammateis*, "secretaries," for other state magistrates. Secretaries are mentioned in two and possibly three inscriptions dating from the middle of the sixth century (*IG* I[3] 507–9).[3] The texts are terribly fragmentary, but each one can be restored with some degree of certainty based on comparison with the preserved parts of the other two. The first inscription does not name a secretary. It states that certain officials, whose names are listed, "made a track" or "conducted a race" for Athena. Following the list of names there appears the phrase "they first instituted the contest for owl-eyed Athena." At least one additional name is preserved on the reverse side of the inscription.[4] The second inscription also begins with the words "they conducted a race," followed by a list of names, probably those of the officials who administered the race. After this list, however, the text states that a certain individual, whose name is lost, served them as secretary.[5] The opening lines of the third inscription are extremely fragmentary, but they too may be restored to correspond with those of the previous two inscriptions. A list of officials is not preserved on the stone, but the text does provide the name of an individual who served as secretary, once again, presumably for the officials responsible for conducting the race mentioned in the earlier two texts.[6]

There is considerable agreement that these inscriptions commemorate some of the earliest athletic contests held at the Greater Panathenaia, the great quadrennial festival to Athena, which was reorganized on a grand scale in the second quarter of the sixth century, perhaps in 566. Likewise, the officials listed in two of the inscriptions are generally thought to have been *hieropoioi*, who supervised many public festivals in later times.[7] But for our purposes the identity of the contest and the officials who oversaw it are of secondary significance to the mention of individuals who worked as secretaries. The Greek word used to describe this activity is *grammateuein*, a word that implies that writing was the primary duty of the individuals whose activity it describes. Written documents, evidently, were used in the administration of the contests commemorated by these inscriptions.

Now, in other city-states we sometimes hear of officials called *mnēmones*, "rememberers," an office whose title has been taken to suggest that these officials once had the duty of remembering, without the aid of writing, items of public business, and rememberers have rightly been seen as important figures in the transition of Greek society from an oral to a literate one. The office of rememberer survived well into the classical and Hellenistic periods, but by the fourth century some *mnēmones* functioned as scribes who kept records in writing.[8] Athens too had its rememberers; a sacred remember (*hieromnēmon*) served as a representative to the Amphictyony at Delphi, and various subgroups of the Athenian state had officials with the same title.[9] But the duties performed by the Athenian rememberers are not well attested, and those rememberers who are attested are not associated with any of the central institutions of the Athenian state. At Athens, the records of state magistrates are intimately tied with *grammateis*, and therefore with writing, from the earliest times.

What types of records were the Athenian secretaries named in the two sixth-century inscriptions keeping? They certainly did more than compose the texts that were inscribed on stone. The verb *grammateuein* regularly described the activity of officials who maintained written records for Athenian public boards and magistrates in later times, and the duties of these later secretaries may serve as some guide to those exercised by these sixth-century secretaries. The Boule chose its own secretary in the fifth century whose duty was to record details of business coming before the Boule and Ekklesia. Judicial magistrates employed secretaries to schedule the cases that came before them, and other Athenian officials, such as the *pōlētai*, *praktores*, and *poristai*, had their own undersecretaries to assist them in the record-keeping requirements of their offices.[10]

Still other secretaries assisted Athenian boards and magistrates by keeping written accounts of the finances managed by them during their term in office.[11] In the fourth century, it was a basic principle of Athenian government that all public officials were accountable for their conduct in office. Magisterial accountability was administered through proceedings called *euthynai*, at which magistrates retiring from office submitted to both a general scrutiny of their conduct and a financial accounting of the public moneys that had passed through their hands. Unfortunately, we do not know when formal audits of the financial accounts of magistrates were instituted. The practice is first attested in the Tribute Quota List of 454/3, which mentions a board of thirty auditors (*logistai*), and regular audits of magisterial accounts is often linked with the reforms of Ephialtes of 462/1. But magistrates were certainly accountable for their activities even earlier, and documents attesting to financial dealings would have provided potentially valuable evidence in the event of charges of malfeasance.[12] How much income and expense a sixth-century official might incur is difficult to gauge, but state festivals like the Greater (and Lesser) Panathenaia will have required both collection and redistribution of a significant amount of resources. Inscriptions of the late fifth century show payments of large sums of money to the *athlothetai* who then ran the festival, and fourth-century inscriptions attest to large prizes of olive oil and cash for victors in the festival's athletic and musical contests. Aristotle also notes that the *athlothetai* oversaw the weaving of a new robe for a statue of the goddess Athena and had made the prize amphoras in which the olive oil awarded to victors was stored, while the archon was responsible for procuring that oil, which he delivered to the treasurers of Athena for storage on the Acropolis.[13] We obviously cannot assume that all these features were in place when the Greater Panathenaia was founded, or that similarly large numbers of goods passed through the hands of sixth-century officials. Nor should we imagine that the system of public audits attested from the middle of the fifth century was already in place in the middle of the sixth century. But sixth-century *hieropoioi* may have found it desirable to maintain simple, written accounts of the goods they handled, either to facilitate their administration of the festival or to protect themselves against charges of corruption or malfeasance; it was to assist with such record keeping that secretaries were enlisted.

Although we do not meet secretaries at Athens again until the mid-fifth century, it is not likely that magistrates abandoned their use, and the use of writing, in the intervening century. Undoubtedly, later *hieropoioi* continued to employ secretaries, but these have left no mark on the scanty literary and epigraphical remains for sixth-century Athens, perhaps because any documents they produced were written on perishable materials. At the same time, we should not assume that the appearance of secretaries in two inscriptions of the mid-sixth century reflects the earliest use of writing or written accounts by Athenian officials. The treasurers of Athena, for example, managed the treasures and dedications deposited with Athena on the Acropolis, and they published detailed records of many of those items in the classical period. They were named in Solon's laws, and they too may have recognized the benefit of keeping written accounts of treasures they administered.[14] Another law of Solon mentions officials called *naukraroi* and a naukraric fund; the origins and duties of these officials are highly disputed, but if the law's authenticity can be trusted, they were concerned with state finances in the early sixth century, duties that will also have benefited from some documentation.[15] In addition, the *pōlētai*, Athenian officials who oversaw the leasing of public land and state contracts in the fifth and fourth centuries, were said to have dated back to the time of Solon, and although they are not mentioned in any of Solon's poems, one fragment of Solon's poetry refers to sacred and public property; these lands may have been leased out already in Solon's day, and the income accruing from those leases may have required written documentation.[16] Finally, Solon's laws included a calendar of sacrifices that fixed the dates of public sacrifices and the types of victims and offerings to be made on particular occasions. Sacrifices sponsored or required by the state involved the collection of the sheep, cattle, or other required offerings, and the officials who oversaw them may have found it convenient, necessary, or desirable to keep track of the goods they received and distributed.[17]

These points are admittedly speculative, and we cannot be certain that these or other Athenian officials were using writing before the middle of the sixth century. Conversely, there is no reason to suppose that the use of writing by Athenian magistrates was limited to or began with the two secretaries who are attested around the middle of the sixth century. The recording of the laws of Drakon and Solon demonstrates a recognition of the potential value of writing in public life, and their legislation may have suggested to some Athenians further possible uses for the written word. Not all Athenian magistrates made use of documents during the sixth century, and the number of those who did was probably quite low. But the fact that seemingly minor officials, such as *hieropoioi*, had resorted to written documents by circa 550 should open the possibility that other officials with more significant duties were also employing writing in the administration of their duties by the same time.

Such a concern for keeping track, in writing, of objects falling under the supervision of magistrates may be indicated by another inscription from the mid-sixth century (*IG* I³ 510). Its text is engraved on a bronze plaque and records that a board of treasurers "gathered together" some bronze objects.[18] The names or parts of names of at least five treasurers are preserved; the original text may have held as many as eight. Scholars usually interpret the inscription as a dedication to Athena, which is probably correct.[19] But its dedicatory nature should not overshadow other features, which suggest that the tablet was accompanied by a catalog drawn up by the treasurers during their term in office. The participle *synlechsantes*, "having gathered together," used to describe the activity of the treasurers derives from the verb *syllegein*. The same verb appears in an account of the treasurers of Athena dating from the late fifth century, where it refers to both income and other objects received by those treasurers during their year in office (the *epeteia*), as opposed to funds they received from their predecessors.[20] In addition, the demonstrative pronoun *tade*, "these things," with which the text of the inscription begins, appears regularly in inscribed inventories of the fifth and fourth centuries, when it introduces lists of objects kept in sacred buildings and administered by the treasurers of Athena. Such a list of objects collected by the treasurers named in this sixth-century plaque does not survive, but the presence of the pronoun *tade* is a strong indication that some such list was set up near or beside it.[21]

The plaque thus commemorates the compilation of a written inventory, now lost, by the treasurers named in the text. We know too little about the management of Athena's treasures during the sixth century to guess how regular such inventories were, and it may be that some extraordinary circumstances demanded a catalog of bronze objects under their care. But it is equally possible that Athena's treasurers had started to maintain more regular written inventories of goods and dedications coming into their possession already in the sixth century. The earliest monumental temple on the Acropolis dates from the middle of the sixth century, and written accounts may have proved useful in maintaining control over dedications and other objects housed within it.[22]

The importance attached to record keeping by some sixth-century Athenians can be discerned in other ways. Three statues of seated secretaries or scribes, one of whom holds a wooden tablet in his lap, were set up on the Acropolis later in the century, and one of these may have been erected for an earlier treasurer by his son.[23] More important, one of the Hekatompedon Decrees of 485/4 instructs certain treasurers to make records of certain bronze (?) objects found on the Acropolis. The frag-

mentary nature of this decree renders interpretation of its contents problematic. The provision calling for the treasurers to make some type of
inventory may direct them to catalog objects they had not inventoried
before. But it may also formalize record-keeping procedures that previously had not been uniform.[24] What is striking, however, is that inscribed inventories of objects on the Acropolis do not survive from
before the 430s, when the great series of Parthenon inventories begins.
The relatively late date of these inventories is not a sign that Athena's
treasurers had not kept written records or used writing in earlier times. It
simply reflects the fact that the Athenians decided to entrust some records to stone at a relatively late date. Some earlier documents and inventories may have been committed to materials like bronze, like the inventory that probably accompanied the bronze plaque set up around the
middle of the sixth century. But the treasurers of Athena may also have
worked more routinely with wooden tablets, a medium whose use is well
attested in both artistic depictions and scattered references in literary
and epigraphical sources.[25] The keeping of rudimentary accounts by
Athena's treasures and other Athenian officials was probably not widespread during the sixth century, but it was almost certainly more common than the few explicitly attested instances indicate.

11. Didascalic Records
and Long-Term Preservation

The absence of accounts or inventories on stone or bronze from the sixth
century, coupled with the possibility that the treasurers of Athena and
other magistrates were nonetheless using writing to keep some basic
form of accounts in the same period, is of interest, because they raise
questions about the general nature of early Athenian record keeping.
Documents engraved on materials like stone or bronze had some chance
of surviving for decades or even centuries, but documents recorded on
wooden tablets or papyrus, we might assume, could last no more than a
few months, years, or decades. Although there is no reason to assume
that the bronze plaque set up by Athena's treasurers in the mid-sixth
century was unique, the overall dearth of documentary, sixth-century
Athenian inscriptions on stone or bronze raises doubts about the general
permanency of any accounts, inventories, or other documents Athenian
officials drew up in this period. We can easily imagine that some magistrates kept written accounts related to their official activities from early
times, but that they erased or discarded whatever texts they created soon

after the transactions recorded in them were completed. Thus, apart from the laws of Drakon and Solon, early Athenian record keeping was generally ephemeral and impermanent in nature.

But some evidence advises caution against downplaying the overall permanence of Athenian documents in this or any period. An inscription of the second half of the fourth century (IG II² 2318), commonly called the Fasti, preserves a list of victors in the dithyrambic and dramatic contests held at the City Dionysia. Names of victorious tribes, poets, and *chorēgoi* are arranged by year and in columns, with the victors in various contests of each year listed under the name of the archon of that year. The inscription was erected sometime around 346, but its contents were kept up-to-date in subsequent years; the last preserved entry dates to 329/8, and it is widely believed that the original text continued down until about 316, when the *chorēgia* was abolished and responsibility for funding the dramatic competitions at the Dionysia was handed over to an official called the *agōnothetēs*.[26]

The earliest victors named in this inscription date from the archonship of Menon (473/2), but the opening columns of the inscription are now lost. Judging from the number of lines per column and estimates of the monument's original size, the text probably listed victors going back to 502/1 and possibly earlier.[27] The interval between the inscription's publication date and the date of the earliest details it records is great, and it should raise questions about the sources on which the published text depended. A work of Aristotle is a possibility. Aristotle wrote several works on Attic drama, including one, the *Nikai Dionysiakai* or *Dionysiac Victories*, whose title reflects the details contained in the Fasti.[28] Unfortunately, we know little of this treatise, and if it dates from Aristotle's last stay in Athens during the years 334–323, as is sometimes thought, it cannot have served as the Fasti's source.[29] But to hypothesize a work of Aristotle as the Fasti's source solves little anyway, since we must still inquire into the sources from which a scholarly work of the fourth century might have obtained a list of past victors. Since we have no evidence that lists of victors were inscribed on stone or bronze before the time of the Fasti's publication, we might suppose that its compilers scoured Athens inspecting choregic monuments and other inscriptions commemorating victories in various contests. Plutarch (*Them.* 5.5) relates that Themistokles commemorated his victory as a tragic *chorēgos* with a dedicatory plaque that included Themistokles' own name, the name of his tragic poet (Phrynichos), and the archonship (Adeimantos, 477/6) in which the victory was won. These details conform precisely to those found in the Fasti. But surviving choregic inscriptions from the fifth century do not regularly mention the names of archons until late in that century, and we can hardly be certain that a complete set of choregic dedications representing every victory won at the Dionysia over the course of the fifth and fourth centuries survived into the 340s. It is possible that private dedications served as the principal source for the Fasti's text, but if we make that assumption we probably also have to admit the possibility that the compilers of the Fasti assigned some victors to years arbitrarily or simply filled in names for contests in years for which they had no evidence.[30]

Given scholarly attraction to theories of forged and fabricated documents in the fifth and fourth centuries, arguments for the unreliability of the Fasti's contents might find some supporters. The inscription was set up at a time when the Athenians were experiencing difficulties in attracting *chorēgoi*, and publication of a list of previous victors may have been intended to inspire contemporary Athenians to mimic the examples set by their ancestors.[31] But authentic records can be just as valuable in promoting patriotism as forged ones, and, unlike other forged documents of the fourth century, no features of the inscription's text point to a fourth-century origin. Some Athenian officials, however, were employing secretaries by the middle of the sixth century, and the Hekatompedon Decrees ordered the treasurers of Athena to draw up some type of documents in roughly the same period in which the Fasti's contents begin. It seems reasonable to suppose, therefore, that the official who administered the Dionysia also kept records related to that festival from the same period. Since the eponymous archon supervised the Dionysia during the classical period, it may also be supposed that records kept by him lay behind the Fasti and other didascalic notices appearing in later sources.[32]

Since the extant fragments of the Fasti go back only to the Dionysia of 473/2, any conclusions about the inscription's entries for earlier years, and the records from which these were compiled, must remain tentative. But the Fasti certainly began before 473/2, and details about pre–Persian War performances at the Dionysia are attested in later times. Aeschylus's first victory was dated to 485/4, and the introduction of comic performances to the City Dionysia was put in the eighth year before the Persian Wars.[33] Both details could have been inferred from the Fasti themselves or from the records on which they drew. In addition, a note in the *Suda*, an encyclopedia of Byzantine date, gives the names of three tragedians who competed in some year during the seventieth Olympiad (500/99–496/5); the names of the several tragedians who competed in the tragic contests of individual years were also preserved in later times, so this detail too may have a documentary origin.[34]

How far back beyond circa 500 these didascalic records went proves more difficult to establish. The foundation of the City Dionysia as a civic festival and the introduction of some type of dramatic competitions are usually thought to have occurred in the late 530s, based on the *Suda*'s entry for the poet Thespis and another mention of Thespis in the Parian Marble, a Hellenistic inscription that provides specific dates for many events of earlier times. But recent scholarship has lowered the festival's foundation date to bring it into accord with the political reform of the Athenian state begun by Kleisthenes in 508/7.[35] An examination of the origins of the City Dionysia cannot be undertaken here, but the revised dating depends in large part on the assumption that the inscribed victor list of the Fasti began in the very year the festival was founded, and that that starting date was 502/1. But that date is not firmly fixed. We do not know the specific year in which the Fasti began, and dates for earlier dramatic performances are attested. The *Suda* dates a victory of the tragedian Phrynichos to the sixty-seventh Olympiad (512/1–509/8), and puts a performance of the tragedian Choirilos in the sixty-fourth Olympiad (524/3–521/0), while the Parian Marble dates the first production of dithyrambic choruses for men to the archonship of Lysagoras (510/9 or 509/8) and names Hypodikos of Chalkis as the poet-producer.[36]

These dates and those given for Thespis have been dismissed as referring to performances put on at the Rural Dionysia,[37] or characterized as unreliable.[38] But it is difficult to see why precise dates for the Rural Dionysia would have survived from the sixth century when we possess so little information about that festival in the better-documented fifth and fourth centuries.[39] Moreover, the dates for Phrynichos's victory and the introduction of dithyrambic choruses are precisely the sort of details that could be inferred from records like those from which the Fasti were compiled; to dismiss them because they fail to conform to a theory about the origins of the City Dionysia, one not supported by any ancient testimony, seems arbitrary. It is of course possible that the inscribed Fasti themselves began in or around 502/1, when the festival was reorganized to make it conform with the new tribes established by Kleisthenes. But that date does not preclude earlier dramatic performances or the earlier keeping of records related to those performances. Absolute certainty on this issue cannot be achieved, and I am not arguing that detailed didascalic records extended far back into the sixth century. But the evidence certainly suggests that documentation existed for some early dramatic performances before a fuller sequence began in or around 502/1.

Whether records of the Dionysia were available from 502/1 or a little earlier, the nature and contents of these records demand closer attention.

The Fasti themselves constitute a victor list, and it might be argued that the didascalic records from which the Fasti were compiled were similar in nature. They commemorated the victors in the contests held at the Dionysia each year, and they were kept to enhance the honor and prestige of victory by preserving the names of victors for posterity. The commemorative value of the list would have been enhanced if it was publicly displayed, perhaps on whitened boards, before being committed to stone in the 340s.[40] If these records were simple victor lists, their broader significance for record keeping by state officials might be considered minimal. But more than the names of victors was preserved into the fourth and third centuries, and this suggests that the Fasti originated in more detailed, administrative records of the City Dionysia.[41] The hypothesis to Aeschylus's *Seven against Thebes*, produced in 468/7, states that it was part of a trilogy that won first prize in the archonship of Theagenides, and it provides the names of the poets who placed second and third in that year, along with the titles of the plays they produced. A didascalic notice for Aeschylus's *Supplices* (*POxy* 2256, fr. 3), performed in 463/2, similarly lists the names of competing playwrights and their plays.[42] The hypotheses to other fifth-century plays preserve similar information. These hypotheses are generally traced back to the Hellenistic scholar Aristophanes of Byzantion and from Aristophanes to Aristotle's *Didaskaliai*, a work that treated tragedy, comedy, and dithyramb. But the contents of the *Didaskaliai*, like those of the Fasti, must have depended ultimately on an official, documentary source. The preservation of details beyond the names of victors shows that didascalic records were not victor lists but fuller collections of records documenting the participants in the contests of the City Dionysia each year.

The completeness of these didascalic records may help to explain how they were used and why they were preserved. Administration of the City Dionysia involved a large number of participants, most of whom changed each year. *Chorēgoi* had to be appointed to sponsor both a boys' and men's dithyrambic chorus from each of the ten Attic tribes, and three sponsored tragic choruses, while from 487/6 five poets were selected for comedy (except during the Peloponnesian War, when only three were chosen). Altogether, at least twenty-eight *chorēgoi* and poets took part in the City Dionysia each year, to say nothing of others who took part as actors and flute players.[43] The number of participants was certainly smaller when the Dionysia was established or reorganized as a state festival in the late sixth century, but probably not by much, and archons may have kept written lists of participants simply to keep track of what individuals were responsible for what performances. Documents might also have been necessary for recording expenditure of public moneys. Although much of the burden of sponsoring dramatic and dithyrambic choruses was borne by individual *chorēgoi*, the state did support poets and actors, and archons, like other magistrates, probably could be called upon to make an accounting of their finances. The general administration of the festival by each year's archon was also subject to scrutiny. Demosthenes in his speech *Against Meidias* refers to a law that required a meeting of the Ekklesia the day after the celebration of the Dionysia, at which the archon could be called upon to defend his administration of the festival.[44] Although the law cited by Demosthenes probably dates from the fourth century, the archon's management of the Dionysia was presumably subject to review in earlier times as well, whether at a special meeting of the Ekklesia or when he stepped down at the end of his year in office. Records of choices for *chorēgoi*, poets, and actors offered potentially valuable evidence that he had fulfilled his duties in accordance with the city's laws.

Records of past competitions also had value for future archons. We do not know what criteria archons applied when they selected the poets or actors who would compete at the Dionysia, but records of earlier years could provide information about the success or failure of particular individuals. After an acting competition was introduced in 449, the winning protagonist was guaranteed a spot in the contest of the following year, and there is some evidence that a poor showing could affect a poet's selection for later contests.[45] Didascalic records may have also proved useful when archons chose the *chorēgoi* for each year's festival. In the fourth century, wealthy Athenians enjoyed some limitations on the frequency with which they could be called upon to perform public liturgies. They were exempted from performing two liturgies in the same year, from performing liturgies in successive years, or from performing the same liturgy twice. Citizens appointed to choregic duty when legally exempt could appeal their selection by a procedure called *skēpsis*, over which the archon presided. We do not know how archons went about adjudicating claims of exemption, but the preservation of records from the contests held at the Dionysia, quite possibly by archons themselves, will have offered at least some evidence on which claims for exemptions could be decided.[46]

Admittedly, we do not hear of archons or other officials consulting didascalic records, and other factors beyond simple, practical concerns may have been involved in their long-term preservation. The Dionysia was a religious festival, so feelings of piety and devotion may have dictated that detailed records had to be kept of each year's festival. But the contents of didascalic records were not inherently religious, as far as we can tell, and sentiments of piety or devotion will not have excluded their practical use by the eponymous archon or other magistrates. The practical value of records for individual years certainly diminished over time, as the citizens named in them died. But it is certainly noteworthy that didascalic records as old as the late sixth century were maintained well into the fourth century. The Athenians did not systematically destroy old records once they had outlived their practical value; in the case of the Dionysia, older records were preserved for well over a century. Why they were preserved at all we can only guess, but their preservation illustrates the weaknesses of attempts to downplay the number of documents the Athenians made, used, or maintained in any period. We know that some didascalic records for the City Dionysia were being kept from circa 500 because Athenians of the fourth century decided to publish some of these records on stone. What we do not know is how many other records Athenian officials were making at the same time and perhaps preserving for equally long periods, without, however, ever publishing them on stone. It would be rash to exaggerate their number, but it would be equally misleading to deny their existence altogether. We must keep in mind that our knowledge of Athenian record keeping depends largely on decisions to publish some texts on stone. The possibility that Athenian magistrates kept other documents that they never published must also be borne in mind.

III. The Archon List

The Dionysiac victor list preserved in the Fasti is arranged according to archon years, and it is natural to infer from this arrangement that the didascalic records from which the Fasti derived were organized or dated by a similar method. This use of archon dating has special relevance to another document from the archaic period, the existence of which in the sixth century has sometimes been doubted. Sometime around 425 the Athenians published on stone a list of their eponymous archons going back into the sixth and possibly seventh centuries. The inscription, which survives only in fragments, preserves a bare list of names, without patronymics, demotics, or other comments. The names are arranged in columns, with the archon of each year listed below his predecessor. The original dimensions of the inscription are unknown, and it cannot be established with certainty when or with whom the list of archons began. One fragment preserves a sequence of the archons from 527/6 to 522/1, and others give the names of archons from earlier in the sixth century, some perhaps even earlier than Solon. The list, therefore, may have gone back to Kreon, who according to Athenian tradition was the first holder of the archonship when the office became annual in 683/2.[47]

The late date at which the list of archons was inscribed on stone has led some scholars to doubt that the Athenians maintained such a list of their eponymous magistrates in earlier periods. The issue is not simply one of chronology; it bears directly on the role of writing and documents at Athens in the archaic period. Was dating based on a fixed list of eponymous officials or did it rely on orally preserved information? Skeptics maintain that the list published around 425 was pieced together only at that time from any of several sources of information; no earlier list existed and the inscribed list's compilers resorted to scattered written texts, oral traditions, or outright fabrication.[48] Almost all arguments against the inscribed list's dependency on a much earlier document allude to Herodotus's failure to express dates in terms of archons in his history: if an archon list had existed, Herodotus surely would have consulted and used it in his work. But this argument is weak. Herodotus ignored many pieces of evidence that a modern historian might consider relevant to his work, and his methods are not a guide to the use or existence of documents in Greek society.[49] Publication of the Fasti in the fourth century demonstrates the upkeep of detailed records in the fifth and fourth centuries long before their publication on stone, so we should not be surprised to find other types of documents in existence for a very long time before being published on stone or bronze.

That this was also true of the archon list is suggested by several considerations. The list of Athenian archons, as known to later authors, shows no signs of manipulation or fabrication; what we know about the list speaks for its antiquity.[50] The names of archons of the seventh and early sixth centuries exhibit no preponderance of names belonging to families or individuals of the fifth century, as we would expect if the list was first drawn up at that time. Kreon, with whom the list of annual archons began, is otherwise unknown, and if the list was created in the 420s, we might expect it to have begun with a more epochal date or with a better known individual, perhaps one belonging to a more prominent family. Nor is there evidence for insertions into the list or for two individuals being assigned to the same year, the types of inconsistencies to be expected in the absence of authentic, authoritative records.

Other features of the archon list as it was known in later times also speak against a late date for its first compilation. According to Aristotle, no archons were elected in the fifth (590/89) and ninth (586/5) years after Solon's archonship, while in 582/1, a certain Damasias was elected archon and then held the office for a total of two years and two months.[51] If the archon list had been drawn up in the years around 425 for the first time, why were these years left blank and Damasias given a term of more than two years? Extended tenures for archons or years in which no eponymous archon was selected are unattested in the years around 425, the time when the archon list was published on stone; surely an editor working without an authentic list would have drawn up a continuous list with no gaps and without one individual being assigned to successive years. Yet the archon list known to Aristotle did just that. The presence of *anarchiai* (years with which no names of archons were associated) in Aristotle's archon list is most easily explained by assuming that the source from which Aristotle's list was compiled, presumably the same source as that from which the inscribed list was constructed, offered a full sequence of archons, but also included some indications that no archons were chosen in some years. An oral source for such *anarchiai* might be posited, but we have little evidence that archon names, much less *anarchiai*, were routinely transmitted in oral traditions; a documentary explanation is preferable.[52] Similarly, the extended tenure of Damasias in the archon list is difficult to explain on the assumption of fifth-century fabrication, but it makes more sense if we accept that Aristotle's knowledge of Damasias depends on an authentic list of archons dating back to the 580s, in which Damasias's name appeared in three consecutive years.[53]

To assume, however, that a list of archons existed and was maintained from the seventh and sixth centuries also assumes that a need for such a list was felt in those centuries; that is, upkeep of an archon list assumes that the archon was already an eponymous official in the seventh or sixth century.[54] But did Athenians actually use the names of archons for dating purposes before the late fifth century? Archon names do not regularly appear in the prescripts of inscribed Athenian decrees until after 421, the very time the archon list itself was published on stone, and this has sometimes been taken to show that the Athenians became concerned with precise dating only in the late fifth century.[55] But archons were regularly used for dating purposes long before the list of archons was published on stone. A set of Athenian regulations governing affairs at Miletos twice names the archonship of Euthynos (450/49).[56] The context in which Euthynos's archonship was named is lost, but its mention implies that henceforth his year was to be a fixed point in relations between Athens and Miletos, a year from which the inscribed regulations would be valid. This, in turn, assumes that the year of Euthynos's archonship could be fixed and computed with respect to the years of other archons.

From the same period, the heading of the first of the Athenian Tribute Lists names the archon Ariston (454/3). Subsequent headings do not give the names of archons, but they are numbered from the first list, so that the absolute date, in terms of the archon-years, could be determined.[57] Earlier in the fifth century, the Hekatompedon Decrees record that their provisions were enacted in the archonship of Philokrates (485/4).[58] Finally, the didascalic records from which the Fasti were compiled show that the contests of the Dionysia were attached to archon names already from around 500 and possibly earlier.[59] Archon dating in Athenian documents was not a phenomenon new to the late fifth century.

These texts take us back to the end of the sixth century. But the use of archon names in Athenian documents goes back further still. Solon's amnesty law applied to all those who were in exile before Solon's archonship, with the exception of those convicted of certain crimes by specific tribunals.[60] Another law of Solon allowed individuals who had not adopted children when Solon entered his archonship to dispose of their property as they saw fit, as long as they met other conditions specified later in the law.[61] References to Solon's archonship in these laws are not intended to date the laws to his archonship. Instead, they establish the year from which provisions of the laws would apply. Thus, the terms of the amnesty law applied only to certain individuals in exile before Solon's archonship; it did not extend to individuals exiled afterward. Likewise, the adoption law applied to those individuals who had not made adoptions prior to Solon's archonship; those who had made adoptions before his year may not have been bound by its terms. The naming of an archonship in early laws shows that archons were already eponymous and used to label individual years, and this presupposes the ability to put individual archons in some type of order. A list of some sort seems to be assumed.[62]

Other areas of Athenian public life in the seventh and sixth centuries may also have required the specific dating an official list will have provided.[63] In the fourth century, citizens liable for military service were organized and called up for service according to age-classes arranged under the names of the archons in whose years they had been enrolled as citizens.[64] In addition, age qualifications existed for many public offices, and, presumably, a candidate's age was determined by reference to the archonship in which he was born or registered as a citizen.[65] Although practices of the fourth century need not be an accurate guide for those of the seventh and sixth centuries, some age qualifications certainly were in force in Athenian society from very early times. Already in the fifth century military service depended at least in part on age-grades, and age qualifications for some magistracies are securely attested from circa 500, and possibly as early as the time of Drakon.[66] Solon was certainly familiar with the idea that certain ages were appropriate for certain activities.[67] It is not necessary to believe that specific ages for different offices or activities were set by law, and early age qualifications may have been dictated by custom alone. But enforcement of even customary practices will have been facilitated by reference to a written list of archons.

A list of archons could theoretically have survived in memory or have been transmitted orally, as some scholars have assumed.[68] But an official list of Athenian archons was written down at some time, and the time of Solon's legislation provides a suitable terminus ante quem for such a step. The overall uniformity of the archon list for all periods, the lack of evidence for manipulation, and the use of archon dating in Solon's legislation all point to the existence and upkeep of an annual archon list from the early sixth century, at the very latest. Evidence for archon dating before the time of Solon is more difficult to come by, but the names of some seventh-century archons are attested, including ones with whom no events of historical significance were associated.[69] The seventh century saw the Athenians and other Greeks begin to write down some of the laws that were to govern their legal and political practices. Although the precise conditions that motivated the Athenians to take this step are unknown to us, the recording of laws was probably due in part to a desire to establish fixed rules where none had existed before, or where earlier practices had been vague, imprecise, or not entirely uniform.[70] The same desire offers a rationale for the creation, preservation, and upkeep of a list of eponymous archons. It is possible that a list was originally preserved orally, but studies of oral traditions suggest that orally transmitted lists and traditions are subject to manipulation and alteration over time: like orally transmitted legal procedures and penalties, oral lists could be subject to arbitrary treatment and application, and this aspect of oral transmission probably was not lost on the same Athenians of the seventh and sixth centuries who called for laws to be fixed in writing.[71] The existence of written laws at Athens already in the seventh century may be the best argument for the creation and upkeep of an annual list of their eponymous officials from the very same period.

IV. Written Records and Kleisthenes' Reforms

The sixth-century documents we have discussed thus far all concern the activities of individual magistrates. But what of written records of laws and other rules governing aspects of life in the Athenian community?

The first decade of the sixth century witnessed the publication of Solon's laws, which provided the Athenians with an extensive body of written rules governing many areas of human activity. Such publication might suggest that henceforth decisions taken or approved by the Athenian people meeting in assembly would be similarly preserved. But we should hesitate before making this assumption. Solon had issued his laws in writing, but he had also received, it seems, a special commission to do so; as far as we know his laws were not debated or discussed in the Ekklesia, and the Athenians simply swore to abide by them en masse.[72] We are otherwise terribly ill informed about legislative procedure during the sixth century. Scholars usually assume that the archon had some control over what business came before the Ekklesia, but how this control was exercised and what effect it had on the written preservation of the Ekklesia's decisions are questions for which our evidence offers no answers.[73] Many of Solon's laws took the form of general, permanent rules governing such areas as the administration of justice, and it seems reasonable to think that proposals treating similar topics, especially those that modified or amended Solon's work, were similarly set down in writing. But other decisions, such as declarations of war or dispatches of embassies, which required immediate action and possessed no permanently binding significance, may not have been written down at all. A vote of the Ekklesia could order a specific action, such as the departure of an embassy, that had no need of a written text for implementation. Writing was not essential to every product of the legislative process.

But the public uses of writing were spreading throughout the sixth century, and it is therefore reasonable to ask whether at least some records of the Ekklesia's business, business that was arguably of greater significance than that of individual magistrates, merited preservation in writing. The Ekklesia certainly met to choose magistrates throughout the sixth century, and even if its choices were limited, preservation of an archon list points to the keeping of some records of elections. The sixth century also saw the institution of new public festivals, among them the Panathenaia. These will have required additional duties for the magistrates involved, and following the precedent of Solon's legislation, regulations governing magisterial duties and public sacrifices may have been committed to writing. In addition, it is unclear whether the Athenians differentiated between legislative acts of permanent validity and general applicability (i.e., laws) and those that were more specific and ephemeral in nature (e.g., a decree calling for the mobilization of the army). Solon's amnesty law, for example, was aimed at specific groups of people and its contents will have lost significance once those recalled by its terms had returned to Athens. But its text was written down and survived for centuries. The Athenians of the sixth century may not have drawn so sharp a distinction between general measures with permanent validity and acts of more limited applicability and duration, as they would in later times. That does not mean that every decision of the sixth-century Ekklesia must have been preserved in writing, but we should not be surprised to find written documentation of the Ekklesia's business becoming increasingly common.

And yet few traces of laws or decrees approved by the Ekklesia survive before the end of the sixth century. Sixth-century Athenian history was dominated by the tyranny of Peisistratos and his sons, and neither they nor the Athenian Ekklesia seems to have engaged in extensive legislative activity. But the lack of evidence for sixth-century laws and decrees need not arise from the failure of the Athenians to write down and keep written records of their public decisions. It may simply reflect the relative inactivity of the Ekklesia. Traditions about the tyranny of Peisistratos support this view. According to several sources, Peisistratos respected the laws of Solon and refrained from changing them.[74] Another tradition held that Peisistratos promoted agriculture with the view to keeping Attic farmers on their land and away from the city so that they would not trouble themselves with public affairs.[75] The institution of traveling deme judges and an imposition of a tax on Attic produce, both attributed to Peisistratos, might have been enacted by decrees, but Aristotle's references to these innovations are too brief to establish what his sources were.[76] Several dates in the chronology of the tyranny of Peisistratos and his sons might also point to documentary sources; it has been suggested, for example, that Aristotle's reference (*Ath. Pol.* 14.1) to a decree of Ariston, by which Peisistratos was awarded a bodyguard before his first seizure of power in the archonship of Komeas (561/0), could have emanated from an inscribed text of the decree; so too the dates for Peisistratos's first exile and his death have been held to derive from popular decrees.[77] But these archon dates could just as easily have survived in the memory of the Athenians, or they could be the product of calculations based on the number of years Peisistratos and his sons were believed to have held power, information that, as Herodotus shows, was preserved in oral traditions.[78]

With the expulsion of Peisistratos's son Hippias in 511/10, however, evidence for Athenian documents increases, perhaps because of growing activity on the part of the Ekklesia. Two inscriptions of the late sixth century preserve sacred laws apparently related to the Eleusinian Mysteries; we do not know what body was responsible for ratifying or setting up these inscribed texts, but the Ekklesia supervised sacred matters and enacted legislation on sacred affairs in later periods, so its hand may be behind both measures. The earliest Athenian decree on stone, which concerns Athenian settlers on the island of Salamis, is also dated to just before the turn of the century.[79] None of these inscriptions can be dated precisely, so a connection between their publication and the overthrow of the tyranny can only be regarded as tentative, but literary sources also point to greater legislative activity in the last decade of the sixth century. Thucydides (6.55.1) refers to a stele set up on the Acropolis pronouncing a sentence of exile on the Peisistratids and their descendants and including a list of those to whom the sentence applied. Thucydides does not relate how this sentence was enacted, but cases of treason and attempted tyranny were later tried before the Ekklesia, which passed judgment on the accused; presumably the Ekklesia was also responsible for the ban on the Peisistratids.[80] Shortly after the expulsion of the tyrants, the Athenians undertook a revision of their citizen rolls with the purpose of depriving of citizenship those who had acquired it fraudulently under the tyrants. Aristotle, our source for this *diapsēphismos*, does not reveal how he knew of the measure, but later revisions of the citizen rolls were carried out after a decree of the Ekklesia, and it is possible that a similar decree served as his source in this instance.[81] Another measure dated to the years immediately following Hippias's expulsion was a decree ratified in the archonship of Skamandrios prohibiting the torture of Athenian citizens.[82] The decree was still valid in 415, when it was cited in a debate in the Boule, and although it is impossible to know in what form its text was available, we have no evidence that the Athenians retained records of legislative acts in their memories alone. Citation of the decree in debate suggests that a written text was available.

Further measures followed in the next several years. In the struggle for power among Athenian aristocrats after the expulsion of Hippias, son of Peisistratos, the Athenian Kleisthenes eventually overcame his opponents in 508/7 and pushed through a series of reforms restructuring the political fabric of the Athenian state. These reforms demand only a brief summary here. Their centerpiece was a tribal reorganization, founded on a territorial basis, of the Athenian people. Athenians were required to register in demes, local villages or towns spread throughout Attica, and membership in a deme henceforth was to serve as the basic criterion for determining Athenian citizenship. The demes themselves were distributed among ten new tribes in such a way that each tribe represented a cross section of the entire population of Attica. The impact of the tribal reform was felt most prominently in Athenian government through the establishment of a council, the Boule of Five Hundred, made up of fifty members from each of the ten new tribes. The Boule exercised a pro-bouleutic function and prepared business for the Ekklesia; it may have also enjoyed some judicial powers. Beyond the tribal reform, the extent of Kleisthenes' work is uncertain. Although some scholars have assumed that Kleisthenes was responsible for redistributing political and judicial power among the city's magistrates, the Boule, the Ekklesia, the Areopagos, and the lawcourts, evidence for such changes is meager, and Kleisthenes may have left many organs of Athenian government, and aristocratic control over them, untouched.[83]

Of greater interest to us is the extent to which Kleisthenes' reforms prompted or required further uses of writing and record keeping by the Athenian state and its magistrates. One area may have required written documents. Kleisthenes made citizenship dependent on an individual's membership in one of the Attic demes, which later numbered 139. In the fifth and fourth centuries, demes kept lists of their member-citizens on registers called *lēxiarchika grammateia*, and it is commonly assumed that their use went back to the time of Kleisthenes himself.[84] But these registers are first attested only in an inscription dated to the 440s, and it has also been suggested that their use was not instituted until a citizenship law, proposed by Pericles, changed the requirements for Athenian citizenship in 451/0.[85] The argument from silence (*lēxiarchika grammateia* are not mentioned until after 450), however, is not conclusive.[86] Athenian officials were using written documents increasingly in different areas of Athenian life throughout the sixth century, so a use of writing for maintaining lists of deme members would not have been out of place; indeed, the keeping of some type of citizenship lists may not have been entirely new in the late sixth century.[87] Ostwald has pointed out that the *lēxiarchika grammateia* were more than citizenship lists. They also listed the property classes to which citizens belonged. These classes went back to the time of Solon, and possibly earlier, and they determined not only what offices citizens were eligible for, but also what financial and military obligations citizens owed to the state. Ostwald argues strongly that lists recording these obligations must have existed even before the *lēxiarchika grammateia* came into use, and he postulates that the *naukraroi*, Athenian officials who played some role in state finances during the sixth century, were responsible for their upkeep. Explicit evidence for naukraric lists is not forthcoming, but a system for specifying the financial and other obligations owed by citizens must have existed; that writing played some role in this system even before the time of Kleisthenes is certainly a reasonable hypothesis.

Use of official, written lists in some form at Athens in the late sixth century may be illustrated in Attic vase painting. A red-figure vase dated to the last decade of the sixth century depicts several young men leading horses toward an individual who is recording information on a writing tablet.[88] The scene is regularly identified with some sort of scrutiny or inspection of Athenian cavalrymen and their mounts, and it suggests that written registers of cavalrymen were in use already in the late sixth century. Arguments by analogy are seldom decisive, but the keeping of some form of written records related to the Athenian cavalry in the late sixth century certainly removes obstacles against believing that Attic demes were capable of keeping similar lists of their own members from the time Kleisthenes gave them a political role.[89]

How far the Kleisthenic reforms affected the keeping of other types of Athenian records, especially laws and decrees, is far less clear. Difficulties arise in part because we do not know the fate of the very measures by which Kleisthenes' reforms were put in place. Kleisthenes probably won support for his work by presenting proposals in the form of decrees to the Ekklesia, and although we hear virtually nothing about the physical disposition of his proposals after their approval, we can probably take it for granted that they were set down in writing at the time. The laws of Solon had been recorded almost a century earlier, and although the contents of Solon's laws were vastly different from the measures promulgated by Kleisthenes, the complexity of his tribal reorganization may have necessitated its explication in writing. But the survival of Kleisthenes' measures into later times is more problematic. They are not referred to by the Attic orators, and one reference to them, mentioned by Aristotle, at a meeting of the Athenian Ekklesia on the eve of an oligarchic revolution at Athens in the year 411 has especially troubled scholars. At that meeting, a certain Pythodoros proposed a decree calling for the appointment of *syngrapheis*, "commissioners," to draft measures for the safety and salvation of Athens. Kleitophon added an amendment to Pythodoros's decree, instructing the commissioners "to investigate . . . the ancestral laws that Kleisthenes had enacted when he established the democracy."[90] The sincerity of Kleitophon's motion is sometimes questioned, and since we hear nothing more of Kleisthenes or his laws in the events that follow, we may wonder whether a search was conducted or whether Kleitophon even intended one to be carried out. But whatever questions we may have about Kleitophon's motives, his motion was approved, and this certainly implies that at least some of the Athenians who voted for it believed that the laws of Kleisthenes existed and could be found if looked for.[91]

To be sure, Kleitophon's motion shows only what some Athenians thought in 411; it does not demonstrate that texts of Kleisthenes' laws actually existed. But other records from the same period did survive, and although this does not prove anything about the fate of Kleisthenes' acts, it suggests that records of state decisions were being recorded and preserved with growing frequency. In the same year or shortly after Kleisthenes carried out his reforms, the Athenians condemned those Athenians who had supported the Spartan king Kleomenes in his invasion of Attica in 508/7. The vote of condemnation was inscribed on a bronze stele set up near the old Athena temple on the Acropolis. The Athenians seem to have used bronze stelai for sentences against traitors and public enemies or for texts of a sacred nature, but we cannot exclude the possibility that bronze was the preferred medium of publication before marble stelai gained wider popularity around the middle of the fifth century; Kleisthenes' reforms may have been published on bronze. Another possibility, however, is that they were published and preserved on wooden boards or even papyrus. The archon (or some other official) had begun to keep records of the performances at the City Dionysia from the last decade of the sixth century, records that had far less practical significance than those carried by Kleisthenes. These didascalic records were not, as far as we know, inscribed on stone or bronze until after the middle of the fourth century, when the Fasti were published, but their survival was in no way hampered by their probable preservation on some other material. Their preservation does not prove the existence of Kleisthenic laws or decrees in the late fifth century, but it does show that long-term survival of uninscribed documents of the late sixth century was a real possibility.

An inscription (*IG* I³ 105) published on stone in the late fifth century and recording a series of regulations delineating the relative powers of the Boule and the Ekklesia offers further evidence for the preservation of sixth-century documents. Its text is poorly preserved, but the archaic wording of parts of it shows that we are dealing with regulations of much older date than the inscription itself.[92] Some portions of the text are part of an oath, and many scholars believe that the inscription actually preserves the text of the Bouleutic Oath, which according to Aristotle was first sworn by the Boule in the archonship of Hermokreon (501/0) and continued to be sworn up to his own day.[93] But the inscription also contains at least two other measures, which are set off from the oath and from each other by a specific enactment formula, "the following things seemed best." These provisions appear to be laws concerning the relative powers of the Boule and Ekklesia, and they probably reflect legislation designed to refine or redefine the Boule's powers in the years following Kleisthenes' reforms.[94] Why would such measures be published on stone nearly a century after their enactment? Possibly, they had originally been inscribed on separate stelai, and the publication in the late fifth century reflects a desire to bring together several related measures onto a single stone. But Immerwahr has pointed out that measures concerning secular and internal Athenian affairs do not appear in the epigraphical record until late in the fifth century.[95] Arguments based on the surviving sample of Attic inscriptions must be deployed with caution, since the inscriptions still extant probably represent only a portion of those that were originally published on stone. But the absence of stelai inscribed with constitutional and nonreligious, legal measures before the late fifth century is nonetheless striking. A more likely hypothesis, and one consistent with the available epigraphical material, is that measures like the Bouleutic Oath and the other provisions related to the Boule's powers found in *IG* I[3] 105 were originally published and preserved only on materials other than stone.[96]

That the Bouleutic Oath was preserved without being published on stone is further suggested by a clause in the Coinage Decree. This decree probably dates from around 420 and it implemented the use of Athenian weights, measures, and coinage throughout the Athenian empire. One provision of that decree calls on the secretary of the Boule to add a clause to the Bouleutic Oath.[97] Since the secretary of the Boule is given responsibility for this addition, the natural assumption is that he had control of or access to the oath's text. But the decree does not instruct the secretary to rewrite or erase any part of the oath; he is simply told to make the specified addition. Addition of a further clause to the oath should have left an earlier text of the oath intact, the same procedure we saw at work with additions made to Drakon's homicide law.[98] The verb used to order the addition to the Bouleutic Oath is also suggestive in another respect. The verb used is *prosgraphein*, which means "to write in addition to" or "to add in writing." *Prosgraphein* sometimes refers to additions made to texts inscribed on stone, but it can also refer to additions made to documents recorded on other materials, including wooden tablets.[99] Quite possibly, then, at the time the Coinage Decree was enacted, the Bouleutic Oath had not been published on stone but existed only in a copy on a wooden tablet or papyrus, to which the secretary of the Boule added the clause ordered by that decree. Preservation in this manner would also explain why the Bouleutic Oath and other measures concerning the Boule were published on stone (*IG* I[3] 105) in the late fifth century: these measures had previously not been so displayed. Their texts had been preserved, but, like the laws of Solon, wood may have been the material of choice.

The Bouleutic Oath itself was not an immediate component of Kleisthenes' reforms, since it was first sworn several years after those were carried in 508/7. But the oath was a direct product of those reforms and perhaps the final step in their implementation. Jacoby believed that these measures could have been found in the archives of the Boule, which he thought came into being at the time of Kleisthenes' reforms, when the Boule replaced the archon as the chief executive of the Athenian state.[100] The Boule certainly had its own archives in the second half of the fifth century, when its secretary managed many types of documents reflecting the central position of the Boule in Athenian government. If we could be certain that this secretary existed from the moment the Kleisthenic Boule was instituted, we would have some reason to believe that business coming before the Boule and Ekklesia was routinely committed to writing and, to some degree, preserved from the same time. Unfortunately, the secretary of the Boule is not securely attested until the middle of the fifth century, when the names of individual secretaries first appear in the prescripts of inscribed Athenian decrees.[101] Evidence for the disposition of Athenian documents in the fifty years following Kleisthenes' reforms is otherwise quite thin and limited to some half-dozen Athenian decrees inscribed on stone. Once again, however, the absence of inscribed laws and decrees is not evidence that texts were not preserved in writing. Publication on stone of an archon list and the Fasti, years after their texts had started to be kept in writing, shows how documents could survive and be maintained without being entrusted to more durable materials. Since the Boule exercised a probouleutic function and supervised many areas of Athenian government, it was the natural body to record and preserve records of decisions approved by itself and the Ekklesia, in whatever form they were kept. Legislative decisions may not have been numerous in the decades immediately following Kleisthenes' reforms, and what records were kept may not have been well organized or cared for. But the survival of didascalic records from the late sixth century indicates that records were being kept in some order, and it is not too hazardous to suppose that the Boule treated decisions of the Ekklesia, like those found in *IG* I³ 105, in a similar way.

Another possibility, however, also merits consideration. Rhodes has argued that the Boule's activities were actually quite limited until the time of Ephialtes' reforms in the late 460s; prior to that time, the Boule considered proposals before they advanced to the Ekklesia for final approval but exercised few other duties. Rhodes also suggests that the system of *prytaneis*, the tribal contingents of fifty men who took turns presiding over meetings of the Boule and Ekklesia, may also have been an innovation resulting from the increased influence granted the Boule by Ephialtes.[102] If this late dating is correct, creation of a Boule secretary might also belong to the post-Ephialtic period, and we might want to consider what other magistrates could have overseen the keeping or publication of earlier decisions enacted by the Ekklesia. The eponymous archon is one possibility. The archon is generally believed to have presided over meetings of the Ekklesia in the sixth century, and he presumably will have continued to do so until he was replaced by *prytaneis* of the Boule.[103] The duty of keeping records of what the Ekklesia decided may also have fallen on archons by virtue of their supervision of its business. Some evidence points in this direction. A decree prohibiting torture of Athenian citizens was known as the decree enacted in the time of Skamandrios, probably the archon, in spite of the fact that in later periods decrees were generally known by the names of their proposers. Similarly, the Hekatompedon Decrees of 485/4 are dated by the name of an archon with no mention of officials of the Boule, although other inscribed decrees regularly use only the names of Bouleutic officials for dating purposes until the late fifth century.[104] The use of archon names for both measures can be explained on the assumption that decisions of the Ekklesia were not only enacted in the archonships of these individuals but also preserved by them in records kept under their names. On this view, the archon maintained not only records from the City Dionysia, which he also supervised, but also measures enacted by the Ekklesia, at least to the time of Ephialtes. This is of course only a possibility, but it is one that accounts for the specific dating of several measures of the early fifth century to archon years.[105]

v. Conclusion

It would be mistaken to exaggerate the extent to which written documents had infiltrated Athenian public life by the end of the sixth century, nor has it been my intention to argue for the survival of large numbers of sixth-century documents into the fifth and fourth centuries or for their widespread consultation by later historians. Athens was a predominantly oral society well into the fifth and fourth centuries, and writing made its way into many areas quite slowly. But the evidence reviewed here suggests that Athenian magistrates of the sixth century had found further uses for writing beyond its earlier function of recording laws, and these uses were not simply symbolic. Laws themselves continued to be written down, although the practice may have become regularized only with an increase in legislative activity at the end of the sixth century. Even earlier, however, some officials had started to keep written accounts of their income and expenditure of public funds and to draw up inventories of dedications and other objects housed in sacred buildings or sanctuaries. By the end of the century other magistrates were making and preserving more general records of public business they oversaw, like those of the City Dionysia, and a list of archons was probably kept up throughout the sixth century as a reference point for dating purposes. These uses were probably not dictated by law, and not all Athenian officials will have used writing consistently or regularly. But the utility of written documents as tools that could assist the administration of official business or provide evidence of a magistrate's actions while in office had gained recognition by 500. We are accustomed to think of the second half of the fifth century, after the implementation of the Ephialtic reforms and the expansion of the Athenian Empire, as the period in which the use of writing became more widespread at Athens for official, administrative purposes, and there can be no doubt that these developments brought with them new situations in which written documents proved increasingly useful. But the sixth century was also a period of rapid growth and change for Athens; it saw the establishment or expansion of several state festivals, the introduction of coinage, the first large-scale building on the Acropolis and in the lower city, and a reform of the political system. Writing was not necessary for these innovations nor was it a necessary component of them. But written documents had started to play further roles in public life. The administrative use of documents attested to by the vast crop of Attic inscriptions of the second half of the fifth century was not a phenomenon wholly new to the fifth century. It had its origins in practices that began more than a century before.

CHAPTER THREE

Records and Archives
in the Fifth Century

About a century after Kleisthenes' reforms, the Athenians initiated several significant projects related to their public records. Between 410 and 399, they undertook a review and revision of their existing laws. Many aspects of this revision are uncertain, but it seems that the Athenians appointed a board of *anagrapheis* in 410 to examine the laws, determine which measures were currently valid, and gather these into a single collection or code. The same decade probably also saw the establishment of the Metroon, the sanctuary of the Mother of the Gods, as a centralized, state archive, in which many important documents were routinely deposited.

Discussion of these events and their relevance to the development of Athens' archives form the subject of the next chapter. They merit attention here, however, because of the role they play in assessments of the nature of Athenian public records before the end of the fifth century. For historians generally see both the revision of the Athenian law code and the establishment of the Metroon as an archival repository as epochal events for Athenian public records and for the transition of Athens from an oral to literate society.[1] Prior to the last decade of the fifth century, the preservation of Athenian documents and records had been haphazard and unsystematic; the Boule may have kept some records in its meeting place, the Bouleuterion, but most state documents were scattered around the city at the offices of different magistrates and published on a variety of media.[2] An extreme view holds that before the late fifth century the Athenians did not keep archives in any sense of the word. Records inscribed on stone were the only permanent texts of many state documents, and texts written on other materials were destroyed as soon as they had served their immediate purpose.[3]

The chief difficulty facing a study of archives in fifth-century Athens is the nature of our sources. Although the number of available sources increases dramatically during this century, especially after circa 450, when the Athenians began to inscribe large numbers of documents on stone, these sources have proved rather uninformative when it comes to questions about the archives of Athens. Earlier studies, for example, have sought to establish what buildings served as archival repositories during the fifth century, but literary and epigraphical texts have little to say about the location of uninscribed texts, so this approach has yielded few definitive answers. Details of decrees inscribed on stone have attracted more attention on the assumption that their features reflect both the disposition and contents of other, archival records. This approach is more promising, but arguments about archival texts based on inscriptions must proceed with caution. The Athenians did not publish all state documents on stone, and those they did inscribe were often extracts taken from fuller texts preserved in some other format. Explicit evidence for these unpublished texts is sparse, but their existence may be deduced from features of epigraphical texts and scattered allusions to them in literary sources.

An examination of these unpublished, archival records forms the subject of this chapter. The first section offers some general observations about Athenian inscriptions and their relationship to other records maintained by Athenian magistrates. It is argued that, however valuable the evidence provided by inscribed documents, a proper assessment of Athenian writing and record keeping must recognize that these texts represent only a portion of the records kept by Athenian officials, most of which were not inscribed on stone but still could be preserved for long periods of time. Discussion then turns in the next two sections to the archives of the Boule, which contained texts of laws and decrees enacted during the fifth century. Attention is focused, however, not on the buildings in which these archives were housed, but on the official, the secretary of the Boule, responsible for their maintenance. Consideration of the duties of this secretary will suggest that he regularly recorded decisions reached by the Boule and Ekklesia; the names of Boule secretaries also provided the system by which texts of fifth-century legislation were organized. Because insights into the records kept by the Boule secretary depend largely on inscribed documents, conclusions can seldom advance beyond the stage of hypothesis. But the investigation will show that behind the inscriptions on stone there flourished an extensive array of other documents, the nature of which demands attention in the study of Athenian literacy, writing, and record keeping.

1. Inscriptions and Archives

One of the distinctive features of the Athenian democracy of the fifth century was its tendency to publish state documents on stone stelai—large, rectangular slabs of marble. The earliest surviving documents on stone date from the end of the sixth century, but their numbers increase dramatically around the middle of the fifth century. The surviving inscriptions represent a wide range of documents: decrees enacted by the Ekklesia, records of state debts lent out by sacred treasuries, and inventories of some of the city's sacred buildings. The sudden rise in the number of inscribed, official documents around 450 is sometimes attributed to the democratic reforms carried by Ephialtes in 462/1, but many inscriptions concern Athens' overseas empire and relations with subject-allies, and the rapid growth of this empire from the 450s played an equally important role in the Athenian predilection to display so many state documents on stone.[4]

Epigraphists have traditionally seen the publication of documents on stone as an attempt to make their texts more accessible to the general public, but they have also recognized that behind the stone texts there lay fuller and more complete documents, including ones stored in archival collections.[5] Some fifty years ago, however, Kahrstedt argued that before the end of the fifth century the Athenians did not have real archives: publicly displayed copies were their only permanent texts of most state documents.[6] Kahrstedt based this view in part on the Athenian practice of citing fifth-century documents by the physical objects, usually the stelai, on which they were published. He also pointed out that when fifth-century decrees were repealed, annulment was accompanied by the physical destruction of the stelai on which their texts were inscribed.[7] The fourth century, however, saw a change in practice. When the orators cited documents in their speeches, they usually did not mention a source for them, presumably because the Metroon, the state archives building, was generally recognized as their place of origin. Similarly, when decrees were repealed in the fourth century, a public slave working in the Metroon took responsibility for their destruction.[8] Kahrstedt inferred that fifth-century inscriptions must have preserved the only texts of the documents they recorded, but that in the fourth century documents were regularly deposited in the Metroon, where their texts were available for consultation.

Initially, Kahrstedt's views won few adherents. But recent years have seen their revival in modified form, especially in works focusing on writing and its role in the predominantly oral society of classical Athens. Their arguments are complex, and a brief review cannot do them full justice. Generally speaking, however, they argue that documents on stone were the principal and perhaps only means by which lasting records were kept during the fifth century. Inscriptions were cited with frequency and constituted the chief administrative documents of the Athenian state. But the same inscriptions were not frequently read or set up to be read; they functioned more as monuments, symbols, and "talismans" that often carried meanings and messages beyond what was stated in their written contents. The fourth century saw some change in practice; archives developed and the Athenians became more "document-minded." But even then the city's archives were disorderly and confused, and inscribed texts continued to be cited as authoritative texts.[9]

A detailed investigation of the function of public inscriptions in Athenian society falls beyond the scope of this work. That inscriptions were physical objects that could be used and viewed in symbolic terms, as recent studies emphasize, is an important observation, although it is hardly new.[10] That they were also considered authoritative documents worthy of consultation is also significant, although this point too is not novel.[11] But the further conclusions drawn from these observations, that inscriptions preserved the only lasting records of documents or that records on other materials were not regularly kept, are insupportable.[12] Inscriptions were set up by state officials and they recorded state documents. If they were erected to make their texts more accessible, as is commonly believed, it was only natural for Athenians to consult and cite their texts. But the citation of inscribed documents reveals nothing about the disposition of other texts of the same or similar documents. We know that documents were recorded on materials like wood and papyrus throughout the fifth century, and although this point is often recognized, its general significance has not received sufficient attention in assessing the nature of Athenian public records. Evidence for the keeping of uninscribed texts of laws and decrees is treated in the next section. But it should prove useful first to consider briefly some aspects of the other types of documents made, used, and preserved by Athenian magistrates throughout the fifth century.

The administration of Athenian government in the fifth century relied heavily on written documents, not from necessity but by choice: the Athenians placed a high value on keeping and maintaining accurate records of many items of state business. This importance is well illustrated by the use of secretaries, *grammateis*, by numerous Athenian boards and magistrates. Secretaries are attested already in the middle of the sixth century, but evidence for their existence proliferates from the middle of the fifth century, when secretaries are found serving the Hellenotamiai, the treasurers of Athena, the *epistatai* or "overseers" of various Athenian building projects, and numerous other officials.[13] We do not know what qualifications were required of these secretaries, but they were Athenian citizens and an individual could serve as secretary for the same official or board for several years.[14] Some secretaries kept records of a judicial nature; thus, Strepsiades daydreams of erasing the text of a lawsuit brought against him as the secretary for an unnamed official writes the indictment down.[15] Others might assist in drawing up state contracts; thus, an undersecretary to the *pōlētai*, the Athenian officials responsible for selling state contracts, is mentioned in a speech of Antiphon dating to circa 420.[16] And still others, who are otherwise unattested, must have kept records related to the administration of Athenian festivals, like those of the Dionysia, which were maintained and updated continually throughout the fifth and into the fourth century.

Some secretaries were involved in keeping records of a financial nature. It was a basic principle of Athenian government that all officials who handled public finances should submit to an audit at the end of their term of office. When this rule came into effect and how widely it was applied are uncertain, but many officials were maintaining written accounts of their income and expenditures by the 450s, when the earliest financial records on stone appear.[17] Secretaries are named frequently in these documents, and their names are placed prominently in the opening lines. They are so named because the inscribed texts were copied from other documents, originally written on wooden tablets or papyri, kept by them throughout the course of the year.[18] These uninscribed documents were examined at the end of each year (and perhaps more frequently) by a board of *logistai* or auditors who examined them for malfeasance and received complaints from citizens about financial wrongdoing.[19] It was these accounts, and not the inscriptions themselves, that were the administrative documents of fifth-century Athens.

The surviving inscriptions are a poor guide to both the amount and types of written documents used by Athenian magistrates, because only a relatively small number of documents were ever inscribed on stone.[20] Consider, for example, the records of the Hellenotamiai, the treasurers of the Delian League and the Athenian Empire, who received tribute payments from Athens' allies. Few, if any, of their records were ever published in permanent form. It is well known that the so-called Athenian Tribute Lists preserve not an annual record of the actual tribute paid by the subject-allies of the Athenians, but merely the *aparchai* or "first-fruits" consisting of one-sixtieth of the tribute that was dedicated to Athena.[21] We have no evidence to suggest that records of the actual tribute paid by Athens' subject-allies were similarly inscribed, but that is no reason to doubt that annual records of payments by allies were not actually kept; they were simply written down on documents made from other materials.[22] Similarly, inscribed records of the assessments imposed by the Athenians on their subjects survive only after 430; earlier assessments were certainly recorded, but they may not have been deemed worthy of publication on stone.[23] The absence of particular types of documents among the surviving inscriptions is not evidence that these documents did not exist or were not preserved. It simply shows that the Athenians did not publish every state document on stone.

Similar observations hold true for other types of inventories and financial documents. The inscribed inventories of the cellae of the Parthenon, made by the annual boards of the treasurers of Athena and surviving on an annual basis from 434/3, do not represent all the records produced by these treasurers.[24] Fifth-century inventories preserve lists of sacred objects and dedications housed in the Parthenon. Accounts of the coined money in Athena's treasury, which made up the bulk of its wealth, do not survive. Close track was presumably kept of money (coined and uncoined) as well as sacred objects, but if accounts were ever published, no trace of them has survived; probably they were simply not inscribed on stone. Inscribed building accounts of the fifth century also point to limited publication. Accounts of income and expenditures are extant for the construction of the Parthenon, the Propylaia, and the Erechtheion, and for the making of the statues of Athena Promachos and Athena Parthenos, among others.[25] Similar, published accounts for secular public buildings, several of which were constructed over the course of the fifth century, are unknown.[26] It is possible that no records of the costs of these buildings were ever drawn up and that the officials who oversaw their construction were not subject to audit. But it is equally and perhaps more plausible to suppose that records for such secular building projects were simply not inscribed on stone.[27]

Some inscribed financial records also represent summaries of more complete sets of documents. The yearly accounts for the construction of the Parthenon, for example, begin with a statement of the income received each year by the *epistatai*, the overseers of construction, broken down by the source for each payment.[28] There follows a list of expenses. These appear as simple figures for such expenditures as stonecutting at the Pentelic quarries, transport of the marble to Athens, unspecified purchases or more specific ones for gold or silver, and payments to workmen. Expenses are not broken down any further, and the names of individuals are not given nor are records of daily wages paid to workmen supplied. Another, more detailed picture of building records kept by fifth-century officials and their secretaries is represented in the accounts of the Erechtheion.[29] These records are not simple summaries; they provide detailed accounts, prytany-by-prytany, of the income and expenditures for the temple's construction. Not only do these accounts list the wages paid in each prytany for different tasks, they also provide the names of individual workers and the wages paid to them. We cannot be certain that the Parthenon's *epistatai* kept similarly detailed records throughout their time in office, but it seems reasonable to assume that they kept more detailed information than what was inscribed on stone. At the end of each year, they condensed their accounts and inscribed a simple overview of their total income and expenditures.[30]

The publication of records on stone by magistrates, whether full texts or summaries, at the end of their time in office raises questions about the fate of the documents from which published texts were taken. In the Hellenistic period, Athenian officials deposited copies of accounts and inventories in the Metroon, and this practice was almost certainly observed during the fourth century.[31] Evidence for fifth-century practice is far less clear. It might be assumed that officials did not maintain any unpublished archives of the transactions they administered. Once they had passed their audits, they simply discarded any documents they had drawn up while in office, leaving only inscribed texts for their successors, or, in cases where no documents were published on stone, no records whatsoever.[32] The destruction of documents by several Athenian officials might support this conclusion. When the *pōlētai* farmed out tax contracts, they wrote up the names of individuals who purchased the contracts with the amounts owed onto whitened wooden boards. The *pōlētai* also wrote up separate tablets for each payment that was to be made: some contracts required payment every prytany and therefore required ten separate tablets, one for each prytany; others were to be paid off in three installments and so were recorded on three separate tablets, while still others were paid off in full in one payment, in the ninth prytany, and were therefore recorded on a single tablet. When payments fell due, a public slave brought the appropriate tablets before the Boule and delivered them to the *apodektai*, the officials responsible for receiving payments owed to the state. The *apodektai* erased the names of those who paid off the debt and handed the blank tablets back to the public slave.[33]

A similar erasure is described in the first of the Kallias Decrees. The opening lines of the first of these decrees call for repayment of moneys owed to the Other Gods from funds held by the Hellenotamiai.[34] The thirty *logistai*, under the supervision of the Boule, are instructed to tabulate the amounts owed to these deities, and the *prytaneis* are ordered to pay back the money in the presence of the Boule. At the time of repayment, the *prytaneis* are called on to erase records of these debts, after they have sought out the tablets and documents on which they were written; the officials possessing such records are similarly ordered to produce them.[35]

Such erasures have suggested to some scholars that the Athenians were not concerned with preserving records of transactions once those transactions were completed.[36] When installments on a public debt were paid off, all records of the debt disappeared along with the debt itself. Finley noted the crudity of this system and took it as a sign of the overall simplicity of ancient documents and ancient record keeping.[37] Thomas interprets the erasure of *pōlētai* documents as paradigmatic of Athenian record keeping in general. The tablets of the *pōlētai* were not documents meant for consultation but "mnemonic aids"; no permanent, written records were kept of these transactions. The procedures illustrate "an absence of an archive mentality" characteristic of the Athenian treatment of written records.[38]

But the overall significance of these erasures should not be exaggerated. The *pōlētai* and *apodektai* did erase some documents recording debts owed to the state, but it is far from certain that the documents they erased were the only records of the debts that were owed. Aristotle's account of the *pōlētai* describes two sets of documents. The first (*Ath. Pol.* 47.2) contained the names of purchasers of tax contracts with the amount they promised to pay for them. The second set of documents (*Ath. Pol.* 47.3) listed the names of purchasers according to the dates on which their payments fell due; these latter documents were those later erased by the *apodektai*. There is no suggestion in Aristotle's account that the earlier documents, which contained a complete record of the purchaser's name and the amount that he promised to pay for the contract, were similarly erased.[39] Similarly, the provisions of the first Kallias Decree concerning the cancellation of documents fail to substantiate claims that no further records were kept signaling the cancellation of those debts. In that decree, the *prytaneis* are instructed to erase the writing tablets and boards recording the debts owed to the Other Gods and supplied by the local priests and sacred officials responsible for the original loans. The search for these tablets was conducted so that the *prytaneis* could corroborate the calculations made by the *logistai* and prevent any future charges or claims that the original debts had not been repaid. The *logistai* are not instructed to establish the amount of moneys owed to the sanctuaries of the Other Gods from these tablets; mention of their activity comes earlier in the decree. That is, the *logistai* must have had their own records from which they tabulated and calculated what was owed.[40] That the records from which the *logistai* made their calculations were also destroyed when payment was made is not stated, and it certainly is not a necessary assumption.[41] Even if they were, it would only show that the Athenians did not maintain permanent records of documents recording payments of debts; the practice says little about the preservation of other types of texts.

We have already seen that records of dramatic contests held at the City Dionysia survived from the end of the sixth century well into the 340s before they were published on stone; similar records of the Lenaia were evidently kept from the 440s. Whatever practical value the records of the contests of individual years may have originally possessed, this value will have disappeared in a few years. Yet didascalic records were kept indefinitely without being published on stone. Their survival demonstrates how perilous it is to assume the widespread destruction of uninscribed documents once their immediate usefulness seems to have passed.[42] Other documents reinforce this point. The Parthenon building accounts span construction over the years 448/7 to 432/1, and they provide an annual (but probably only summary) account of the income and expenditures of the *epistatai* responsible for the temple's construction. But the entries for the first five years seem to have been inscribed in the same hand and at the same time.[43] The accounts of the statue of Athena Promachos similarly span a period of at least nine years, but they too may have been published at a single time.[44] If the Athenians destroyed administrative documents as soon as the transactions they recorded were completed, we should have expected the officials who oversaw both projects to have published their accounts immediately when they passed their audits each year and to have discarded unpublished records at the same time. But this was not the case with either the Parthenon or Promachos accounts. In neither instance were the accounts of each year's board immediately published on stone, but records of several years' accounts were preserved. Publication on stone was neither immediate

RECORDS IN THE FIFTH CENTURY

nor automatic. Preservation in some type of archive, however, was apparently more routine.

It might be argued that the Parthenon and Athena Promachos accounts were preserved archivally pending their eventual publication on stone. Publication was always intended, and once the accounts of each year were inscribed, any other, archival texts were destroyed. This possibility cannot be denied, but the argument is weak in two respects. First, it interprets intentions from results. The Athenians chose to inscribe these accounts a few years after they were drawn up. We are not informed of the reasons for the delay or what ultimately prompted the Athenians to publish them, and to assume that the records were kept only pending later publication simply assumes what needs to be proved. Second, the suggestion that archival documents were destroyed once copies of their texts were inscribed is not stated or implied by any ancient evidence. In the case of the Parthenon and Athena Promachos accounts it is certainly conceivable that any unpublished records related to both projects were destroyed once construction was completed, so that the accounts published on stone were the only lasting texts. That, however, is simply a conjecture, and it would be rash to apply it to all Athenian documents. It is equally possible that copies of these building accounts were deposited elsewhere, perhaps with the *logistai* or the Boule, the latter of which exercised supervision over many public works. We simply do not know what happened to the texts of Athenian documents not inscribed on stone, and to assume systematic destruction goes beyond the available evidence. Our knowledge of most documents depends on a decision to have them inscribed on stone, a decision sometimes taken years after they were created. How many other documents sat in the archives of magistrates for which no such decision was made we cannot know, but their existence cannot be too lightly ignored.

But leaving questions of stone publication aside, we ought not overlook the fact that many uninscribed documents retained practical value for a considerable number of years. The *pōlētai*, for example, drew up leases lasting for periods of five, ten, and twenty years (or more); certainly, the Athenians kept track of payments on these leases, using written records, throughout their duration.[45] A better illustration of preservation and consultation of older, unpublished documents is offered by the Logistai inscription (*IG* I³ 369). Dating from 422/1, it preserves a record, drawn up by the *logistai*, of moneys lent out by the treasurers of Athena and the treasurers of the Other Gods over the previous four years (426/5–423/2). The text records the precise dates on which loans were made and calculates the interest owed at the end of the four-year period.[46] The *logistai* presumably drew up the inscription's text from other documents, written on wooden tablets or papyri and kept by them or by the treasuries mentioned in the text. But the text of the Logistai inscription also made use of documents dating back even earlier, to the year 433/2. For it contains calculations of interest owed to different sacred treasuries as a result of outstanding loans made in the period 433/2–427/6, and final calculations of the interest for the eleven-year period (433/2–423/2).[47] It is reasonable to assume that the *logistai* did not make these calculations in their heads or base their figures on memory alone. They consulted records they themselves had kept or ones maintained by individual treasuries; working from such records they determined when outlays had been made and tabulated what interest had accrued since the loans had been made. As a multiyear record of state debts to sacred treasuries the Logistai inscription is unique, but it illustrates well how detailed the financial records of Athenian officials were and how uninscribed documents could be consulted years after their creation.

Athenian magistrates had been using written documents since the sixth century, and from the middle of the fifth century the administration of the Athenian Empire and the internal workings of Athenian government relied more heavily on them, especially where the financial activities of magistrates were concerned. Documents were made, kept, and preserved for as long as they were thought useful, but we seldom know how the Athenians defined utility, and the long-term preservation of records from the City Dionysia for centuries shows that seemingly obsolete records could be kept far longer than might seem practical—to us. Inscriptions were a part of the system of Athenian documents, but they represent only a fraction of the documents that once existed, and writing was used far more widely and extensively than the study of inscriptions alone suggests. Obviously, the use of written documents in the administrative life of the city did not bring an end to oral modes of communication, nor did the Athenians cease to employ the spoken word in public life. Athenian accounting practices might also appear crude and unsophisticated by modern standards, but such an assessment should not diminish the fact that written documents found widespread, practical use throughout the fifth century. Some of these documents were deemed worthy of more prominent display on stone stelai, many of which survive to the present day. The impressiveness of these inscriptions, however, ought not diminish the significance of the far more numerous documents that were never graced by the mason's chisel.

11. The Archives of the Boule

Like accounts and other records of Athenian magistrates, laws and decrees were also preserved archivally during the fifth century. Some historians have denied this and argued that the principal copies of laws and decrees during the fifth century were those inscribed on stone.[48] This view is thought to be supported by the fact that Athenians often refer to inscribed stelai and not archival texts when they cite documents, and by the paucity of explicit testimony about archival texts in general. But arguments built on negative evidence such as this are weak, and they overlook some basic aspects of Athenian publication practices that merit further discussion.

The display of laws and decrees on stone was in fact probably quite limited in scope. Before the end of the fifth century, we have no evidence that the texts of laws and decrees ratified by the Ekklesia were automatically inscribed.[49] Among the laws and decrees surviving from the fifth century, decrees honoring foreigners or related to foreign affairs predominate and are followed in number by measures related to Athenian sanctuaries and regulating religious affairs.[50] Laws and decrees related to secular and domestic matters are almost entirely absent from the epigraphical record before the last decade of the fifth century.[51] It is not unlikely that most of the business of the Ekklesia and Boule focused on enacting decrees awarding honors, regulating religious matters, or administering the empire. But measures treating secular matters are also attested in literary sources, and the dearth of such measures among the extant inscriptions is difficult to explain by appeals to the accidents of survival alone.[52]

The epigraphical record of the fifth century is of course incomplete, and it would be dangerous to put too much weight on evidence supplied by surviving inscriptions alone. The Thirty Tyrants destroyed some documents, and the Athenians themselves occasionally tore down inscriptions;[53] many more were removed and broken up, from the Roman period to modern times, to be used as construction material in later buildings. But our sources do not suggest that certain types of inscriptions were destroyed with greater frequency than others, and in the absence of other evidence we have no better guide by which to judge what types of documents were routinely inscribed than the extant inscriptions themselves. The survival of large numbers of inscriptions with texts reflecting certain areas of Athenian legislation and the near complete absence of inscriptions representing other areas are difficult to explain unless we assume that underrepresented types of documents were seldom inscribed on stone in the first place. That is, the Athenians may have been more inclined to inscribe documents granting honors to state benefactors, governing their empire, or overseeing their sacred affairs. The available inscriptions, however, do not support the view that laws and decrees dealing with domestic, nonsacred issues, such as citizenship, the administration of justice, or the institution of jury pay, all of which were the subject of legislation in the fifth century, received permanent publication on stone.

But written records of such measures certainly existed. Many may have been displayed on wooden tablets, as were the laws of Solon. All, however, could have been preserved in archives kept by the Boule. In the fifth century, the secretary of the Boule, *ho grammateus tēs boulēs*, served as the chief secretary of the Athenian state. His principal duty, as the title of his office indicates, was to write down and keep records of business that came before both the Boule and the Ekklesia. The significance of an official with these duties cannot be underestimated. The recording of the state's most important decisions was institutionalized and became a part of the machinery of Athenian government, just as the existence of judicial officials with competence over specific areas of law reflected the state's concern for the administration of justice. The existence of a state secretary does not guarantee that his records were accurate and well kept, but it implies a recognition that the state's business, as conducted by the Boule and Ekklesia, merited some degree of preservation in writing. A Boule secretary is first attested in a decree of the 460s, but the office may be earlier in date and perhaps goes back to the establishment of the Boule by Kleisthenes.[54] Throughout the fifth century and until the 360s, Boule secretaries were chosen from the Boule itself. They served for a single prytany, and they were elected from a tribe that was not holding the prytany.[55] Since a citizen could only serve as a *bouleutēs* or councillor twice in his lifetime, iteration in the office of Boule secretary was possible, though it is unattested. Frequent turnover may have brought discontinuity and instability to the records kept by these officials, but if so, it took the Athenians more than a century to attempt to rectify these failings. Consistency might have been achieved if the secretary was assisted by more experienced secretaries; no assistants are explicitly attested during the fifth century, but other magistrates were aided by cosecretaries and undersecretaries, so it is not unlikely that the secretary of the Boule was similarly assisted by a small staff.[56]

Since both Boule and Ekklesia conducted business by means of decrees (*psēphismata*), the secretary concerned himself primarily with recording these documents. This concern is reflected in two formulae found in the inscribed copies of fifth-century decrees. The prescripts of decrees routinely contain the formula "so-and-so served as secretary."[57] This phrase denotes that the named individual had been responsible for keeping a written record, including the text of the decree that follows, of the business transacted at that particular meeting of the Ekklesia. Decrees also regularly include provisions calling upon the secretary of the Boule to have their texts published on stone. Secretaries did not inscribe the texts themselves; contracts for inscribing were let out by the *pōlētai*, and the secretary simply produced a copy of a decree from his records, which he delivered to the stonemason who undertook the actual engraving. Instructions for publication are the best attested of the secretary's duties, but they derive from his more general role as the recorder of the Boule's and Ekklesia's decisions.

Decrees on stone provide most tangible evidence of the secretary's activities, but stone inscriptions were not the only copies of such measures.[58] In the classical Athenian democracy, all business to be treated by the Ekklesia, including proposals for decrees, was first brought before the Boule.[59] If the Boule approved a proposal and passed it on to the Ekklesia, it made a preliminary motion, a *probouleuma*, which the Ekklesia was free either to accept, reject, or amend.[60] The entire enactment process involved writing. Inscriptions generally introduce the texts of motion with the words *ho deina eipe*, "so-and-so spoke."[61] The phrase probably reflects a time when proposals were delivered orally by a proposer in the Boule or Ekklesia. But literary sources preserve another phrase, *graphein psēphisma*, "to write a decree," in connection with the introduction of proposals. The earliest use of this phrase occurs in Aristophanes' *Clouds* (423 B.C.), and it appears frequently in the fourth-century orators, for whom it formed the standard idiom to designate the proposal of a motion.[62] The phrase "to write a decree" suggests that proposers submitted proposed decrees in writing, and we can well imagine that the practice originated around the middle of the fifth century, when the activities of the Ekklesia increased as a result of the reforms of Ephialtes or the expansion of Athens' overseas empire.[63] The submission of written texts of proposals is illustrated by an anecdote in Aeschines' speech *On the False Embassy*; Aeschines recalls how Demosthenes had once asked Amyntor whether he (Demosthenes) should hand in a proposed decree, on which Demosthenes' name was written, to the chairmen of the Ekklesia.[64] Sometimes, however, individuals might simply make a proposal orally, leaving to the secretary the task of drawing it up in writing. Thus, in Aristophanes' *Thesmophoriazusai*, a speaker suggests that the secretary could assist him (or her) later in drafting a motion.[65] But whether a proposer submitted a written text or made a motion orally, the *grammateus* of the Boule surely kept records of proposals that were ratified, a duty implicit in his title.

Suppose a proposal was ratified. What happened to the text received or drawn up by the secretary during the enactment process? If we assume that stone inscriptions preserved the principal and only copies of all fifth-century Athenian decrees, we must assume that a secretary's text of a ratified proposal that contained no provisions for its publication on stone was erased or discarded. But there is no evidence for such routine erasure. The decree of Patrokleides (Andok. 1.77–79), passed in 405, does include provisions calling for the destruction of some documents, including decrees, and other texts prescribe the destruction of inscribed stelai when the terms inscribed on them were revoked.[66] But the erasures of Patrokleides' decree took place long after the concerned decrees had been enacted, and Patrokleides' decree itself was a product of a crisis situation: Athens' pending defeat in the Peloponnesian War. Its provisions are hardly indicative of how Boule secretaries handled decrees in the normal course of business.

The preservation of decrees not initially published on stone, however, is attested in the fifth century. An inscription of 423/2 preserves two decrees and the prescript of a third regulating Athenian relations with the city of Methone in Macedonia.[67] None of these decrees contains a clause ordering their publication on stone, and a fourth decree, once inscribed on a portion of the stele now lost, presumably included some such instructions. Evidence for the fourth decree appears in the form of the secretary, Phainippos, who is named in a heading above the entire text but who is not named in any of the three preserved decrees. Phainippos is mentioned by Thucydides (4.118.1) as secretary when the one-year truce was concluded between Athens and Sparta in 423, so this year should provide the date at which all the decrees were published on stone together. But the earliest of the Methone Decrees was passed between 430 and 426, while the second and third decrees were probably ratified in 426/5 and 425/4.[68] When the three earlier decrees were first enacted, the Athenians evidently did not deem them important enough to be inscribed on stone; the first two decrees, at least, do not contain such instructions. But their texts were preserved for several years, so that when a fourth decree was passed, it was also decided that the earlier decrees concerning Methone also merited publication. At that time the secretary Phainippos searched through records left by his predecessors, found the relevant decrees, and had them published together with the fourth decree.

A skeptical reader might want to discount the Methone Decrees as an isolated occurrence. Others might suggest that the earlier texts were not preserved in an Athenian archive but by the Methoneans, from whom the published texts were taken. But such skepticism is misplaced. It would be difficult to explain why greater care for the preservation of documents should be attributed to the citizens of Methone than the Athenians, especially when the names of at least four Athenian secretaries appeared on the stone. The most likely source for these decrees is the records kept by the secretaries named in the inscriptions themselves. In addition, we know of the first three Methone Decrees only because a later, fourth decree specified their publication on stone. That other decrees sat in the archives of the secretary of the Boule but never received orders for later publication is hardly unlikely. Other possible instances of unpublished decrees stored within these archives may be advanced. The Bouleutic Oath and several laws concerning the powers of the Boule, measures dating from the late sixth and early fifth centuries, were inscribed on a single stele only at the end of the fifth century. The disposition of these measures before publication cannot be established with certainty, but one possibility is that they sat in some sort of archive until they were finally published on stone.[69] Aristotle also mentions several laws from the first half of the fifth century, laws that opened the archonship to citizens belonging to a lower census class, established traveling deme judges, and changed the requirements for citizenship.[70] Aristotle's sources for these laws are uncertain, but measures of similar content are not represented among the surviving inscriptions of the fifth century, and his knowledge of them may derive ultimately from records preserved by the secretary of the Boule. Another reference to a fifth-century decree is especially telling. Andokides (2.23) mentions a decree of Menippos that was still preserved in the Bouleuterion but was no longer in force. The relevance of this decree to Athens' fifth-century archives will be discussed in more detail later, but the obsolescence of the decree at the time of Andokides' speech is noteworthy: it was neither inscribed nor valid, but a copy was still available in the Bouleuterion.

Our evidence for these archives is admittedly sparse, but there are no reasons for assuming that Boule secretaries recorded and preserved decrees selectively or discarded texts of measures that happened to be inscribed on stone, so as to make inscribed decrees the only texts of those documents. Several decrees of the early fourth century may also offer an indication of the extent to which texts were routinely maintained in the Boule's archives. These decrees appear to be republications of decrees originally enacted in the fifth century, and one of them states explicitly that the stele onto which its text had been previously inscribed was torn down under the Thirty Tyrants; the same or similar words may be restored in several other inscriptions.[71] If the stelai on which these decrees were published had been destroyed, where, we may ask, were the republished texts to come from? Honorands sometimes received copies of decrees on their behalf, and individuals honored by fifth-century decrees may have presented such texts when petitioning for republication early in the fourth century.[72] But we do not hear of such petitions or of privately held records, and another possibility is that copies of these decrees were found in the Boule's records. In several of the republished decrees, the secretary of the Boule is instructed to see to the republication; as I have noted already, the secretary normally attends to publication because he was responsible for drawing up and keeping texts of ratified decrees. For the same reason, we may suppose, fourth-century secretaries were ordered to republish fifth-century decrees: the texts were preserved in their records. The argument is admittedly not conclusive, but it explains the available evidence without resorting to unsupported hypotheses.

This interpretation of the Boule's archives requires that we think of the inscribed texts of decrees as copies of other, archival texts created and preserved by the state secretary. The derivative quality of inscribed texts, however, hardly diminished their authenticity or authority. Both Kahrstedt and Thomas were struck by frequent references to inscribed, as opposed to archival, texts in the orators. Kahrstedt inferred from these citations that archival texts of these documents did not exist. Thomas recognizes that archival texts existed even in the fifth century, but she takes the citation of inscriptions as indicative of a more primitive attitude toward records, one that does not recognize the value of archives.[73] This is an odd line of reasoning. The secretary of the Boule copied texts for publication out of his own, official records. He did so, presumably, so that these texts could be more visible and accessible to the public. This, at any rate, is the implication of the phrase *tōi boulomenōi skopein*, "for whoever wishes to examine," which is sometimes used to describe the reasons why Athenian documents were published, whether on wooden tablets or stone stelai.[74] The intent of these words could not be more clear: some documents were inscribed on stone so that, if necessary, they could be read and examined by any concerned citizens.[75] The fact that Athenians consulted and cited inscribed documents may simply indicate that inscriptions were serving the purpose for which they were erected. Why should consultation of an archival text be expected when another text, issued by an official authority and displayed in a public place, was more readily accessible? Athenians cited inscriptions because the inscribed copies of state documents were official, available, and visible: the practice implies nothing about the existence or nonexistence of noninscribed, archival texts in the fifth or later centuries.[76]

So too the destruction of stelai when their texts became obsolete reveals little about the contents or disposition of archival texts. Kahrstedt interpreted this practice as evidence of the nonexistence of archives in the fifth century; Thomas sees the practice as directly opposed to an "archive mentality."[77] Let us step back, however, for a moment and consider this practice. The inscribed copies of laws, decrees, and treaties derived from official and authoritative documents. Their public display surely implied that their texts were valid and in force. If a treaty or other decree was rescinded or abrogated, the continued display of an inscription carrying its texts might lead to confusion; at the very least, continued display contradicted the existing state of affairs. Hence, inscriptions were sometimes destroyed as a purely practical matter. A certain degree of symbolism might have been associated with their removal, as when the Athenians cast the stelai recording the curses against Alkibiades into the sea on his return to Athens in 407. Their removal supplied a symbolic counterpart to the vote of the people canceling those curses. But the act of destruction hardly implies that the stone copy of the law or decree was the only or principal text of that measure.[78]

Much of the confusion surrounding the state of fifth-century Athenian archives arises from the mistaken view that stone inscriptions were the only, or at least the principal, permanent records of fifth-century Athens. But the secretary of the Boule, who oversaw publication of decrees on stone, also dealt with documents on other materials. He attended meetings of the Boule and Ekklesia, of which he kept "minutes," presumably on wooden tablets or papyri, in the form of decrees proposed and ratified by both bodies.[79] He received proposals that were submitted for approval, as we have seen, and he helped compose drafts of measures that were introduced orally. He also made and distributed copies of decrees after ratification. A decree of the late fifth century orders the Boule secretary to prepare a copy and to deliver it to the Samian Poses, who was honored earlier in the decree.[80] The practice of distributing copies of honorary decrees to honorands is not otherwise attested, but there is no reason to doubt that other individuals awarded honors by the Athenians also received written copies of the decrees in their honor. Athenian officials may also have received texts of decrees outlining their duties. In a scene from Aristophanes' *Birds*, an *episkopos*, an official involved in the administration of Athens' empire, arrives in

Cloudcuckooland armed with a decree containing his orders. When questioned, he cites this decree, "a wretched paper of Teleas," referring to a papyrus copy of the decree that he seems to hold in his hand.[81] Aristophanes' purposes are comic, but the passage should reflect a common sight: Athenian officials traveling throughout the empire and carrying with them texts of decrees spelling out their duties. The secretary of the Boule was presumably responsible for making such copies.[82] Some decrees of the fifth century also required publication in cities other than Athens, and here too the secretary will have prepared copies to be sent out and distributed abroad.[83]

In addition to making copies, secretaries also consulted and conducted searches through their own records and those of their predecessors for a variety of reasons. When the fourth of the Methone Decrees gave instructions for the publication of three earlier decrees, the secretary will have had to search for these texts, if they had not already been produced during debate. A provision of the Coinage Decree instructs the secretary of the Boule to add a provision to the Bouleutic Oath, presumably because this oath was found in the Boule's archives: its text had to be retrieved and modified.[84] A decree of 411 honoring a certain Pythophanes prescribes its own publication and that of an earlier decree for Pythophanes. We do not know when the earlier decree on Pythophanes' behalf was enacted, but its text will have had to be located to be added to the inscription.[85] Still another decree of the last decade of the fifth century orders the secretary of the Boule to erase the names of Selymbrian hostages.[86] There is no indication that these names were inscribed on stone, and presumably the secretary had a list of them somewhere in his records. The frequency with which secretaries conducted such searches is difficult to gauge, but the attested cases need not be taken as isolated events; searching for, copying, and erasing uninscribed texts may have occupied much of a secretary's time.

This last search also shows that documents other than decrees were present within the archives of the Boule. The secretary was to erase a list of Selymbrian hostages held at Athens, presumably because the list was found in the Boule's archives. Other lists were also kept by the Boule secretary. Another decree of the last decade of the fifth century honors the Samians for their loyalty to Athens and tells Samian ambassadors to hand over to the secretary of the Boule a list of Athenian trierarchs whose triremes were being delivered to the Samians.[87] The decree does not state what the secretary was to do with this list, but later in the decree the neōroi, the dockyard superintendents, are instructed to erase all documents recording the obligations of these trierarchs; presumably the secretary of the Boule received a copy for a similar reason. The Boule took an active role in the administration of the Athenian navy, and this provision may imply that the secretary of the Boule sometimes kept records of the trierarchs of each year.[88] The Boule also received a record of demes and cities that delivered firstfruit offerings to Eleusis; whether this practice was regular is not clear, but it is in accord with the Boule's general oversight of the Eleusinian sanctuary.[89] The Boule may also have received records of tribute payment. It was responsible for seeing that the tribute was collected and delivered safely to Athens, and payments were made in its presence.[90] The Boule also played a role in the assessment of tribute to be paid by allied cities, and it received a list of *eklogeis* or "collectors" who were responsible for bringing allied tribute to Athens.[91] Although the Hellenotamiai probably kept their own records of tribute payments by individual cities, the Boule too may have kept similar records by virtue of its supervisory role in tribute collection.[92]

But where were these archives kept? In the fourth century the state archives were housed in the Metroon, and some scholars have supposed that this building also served as an archives building in the fifth century.[93] There is no evidence, however, for a building of this name or for the public worship of the Mother of the Gods until the fourth century, and all available evidence indicates that the relationship between the Metroon and the city's archives dates from that century. Some fifth-century records, however, are attested in the Bouleuterion. The decree regulating offerings of firstfruits to the Eleusinian goddesses calls for the deposition of a list in the Bouleuterion.[94] The decree of Kleonymos of 426 prescribes that a list of tribute collectors should be written up in the Bouleuterion.[95] Deposition of these documents in the Bouleuterion reflects the general supervisory role exercised by the Boule over both the Eleusinian Mysteries and the administration of the Athenian Empire. But it also suggests that the Bouleuterion, the Boule's meeting place, had come to serve as a place for the storage and keeping of the Boule's documents.[96]

Decrees too were housed in the Bouleuterion. Three fifth-century proxeny decrees, their texts in extremely poor condition, seem to specify double publication, with one text to be inscribed on stone and set up on the Acropolis, while the other was recorded on a wooden tablet and placed in the Bouleuterion.[97] Some scholars have taken this display as evidence for the Bouleuterion's archival function during the fifth century.[98] I am not convinced that this must be the case. If the normal duty of the secretary of the Boule was to keep track of decrees and to deposit them among his archives in the Bouleuterion, as the title of his office implies, it was hardly necessary to instruct him to carry out this duty in the texts of decrees, and instructions of this sort are not otherwise attested in inscribed Attic decrees. Wilhelm also suggested that in these cases of double-publication the second copy of the decree, written on a wooden tablet, represented not archival deposition but public display of the decree for a temporary period of time.[99] On this view, publication of three proxeny decrees in the Bouleuterion is not evidence for the storage of documents in the Bouleuterion, but it may reflect an otherwise poorly attested practice of displaying newly enacted decrees on wooden tablets on a wall in the Bouleuterion for a short amount of time.[100]

Still, the Athenians were not always strict in the drafting and formulation of their decrees, and possibly for some unknown reason the proposers of these decrees included mention of their archival deposition, and these passages were not edited out by secretaries responsible for drawing up the texts that were later published on stone. But better evidence for the Bouleuterion's archival function is found in Andokides' speech *On His Return*, delivered between 410 and 405. In the course of this speech, Andokides refers to a decree of Menippos, which, he claimed, granted him some form of immunity from prosecution. The decree had been revoked, but Andokides asks that its terms be reconfirmed. He calls for the decree's text to be read out, saying that it was still to be found "in the Bouleuterion."[101] The verb that Andokides uses to describe the disposition of the decree, *eggraphein*, invites brief discussion. *Eggraphein* is seldom used to refer to the display of documents on stone in a public place; it is used, however, to denote the recording of texts that were written down and kept in the custody of public officials. Thus, when young men came of age and were registered onto the *lēxiarchika grammateia*, *eggraphein* is the technical term used to describe their registration.[102] The same verb is found in Aristotle's account of the review and registration of members of the cavalry (*Ath. Pol.* 49.2). Names of cavalrymen were recorded on a sealed *pinax*, a wooden tablet; those whose names had been listed previously (*tōn proterōn eggegrammenōn*) had their names erased when they were no longer fit to serve, while the names of new members were added to the *pinax* (*eggraphousin eis ton pinaka*). Generally, the verb *eggraphein* refers to information recorded or registered on documents that were stored away and not set out in public, and Andokides' use of the same verb to describe the disposition of the decree of Menippos should indicate that its text was not published or displayed on stone, but recorded and preserved in the Bouleuterion, probably among the records and archives kept by the secretary of the Boule.[103]

Excavations in the Athenian Agora have uncovered the remains of the

RECORDS IN THE FIFTH CENTURY

Bouleuterion, and, thanks to recent studies, we stand in a better position to understand its building history.[104] The building identified as the Bouleuterion was constructed in the southwest corner of the Agora around 500, was destroyed by the Persians in 480 and 479, but was rebuilt soon thereafter. The building forms a large square, measuring a little over twenty-three meters on each side. The south side of the building, however, was used as a porch, measuring about five meters in width, so that the main chamber of the building was somewhat smaller.

Little survives of the Bouleuterion above foundation level, so we are in no position to discuss how or where documents were stored within it. But since the building served primarily as the meeting place for the Boule's five-hundred members, there could not have been much room for the storage of documents. Possibly, documents were stored or arranged on shelves or in cabinets on the walls of the building or in its interior porch, but even so, space was limited.[105] In this context, mention should also be made of a smaller building located immediately to the north of the Bouleuterion. This building is rectangular and is oriented on an east-west axis; it measures approximately seven by eighteen meters.[106] When discovered, it was dated with the Bouleuterion to circa 500 and identified as a shrine of the Mother of the Gods. The building, like the Bouleuterion, seems to have been destroyed around 480, but its later history is uncertain. Thompson, its excavator, initially thought that it was never rebuilt, but the remains are so exiguous and were so obliterated by a Hellenistic structure built over it that it is possible the building was reconstructed after its destruction by the Persians. In addition, the building's identification as a sanctuary of the Mother of the Gods is subject to serious doubts. Evidence for public worship of the Mother of the Gods at Athens before the late fifth century is weak, and it is unlikely that this small building served as her shrine at such an early date. The building's location and orientation, however, indicate that it was closely tied to the Bouleuterion, and possibly it served as an annex to the Bouleuterion where equipment or objects associated with the Boule, including its records, may have been kept.[107]

III. Organization and Dating of Fifth-Century Decrees

The location in which the archives of the Boule were kept during the fifth century is, in a sense, of secondary importance. Written records existed and were being kept, and the Athenians had many buildings in which to house them. Of greater interest is how, if at all, documents in these archives were arranged and organized. On this issue, scholars have reached largely negative conclusions. When a board of *anagrapheis* was ordered to publish Drakon's homicide law in 409/8, it was told to obtain a text of the law from the king archon, the Athenian official who oversaw homicide cases. In the same way, we might suppose, other magistrates kept copies of laws that they administered at their offices, so that all the city's laws were not housed together in a single location.[108] Decentralization does not mean that individual collections of laws were themselves poorly organized; we have no evidence of how magistrates maintained copies of laws in their possession, so it is safe to attribute to them neither too high nor low a degree of order. But decentralization could have created uncertainties about what laws were valid or where the texts of particular laws could be found, and problems arising from such difficulties may have contributed to the Athenians' decision to review their laws in the last decade of the fifth century.

It will be noted, however, that the law on homicide which the *anagrapheis* are called on to publish was enacted long before the establishment of the Kleisthenic Boule. The Boule's secretary, as I have argued, was responsible for recording laws and decrees enacted by the Boule and Ekklesia, and he will have performed this duty from the time his office was created. He may have distributed copies of newly enacted laws and decrees to other officials, but there is no reason to suppose that, having distributed such texts, he then discarded his own copies of the same measures. Since the Boule and its secretary postdated the earliest Athenian legislation, not all the city's laws were found in its archives. But they probably contained many if not all laws and decrees ratified during the fifth century. How, then, were these archives organized?

Details found in the prescripts of Athenian decrees published on stone may offer a clue. By the term "prescript" I mean those details of an inscribed decree's text that precede the name of the proposer and the motion itself.[109] In the fifth century, decree prescripts generally included the name of the secretary of the Boule in office when the decree was enacted, the name of the tribe that held the prytany at the same time, and the name of the chairman (*epistatēs*) of the *prytaneis* who presided at the meeting of the Ekklesia at which the decree was ratified. The order in which these items appeared shows some variation, and occasionally one or more items are left out. But each of them is generally present, and since it is generally agreed that prescripts were added to the texts of decrees by the secretary of the Boule himself, their contents may offer some insights into the records from which published decrees were copied.[110] What has especially struck some scholars is that prescripts do not include the names of archons until after 421, and that the practice becomes common only in the last decade of the fifth century.[111] Since archon names were the chief means by which Athenians dated events to specific years, their absence from decree prescripts has been taken as a sign that Athenian decrees were generally undated before that time. Without dates, it will have been difficult to organize decrees in any meaningful way, and without an even rudimentary system of organization consultation of archival texts will have proved difficult if not impossible.[112]

But the absence of archon names from the prescripts of fifth-century Athenian decrees is not evidence that unpublished, archival texts were undated or poorly organized, since the names of several of the officials mentioned in decree prescripts corresponded to specific dates. The chairman of the *prytaneis* presided over the Ekklesia for a single day, so decrees to which his name was attached were enacted on the same day. Each of the ten Attic tribes held the prytany for one-tenth of a year, so the mention of a tribe would indicate at what point in the year a decree was enacted. The secretary of the Boule also served for a single prytany, so his name too, along with that of the tribe in prytany, could offer an indication of the decree's date. It is not difficult to imagine that decrees enacted on the same day were grouped together and differentiated from one another by the names of those who had presided over individual meetings of the Ekklesia, and that decrees enacted in the same prytany were arranged under the name of the tribe in prytany or of the secretary who held office during that prytany. For such a system to work would require some knowledge of the order in which different secretaries held office, knowledge that would have been enhanced by the keeping of regular lists of secretaries. No such lists or finding aids are attested, but lists of other officials are known from fifth-century Athens. In addition to the archon list, annual lists of generals were being kept, and financial documents on stone regularly include the names of treasurers or other officials in office during the year they were created.[113] Modern scholars have been able to reconstruct a list of names of a large number of secretaries and their tribes from the 450s to the 360s;[114] if fifth-century Athenians wanted to determine when a particular secretary held office, they will not have had much difficulty in doing so.

That the names of secretaries, at least, were used in a simple filing system is indicated by a decree of the 440s which preserves a series of regulations for the founding of an Athenian colony at Brea (*IG* I^3 46). One provision of the decree calls upon allied cities in Thrace to come to the aid of the colony in the event of an attack, in accordance with agreements made while an individual, whose name is lost, served as secretary.[115] We have no evidence that these agreements were inscribed on stone, and the decree does not refer readers to a stele on which the Thracian agreements were inscribed. The agreements were probably stored in the Boule's archives under the name of a secretary in whose tenure they were ratified.[116]

Unfortunately, the stone is damaged at the very point where the secretary's name was mentioned, and different restorations are possible. The text could have named the secretary during whose time in office the agreements were ratified. This restoration, if correct, would suggest that decrees were regularly arranged in batches corresponding to names of the secretaries who were responsible for recording them. But the text can also be restored to make it refer not to the secretary in whose prytany the Thracian agreements were enacted, but to the secretary who served in the first prytany of that year.[117] This may require some explanation. During the fifth century, the Athenians used two different calendar systems.[118] The regular Athenian calendar was a lunar one of twelve or thirteen months, in which years were identified by the name of the archon of the year. This, the festival or archontic calendar, was used for religious and other purposes and was the normal calendar of daily life in Athens. But many items of state business operated on a separate calendar based on the Boule's prytany system. This calendar followed the solar year and was divided into ten prytanies, with each prytany lasting either thirty-six or thirty-five days. Both the Boule and Ekklesia used this, the bouleutic calendar, to date and administer the business they conducted. The archontic and bouleutic calendars were not coterminous until 407/6; they did not begin and end on the same day, so the name of an archon did not always provide an accurate indication of the date of a decree enacted by the bouleutic calendar. To obviate this difficulty, the Athenians designated years of the bouleutic calendar by the names of the secretaries of the Boule who held office in the first prytany of each year. A first Boule secretary is named in the prescript of a decree of 433/2, but the dating of other documents to years identified by first secretaries occurs even earlier: inscribed financial records dating from the 440s already designate their year by the name of the first secretary of the Boule of the bouleutic year.[119]

Since the text of the Brea Decree is damaged at the crucial point, we cannot be certain whether it referred to agreements arranged under the name of a first Boule secretary, or a secretary who held office for a single prytany later in the year. But some sort of filing system based on secretary names is implied, and this itself is significant. Athenian financial documents on stone are regularly grouped under the names of the secre-

RECORDS IN THE FIFTH CENTURY

taries who produced them, so there is no difficulty in assuming that the Boule employed a similar principle with its records. But the Boule had ten secretaries, and therefore ten sets of records, per year. Such a system, however, does not exclude the possibility that decrees were also arranged in annual groups. Many financial records also indicate the years to which they belong by referring to the first Boule secretary of the year,[120] so it is not unreasonable to suppose that the Boule employed a similar method to arrange its own records of decrees. Decrees of individual prytanies were kept under the names of the secretaries who recorded them, and decrees enacted in a single, bouleutic year were stored under the names of the first secretaries of those years.

Still, archon names were the primary means by which Athenians identified individual years, and a system based on Boule secretaries to organize the Boule's archives could have been a source of confusion for potential consultants. Synchronization, however, between the bouleutic and archontic years is well attested, and we should not immediately assume that it was impossible to date individual measures to archon years before the practice of including the names of archons in decree prescripts became common. The accounts of the Parthenon from 437/6 to 433/2 include the names of both the archon and the first secretary of the bouleutic year; the headings of earlier lists are terribly fragmentary, but similar equations cannot be ruled out.[121] A similar equation between archon and first Boule secretary is found in the accounts for the expedition to Kerkyra (*IG* I³ 364; 433/2) and is restored with some likelihood in the accounts for the Samian War (*IG* I³ 363; 441/0–440/39). Archon and first Boule secretary are named in the prescript to an Athenian treaty with the Sicilian city Leontinoi in 433/2, and the tribute reassessment decree of 425/4 refers to assessments by the name of archon and first secretary. Moreover, literary sources provide dates for several pieces of fifth-century legislation by archon names, despite the fact that decree prescripts of the same period do not include archon names.[122] The absence of archons from the prescripts of decrees probably reflects the fact that the archon played no role in the legislative process and that the archon's name was not meaningful to the bouleutic calendar by which decrees were enacted. But that absence offers no evidence for the ability or inability of Athenians to provide dates for decrees by archon years based on other information possibly contained in the Boule's archives.

The system here suggested relies heavily on the assumption that the archives of the Boule contained more details than the texts of fifth-century decrees on stone. That this assumption is justified is indicated by consideration of the dating of documents to specific days within the year, by either the bouleutic or archontic calendar.[123] The prescripts of inscribed decrees omit such dates until the fourth century, and this omission has led some scholars to believe that archival texts of decrees also lacked specific dates; the Athenians, it has been argued, did not think precise dating of documents necessary, a further reflection of the inadequacies of Athenian record keeping.[124] But the Athenians did have a calendar and they did use it to date matters of public business. The accounts of the *logistai* covering the period 426/5 to 423/2 name the specific days in each prytany on which payments and loans were made from different sacred treasuries.[125] Other accounts of the treasurers of Athena from the last decade of the fifth century also provide the dates on which payments were made by the treasurers according to both the bouleutic and archontic calendars.[126] So too the Attic Stelae, which record the sale of property of those condemned for profanation of the mysteries in 414/3, date some sales by both the festival and bouleutic calendars.[127]

Administrative practices also required dates to be specified in decrees, and the provisions of several decrees sometimes assume that such dates could be determined. The *prytaneis* published the agenda of meetings of the Ekklesia four or five days in advance of meetings; certainly, such postings required reference to a specific date by either the bouleutic or archontic calendar, or both.[128] A decree of the 440s required Kallikrates to draw up plans for work on the Acropolis and the *pōlētai* to let out a contract so that the work could be completed within sixty days;[129] the date of the decree's enactment is not mentioned in the text inscribed on stone, but the time limit imposed on construction suggests that it could be fixed, possibly from records kept by the secretary of the Boule. Other fifth-century decrees also contain provisions requiring specific actions to be taken within a fixed number of days, and these provisions make sense only if dates of these measures were recorded and preserved in the records kept by the secretary of the Boule.[130]

Positive evidence for the presence of specific dates within the archival records, in spite of their absence from decrees published on stone, is provided by the texts of two documents known from literary sources. Thucydides supplies texts for both a one-year truce concluded between Athens and Sparta in 423 and the fifty-year peace (the Peace of Nikias) concluded by the same parties in 421. Leaving aside questions raised by these documents in terms of the composition of Thucydides' work, the texts of both measures illustrate the precision with which Athenian decrees could be dated.[131] Thucydides quotes both the terms of the one-year truce of 423 and the Athenian decree ratifying it. The decree begins with a standard fifth-century prescript, including the name of the tribe in prytany, the secretary in office, and the chairman who presided at the meeting of the Ekklesia; the name of the archon and specific day of the year on which the decree was enacted are not mentioned. But the text of the truce itself contains a provision stating that it was to be in force from the day of its enactment, 14 Hekatombaion.[132] Thucydides' text of the Peace of Nikias offers a similarly precise date. It does not include an Athenian decree ratifying its terms, but it does record a provision declaring that the peace terms were to be in force from 25 Hekatombaion in the archonship of Alkaios (422/1).[133] The appearance of specific dates in both documents is striking, because fifth-century Athenian treaties and other documents related to foreign affairs on stone do not mention the specific days of the year on which their terms were to go into effect. Scholars debate when and how Thucydides obtained his texts of the truce of 423 and the Peace of Nikias, but the discrepancy in terms of dating practices between his texts of these documents and inscribed fifth-century documents of similar contents suggests strongly that his sources did not depend on inscribed copies of either text.[134] But the references to precise dates do show that secretaries who recorded decrees sometimes included the days on which decrees were enacted when fixing those dates was important. They may have simply omitted such details from the texts delivered to masons for inscribing.[135] Prescripts of inscribed decrees, therefore, need not preserve completely all the elements recorded by Boule secretaries, and any assessments of the organization of the Boule's archives cannot rely on features of prescripts alone.

A recently discovered inscription of the fifth century lends this hypothesis further support. The inscription itself dates from circa 400, but it records an earlier decree enacted in 422/1.[136] This earlier decree was proposed by Alkibiades but begins with a heading, "in the archonship of Alkaios, on the nineteenth of the prytany." Next follows a prescript typical of those found in other fifth-century decrees, with an enactment formula and the names of the tribe in prytany, secretary, *epistatēs*, and proposer. The reference to both an archon and a prytany date in the heading of the decree is highly unusual but also extremely significant. Alkaios was archon in 422/1, a year before the earliest secure attestation of an archon name in a prescript of an Athenian decree on stone, and nearly a half century before precise prytany dates find routine mention.[137] We do not know in what form the decree survived from the time of its enactment until the time of its publication, but its preservation in the archives of the Boule is a likely explanation. Whatever the source of the inscribed text, it must go back to a decree recorded in 422/1, and its mention of an archon and prytany date shows that some texts of that year were already including these elements, even though the prescripts of inscribed decrees of the same year fail to include either. That does not prove that all Boule secretaries always recorded these dates in their minutes of meetings of the Ekklesia, but it does illustrate how overly simplistic it may be to regard the contents of decree prescripts as a full indication of the contents of the Boule's archives. Henry concluded his study of the prescripts of Athenian decrees with the observation that secretaries were never bound to include all the information at their disposal in the prescripts of inscribed decrees.[138] Their failure to include a particular detail, however, is not evidence that the same detail was not preserved in other records of the same decrees they may have kept or distributed.

Of course, the freedom enjoyed by secretaries in selecting which details they included in the prescripts of inscribed decrees could also reflect a similar latitude in their drafting of the actual minutes of the meetings of the Boule and Ekklesia that they attended, and inconsistencies could have had an effect on how texts of decrees and other documents were organized in the Boule's archives. The secretary of the Boule was, after all, not a professional, and he held office for little more than a month; although I think it likely that he was assisted by undersecretaries or others already in the fifth century, regular turnover in the position of the chief state secretary could only have been unsettling. We need not assume that every decree enacted during the fifth century was neatly filed under its secretary's name or according to its year of enactment, and by modern standards the Boule's archives may have seemed confused and disorderly. But hypothetical problems of this sort cannot be taken too far. We do not hear of problems with Athens' public records before the late fifth century, and our difficulties in reconstructing the form and appearance of archival records before that time reflect in large part the inadequacies of our sources. Political and forensic speeches are lacking before the late fifth century, and inscriptions serve as our primary source material. But inscriptions represent only a fraction of fifth-century Athenian documents, and their contents do not always reflect fully the information available in other records. Only by penetrating beneath the surface of inscribed texts can we begin to recover the complexity of Athenian record keeping and archival practices. Because these archives have not survived, there is a danger of attributing to them too high a degree of order and creating a sophisticated system where none existed. But it is equally misleading to dismiss evidence for the dating of archival texts and to deny the Boule's archives any system of organization. The didascalic records of the City Dionysia were arranged by archon years already from the start of the fifth century. Athenian financial documents were published on stone in annual sets of records from the 450s. Records of loans and payments made by Athenian officials preserved specific dates on which transactions were conducted. We have seen some evidence that archival records of fifth-century Athenian decrees, whose texts were not automatically inscribed on stone, exhibited similar characteristics; it is not too hazardous to assume that the few attested instances reflect more widespread practices.

IV. Conclusion

This chapter has focused primarily on laws and decrees, texts of which, I have argued, were maintained by the secretary of the Boule in the Boule's archives throughout the fifth century. But laws and decrees were not the only types of documents produced and preserved during the fifth century. Demes maintained registers of their members and possibly records of deme decrees and financial affairs. The polemarch and possibly individual demes also kept lists of metics (resident aliens) residing in Athens. Generals and taxiarchs drew up lists of citizens called up for service on military campaigns, and other magistrates and official boards maintained archives related to the business they oversaw. Apart from those documents which happened to be inscribed on stone, we know little about these other records, and to speculate, in positive or negative terms, on their longevity, their organization, or their detail, would not be useful. But it seems safe to say that written documents were very much a part of the civic life of fifth-century Athens.

Records of decisions of the Athenian people as a whole, however, arguably constituted the most important documents of fifth-century Athens, and their preservation was a matter of some concern. The Athenians published many legislative measures on stone stelai, and these stone documents afford us a glimpse of legislative records produced during the fifth century. But that glimpse is only a partial one. There is no evidence, in either literary sources or the surviving inscriptions on stone, that the fifth-century Athenians sought to publish systematically all decisions of the Ekklesia on stone. The Athenians did, however, have a secretary, the *grammateus* of the Boule, whose responsibility it was to record the Ekklesia's decisions. We find this secretary frequently mentioned in Athenian decrees where he is called upon to publish decrees on stone, but these instructions are a product of his more basic duty of keeping records of the Ekklesia's decisions. We have no evidence, and no reason to believe, that secretaries approached this duty with indifference or that they were selective in the decisions they recorded and preserved.

Records of decrees, only a fraction of which were inscribed on stone, were routinely drawn up and maintained, and these formed the archives of the Boule, the chief archives of fifth-century Athens.

These archives may have originated with the creation of the Kleisthenic Boule in the late sixth century, but their size undoubtedly grew as the development of the empire during the 460s and 450s increased the decision-making powers of both Boule and Ekklesia. The reforms of Ephialtes too, although their precise nature is lost to us, may have enhanced the role in government of both council and people, and any increase in power will have brought with it an increase in the volume of records produced by both bodies. Ephialtes' reforms may also have provided the impetus for the creation of the prytany system and the bouleutic calendar, which provided the framework around which decrees within the Boule's archives were organized.

This assessment of the Boule's archives is undoubtedly an optimistic one, and I do not mean to minimize deficiencies that necessarily existed, some of which will receive attention in the following chapter, or to impute to these archives a sophistication that they could not possibly have obtained. The rotation of secretaries in and out of office ten times each year and the holding of this office by nonprofessionals must have brought inconsistencies. The form of documents may have varied from secretary to secretary, documents were misfiled or lost, and important details were sometimes omitted. The means by which decrees were physically stored is also wholly unattested, and the Athenians could not have overcome the physical limitations on preservation imposed by the conditions of their day. But an awareness of any limitations does not invalidate evidence for the archival preservation of decrees, many of which were never inscribed on stone but still were kept for very long periods. In the late fourth century, the Macedonian Krateros compiled a collection of fifth-century Athenian decrees in nine books.[139] Krateros may have obtained some texts from copies of decrees set up on stone, but inscriptions will not account for all the decrees included in his collection.[140] Had the preservation of archival texts of decrees throughout the fifth century been wholly haphazard and disorderly, Krateros could hardly have filled the nine books attested for his work.

CHAPTER FOUR

The Athenian Law Code and
the Foundation of the Metroon

The preceding chapter argued that the Athenians maintained written records of fifth-century laws and decrees in the archives of the Boule. This chapter turns to two developments of the last decade of the fifth century, both of which were directly related to the ways in which public records were preserved in those archives. First, in the period between 410 and 399, the Athenians reorganized their law code and set out to establish what laws were actually valid on different subjects; when the revision was completed, the Athenians possessed a uniform body of written laws. Second, at some time in the closing years of the fifth century, the Athenians dedicated a single building to the storage of many important public records; by the middle of the fourth century, this building was known as the Metroon, the sanctuary of the Mother of the Gods. The motives for both the revision of the law code and the foundation of the Metroon are not discussed in our sources, but scholars have generally assumed that both were the product of the scattered disposition of Athenian documents during the fifth century, and a desire to bring some order to the city's public records. Previously, state documents, including the texts of laws, had been dispersed widely at the offices of different magistrates, where they were published on stelai and perhaps other media. From the end of the fifth century, laws and other state documents could be found in a single, centralized location.

This chapter reexamines both the revision of the law code and the creation of a state archives building in the last decade of the fifth century. It argues that although many Athenian documents, including texts of laws, had been dispersed widely at the offices of individual magistrates during the fifth century, a desire for centralization alone will not fully account for the revision of the laws and the Metroon's foundation at the end of the fifth century. Some centralization certainly was achieved, but both developments are more readily explained by the vast quantity of documents that had accumulated in the archives of the fifth-century Boule, and by a particular shortcoming in the way in which some of these records, especially texts of laws, were organized.

1. The Revision of the Athenian Law Code

In 411, the Athenian democracy was overthrown and replaced by a more restrictive form of government. This government, generally known as the Four Hundred from the four hundred citizens who held supreme power, sought to limit officeholding and the franchise to individuals of hoplite status—that is, to citizens who could serve the state without pay or financial support. The number of these citizens was to be limited to five thousand, who were thus known as the Five Thousand. Although the impetus for this coup derived from a desire to strengthen the financial resources of the city, the leaders of the revolution soon demonstrated their unwillingness to share power. The Four Hundred never summoned the Five Thousand but instead ruled Athens as a narrow oligarchy. After four months the Four Hundred themselves were overthrown and replaced by a broader form of government, perhaps made up of the Five Thousand to whom the Four Hundred originally promised to hand over power. By the spring of 410, however, the democracy was fully restored to its pre-411 form.[1]

One of the immediate results of the oligarchic coup was the revision of the Athenian law code. In their quest for power, some of the oligarchs of 411 appealed for the restoration of the *patrios politeia*, the ancestral constitution of the Athenians as it had operated before the radical, democratic reforms of Ephialtes. Thus, a decree moved by Pythodoros on the eve of the revolution prescribed the appointment of *syngrapheis*, "commissioners," who were to draw up a new constitution. Kleitophon proposed an amendment to Pythodoros's decree instructing the *syngrapheis* to look into the laws of Kleisthenes, and the wording of his amendment suggests that a similar investigation into Solon's laws may have been mentioned by Pythodoros.[2] The sincerity of the proposers of these measures is uncertain, since neither the actions of the Four Hundred nor the documents they produced, some of which are reproduced by Aristotle, betray an intimate knowledge of Solonian or Kleisthenic legislation.[3] But their appeals to old laws may have highlighted for some Athenians their own ignorance of their laws and which ones were actually in force, and this realization may have played a role in the decision to review laws more systematically once the oligarchy was overthrown.[4]

Reasons for uncertainty about what the law stated on individual subjects are not difficult to discern. Doubts resulted largely from the manner in which the Athenians preserved legislative acts. Many laws and decrees had been enacted over the fifth century, and secretaries of the Boule regularly kept copies of these texts. The Boule's archives, however, probably included only texts of measures enacted since the Boule assumed its role as the chief executive body of the Athenian state, a development that took place no earlier than the time of Kleisthenes' reforms. Laws and decrees passed before that time were housed separately. The *axones* on which the laws of Drakon and Solon were written survived to the late fifth century and were probably preserved in the Prytaneion; the *kyrbeis*, if they were separate objects from the *axones*, were probably housed in the Royal Stoa.[5] It is not known where or how laws and decrees enacted between the time of Solon's lawgiving and the establishment of the Kleisthenic Boule were stored; if a Solonian Boule kept any records, these texts may have been transferred into the archives of the Kleisthenic council. Conversely, the chief archon, who probably presided over the Ekklesia during the sixth century, may have kept records of some sixth-century measures.[6] Possibly, however, the only copies of sixth-century laws and decrees were those that individual magistrates had copied and received, or others that had been inscribed and publicly displayed on stone or some other material.[7]

To determine the valid law on a particular subject, a citizen might consult the *axones* or *kyrbeis* at the Prytaneion or Royal Stoa, or copies of the laws taken from the *axones* or *kyrbeis*; although we do not hear of such consultation, access to Solon's laws need not have posed a major difficulty. More serious problems confronted those wanting to know how the laws of Drakon or Solon had been affected by subsequent legislation.[8] The disposition of sixth-century legislation cannot be determined, but the numbers of texts could not have been very large to begin with. Written records of legislation enacted during the fifth century presented greater obstacles. Some laws may have been displayed on stone stelai, but since the Athenians displayed laws in places where their texts were meaningful, locating relevant statutes could not have been difficult. But we have no evidence that publication on stone was routine or automatic for all legislation during the fifth century, and texts preserved in the archives of the Boule may have constituted the only copies of many acts.[9] These archives probably dated back to the time of Kleisthenes, but the administrative requirements of Athens' naval empire and the radicalization of the democracy by Ephialtes greatly enhanced the legislative capacity of the Ekklesia, and hence, the amount of records it produced. Texts housed in the Boule's archives were not without some principles of organization, as I have argued in the preceding chapter; decrees were kept in prytany batches under the names of the secretaries in whose tenure they had been enacted, and probably in yearly batches under the name of the first secretary of the Boule of that year.[10]

This system, however, was not without difficulties. Its principal drawback was its failure to distinguish between enactments of different types. In the fourth century, the Athenians drew a distinction between *nomoi*, "laws," and *psēphismata*, "decrees." *Nomoi* were enacted by *nomothetai*, "lawmakers," and, generally speaking, consisted of enactments of permanent validity that were binding on all citizens. *Psēphismata* were enacted by the Boule and Ekklesia and were, in general, more specific measures directed toward a particular individual or specifying some immediate action.[11] In the fifth century, however, the Athenians did not draw a sharp distinction between *nomoi* and *psēphismata*, at least not in terms of the procedures by which each type of measure was enacted: measures considered *nomoi* according to fourth-century definitions were voted upon and ratified by vote of the Boule and Ekklesia in the same way as *psēphismata* or decrees.[12] This lack of a procedural distinction presumably carried over into the records kept by the secretary of the Boule. Measures that by their contents were *nomoi* or "laws," measures of general applicability, were not distinguished from *psēphismata* or "decrees," enactments with more specific contents. Both were housed without distinction within the records of the particular secretary under whom they had been ratified.

Let us consider laws on inheritance as an example of how the system worked. Solon had treated inheritance, and anyone wanting to know his provisions might consult the relevant laws on the original *axones* or possibly at the office of the archon, who oversaw inheritance disputes.[13] But suppose inheritance had been the subject of legislation in the fifth century. To find post-Solonian legislation, an interested citizen had to work through a vast quantity of fifth-century records, undifferentiated by content. Fifth-century changes or additions to Solon's laws will have been found among proxeny decrees, decrees ordering architectural changes in building projects, treaties with foreign states, and other documents reflecting business handled by the Ekklesia. Without knowing which Boule secretary under whom Solon's laws on inheritance had been revised, finding such a text entailed an enormous, and perhaps insurmountable, task.

To be sure, the archives of individual magistrates might have contained legislative texts in areas over which they had jurisdiction, and individuals could inquire about relevant laws from these officials.[14] But Athenian officials were not legal specialists, and they generally served in office for a single year; they cannot be assumed to have been familiar with the texts of all legislation relevant to their offices. For litigants, this state of affairs brought a considerable degree of uncertainty, since it might be unclear how Solonian laws had been modified by subsequent legislation. For politicians, the lack of a single, coherent body of currently valid laws made it difficult to know whether a proposed law or decree contravened some earlier statute.[15] For others, such as the oligarchs of 411, the inability of Athenians to distinguish which of their current laws were currently in force provided opportunities for manipulation, propaganda, and coercion.

Events of the year 411 may have prompted the Athenians to embark on a review of their existing laws, but the revision addressed deficiencies in the disposition of Athenian laws that long predated the oligarchic coup. A mass of legislation had accumulated in the Boule's archives since the time of Ephialtes, and it was difficult if not impossible to know how Solon's laws had changed. In the fifty-year period (460–410) preceding the start of the revision alone, some five hundred Boule secretaries had held office. We need not assume that every secretary left behind some documents, but there is no reason to deny that most secretaries produced some records of the decisions of the Boule and Ekklesia enacted during their one-prytany tenure. Some archival texts may have been damaged or lost, and it is quite possible that the only existing copies of some measures were texts published on stone or disseminated on papyri or wooden tablets and kept by individual magistrates. But we do not hear of such damage or loss, and publication on stone was not automatic. The best source for fifth-century legislation was the records drawn up by Boule secretaries.

The Athenians started review and revision with the restoration of the democracy in 410. They appointed a board of *anagrapheis*, "recorders," and assigned to them the task of investigating and recording the city's laws.[16] Our understanding of their work derives from three sources: Lysias's speech *Against Nikomachos*, passages of Andokides' speech *On the Mysteries* (including some documents quoted therein), and fragments of several inscriptions that are generally taken to be the product of the revision.[17] From Lysias's speech, delivered by an unknown speaker at the trial of Nikomachos, one of the *anagrapheis*, we learn the chronology and duties of the *anagrapheis*. According to the speaker, the *anagrapheis* served for two terms, with the first term lasting six years and ending with the Athenian defeat in the Peloponnesian War and the rule of the Thirty Tyrants in 404. After the Thirty's overthrow and the restoration of the democracy in 403, the *anagrapheis* were reappointed and served for four more years. In their second term they seem to have concentrated on drawing up and publishing a sacrificial calendar on stone.[18] In their first term, however, the speaker claims that their task had been "to write up the laws of Solon."[19] What this charge meant and whether it reflects accurately the duties assigned to the *anagrapheis* are unclear. But to the fourth-century orators "the laws of Solon" meant all Athenian laws that were currently valid, and Lysias's description of the duties of the *anagrapheis* probably should be understood in that way: the Athenians appointed the *anagrapheis* to draw up and record texts of Athenian laws that henceforth were to be considered valid and binding on all Athenian citizens.

To complete this task, the *anagrapheis* first must have established what the laws of Solon stated on particular subjects. Then, they worked through subsequent legislation to determine how Solon's laws had been amended, and to see what new measures had been enacted on topics not treated by Solon.[20] Most post-Solonian legislation probably belonged to the fifth century, and all available decrees of the Ekklesia had to be examined. Although the *anagrapheis* were not interested in ephemeral, temporary, or specific measures, such as honorary decrees, treaties, and declarations of war, they needed to sift through these types of measures, since fifth-century *nomoi* in the technical sense were not distinguished from *psēphismata* in the Boule's records. Lysias claims that the *anagrapheis* were initially appointed for a period of four months, but that Nikomachos had remained in office for six years. This statement has been challenged as simple rhetorical exaggeration, but it may reflect the failure of the Athenians to realize how vast a quantity of records had piled up over the past one hundred years.[21]

Actual revision of laws, however, was probably not among the duties of the *anagrapheis*. To a large degree they simply gathered together what laws were currently valid: they did not have the power to make or rescind laws.[22] Starting from the laws of Drakon and Solon, they traced later supplements to these laws and which provisions were still in force. In cases where ambiguity or uncertainty existed, they may have been required to defer to the Boule and Ekklesia for a final decision, though appeals of this sort are unattested in our sources.[23] More often, however, they simply checked later legislation against the Solonian (and possibly Drakontian) originals; in cases where a law of Solon clearly had been superseded, its text was omitted from their compilation in favor of the more recent enactment. In cases where the *anagrapheis* found a later law on a subject not treated by Solon, they included this too in the appropriate place of their collection.[24]

The work of Nikomachos and his colleagues was interrupted by the end of the Peloponnesian War in 404 and the subsequent oligarchy of the Thirty Tyrants. We do not know how far their work had progressed or how it was affected by the oligarchic regime. The Thirty themselves were originally appointed to draft laws for a new constitution; they revoked some portions of Solon's laws that they thought were especially ambiguous, and they tore down some stelai, including, perhaps, those on which the laws of Ephialtes were displayed.[25] But it is unclear how these activities affected what the *anagrapheis* had accomplished in their first term, and the actions of the Thirty may have had little impact. Subsequent events suggest that the *anagrapheis* had nearly completed or already finished their assignment when their first term came to an end. For when the *anagrapheis* were reappointed to a second term after the restoration of the democracy, they focused their energies largely on the text of a sacrificial calendar.[26]

After the overthrow of the Thirty Tyrants and the restoration of the democracy in 403/2, the Athenians did, however, return to their secular laws. Andokides, in his speech *On the Mysteries*, discusses these events.[27] He says that the Athenians voted to live by the laws of Drakon and Solon until new laws could be passed. Soon, however, it was discovered that some Athenians were liable for prosecution under existing laws as a result of their actions during the disturbances of 404 and 403. So, according to Andokides (1.82; cf. 85), the Athenians decided to review their laws and "to write up in the Stoa" those that were approved. Andokides cites a decree moved by Teisamenos to support his outline of events. This decree, a text of which is preserved in Andokides' speech (1.83–84), calls upon the Athenians to live according to their traditional institutions and by the laws of Solon and Drakon, which they had used before. It then lays down procedures for making new laws. Wherever additions were thought necessary, a board of *nomothetai*, chosen by the Boule, was to make proposals by writing them up on wooden tablets and displaying them at the statues of the Eponymous Heroes. These proposals were to be examined by the Boule and a second board of *nomothetai*, this one chosen from the demes, and private citizens were to be given the opportunity to express their views on the proposed laws. After these proposals were ratified, the Areopagos was to see that the magistrates abided by the newly enacted laws. The final clause of the decree stipulates that "those laws being ratified are to be published on the wall where they had been published previously, for anyone who wants to examine them."[28]

Although the decree of Teisamenos does not mention Nikomachos and his fellow *anagrapheis*, its provisions may be considered an extension of their work. Teisamenos called on the Athenians to use the laws of Drakon and Solon that they had used before; since the Athenians commonly referred to their currently valid laws as the laws of Solon, this provision may refer to the collection of Athenian laws compiled by Nikomachos and his fellow *anagrapheis* in their first term. In addition, Teisamenos's decree does not require, although Andokides seems to say so, that all currently valid Athenian laws should be reexamined—that is, it does not prescribe an entirely new review and republication of all existing laws. Rather, the decree makes provisions only for the addition of new laws to a body of laws (those of Drakon and Solon) that already existed. The need for additions, as opposed to full-scale review and rewriting, is intelligible if we assume that the *anagrapheis* had finished some or even most of their work with Athens' secular laws during their first term, regardless of how this work was affected by the Thirty during their time in power.[29] Moreover, since the *anagrapheis*, who were reappointed after the restoration of the democracy, were not empowered to make, approve, or revoke laws, they themselves could not make any additions to the laws that were collected, even when deficiencies were discovered. For this reason, the two boards of *nomothetai* were appointed after the restoration of the democracy, one to draw up new proposals and the other to review and ratify them.[30] Through these boards, the Athenians effected additions they believed necessary to the laws already compiled by the *anagrapheis*, and brought their work to a conclusion.

Andokides does not describe all the additional laws proposed and enacted under Teisamenos's decree, but he does list five supplementary measures that were enacted after it and perhaps by virtue of it.[31] Three of these concern us here. One prohibited Athenian magistrates from applying any unwritten law (*agraphos nomos*) on any topic.[32] This prohibition against the use of unwritten law does not mean that the Athenians ceased their respect for unwritten customs and no longer took them into consideration in the administration of justice. Instead, the provision was intended to prevent magistrates from applying laws not included in the collection of the *anagrapheis* or added to it by virtue of Teisamenos's decree. Another of the supplementary laws was related to the first one; it required magistrates to apply the laws from Eukleides' archonship (403/2).[33] This measure did not nullify legislation enacted before the year of Eukleides, as Andokides would have liked his listeners to believe; laws enacted prior to Eukleides' archonship were still valid, provided that they had been reviewed by the *anagrapheis*. The purpose of such a measure was to ensure that magistrates applied laws only to offenses committed from the year of the archonship of Eukleides and afterward; a law included in the code could not be used to prosecute a crime committed prior to Eukleides' archonship. A third supplementary measure concerned the relationship between laws and decrees. The Athenians did not draw a procedural distinction between laws and decrees in the fifth century, and it is unclear whether they drew any distinction by content. Henceforth, however, laws were to possess a greater validity than decrees, and no decree could contravene an existing law; a distinction between the two types of legislative acts is firmly established.[34]

These supplementary measures provided the natural conclusion to the work of the *anagrapheis* in their first term and to any new enactments added by the *nomothetai* named by Teisamenos's decree. From 403/2, the Athenians were to possess a uniform and distinct body of written laws, one compiled by the *anagrapheis* of 410–404 and supplemented by measures resulting from the procedures outlined by Teisamenos. Magistrates were to observe only these laws in their administration of justice, and laws not included in this collection were invalid. Moreover, this body of law was distinct from other types of enactments and possessed a higher degree of authority; the laws could not be contravened by a decree of the Boule or Ekklesia. All that is missing from these supplementary laws is reference to a procedure by which new laws could be enacted in the future. In the fourth century, this duty fell to bodies of specially appointed *nomothetai* selected from a year's pool of dikasts. When these procedures were instituted is not known, but it is possible that the law(s) governing fourth-century lawmaking (*nomothesia*) were included in the additional laws drawn up by the *nomothetai* by virtue of Teisamenos's decree.

Confirmation of the validity of the work of the *anagrapheis* and the supplementary measures enacted by *nomothetai* under the provisions of Teisamenos's decree was provided by a law moved by a certain Diokles in 403/2 or shortly thereafter. This law stipulates that "laws enacted under the democracy before Eukleides' archonship, and as many as were enacted in Eukleides' archonship and have been written up, are to be valid."[35] Since the duty of the *anagrapheis* in their first term (410–404) had been to compile all currently valid Athenian laws, Diokles' law essentially ratified their work. Diokles' does not guarantee the validity of all laws enacted before Eukleides' archonship, however, but only those enacted "under the democracy"; the qualification effectively nullified any laws added to those collected by the *anagrapheis* under the oligarchy of the Thirty Tyrants.[36] In addition, Diokles' reference to laws enacted and written up during Eukleides' archonship is strikingly reminiscent of the provisions of Teisamenos's decree, which provided for the ratification and publication ("writing up") of additional, new laws.[37] His law made these valid too, but only if they had been "written up." It is possible that the law of Diokles was the final measure of the *nomothetai* named in Teisamenos's decree by which their work and that of the *anagrapheis*, which had formed a starting point for the *nomothetai*, were made valid and binding.

Ostwald has characterized the revision of Athens' laws as the final step in the victory of "rule of law" over popular sovereignty.[38] On a more practical level, the revision of the Athenian law code and the supplementary measures described by Andokides rectified, or sought to rectify, some of the problems that had led to the appointment of the *anagrapheis* in the first place. Prior to their appointment, Athenian laws, in the sense of measures of permanent validity with general applicability, were not clearly distinguished from decrees, enactments with more specific application and calling for immediate action. The laws of Drakon and Solon, published on their *axones* and *kyrbeis*, may have formed a distinct body of laws before the fifth century, but laws enacted subsequently were less easily distinguished in the city's archives. From 403/2, however, as a result of the work of the *anagrapheis*, Athens' laws formed a single collection distinct from decrees and possessing a greater degree of authority. This distinction carried through into the fourth century, when laws and decrees were enacted by separate procedures, and when the laws themselves were arranged and organized according to their own, unique system.[39]

But the revision of the Athenian code and the distinction between laws and decrees that resulted from it raise a further question: what form, in physical terms, did the laws compiled by the *anagrapheis* from 410–404 and the additional laws enacted as a result of Teisamenos's decree in 403/2 take? In the fourth century, Athenian laws were housed and preserved in the Metroon, and new laws were sometimes published on stone stelai. But there is no talk of the Metroon or any other archival repository in our sources for the codification of the late fifth century. Instead, our sources seem to speak of publication alone, and scholars have traditionally believed that the *anagrapheis* of 410–404 were appointed not only to compile all currently valid Athenian laws but also to inscribe their texts on stone.[40] Thus, Lysias says that Nikomachos and his fellow *anagrapheis* were appointed to "write up" (*anagrapsai*) the laws of Solon;

the same verb is regularly used in connection with the publication of Athenian decrees and other documents on stone stelai.[41]

Originally the *anagrapheis* published some laws on individual stone stelai; they were responsible for inscribing Drakon's law on homicide, and the stele recording a series of older regulations concerning the powers of the Boule, published around the same time, may also be a product of their efforts.[42] The *anagrapheis* have also been associated with fragments of a series of joining stelai that formed a wall or several walls. These fragments are inscribed on both faces, with the texts on one side written in the old Attic alphabet and including a trierarchic law, a law dealing with several types of taxes, and parts of a sacrificial calendar. On the opposite side, the original text has been erased, and in the erasure a sacrificial calendar has been inscribed in the Ionic alphabet.[43] Since the Ionic alphabet came into official use at Athens from 403/2, the normal assumption has been that the texts in the old Attic alphabet derive from the first term of the *anagrapheis*, while those in Ionic are the product of their second term, when they drew up a calendar of sacrifices.[44] This wall of stelai, it has been thought, is the same wall where new laws were to be published according to the final provision of Teisamenos's decree, which was located in a stoa where, according to Andokides, all newly ratified laws were published. Several ancient sources combine to suggest that this stoa was the Stoa Basileios, the Royal Stoa, office of the king archon.[45]

The nature and location of the wall mentioned in Teisamenos's decree have recently been the focus of considerable debate. Whereas scholars have traditionally assumed that the *anagrapheis* published their work on a wall of stone stelai in or near the Stoa Basileios and that this publication is reflected by the wall named in Teisamenos's decree, recent scholarship has argued that Teisamenos's decree orders not the publication of laws on stone, but simply the temporary display of proposed or newly ratified laws.[46] Robertson goes further and claims that Andokides' assertion that the Athenians had published all ratified laws in a stoa is either intentionally misleading or a falsehood; no attempt was made to publish laws on stone by virtue of Teisamenos's decree. Even the laws collected by the *anagrapheis*, Robertson argues, in their first and second terms were not automatically published on stone. The goal of the *anagrapheis'* work and the decree of Teisamenos was to compile laws for the newly founded state archive.[47]

Andokides' claim that laws were published in a stoa is probably not false, given that the statement was made shortly after publication had taken place to an audience that was in a position to know. But I am not convinced that either Andokides or the decree of Teisamenos must be understood to refer to publication on stone of all Athenian laws. Neither mentions a stone wall or stelai, and only the appearance of the verb *anagraphein* in their accounts suggests publication on stone. This verb is regularly used in connection with the publication of documents on stone, but it can also be used for the recording or display of documents written on other materials; Andokides' stoa and the wall of Teisamenos's decree need refer only to publication on wooden tablets or a whitened, plastered wall.[48] Publication on stone of many Athenian laws, however, certainly formed a component of the work of the *anagrapheis*, as the epigraphical evidence indicates. But even if we add up all the measures attributed to them, the individual stelai and the wall of joining stelai do not amount to a publication of all Athenian laws, secular and sacred. The fragments of the inscribed wall written in the old Attic alphabet are disproportionately concerned with expenditure, especially on ritual matters, and it may be that as the work of the *anagrapheis* advanced, it was decided to publish only those parts of the code that treated expenditures of state moneys and obligations owed to the Athenian state.[49]

Nonetheless, very little of the wall of joining stelai actually survives, so it is probably best not to draw extreme conclusions about the comprehensive or noncomprehensive publication of Athenian laws by the *anagrapheis* based on fragmentary contents of the wall of stelai; their original texts may have been more comprehensive than the surviving fragments imply.[50] But even if all the laws compiled by the *anagrapheis* and enacted under Teisamenos's decree were published on stone, there should be no doubt that uninscribed, archival texts of these laws were preserved in archival form. Hansen has pointed out that we do not meet a law code published in the Royal Stoa in the orators after Andokides' speech, and he suggests that after the code had been inscribed, changes to it forced the Athenians to abandon the idea of a full publication of all laws on stone; henceforth, they chose to deposit laws written on papyri in the Metroon.[51] This suggests a two-staged development: laws were originally published on stone and only later housed in an archive. But publication of laws on stone and their simultaneous deposition in an archive are not mutually exclusive, and the Boule's archives may have received copies of the revised code throughout the entire review process.

We do not know what role the Boule played in the approval of the laws gathered by Nikomachos and his colleagues, but the Boule did participate in the ratification of new laws under Teisamenos's decree. So, it is reasonable to suppose that the secretary of the Boule kept a record of laws it approved under this decree, as he regularly did with other docu-

ments approved by that body and the Ekklesia. The secretary also coop-
erated with the *anagrapheis* in the publication of Drakon's homicide law,
and he was responsible for the code after its ratification in 403/2. Thus,
the law of Diokles, whose text I have referred to above, contains a provision stipulating that laws enacted after the archonship of Eukleides were
to be valid from the day on which they were enacted, unless some other
date was specified.[52] The secretary of the Boule is instructed to add this
statement to the existing laws within thirty days, and future secretaries
are required to add the same statement to new laws immediately upon
their enactment. It is also noteworthy, however, that statements specifying the effective dates of laws do not always appear in the inscribed texts
of Athenian laws of the fourth century,[53] so the requirement to specify
the effective dates of existing and future laws should refer to texts other
than those on stone. Since the secretary of the Boule is the official required to add this statement to both existing and future laws, then it
must be to texts he maintained, in the archives of the Boule, that enactment dates were to be added.[54] Such preservation of Athenian *nomoi* in
the Boule's archives was not a great innovation, if, as I have argued,
enactments approved by the Ekklesia were already being recorded and
preserved by the secretary of the Boule throughout the fifth century. The
principal effect of the revision of the laws, then, in terms of the preservation of their physical texts, was an administrative one. Laws (*nomoi*)
were not written down and preserved in archival form for the first time,
but from 403/2 they formed a separate and distinct part of the archives
maintained by the Boule.

II. The Foundation of the Metroon

On the most fundamental level, the revision of the Athenian law code
illustrates a concern on the part of the Athenians for the organization of
some of their most important public records. But the revision was not an
isolated event. Many of the city's public records, including its laws and
decrees, were housed in the Metroon in the fourth century. The disposition of laws and decrees in the fifth century is less clear, but the secretary
of the Boule was the record keeper of the Boule and Ekklesia, which
enacted laws and decrees, and it seems likely that this official kept copies
of both measures in or near the Bouleuterion.[55] We possess no direct or
explicit testimony concerning the date at which the Metroon replaced
the Bouleuterion as an archival repository, but many scholars have tied
this development to the revision of the law code in the years 410–399.
The dating has a certain degree of plausibility in and of itself, since we

know of no other large-scale work associated with Athenian public records in the late fifth or fourth centuries.[56] Several pieces of evidence independent of the revision of the law code also point to this period as the time when a Metroon was founded and came to be used as a central archival repository.

Andokides spoke of a decree of Menippos that was still in the Bouleuterion sometime around 410, but the earliest reference to a document housed in the Metroon does not occur until the 340s.[57] Even then, however, the title "Metroon" for the city's archives building may not have been universally acknowledged; Aeschines refers to several documents that are otherwise attested as being stored in the Metroon as being in the Bouleuterion.[58] But other sources indicate that a Metroon existed in the Agora much earlier in the fourth century. A law of 353/2, whose text is preserved on stone, prescribes that a copy of its text should be inscribed on a stone stele in front of the Metroon.[59] Still earlier, an inventory of the treasures of the Other Gods housed in the Hekatompedon and dating from 375/4 mentions a wash basin "from the Metroon," and a similar inventory of the 390s can be restored in similar fashion.[60] By the 370s and perhaps as early as the 390s a building with which the name "Metroon" could be connected stood in the Agora.

This dating is strengthened by the archaeological remains of the Bouleuterion-Metroon complex. In the closing decades of the fifth century the Athenians constructed a large building immediately to the west of and similar in shape to the Bouleuterion. The remains of this new structure are scanty, but pottery finds associated with its construction support a construction date in the last decade of the fifth century.[61] The building stands precisely where Pausanias puts the Bouleuterion in the second century after Christ, so scholars have assumed that it served in this capacity from the date of its construction. At that time, it is supposed that the original Bouleuterion, to which moderns assign the name "old" Bouleuterion, ceased to function as a council chamber. It continued to stand for several centuries, until it was torn down in the second century and a new, larger structure was constructed over its remains. Pausanias identifies this newer building as the Metroon. But since a Metroon is attested in the Agora from the early fourth century, it is normally assumed that the old Bouleuterion acquired the name Metroon over the course of the fourth century, probably because a shrine of the Mother of the Gods was located inside it, and that the second-century Metroon was simply built over the old Bouleuterion/Metroon.

A close connection between the Bouleuterion and Metroon suggested by this reconstruction of their building history is borne out by references to the Mother of the Gods and the Boule in fourth-century sources. From Demosthenes and Theophrastos we learn that the *prytaneis* offered sacrifices to the Mother of the Gods,[62] and a law on silver coinage of 375/4 prescribed that counterfeit coins were to be sacred to the Mother of the Gods and deposited with the Boule; perhaps they were actually put in the Metroon.[63] In addition, the orator Lykourgos, when on his deathbed, was said to have asked to be brought into the "Bouleuterion and Metroon" so that he could render an account of his public services. Lykourgos's association of Bouleuterion and Metroon almost suggests that the two were one building, or, at the very least, that they stood in very close proximity.[64]

The close, physical proximity of the Bouleuterion and Metroon is further highlighted by foundation legends for the cult of the Mother of the Gods at Athens. According to one version of this legend, a priest of the Mother of the Gods appeared in Athens and began to initiate Athenian women. The men of the city became disturbed, so they murdered the priest. A plague ensued, and when the Athenians consulted an oracle, they were told to propitiate the murdered man. So the Athenians built a Bouleuterion, fenced off an area and dedicated it to the Mother of the Gods, and set up a statue for the murdered man. Thenceforth, the story went, the Athenians used the Metroon as an archive and repository for their laws.[65]

Mention of a plague in this story about the Metroon's foundation naturally suggests some connection with the great plague that struck Athens in the opening years of the Peloponnesian War, and this has led some scholars to suppose that a cult of the Mother of the Gods was introduced to Athens in this period.[66] Although other evidence may support this dating, we must question whether a foundation legend could preserve accurate information about a historical plague of any date. Not only are plagues and oracles common in legends about the origins of religious rituals and cults, but also this version of the Metroon's foundation does not appear until the eighth century after Christ; earlier versions of the story speak only of a priest of the Mother of the Gods and his murder, but make no mention of a Bouleuterion or Metroon.[67] The building of a Bouleuterion to appease the murdered man and the concomitant dedication of a Metroon, as related in the myth, do bear a striking resemblance to the building history of the Bouleuterion and Metroon, as interpreted by modern archaeologists, and this might suggest that the myth preserves some kernel of historical truth. But the story speaks of the Metroon as if it were a fenced off area or precinct within the Bouleuterion itself, whereas the archaeological remains indicate that they were separate buildings. The Metroon's foundation legend is best understood as reflecting and arising from the close connection that existed between that building and the Bouleuterion, an association attested in fourth-century sources (presumably the same ones available to Byzantine scholars); these legends do not offer good evidence for the date of the cult's foundation or the establishment of the Metroon as an archives building.

Still, a late fifth-century date for the establishment of a Metroon is supported by other evidence relating to the cult of the Mother of the Gods at Athens.[68] Evidence for her worship is weak until the late fifth century, when Athenian authors displayed a growing awareness of the Mother of the Gods, especially in her manifestation as the Anatolian Kybele. Fragments of the comic poet Kratinos refer to features of the worship of Kybele, and Aristophanes, Euripides, and Sophocles all refer to her in plays of the last third of the fifth century, sometimes assimilating her to the native Greek goddesses Rhea, Earth, or Demeter.[69] In the same period several foreign cults, most notably those of Asklepios and Bendis, were making inroads into Athens, and references to Kybele in authors at this time may reflect a similar development on the part of her cult.[70] More informative, however, are details concerning the cult statue of the Mother that was set up in the Metroon. The dedication of a cult statue is appropriate for the foundation of a new cult or cult building, so its date may provide some indication of the date when a Metroon was actually founded. According to Pausanias, the statue was the work of Pheidias, but Pliny attributes it to Pheidias's student Agorakritos. If the cult statue of the Mother of the Gods was the work of Pheidias, its dedication would have to date to the 430s or earlier, since Pheidias had fled Athens on charges of corruption before 432. We do not have any specific dates associated with Agorakritos's career, but Pliny tell us that he was a student of Pheidias; this should allow his activity to extend over most of the second half of the fifth century. Although this does not fix the date of the Metroon's establishment more precisely, it does conform to the remains of the Bouleuterion-Metroon complex, which also point to building activity toward the end of the fifth century.[71]

A more precise date for the Metroon's foundation has been suggested on the basis of two decrees of 405. The first, a decree moved by Patrokleides, is preserved in Andokides' speech *On the Mysteries*.[72] It grants and restores to the rights of full citizenship certain classes of disfranchised Athenian citizens and calls for the erasure of records of those disfranchisements from wherever they are *en tōi dēmosiōi*, "in the *dēmosion*." Similarly, another decree of the same year proposed by Kleisophos awards a series of honors to the Samians, including a grant to them of twenty Athenian triremes then stationed at Samos.[73] According to the terms of the decree, the Athenian trierarchs who had commanded those triremes were freed from their obligations, and any records found *en tōi demosiōi*, "in the *demosion*," testifying to their possession of naval gear were to be erased.

What is meant by the phrase "in the *demosion*"? *Demosion* can be a difficult word to translate. Sometimes it refers generally to the "state" or "public domain."[74] Frequently, *demosion* is used in connection with state debtors, who are routinely described as owing money *tōi demosiōi*, where *tōi demosiōi* means "to the public treasury."[75] In other passages, *demosion* seems to refer to a specific place or building, including the Athenian state prison.[76] When used with respect to documents, however, *demosion* can also denote an archives building. Klaffenbach has cited inscriptions from Miletos, Priene, and other Greek states, where documents are required to be written up *en tōi demosiōi* or *eis to demosion*; in each case, *to demosion* refers to a building where documents were stored.[77] Similarly, some documents occasionally call for their deposition *eis ta demosia grammata* or *en tois demosiois grammasi*, "in the public records," where *ta demosia grammata* probably refers to a specific archival collection—that is, a city's public archives. Klaffenbach dealt with the Athenian evidence only in passing, but the applicability of his conclusions for Athens is supported by the usage of the orators. Demosthenes, in his speech *On the Embassy*, mentions a document housed "in your public records in the Metroon,"[78] while in the speech *On the Crown*, he refers to documents deposited *en tōi demosiōi*, by which he claims that he shall convict Aeschines.[79] Similarly, Aeschines several times refers to state documents kept among *ta demosia grammata*, "the public records." Many of the documents cited by Demosthenes and Aeschines were also housed in the Metroon, so their use of these phrases probably reflects circumlocutions for the Metroon and the archives stored within it.

Based on the examples cited by Klaffenbach and fourth-century Athenian usage, Boegehold has argued that the appearance of the phrase *en tōi demosiōi* in decrees moved by Patrokleides and Kleisophos should be understood in a similar way, as referring to documents deposited "in the state archive." Boegehold also argued that the dates of these decrees, both of which belong to the year 405, provided the earliest evidence for the existence of a centralized archive building in Athens, one that was distinct from the Bouleuterion and later became known as the Metroon. These references, combined with Andokides' reference (2.23) of a decree that was "still in the Bouleuterion" sometime around 410, provide the termini for the establishment of a centralized archive in the years between 410 and 405.[80]

Boegehold's interpretation of the phrase *en tōi dēmosiōi* as meaning "in the state archive" has won wide acceptance among scholars. Although I am inclined to accept his arguments and his dating, interpretation of *dēmosion* as "state archive" in both decrees is problematic on several counts, and these need to be spelled out in more detail: because *to dēmosion* can refer to a "state archive" in some instances does not prove that it must do so in all instances (as Boegehold recognized). Thus, in Kleisophos's decree, Athenian ambassadors are instructed to make a list of the Athenian trierarchs who commanded the triremes being transferred to the Samians; copies of this list were to be handed over to the secretary of the Boule and to the generals. The decree then instructs the *neōroi*, the superintendents of the dockyards, to erase any records of the trierarchs' responsibility for these triremes found *en tōi dēmosiōi*.[81] In the fifth and fourth centuries, the secretary of the Boule and members of his staff were responsible for records in the Boule's archives and in the Metroon, so that, if we interpret the phrase *en tōi dēmosiōi* to mean "in the state archive," we should expect either the secretary or one of his assistants to be charged with carrying out the erasure. The dockyard superintendents, on the other hand, will have been responsible for documents under their own care, which they will have erased; why the *neōroi* are asked to erase documents *en tōi dēmosiōi*, as meaning "in the state archive," is not clear. It is conceivable that the instructions to the *neōroi* reflect a period of transition for the newly founded state archive, and that responsibility for its records was not firmly delineated. It is possible too that the *neōroi* stored records they had drawn up with records of the Boule, which oversaw naval matters. But the simplest explanation may be to understand the phrase *en tōi dēmosiōi* in this context more generally, as simply denoting "in the public domain." The secretary of the Boule and the generals received copies of the list of trierarchs in order to update their own records, and the dockyard superintendents are then ordered to erase any related records found in their own archives, which are loosely labeled *en tōi dēmosiōi*, meaning "in the public domain." A meaning "state archive" cannot be excluded for *to dēmosion* in this passage, but the context in which it appears renders such an interpretation unlikely.[82]

Reference to the *dēmosion* in the decree of Patrokleides is also problematic, but here its interpretation as "state archive" seems somewhat more likely. Patrokleides outlines several classes of individuals to whom his proposed amnesty would apply, among them state debtors, magistrates subject to fines resulting from *euthynai* proceedings, and individuals who had committed crimes under the regime of the Four Hundred.[83] He also specifies other classes of individuals who were to be excluded from the amnesty's terms. After listing the excluded categories, Patrokleides' decree returns to those to whom his amnesty applied and instructs the *praktores* and the Boule to erase everything "from everywhere as has been stated, wherever anything is in the *dēmosion*, and if there is a copy anywhere, the thesmothetai and other magistracies are to provide it."[84]

If we accept the translation of *dēmosion* as "state archive," the role of the *praktores* in the cancellation of these documents is difficult to explain: the *praktores* were officials who collected money owed to the state, and, technically speaking, like the dockyard superintendents they should be responsible for their own records, not those "in the state archive." But the decree also instructs the Boule to see to the erasure of some documents, and Boegehold suggested that while the *praktores* were responsible for canceling records of state debtors, which were kept on the Acropolis, the Boule was to oversee the erasures of other documents found anywhere "in the state archive."[85] Such documents will have consisted primarily of decrees, and Andokides himself (1.76) explicitly mentions the erasure of both decrees and their copies when he introduces the terms of Patrokleides' decree, an allusion to its cancellation clause. At the time of Patrokleides' decree, therefore, it seems that some documents were being stored in a building called *to dēmosion*, over which the Boule had supervision. Based on the date of Patrokleides' decree and Andokides' reference to a decree in the Bouleuterion in an earlier speech, the foundation of this building can be narrowed to the period 410–405.

Use of the term *to dēmosion* to designate this archival repository in Patrokleides' decree also helps to explain why we do not hear of documents housed in the Metroon until the 340s, more than fifty years after the archive's foundation. The remains of the Bouleuterion-Metroon complex in the southwest part of the Agora suggest that a new Bouleuterion was constructed in the last decade of the fifth century, while the old Bouleuterion continued to stand. Since, however, the old council chamber could no longer be called the Bouleuterion, another name was necessary. Evidently, it was first known by the generic title, *to dēmosion*, "the public building." An inventory of 375/4 suggests that the same building could be called the "Metroon," probably because the cult statue made by Agorakritos stood inside it, but this usage may not have enjoyed universal or popular support.[86] We know nothing of the internal arrangements of the building, and it may be that originally the Athenians made no direct association between the archives and the Mother of the Gods, though they were housed inside the same building. The statue of the

Mother of the Gods may have occupied only a small part of the building, so that only gradually did the name "Metroon" come to denote the entire building and to be connected with other objects, including the archives, housed within it.[87] But even after 350, mention of the Metroon and its archives is infrequent, and our understanding of its holdings depends largely on chance references in a scattered array of sources. The absence of specific references does not mean that the archives did not exist, were not functioning, or were a muddled mass of records; it simply reflects a frequent practice of Greek orators (and historians) not to cite the sources on which they relied.[88]

This reconstruction of the history of the Metroon's nomenclature raises one further question, one that concerns the relationship between the archives housed in the Metroon and the Mother of the Gods, who gave her name to the building. What connection was there between the city's public records and the Mother of the Gods? Authors of the late fifth century show an increasing familiarity with the Mother of the Gods qua Kybele, the Anatolian Mother goddess, and a cult statue of the Mother of the Gods was dedicated in the same period. Some scholars have suggested that Kybele's worship led to the foundation of a temple in her honor; others have tried to draw a close connection between the spheres of activity overseen by Kybele and the archives in the Metroon.[89] But a close connection between Kybele and Athens' archives is difficult to uphold. The building in which Athens' archives were housed was not a temple of Kybele; it was a Metroon, a shrine of the Mother of the Gods. The two goddesses were undoubtedly closely connected in popular imagination and they shared many of the same attributes, but the Mother goddess whose cult was located in the Metroon is not called Kybele in the orators or in inscriptions, and it is difficult to believe that the Athenians ejected the Boule from its headquarters in the heart of the city in order to make room for a new, foreign goddess. This is not the place to examine the cult of the Mother and her origins, but the goddess does seem to have been an ancient, native goddess onto whom was grafted features of Kybele, the popular Anatolian mother goddess.[90] Increasing familiarity with Kybele in the late fifth century may have contributed to the prestige of this old mother goddess, who was sometimes identified with Kybele, and this enhanced standing may have played a role in the decision to grant the goddess a cult statue. But the building later known as the Metroon need not have served solely as a shrine to this divinity from the time it ceased to serve as a council chamber, and an intimate connection between the cult of the Mother and the records housed within the same building is difficult to substantiate.

If religious considerations played little role in the conversion of the old Bouleuterion into an archives building, which later acquired the name Metroon, the growth in the size of the Boule's archives throughout the fifth century was certainly a more crucial factor. Robertson has suggested that the purpose of the revision of the law code by the *anagrapheis* of 410–399 was to compile texts of laws for the new state archive.[91] The coincidence in dates is striking, but the later Metroon housed more than texts of *nomoi*, and since we cannot pinpoint precisely when the decision was made to convert the old Bouleuterion into an archives/Metroon, this suggestion can only be regarded as tentative. But motives similar to those that led the Athenians to appoint the *anagrapheis* in 410 may also have indicated the need for devoting a single building to the preservation of their public records. Whereas the revision of the law code by the *anagrapheis* was in part a response to problems of organization that prevailed in the archives of the Boule, construction of a new Bouleuterion and conversion of the old one into an archives building was also a reaction to the state of these archives. Quite simply, the archives of the Boule had become too extensive and required more room. Boule secretaries are attested from the middle of the fifth century, and some of the documents in the Boule's archives, like a text of the Bouleutic Oath, may have dated back almost a century. The notion of keeping records, apart from those inscribed on stone, was not a new development of the late fifth century, but one that dated back well into the archaic period. If the Athenians had only started to keep archival records of public business in the last decades of the fifth century, there will have been no need for additional space to store the city's records. If, however, the secretary of the Boule had regularly kept texts of measures approved by the Boule and Ekklesia, a duty his title implies, the amount of legislation enacted in the second half of the fifth century alone would have been tremendous. The preservation of such archival texts of these enactments, whether in the Bouleuterion or in a nearby building, allowed them little space, especially as their numbers grew. The decision to convert the old Bouleuterion into an archives building does not represent a recent interest in keeping archival records but was the culmination of developments reaching back a century. How precisely creation of an archives building tied in with the work of the *anagrapheis* we cannot say, but both the revision of the law code and the establishment of a separate archives building may simply reflect a desire to offer more order and space to an ancient but growing body of documents.[92]

CHAPTER FIVE

The Archives in the Metroon

Although it proves impossible to fix the precise year in which the Athenians dedicated a single building to their state archives, a building we shall call the Metroon after its fourth-century name, a date in the last decade of the fifth century is supported by an impressive combination of sources. But simply dating the archive's foundation explains very little. The decision to devote a single building, or portions of it, to the storage of documents signals some recognition of the value of keeping public records, but it leaves unanswered the question of how archival practices actually changed. If all that was involved was the transfer of the Boule's archives into new headquarters, as Jacoby suggested, the overall impact on Athenian record keeping may have been minimal; the Boule kept the same types of records as it had before, except that these were now housed in a separate building.[1] But if the new archive building received types of documents that previously had not been preserved in archival form, either centrally or in the archives of different magistrates, its foundation was far more consequential; Athenians of the fourth century had begun to recognize the value of written records and were now taking steps to see to their preservation.

To assess the impact of this new archival building on Athenian documentary habits, we must start by examining how the records housed in the fourth-century Metroon differed from the types of documents maintained by the Boule or other bodies in the fifth century. Unfortunately, the fifth-century evidence for Athenian archival practice is not extensive; I have argued that the secretary of the Boule regularly kept uninscribed copies of Athenian decrees throughout the fifth century, and that the Boule's archives may have contained a few other documents, but beyond those points, evidence for fifth-century practice offers few specific details. Our sources for the Metroon are better, but important aspects of its archives remain unclear. Some scholars suggest that the Metroon's holdings were extensive and ranged from laws and decrees to texts of tragedies produced by Aeschylus, Sophocles, and Euripides.[2] Others assert that the Metroon's archives were limited to decrees of the Ekklesia, and that other texts attested within it represent later accretions to its archives.[3] But these conclusions have seldom relied on critical examination of the evidence for the Metroon's contents; such an examination provides the focus of this chapter.

It may be useful first to consider some of the criteria by which the Metroon's contents may be determined. Explicit references to texts kept therein obviously provide the most valuable evidence. But all such references cannot be given the same weight. Many appear in sources of the Hellenistic or later periods, and some allowance must be made for the evolution of the Metroon's holdings over the course of its history. Our focus here is on Athenian archives of the fourth century, so primacy will be given to sources of that period, and only then to those sources of later date whose testimony is corroborated by fourth-century authorities.

A direct reference to the Metroon, however, may not always be necessary to conclude that a particular type of document was regularly deposited in that building. The decrees of Patrokleides and Kleisophos refer to documents kept "in the *dēmosion*," and at least in Patrokleides' decree there is some reason to understand this phrase to mean "in the state archive." A related phrase, *ta dēmosia grammata*, "the public records," also appears in speeches of Demosthenes and Aeschines, where it too is used in conjunction with several types of documents, including decrees, that are otherwise attested as being in the Metroon; it too probably represents a circumlocution for the Metroon's archives. Not every document said to be in the *dēmosion* or among the *dēmosia grammata* must be interpreted as located in the Metroon, as the difficulties raised by Kleisophos's decree shows, and individual cases will have to be examined on their own merits. But consideration of the nature of certain documents associated with *dēmosion* or *dēmosia grammata* will sometimes allow us to assume that they too formed part of the Metroon's archives.

The personnel associated with the Metroon and its archives may also provide clues to the types of records its archives contained. Demosthenes, for example, once refers to a public slave working in the Metroon. Public slaves are also found working with other state documents, in contexts, however, in which the Metroon is not mentioned; in some instances, the regular presence of those other documents in the Metroon may be inferred. Similarly, the secretary of the Boule is frequently associated with documents, namely laws and decrees, whose presence in the Metroon is known from several sources. But the state secretary also handled other public records that are not explicitly attested in the Metroon. Given the secretary's connection with texts that were kept there, we may occasionally suppose that these records too found their way into the Metroon's archives.

1. Laws, Decrees, and the Records of the Boule and Ekklesia

Foremost among the records preserved in the Metroon were *nomoi*, or laws in their fourth-century, technical sense.[4] As we saw in the previous chapter, the chief result of the late fifth-century revision of the Athenian law code was the compilation of all currently valid Athenian laws into a single collection. Thereafter laws were distinguished from decrees and were to have a greater degree of authority, and magistrates were to apply only those laws included in the code in their administration of justice. This distinction between laws and decrees was largely maintained throughout the fourth century by means of the process of *nomothesia*; unlike decrees, which continued to be enacted by the Boule and Ekklesia, laws were enacted by specially appointed boards of *nomothetai*.[5]

After their enactment, laws were deposited in the Metroon. Authors of the Roman and Byzantine period generally recognize the Metroon as the repository for Athenian laws. Demosthenes, the imaginary speaker of a declamation of Libanios, defends himself by pointing out that "the Metroon is full of my laws and decrees," a statement that seems to recall the fourth-century distinction between the two types of enactments.[6] Among the lexicographers, Harpokration, Photios, and the *Suda* not only put Athens' public records (*dēmosia grammata*) in the Metroon, they also refer specifically to the city's laws as being found there. The same works also mention lost speeches of fourth-century orators in support of their claims; all three cite Lykourgos's speech *Against Aristogeiton*, while Harpokration reinforces his note that the city's laws were placed in the Metroon by stating "Deinarchos makes this clear in his speech *Against Pytheas*."[7]

Sources of the fourth century itself also locate Athenian *nomoi* inside the Metroon. Lykourgos, in his speech *Against Leokrates* of 330, warns the jury of dikasts that his opponent Leokrates, who stood accused of treason for fleeing Athens immediately after the battle at Chaironeia, might claim that his actions were of little consequence and brought no serious harm to anyone. Lykourgos counters this hypothetical argument by declaring that the issue is not the enormity of Leokrates' crime but the simple question of whether Leokrates had broken the city's laws, and he compares Leokrates' crime to someone entering the Metroon and physically destroying the text of a law preserved there.[8] The speaker of the first Demosthenic speech *Against Aristogeiton* refers to the laws in the sanctuary of the Mother in similar terms. As he concludes his speech, he asks those dikasts who intend to vote for Aristogeiton's acquittal how they will face their fellow citizens and any other person they may meet as they leave the court, and how they will enter the Metroon "to find laws that are valid."[9] The speaker's intention is to equate a vote for acquittal with a betrayal of the laws, and although he does not state explicitly that the laws were found in the Metroon, that is the clear implication of his argument.

If, however, the Metroon's holdings consisted simply or primarily of the archives of the Boule and Ekklesia, as is commonly believed, then we may have to explain why laws were kept there. In the fourth century, laws were not enacted by votes of the Boule and Ekklesia, but by specially empaneled boards of *nomothetai* chosen from the pool of dikasts for a given year. The speeches of Lykourgos and Deinarchos date from the second half of the fourth century, and the relatively late dates of these speeches might suggest that the deposition of laws in the Metroon represents a later practice, and one that was not in use from the time of the Metroon's foundation and the revision of the law code in the late fifth century.[10] But this is improbable. The revised law code of the late fifth century may have been published in its entirety in or near the Stoa Basileios, and laws enacted in the fourth century were sometimes set up on stone stelai. But publication on stone does not exclude the deposition of laws in the Metroon from the time of its foundation. The secretary of the Boule was responsible for the texts of Athenian *nomoi* from the late fifth century. This, at any rate, is the implication of the law of Diokles, dating from 403/2 or shortly thereafter, which instructs the secretary of the Boule to add clauses to the existing laws concerning their effective dates; future secretaries are instructed to do the same for future laws. Statements specifying the implementation dates of *nomoi* are not regularly included in the inscribed versions of Athenian laws, so the order must pertain to archival texts of laws kept by the secretary.[11] Moreover, although the Boule and Ekklesia did not approve new laws in the fourth century, both bodies did play a role in their enactment, since *nomothetai* could only be appointed by a vote of the Ekklesia.[12] The secretary of the Boule was also responsible for seeing to the publication of fourth-century *nomoi* on stone, another indication that this official retained responsibility for their texts.[13] Archival texts of laws were housed in the Metroon from the end of the fifth century.

In addition to *nomoi*, the Metroon held texts of *psēphismata* or decrees.[14] Apart from the late testimony of Libanios cited earlier, ample evidence of the fourth century attests to their presence. In the speech *On the False Embassy* of 343, Demosthenes relates that after the return of the second embassy to Philip in 346 both he and Aeschines were appointed to serve on a third embassy to Philip and the Amphictyonic Council. Demosthenes claims that he immediately declined the appointment, but Aeschines only later swore that he was sick and unable to serve, when his brother was elected to go in his place.[15] To support his version of events, Demosthenes appeals to the decree appointing him and Aeschines to the embassy and Aeschines' disavowal of his appointment, claiming that both were preserved "in your common records in the Metroon, over which a public slave is set."[16] The decree is read out to the court shortly afterward. Courtroom speakers seldom offer an indication of the sources from which they obtained the documents they cite; Demosthenes' words provide valuable evidence that some were taken from the Metroon. Moreover, Demosthenes cited this decree, which appointed ambassadors to serve on an embassy, three years after it was proposed. It hardly had any long-term significance, but its text still could be found in the Metroon.[17]

Later in the fourth century, Deinarchos refers to another decree housed in the Metroon. In the speech *Against Demosthenes*, delivered in 323, Deinarchos accused Demosthenes of having accepted a bribe from Harpalos, the fugitive treasurer of Alexander the Great who found his way to Athens.[18] When the Macedonians demanded his surrender, Demosthenes proposed that Harpalos be allowed to stay and his money be put on the Acropolis for safekeeping.[19] When Harpalos fled, the amount of money was discovered to be half of what Harpalos had brought with him, and several leading Athenians, including Demosthenes, were accused of accepting bribes. So Demosthenes proposed a decree calling on the Areopagos to conduct an investigation, and he specified death as the penalty for anyone found guilty of wrongdoing.[20] Deinarchos refers to this decree several times, and he claims that by proposing it Demosthenes had "put agreements with the people, by writing this decree against himself, in the care of the Mother of the Gods, who is established as guardian of all the rights in these writings."[21] Deinarchos likens the decree of Demosthenes to a contract drawn up and deposited with a third party; that the third party with whom the decree is deposited is the Mother of the Gods is a strong indication that her sanctuary was the normal location for the deposition of Athenian decrees.[22]

Epigraphical evidence also attests to the keeping of decrees in the Metroon, some of them for extended periods of time. In one decree of the late fourth century, a public slave is instructed to deliver a copy of an earlier decree granting an unnamed foreigner the right of *isoteleia*, "equal taxation," so that the earlier decree could be inscribed along with the present one. The Metroon is named only in a restoration, but the reference to a public slave is preserved, and since Demosthenes (19.129) states that a public slave was in charge of the records in the Metroon, including decrees, the restoration should carry some weight.[23] The date of the original grant of *isoteleia* is unknown, and we cannot date the preserved decree itself more precisely. But its call for publication of an earlier decree shows that, although honorary decrees were not automatically published on stone in the fourth century, there existed archival texts, which later could be retrieved from the Metroon and published.

Long-term preservation of a decree housed in the Metroon is further illustrated by an inscribed decree of 140/39. The decree itself records a grant of Athenian citizenship to Telesias, a native of Troizen. According to its text, this award was made not because of any particular deeds performed by Telesias for the Athenians, but because an ancestor had rendered services to Athens and received a grant of citizenship in return. This grant had been proposed by Stratokles of Diomeia, and, according to the restoration, a certain Onasos found this decree and produced its text from the Metroon.[24] That the earlier citizenship decree was moved by Stratokles is of considerable interest. Stratokles was a prominent Athenian politician in the late fourth century, and in the last decade of the fourth century he was the author of numerous decrees, including several that awarded citizenship to foreign supporters of Demetrios Poliorketes.[25] Whether or not Telesias's unnamed ancestor was another supporter of Demetrios cannot be established, but the original citizenship decree should belong to the same period.[26] We do not know if the original decree had been inscribed on stone, but a text apparently did remain in the Metroon for over 150 years.

The Athenians also deposited treaties, alliances, and interstate agreements in the Metroon. In one sense, this is to be expected: treaties and alliances were ratified by the Ekklesia in the form of decrees, so their preservation in the Metroon conforms to ordinary practice. But the Metroon also contained texts of agreements or decisions of Panhellenic congresses and bodies to which the Athenians were party. An Athenian inscription of the second century preserves two *dogmata* or decrees and a letter from the Delphic Amphictyony concerning the rights and privileges of the *technitai* of Dionysos, an actors' guild, at Athens.[27] The lettering of the inscription suggests that it was inscribed in the second half of the second century, but the first *dogma* on the stone dates from circa 278/7. It grants the guild of actors *asylia*, *asphaleia*, and *ateleia*, immunity from certain types of reprisals and obligations. It also stipulates that one copy should be set up on stone at Delphi and another, sealed copy sent to Athens.[28] Appended to this *dogma* is a letter from the Amphictyonic Council dated to the year 130/29, which, in turn, is followed by another *dogma* of the same year renewing the rights and privileges of the earlier *dogma*. Its text also calls for publication at Delphi and the dispatch of a copy to Athens.[29] The fate of the copies sent to Athens is provided by the inscription itself. At lines 2 and 40, before the first decree and the letter from the Amphictyons, appears the phrase *ek tou Mētrō-iou*, "from the Metroon." These words do not mean that the inscription was set up in the Metroon, but that the texts inscribed on it were taken from the Metroon and the archives it housed.[30] How frequently Athenian representatives brought back decisions from the Amphictyons we cannot say, but the deposition of such documents in the Metroon indicates that non-Athenian texts also found their way into the Metroon, where, like the *dogma* concerning the artisans of Dionysos, they could remain for centuries.

The Hellenistic date of these Amphictyonic texts should not lead us to suppose that their preservation in the Metroon was a postclassical or later development; even in the fourth century, similar types of documents were being kept in the Metroon. Aeschines recounts in his speech *On the False Embassy* (343) how on the first embassy to Philip he had reminded the Macedonian king of the injustice of his continued occupation of Amphipolis. Aeschines reasserted Athens' rights to that city by noting that Philip's father Amyntas had once recognized the Athenian claim in a congress of Greek states held at Sparta around 370. In support of the Athenian claim Aeschines supplied a *dogma* enacted by this congress, which he had obtained "from the public records."[31] Given the deposition of Delphic documents in the Metroon early in the next century, Aeschines' reference to "public records" in this passage should indicate that building's archives; the decisions of Panhellenic bodies, it seems, were being kept in the Metroon from early in the fourth century.

The deposition of such agreements in the Metroon may be explained in part by the role played by the Boule in the supervision of Athenian envoys. Athenian ambassadors to Panhellenic congresses or serving on embassies to foreign states routinely reported to the Boule and sometimes the Ekklesia on their return to Athens.[32] They presented a summary of what was decided at those gatherings and probably delivered documents recording those decisions, which were then deposited in the Metroon, perhaps as part of the normal record made of the Boule's or Ekklesia's business. Thus, Aeschines, who served as an Athenian delegate to a meeting of the Amphictyonic Council at Delphi in 340/39, relates how he brought back a *dogma* passed by that council against the Amphissans and had its text read out to both the Boule and Ekklesia. A text of this Amphictyonic *dogma* was still available in 330, when Aeschines had its text read out at the trial of Ktesiphon; probably, he had submitted a copy of the *dogma* on his return to Athens in 340/39, when its text was deposited in the Metroon and from where he retrieved it a few years later as he prepared his case against Ktesiphon and Demosthenes.[33]

Aeschines' reference to a Panhellenic *dogma* and Athenian decrees taken from *ta dēmosia grammata*, the "public records," and the probability that these public records were the very archives housed in the Metroon, offer further insights into the contents of these archives. Throughout the speeches *On the False Embassy* and *Against Ktesiphon*, Aeschines cites numerous documents in support of his arguments, and on several occasions he indicates that the texts of these documents were taken from the *dēmosia grammata*. Although we need not accept blindly the version of the events put forward by Aeschines, there is no reason to reject his statements that the documents he cites came from the city's public records. Among these were not only decrees enacted by the Ekklesia, but also *probouleumata* or preliminary decrees of the Boule.[34] The *dēmosia grammata* also included the names of the proposers of these decrees, the officials who put them to a vote, and the dates on which they were ratified.[35] Details related to the election of magistrates could also be found among the *dēmosia grammata*. Thus, Aeschines recalls the specific year, month, and day on which Demosthenes was elected one of the controllers of the Theoric Fund; it is these items, he says, "the public records," which convict Demosthenes.[36] In addition, the names of special envoys elected by the Ekklesia for missions to other Greek cities, together with the dates of their election and the dates on which they were sent out were to be found in the *dēmosia grammata*.[37] Finally, Aeschines' account of the downfall of Kersebleptes refers to a letter sent by the Athenian general Chares; this letter is read out to the dikasts, and it seems to be included in Aeschines' general references to the *dēmosia grammata* in the preceding and succeeding passages.[38]

Nowhere in these passages does Aeschines mention the Metroon by name, but many of the items that he associates with the *dēmosia grammata* were decrees or related to decisions of the Boule or Ekklesia. Since decrees were known from other sources to have been kept in the Metroon, Aeschines' use of the phrase *dēmosia grammata* is best understood as an alternative expression for the archives of the Metroon. When we put all of the documents mentioned by Aeschines together, his references confirm that that building's holdings included a range of documents, not simply decrees, reflecting the activities of the Boule and Ekklesia. We might characterize these records as "minutes" of their meetings. By minutes I do not mean detailed commentaries on all matters treated or discussed at meetings of either body; we have no evidence to suggest that secretaries recorded the names of individual speakers or took notes on debate. Rather, minutes refers simply to records of actions taken by the Boule and Ekklesia, usually in the form of decrees, and other documents reflecting other business handled at their meetings. Decrees will have formed the bulk of these minutes, but other texts—laws, election results, appointment of ambassadors, interstate agreements—emanating from the powers of both Boule and Ekklesia formed part of the minutes, and all these were regularly deposited in the Metroon.

11. Financial Records and Accounts

The archives in the Metroon were not limited to laws, decrees, and other documents emanating from the activities of the Boule and Ekklesia. From the middle of the third century some evidence suggests that the Metroon received documents related to the financial activities of magistrates and their inventories of sacred and secular buildings.[39] Thus, an inventory from the Athenian Asklepieion, dating to the year 245/4, is prefaced with a decree appointing a special commission that was to undertake an inventory of the Asklepieion, remove old dedications from within the sanctuary, and make new dedications out of old ones.[40] The decree also instructs the commission, which included members of the Boule, to deposit a record of their findings into the Metroon. Unfortunately the inscription breaks off at that point where the specific type of document to be deposited was specified, but we may be confident that it was an account or inventory of the commission's work.[41]

A decree of the early second century refers to another special inventory whose text was deposited in the Metroon. It honors three *bouleutai* who had been elected to replace the bedding within the Tholos and to make a list of equipment kept therein; they are also commended for having deposited their accounts in the Metroon.[42] Similar actions are reflected in a decree of the Boule dating from the late second century.[43] In the latter decree, a priest of the "Hero Doctor" had approached the Boule and pointed out that many of the votives in his sanctuary were worn out and useless because of their age. He asked for the appointment of a commission consisting of three members of the Boule, a public slave, and other magistrates to oversee the repair and restoration of these objects. The Boule agreed to the request and appointed the commission, and in its instructions it called upon the commissioners to deliver an account of their work to the Metroon and to inscribe the same account in the sanctuary. Presumably, the account or *logos* deposited in the Metroon consisted of a list or inventory of those objects that had been repaired and was identical with the inventory appended to the end of this decree.[44]

The documents deposited in the Metroon in these three cases all represent extraordinary or special inventories conducted by special commissions, which, in at least the latter two cases, included members of the Boule. Deposition of more regular inventories, recording the annual transfer of objects in a particular shrine, sanctuary, or public building, when the officials overseeing them changed office, is suggested by a decree of the late second century.[45] It calls for the replacement of official sets of public weights and measures and prescribes their placement in four locations; public slaves are put in control over these standards in each location and ordered to make copies for state officials. The decree also stipulates that when these public slaves retired from their positions, they were to hand over all the weights and measures in their possession to their successors, together with a list of these objects; they were also instructed to make a text of what they delivered and received, and to deposit that text in the Metroon.[46] It is unclear how often public slaves rotated from position to position in the Hellenistic period, but the type of transfer described is reminiscent of the annual transfers (*paradoseis*) of objects in sanctuaries and other public buildings, and the decree's requirements that public slaves place inventories of objects under their care in the Metroon when they leave office may reflect what Athenian magistrates and priests, who were responsible for sacred or public objects, were normally required to do each year.[47]

Evidence for the deposition of some types of accounts in the Metroon by Athenian officials is provided by a decree of 215/14. It honors the *epimelētai* of the Eleusinian Mysteries for having supervised successfully the celebration of the Mysteries.[48] According to the decree the *epimelētai* had conducted the proper sacrifices, overseen the sacred procession, and paid for certain sacrifices and items from their own funds. In addition, the *epimelētai* rendered their accounts to the *logistai* and to the Metroon and faced their *euthynai* in a lawcourt "in accordance with the laws."[49] What laws were these? Possibly, they were laws governing the administration of the Mysteries that required presiding officials to submit their accounts to the *logistai* and to the Metroon. It is equally possible, however, that the laws specified were ones binding on all Athenian magistrates, which required them to submit accounts for scrutiny at the end of their term in office. A similar phrase appears or is restored in several other inscriptions.[50] Thus, a decree of 161/0 honors Nikogenes of Philaidai for his service as *agōnothetēs* for the Theseia.[51] It relates that he sent off the procession in elegance, conducted the sacrifices in accordance with ancestral customs, and administered the games with forethought. In addition, "concerning all things which he administered, he handed in accounts to the Metroon and the *logistai*, and underwent his *euthynai*."[52] Some years later, probably in 149/8, another *agōnothetēs*, Miltiades of Marathon, was honored for similar reasons, including his deposition of accounts in the Metroon,[53] and the same formula may have occurred in a third inscription whose text, however, is too fragmentary to be certain.[54]

The texts delivered by magistrates to the Metroon could also include more than simple accounts or inventories of public moneys or property under their supervision. An inscription of the late third century from the Thessalian city of Gonnoi preserves an Athenian decree calling for honors to be granted to the foreign hosts (*hoi theōrodokountes*) of Athenian envoys (*spondophoroi*) who announced the sacred truces preceding the Athenian festivals of the Eleusinia, Panathenaia, and Mysteries.[55] To ensure that these hosts are duly recognized, the envoys are instructed to include a list of their names in the accounts they deposit in the Metroon when they return to Athens. The verb used to refer to this list of hosts, *prosapopherein*, however, means "to report in addition"; the *spondophoroi* reported the names of those who had entertained them in addition to something else, which can only be the names of those cites that had accepted the truces, as the decree's text indicates.[56] The accounts of these *spondophoroi* may have had a financial component, since *spondophoroi* did receive expense money for their travels, so their deposition in the Metroon would reflect normal practice.[57] But they might also have included nonfinancial information related to the actions carried out by individual officials.

Each of these cases illustrates practices of the Hellenistic period. Can we assume that Athenians of the fifth and fourth centuries were already depositing accounts in a central archive? Some scholars have thought so. Curtius, for example, argued that when the dying Lykourgos asked to be brought into the Metroon and Bouleuterion to render an account of his political activities, it was because the accounts of his administrative activities were housed in the Metroon.[58] Dziatzko noted that an entry in the Erechtheion accounts of 408/7 mentions the purchase of two rolls of papyrus to be used for making copies, and he supposed that one copy was intended for the *logistai*, the other for the Metroon; he cited several of the Hellenistic inscriptions discussed here to support his conjecture.[59] Since we are not told where these copies were to go, we cannot be certain, but several texts show that the Metroon was receiving accounts during the fourth century. One, an inscribed, Athenian law dating from the first half of the fourth century, opens with several provisions regarding the activities of *spondophoroi* for the Eleusinian Mysteries.[60] The text is extremely fragmentary, so we must proceed with caution, but one section seems to refer to the deposition of a written list with a secretary.[61] Since *spondophoroi* included lists in the accounts they submitted to the Metroon during the Hellenistic period, it is not unreasonable to identify this secretary with the secretary of the Boule, who oversaw Athens' public records, and to see in this law a fourth-century predecessor to Hellenistic practice.

A decree of 353/2 ordering an inventory of objects in the Chalkotheke, a building on the Acropolis in which bronze objects were housed, suggests that some inventories were being deposited in the Metroon already in the fourth century.[62] It instructs the *prytaneis* to name a day on which the inventory was to be conducted, and a public slave named Eukles is charged with cataloging all objects found within the building. Next, the secretary of the Boule is ordered to make a copy of the inventory, from which the secretary of the Boule and several other secretaries "in charge of the public records" (*epi tois dēmosiois grammasi*) are to make their own copies. The secretary of the Boule is to publish the inventory on a stone stele, and he is to make copies of the Chalkotheke's contents according to the stelai published by the treasurers of preceding years. The *prytaneis* are to fix a day on which the inventory is to be read out before the Boule, and the inventory drawn up by Eukles is to be compared with those published on the individual stelai. If any objects are damaged or missing, the Boule is to consult the Ekklesia about what steps should be taken.

The circumstances prompting a special inventory of the Chalkotheke in 353/2 are not preserved. We may suppose, however, that some items were thought to be missing from the building so that a new inventory had to be drawn up. The situation seems similar to the inventories prescribed by some of the Hellenistic decrees discussed earlier, in which special commissions were appointed to examine and inventory the contents of certain sanctuaries and public buildings. And although the Metroon is not mentioned in the Chalkotheke Decree, the role it gives to a public slave suggests that the inventory to be drawn up was destined for its archives; several of the Hellenistic decrees ordering inventories of sanctuaries require participation of a public slave, and Demosthenes (19.129) mentions a public slave in charge of the records in the Metroon just a decade after the Chalkotheke Decree. We need not assume, however, that no archival records of the Chalkotheke's contents existed prior to the date of this decree.[63] It is true that the inventory drawn up by Eukles was to be compared with the annual inventories published on stone, a practice that seems to imply that the inscribed inventories alone, and not archival records preserved either by the treasurers of Athena who superintended the Chalkotheke or the Boule, preserved the authoritative texts of the contents of the Chalkotheke, but this fact does not exclude the possibility that other copies once existed. The treasurers of 354/3 may have discovered discrepancies between what they found in the Chalkotheke and what was recorded in their records, inscribed or otherwise, that had been delivered to them by their predecessors. If these earlier, uninscribed records were thought to be inaccurate, then the Boule may have decided that its records too, kept in the Metroon and sent there by earlier boards of treasurers, were similarly inaccurate, and for this reason it decided to start anew and conduct a special inventory of the Chalkotheke's contents.

Finally, a passage of Aeschines' speech *Against Ktesiphon* may indicate that Athenian magistrates regularly submitted copies of their accounts to the state secretary already in the fourth century. In the fourth century, public officials were required to submit to a scrutiny of their conduct at the end of their term in office. This examination consisted of two parts: a board of auditors (*logistai*) reviewed financial records, and officials called *euthynoi* received more general complaints concerning a magistrate's general conduct.[64] According to Aeschines, one of the laws governing these proceedings stated that all officials who administered some public business or presided over a lawcourt were required "to write an account to the secretary and the *logistai*."[65] Who is the secretary mentioned in this law? Hellenistic inscriptions mention the *logistai* and Metroon, but no secretary, in connection with the accounts of magistrates. But the secretary of the Boule was responsible for the city's public records, including those kept in the Metroon, so the secretary named in the law cited by Aeschines was quite possibly the chief state secretary, who received magisterial accounts after officials retired from office. Indeed, the law cited by Aeschines may be the very same law according to which the *epimelētai* of the Eleusinian Mysteries and other officials deposited their accounts in the Metroon in later periods.[66] If so, the deposition of accounts in the Metroon does not reflect an innovation of that period but the continuation of a practice already in use in the fourth century.

But can we push the practice back earlier? That is, was the Boule receiving copies of magistrate's accounts already in the fifth century? The *euthynai* procedures by which all magistrates were scrutinized when they left office may have undergone some changes around the year 400, so it is possible that the transfer of accounts and inventories to the secretary of the Boule and Metroon reflects fourth-century practice.[67] But the financial accounts of magistrates did follow the bouleutic calendar from the mid-fifth century, and the Boule's interest in financial matters is well attested from the middle of the fifth century: that the Boule sometimes received reports on the financial activities of state officials before the fourth century must be considered a strong possibility.[68] The decree of Drakontides may shed some light on the question. This decree required Perikles, suspected of malfeasance in his oversight of work on the Parthenon, to submit his accounts to the *prytaneis* for a special examination.[69] The date of the decree cannot be fixed definitively, but it probably belongs either to 438/7 or 430/29,[70] and the role it assigns the *prytaneis* is suggestive. The audit ordered of Perikles' accounts is an extraordinary one, but the involvement of the *prytaneis*, a subcommittee of the Boule, may not have been unusual; it possibly reflects the more regular deposition of at least some magisterial accounts centrally, with the Boule and in its archives, from the mid-fifth century.[71] On this view, the later but better-attested conveyance by Athenian magistrates of their accounts to the Metroon was not an innovation of the fourth century or Hellenistic period, but the development of a practice dating back to the heyday of the democracy.

III. *Pōlētai* Documents

The Metroon also contained records associated with the leasing of public lands, mines, and tax contracts let out by the *pōlētai*.[72] Aristotle relates that when the *pōlētai* leased out a tax contract, they wrote down the name of the lessee and the amount that he paid for the lease onto a whitened tablet, which they handed over to the Boule. Separate tablets were made for each payment owed, so that contracts fulfilled with one payment had one payment tablet, those with payments due three times in a year had three tablets, and those with payments due each prytany had ten separate tablets. These payment tablets were kept by a public slave, and when individual payments fell due, the slave took down the tablets at the appropriate time and erased the names of those who paid off what they owed.[73] Aristotle's discussion of the separate payment tablets drawn up by the *pōlētai* refers specifically to tax contracts, but the *pōlētai* also let out contracts for mines, leases of public land, and the sale of confiscated property. These were let out for periods of anywhere from three to ten years, and presumably a similar type of recording system was used to keep track of payments due on them.

The Metroon is not mentioned in Aristotle's account of the *pōlētai* and their records. But its preservation of some of the records drawn up by the *pōlētai* is indicated by two features of Aristotle's account. First, Aristotle states that tablets recording the names of lessees and the price of their leases were handed over to the Boule; later he says that separate payment tablets were also brought into the Boule.[74] When Aristotle says that these documents were given to the Boule, it is possible that this means they were kept in the Bouleuterion. But since many of the Boule's documents, such as its decrees, were kept in the Metroon in the fourth century, it seems safe to assume that these *pōlētai* documents were to be deposited there.[75] This assumption is lent some support by a second feature of Aristotle's account, for he says that a public slave watched over *pōlētai* documents that were delivered to the Boule. Not only is a public slave associated with the Metroon and several of its documents in several sources, as we have seen, but a decree of the year 304/3, which concerns repairs on Athens' city walls, also seems to refer to a lease or contract that was to be handed over to the public slave in the Metroon.[76] The text of the inscription is extremely fragmentary, but immediately following the reference to a public slave we find references to leasing contracts and moneys owed on them; the procedure seems similar to the process described by Aristotle and to involve the deposition of a contract in the Metroon.[77]

The keeping of records drawn up by the *pōlētai* in the Metroon at first seems unusual for two reasons. First, if the Metroon's archives consisted primarily of documents reflecting the activity of the Boule and Ekklesia, the deposition of *pōlētai* documents there is anomalous; records of the *pōlētai* should have been kept in the *pōlētai*'s own office, the Poleterion.[78] But we do not know that the *pōlētai* did not keep separate copies of their records in the Poleterion, and the keeping of records related to state contracts in the Boule's archives suits well the Boule's overall concern for state finances. Tax contracts were among the chief sources of income for the Athenian state, and they were drawn up and paid off in the presence of the Boule; it would have been natural for the Boule to keep its own records of these transactions.[79]

A second feature of the *pōlētai* documents that makes their presence in the Metroon appear atypical is their lack of permanency. Whereas laws, decrees, and certain other documents preserved in the Metroon were kept there for very long periods of time, some of the documents drawn up by the *pōlētai* were erased as soon as payments were made. Although it is not clear that all records of leases or tax contracts were destroyed on payment, the payment tablets that Aristotle describes were erased once lessees or contractors paid what they owed.[80] The Metroon's archives did not consist solely of documents that were deposited there but only consulted when a need for them happened to arise: its holdings included texts that were used, consulted, and, in this case, erased on a regular, systematic basis.

When the Boule began to keep its own copies of documents reflecting the activities of the *pōlētai* is not attested, but we need not assume that the practice originated only in the fourth century. The Boule had some authority over state income throughout the fifth century, and is connected with the *pōlētai* in several fifth-century documents. Although certainty is impossible, the Boule's maintenance of its own copies of some leases and contracts leased out by the *pōlētai* already during the fifth century must be considered a real possibility.[81]

iv. Other Documents

In addition to "minutes" of meetings of the Boule and Ekklesia, accounts of magistrates, and some documents concerned with state income, several other types of records are attested among the Metroon's contents. The evidence for these texts, however, which include lists of ephebes, records of judicial proceedings, and at least one private document, requires closer scrutiny. The sources for their preservation within the Metroon are generally late, and often no ready parallel can found from the classical period. In different cases, we may be dealing with texts erroneously located in the Metroon by an ancient source, or an expansion of the Metroon's holdings after the classical period.

Lists of Ephebes

An inscription of A.D. 61/2 mentions that Epiktetos, *kosmētēs* of the ephebes, had "handed over the following ephebes to the Metroon," meaning, presumably, that Epiktetos had deposited in the Metroon a list of ephebes of that year; a copy of this list appears lower on the stone.[82] The late date of this inscription and the absence of earlier evidence for the deposition of such lists, however, is troubling and forces us to question whether the practice was in use in the classical or even Hellenistic periods. Lists of ephebes were kept in the classical period, but it is unclear whether the Boule was responsible for their preservation. In Aristotle's time, the names of the ephebes of a given year were inscribed on a bronze stele under the name of an eponymous hero assigned to that year and the name of the archon in whose year the class had been registered as citizens. In earlier times, according to Aristotle, these lists were kept on whitened wooden tablets.[83] Aristotle does not indicate what body or which magistrates were responsible for inscribing the lists of ephebes on bronze stelai in his own day, or for the keeping of the earlier lists that were written on whitened tablets. Possibly, these earlier lists on wood were kept by the generals and taxiarchs, the officials who oversaw military mobilizations; the same officials may also have published the lists of ephebes on bronze.[84] The deposition of a list of ephebes in the Metroon could have been the result of Hellenistic reforms of the *ephēbeia*, when service was no longer compulsory and the military importance of the *ephēbeia* had diminished. At that time, each year's ephebes no longer paraded before the Ekklesia in the Theater of Dionysos, as they had in the fourth century, but only before the Boule.[85]

Still, the possibility that the Boule (and Metroon) received lists of ephebes in the fourth century deserves consideration. Although the *ephēbeia* must have existed in some form as early as the fifth century, it underwent a radical reform after the Athenian defeat at Chaironeia in 338. Our knowledge of the *ephēbeia* before that time is slim, but the reform may have been intended to bring military training under tighter and more centralized state control.[86] The Boule took some interest in the training of the ephebes, and a gloss in Harpokration's *Lexicon* may suggest that it received a list of ephebes from the time of the reform. Harpokration provides virtually the same description as Aristotle of the registration of ephebes, and he cites Aristotle as his authority. But whereas Aristotle says that in his day the names of ephebes were posted on bronze stelai in front of the Bouleuterion and beside the statutes of the Eponymoi, Harpokration's gloss says only that these lists were recorded *eis tēn boulēn*, "in" or "with the Boule."[87] It is difficult to know what emphasis to place on this discrepancy. Harpokration may have abbreviated Aristotle's statement that the stelai bearing ephebes' names were displayed before the Bouleuterion with the words "with the Boule." But Harpokration may also have used a different edition of the *Athēnaiōn Politeia* than that which we now possess, and possibly his edition noted only the deposition of lists of ephebes with the Boule, whereas a later edition changed that reference to accommodate the recent publication of their names on bronze stelai.[88] If this is the case, Harpokration would provide evidence for the fourth-century preservation of lists of ephebes by the Boule and possibly in the Metroon.[89] Such a practice could have been a result of the reform of the 330s, when the *sophronistēs* and *kosmētēs* who supervised the training of the ephebes were elected by the entire citizen body and were presumably accountable to the Boule and *dēmos* for their conduct in office. A transfer of lists of ephebes to the Boule would thus reflect the normal deposition of accounts into the Metroon by other Athenian officials.

Judicial Records

Late sources suggest that some judicial records were also kept in the Metroon, and their statements have convinced some scholars that such a practice goes back to the classical period.[90] The possibility that records of this type were kept in the Metroon is significant; if the Metroon did contain records of lawsuits and judicial proceedings, this would show that the Metroon's archives extended beyond those of the Boule itself and included those of other Athenian magistrates: the Metroon truly was a central archive of all Athenian public documents. Unfortunately, the evidence is not convincing. An anecdote told by Chamaileon of Herakleia and preserved in Athenaios relates that when Hegemon of Thasos, a fifth-century parodist and friend of Alkibiades, was indicted for an unspecified offense, Alkibiades strode "into the Metroon, where they kept texts of indictments, and wetting his finger from his mouth, wiped away the charge against Hegemon."[91] If we could be certain that this story referred to actual historical events, it would show not only that the Metroon had been founded by 406, when Alkibiades last departed from Athens, but also that its archives contained texts of indictments and perhaps other types of records associated with the activities of Athenian lawcourts.

The anecdote's historicity, however, is dubious. Chamaileon was a student in the school of Aristotle and the author of numerous works on poetry, including biographies of ancient poets. None of these works survives, but from their surviving fragments it seems that Chamaileon sometimes extracted details about the lives of these poets from passages of their poetry.[92] Athenaios, our source for the story about Hegemon, Alkibiades, and the Metroon, indicates that it came from the sixth book of Chamaileon's work on ancient comedy, and this may suggest that the story is based on a work of Hegemon, the author of parodies and possibly comedies. Indeed, not only is the behavior attributed to Alkibiades highly improbable, it is also reminiscent of a passage in Aristophanes' *Clouds*, where Strepsiades imagines using a mirror to melt away the record of a suit brought against him.[93]

One aspect of the story is clearly anachronistic. When Hegemon was indicted, he is said to have gathered together some Athenian actors and to have gone with them to solicit Alkibiades' help. The phrase used by Chamaileon to describe the Athenian actors is the same used to describe the Hellenistic actors' guild or association, the artisans of Dionysos (*technitai peri ton Dionyson*). This guild, however, seems to have been organized only in the early third century.[94] Even if the anecdote preserves some kernel of historical truth, and Hegemon was charged with some offense and did enroll Athenian actors to support him, Chamaileon's reference to the *technitai peri ton Dionyson* shows that he has colored his account with anachronistic details. The same may also be true of his reference to the Metroon: because Chamaileon knew that the Metroon housed some types of records, he mistakenly inserted a reference to that building in a story about Alkibiades' involvement in a suit against Hegemon. Without further evidence about the origins of the story, its value as evidence for the holdings of the Metroon must be rejected.

The preservation of judicial records in the Metroon, however, is also suggested by Diogenes Laertius's statement that the indictment against Socrates was also preserved there.[95] Diogenes cites Favorinus as his authority for this claim. Favorinus was a well-known rhetorician of the second century after Christ, and he is known to have spent time in Athens, so his testimony merits some respect.[96] But we must ask whether the indictment seen by Favorinus was the original indictment against Socrates or a later copy set up for antiquarian reasons. For unlike other evidence of Hellenistic and Roman date which located certain types of documents in the Metroon, Diogenes' testimony about the indictment of Socrates finds no corroboration in reliable, fourth-century sources. Athenian judicial magistrates did keep some records, and it is conceivable that they delivered copies of these records to the Boule as part of the accounts they submitted to the secretary of the Boule and Metroon.[97] But our knowledge of such judicial records is extremely poor, so this point cannot be pushed too far. Later Athenians would certainly have been capable of reconstructing a text of Socrates' indictment from passages of Xenophon or Plato; how such a text ended up in the Metroon is less certain, but its presence there may be explained on the assumption that it was intended to satisfy the curiosity of the many foreigners who came to Athens to study in the tradition of the great philosophical schools that traced their origins back to Socrates.[98]

If the Metroon preserved any records of a judicial nature, these will have been records of trials that were initiated or conducted before the Boule or Ekklesia.[99] The Boule was competent to hear certain types of judicial cases in which the penalty did not exceed a fixed amount; it also had the power to punish individuals who committed offenses in areas over which it had authority. Likewise, the Ekklesia heard trials resulting from *eisangeliai* or indictments on charges of treason and other high crimes against the state, and records of these proceedings will have been included in the normal minutes of the meetings of these bodies.[100] Other magistrates may have preserved records of proceedings that took place in courts over which they presided, but we cannot assume that these were routinely transmitted to the Metroon.

Private Documents

Diogenes Laertius preserves a text of the will of Epikouros, in which Epikouros entrusted his property to Amynomachos and Timokrates "in accordance with a grant [*dosis*] that is recorded in the Metroon."[101] The *dosis* referred to in Epikouros's will is not the will itself, but a separate bequest or gift made by Epikouros that was to become active upon his death.[102] The deposition of a document of this type in the Metroon is unparalleled, but there is no reason to doubt the authenticity of Epikouros's will or to challenge its reference to the Metroon. In fact, according to a gloss in Harpokration, which cites the fourth-century orator Deinarchos, *dosis* was a special term used to describe "a written agreement, when someone gives his property to someone through the archons."[103] This suggests that in the fourth century, individuals could register certain gifts or bequests with a magistrate or official boards.

A speech of Isaios illustrates a similar practice at an earlier date. The speaker of Isaios's speech *On the Estate of Kleonymos* states that Kleonymos, whose property was under dispute, had deposited a will with certain state officials, probably the *astynomoi*, but that he had not had time to change the terms of that document before his death.[104] The validity of the will is challenged in the present speech, since the heirs named by the will were more distant relatives than the speaker and his brothers, who by virtue of their closer relation claimed the inheritance as rightfully their own. There is no suggestion, however, that the deposition of this document was required by law, and perhaps it was to guard against such claims that Athenians sometimes deposited documents with public officials. Both Kleonymos and Epikouros were childless, and since the property of childless Athenians who died intestate was distributed to their next of kin, their deposition of documents with public authorities may reflect a desire to give these documents a greater degree of security than if they had been deposited in private hands, as was normal practice.[105]

Why, however, Epikouros's *dosis* was deposited in the Metroon, as opposed to the office of some magistrate, we cannot say. It is unlike any other document housed and preserved in the Metroon, and both Harpokration's gloss on *dosis* and Isaios's speech refer only to documents deposited with magistrates, not in the Metroon. Ferguson suggested, on the basis of developments in the texts of security *horoi*, that Demetrios of Phaleron promulgated laws for the Athenians in 316/15 that required the registration of certain types of private transactions with third parties, including public officials, in order to protect property rights, and it may be that in the Hellenistic period the Metroon began to attract types of documents that previously had been deposited with other magistrates.[106] The deposition of a wide variety of documents recording private transactions—contracts, bills of sale, manumissions, wills—in centralized, archival establishments is well attested in Greek cities throughout the Hellenistic period, and it would be unusual if Athens did not share in this development. But additional evidence for any such development at Athens is not forthcoming.[107]

Tragedies

Among the several laws attributed to the fourth-century orator and statesman Lykourgos was one calling for the erection of statues of the poets Aeschylus, Sophocles, and Euripides, and the recording and preservation of official texts of their tragedies. These texts were to be used by the "secretary of the city," who was to read them to actors; actors were expected to abide by these official texts in their productions.[108] The purpose of the law was undoubtedly to bring an end to frequent interpolation, but some scholars have cited it as evidence that texts of tragedies produced by the three great fifth-century tragedians were deposited in the Metroon.[109] For the law stipulated, according to Plutarch, that the texts of tragedies were to be written down *en koinōi*, "in common" or "in public." This phrase is reminiscent of the phrase *en tōi dēmosiōi*, which, we have seen, sometimes served as a circumlocution for the Metroon itself. But there is a slight difference. The phrase *en koinōi* lacks the definite article *to*, and it may mean "in public" or "publicly," with no specific location being defined; the word implies simply that whereas before the law's enactment the texts of tragedies had been transmitted only in private hands, now they were to be written down and preserved by a public authority, to ensure their accurate preservation for performances.[110] What body or official was required to write down and preserve these texts we do not know, but since the chief archon was responsible for selecting the poets and actors who performed at the City Dionysia, official texts of tragedies may have been kept in his archives.[111]

v. Conclusion

Before turning to the personnel and organization of the Metroon in the following chapter, a few features of its archives call for a brief discussion. The records housed in the Metroon embraced a wide range of texts, from laws and decrees to some financial accounts and inventories. It was not simply an archive of decrees of the Ekklesia. Most of its documents, however, were in some way connected to the probouleutic, legislative, and administrative powers of the Boule. Decrees began as preliminary decrees of the Boule, and treaties, *dogmata*, and official letters were often introduced to the Boule before being presented to the Ekklesia. Even laws, though enacted by special boards of *nomothetai*, had originated in decrees that called for the appointment of *nomothetai* and set the legislative process in motion. *Pōlētai* contracts, magisterial accounts, and possibly ephebic lists were likewise related to the Boule's duties, so that the Metroon's contents were essentially the archives of that body. But the Boule had broad responsibilities in the administration of Athenian government, so it is legitimate to characterize its archives as the principal or central archives of the Athenian state.

The Metroon, however, did not contain texts of all public documents. Demes, official boards, and individual magistrates made and kept records related to their activities. Copies of many records were transferred to the Metroon as part of the accounting process which all Athenian magistrates went through, but nonetheless not all documents found their way to its archives. In some cases, the absence of certain types of documents from the Metroon seems odd. The Athenians, for example, do not seem to have maintained a central register of citizens, despite the fact that the Boule played a role in the examination of young men when they came of age.[112] As far as we know, demes maintained control over citizen registers, the *lēxiarchika grammateia*, throughout the history of the classical democracy. Another instance of the lack of centralization in an area in which the Boule exercised some supervisory control is illustrated by the Athenian cavalry register. The Boule conducted an annual review of the horses and men who served in the Athenian cavalry. Individuals no longer fit to serve were erased from the official list of cavalry members and new members were added, all in the presence of the Boule. The official list of cavalrymen, however, seems not to have been kept by the Boule: Aristotle says that cavalry commanders brought the list with them to the Boule when the review took place.[113] These officials presumably stored this and other records related to the cavalry in the Hipparcheion, the office of the cavalry commanders, just as other officials continued to maintain records related to their duties at their offices in the same period.[114] The factors that dictated what types of records were transferred to the Boule and its archives in the Metroon cannot always be determined. Full centralization, however, even of records of business in which the Boule had some interest, was never wholly achieved.

At the same time, we should not think that our sources provide anywhere near a complete picture of every type of document housed in the Metroon. Both Deinarchos and Demosthenes, for example, cite the texts of oracles in their speeches.[115] Where they obtained these texts they do not say, but if the Athenians sent envoys to consult an oracular shrine, it is reasonable to suppose that those envoys brought back with them texts of responses, which they presented either to the Boule or Ekklesia on their return, just as other envoys did with documents they brought back from embassies. The Metroon, then, would be a likely place of preservation for oracular texts.[116] In similar fashion, the Metroon may have received copies of letters from other Greek cities or foreign kings; several such letters are cited in the speeches of Aeschines and Demosthenes.[117] The Boule may also have maintained its own copies of certain types of naval records. The decree of Kleisophos of 405, discussed in the preceding chapter, required Samian ambassadors to give to the secretary of the Boule a list of trierarchs whose triremes were being taken over by the Samians; we are not told what the secretary was to do with such records, but the order surely implies that the Boule possessed a list of the trierarchs of the year.[118] A decree of 346 similarly gives ambassadors of Spartokos and Pairisades, rulers of the Bosporos kingdom, the right to recruit naval specialists at Athens on the condition that they hand over a list of those recruited to the secretary of the Boule.[119] The conveyance of such documents to the secretary of the Boule is not widely attested, but the Boule played an active role in naval administration, and its receipt of documents related to naval affairs in these individual cases is all the more comprehensible if we assume that the Boule, and its archives in the Metroon, kept detailed records regarding the status of the Athenian navy.[120]

Another outstanding feature of the Metroon's archives was their longevity. Documents survived in the Metroon for considerable periods of time. Long-term preservation is best represented by the early third-century *dogma* of the Delphic Amphictyony which was taken from the

Metroon around 130 and republished on stone (*IG* II² 1132). So too a citizenship decree of the late fourth century was consulted in the Metroon 150 years after its enactment (*IG* II² 971). Similar, extended preservation is not attested earlier, but even in the fourth century documents remained in the public archives of the Metroon for periods of several years. Aeschines relates (2.32) how in 346 he had read out to Philip of Macedon a *dogma* enacted twenty years earlier, one that he says came from "the public records." Aeschines also cites (2.91–92) a decree of the Boule from 346 which ordered the departure of an embassy to Philip, which he suggests was also taken from "the public records." Such a decree had purely ephemeral value; after the embassy had departed, the decree's terms were fulfilled, and its utility had expired. But Aeschines could still obtain it from the public records a few years later. The Athenians could not overcome the limitations on preservation imposed by natural factors such as decay, but we have no grounds for believing that the storage of *dēmosia grammata* was not routine for many types of documents, and perhaps for indefinite periods of time.

What we should like to know is the extent to which the deposition of certain types of documents and their preservation were innovations of the fourth century or practices carried over from the fifth-century archives of the Boule. That is, did the Metroon's establishment bring with it a drastic change in ways that the Athenians, or the Boule, kept and maintained texts of public records? In one case the answer to this question must be in the affirmative. The Boule's archives of the fifth century probably did not contain texts of laws or decrees enacted before the Kleisthenic Boule came into existence, such as the laws of Drakon and Solon. But the Metroon probably did hold texts of all Athenian laws (*nomoi*) from the end of the fifth century, so its foundation did represent a move toward greater centralization. In other respects, however, the dedication of a single building may not have brought with it sudden changes in archival practice. The Boule was already keeping archival texts of decrees in the fifth century, as both the Methone Decrees (*IG* I³ 61) and Andokides' reference (2.23) to the decree of Menippos suggest. In the same way, it is not unlikely that texts of other laws and decrees enacted during the fifth century were kept by the Boule and its secretary.[121] Indeed, the preservation of documents on materials other than stone was not wholly new to the late fifth or fourth centuries. The laws of Drakon and Solon, including some obsolete measures, survived from the late seventh and early sixth centuries, and the Bouleutic Oath, first issued in the late sixth century, was available for publication on stone in the late fifth century.[122] We cannot know how full or detailed the archives of the

Boule or other magistrates were before the late fifth century, but there is no reason to think that the last decade of the fifth century witnessed a sudden shift from preserving documents on stone to depositing them on wood or papyrus and in archival form. The fourth century may have seen some increase in the deposition of magisterial accounts and inventories with the Boule and into its archives, but the near silence of fifth-century sources is not conclusive evidence that the practice was not already current during the second half of the fifth century. The Boule's oversight of many areas of Athenian government long antedated the Metroon's foundation, and the administration of its responsibilities certainly required scrutiny of some written documentation from several different boards and officials.[123]

All this is not to say that the fourth century did not witness any changes in attitudes toward writing or written records. The uses of the written word were certainly expanding, and the numbers of written texts produced in the fourth century must have greatly surpassed those of the fifth century. When the Athenian general Nikias wrote a letter to the Athenians while campaigning in Sicily in 414, Thucydides depicts this action as unusual and worthy of comment; by the fourth century, the dispatch of written letters by Athenian generals had become more routine.[124] Many documents were probably written down, recorded, and kept archivally for the first time in the fourth century, so that the contents of the Metroon differed, in quantity and quality, from what the Boule had preserved in the fifth century. But the keeping of uninscribed texts was not a practice invented with the Metroon's foundation; it enjoyed an antiquity dating back to the time of Drakon and Solon.

CHAPTER SIX

Personnel and Organization

The broad range of written records housed within the Metroon leads naturally to consideration of how, if at all, these archives were arranged and organized. The issue has received little attention from scholars, a reflection, perhaps, of the very inadequate nature of the available sources. For although the Metroon's contents can be reconstructed with a fair amount of certainty, how the records located inside the Metroon were arranged, organized, or administered are questions for which little explicit testimony exists. Not surprisingly, scholarly views have varied. Some scholars have assumed that the Metroon's archives displayed a well-administered system of organization. Others postulate a random and haphazard collection of texts.[1] When our sources have so little to offer, it is probably best to avoid extreme positions in either direction, but some evidence does indicate that the Athenians did not wholly ignore the administration of their state archives. First, several fourth-century officials are associated with documents that are otherwise attested as being inside the Metroon. Although the specific duties of some of these officials are uncertain, their very existence implies some concern for the maintenance of the types of documents housed in the Metroon. Second, it is possible to deduce from several sources some basic principles by which Athenian laws and decrees were organized during the fourth century. The same sources do not reveal how well a system based on these principles worked in practice or how they did or did not facilitate consultation. But the very possibility that the Metroon's archives exhibited some form of organization certainly merits attention within a broader discussion of Athenian record keeping and archival practices.

1. Personnel

A basic principle of the ancient Athenian democracy was its reliance on nonprofessionals in virtually all areas of administration. Professionalism was incompatible with democracy, and most state offices were manned by citizens who served for a single year, and many of whom acquired their posts by lot. The same was true of Athenian record keeping. In the fourth century, the Athenians employed several citizen-secretaries to keep records of laws, decrees, and other state documents. None of these is explicitly linked to the Metroon or its archives, but each of them worked with documents whose presence in the Metroon is well attested, so a discussion of their duties and responsibilities is here in order.[2]

Overall responsibility for Athenian public records at the time of the Metroon's establishment fell to the secretary of the Boule. This secretary had served as the chief secretary of the Athenian state throughout the fifth century, when his primary duties entailed keeping records of laws, decrees, and other items of business that came before the Boule and Ekklesia. The secretary of the Boule was elected from the current councillors and served for a single prytany, but he could not belong to the tribe holding the prytany. This official is best known for his role in publishing Athenian decrees on stone, but his duties extended beyond drafting texts for publication and entailed general oversight of Athenian laws and decrees. As far as we know, neither the establishment of the Metroon nor the revision of the Athenian law code at the end of the century affected the duties of this secretary in any significant way, except that from the late fifth century he superintended both the revised law code and new laws in addition to texts of newly enacted decrees.[3]

In the course of the fourth century, the chief secretaryship underwent changes.[4] In 368/7 we have evidence for two different secretaries serving in two different prytanies. By 363/2 a single secretary holds office for an entire year.[5] In the 350s, references appear for a previously unattested secretary, the secretary *kata prytaneian*, who performs many of the same duties previously carried out by the secretary of the Boule. A secretary *kata prytaneian* is named in a catalog of Boule officials dating from 343/2, and comparison with other documents of that year shows that this official is the same secretary named in the prescripts of Athenian decrees.[6] This secretary was not a member of the Boule, and when Aristotle discusses Athenian state secretaries in the *Athēnaiōn Politeia*, he does not mention the secretary of the Boule but describes instead the secretary *kata prytaneian*, who he says used to be elected but was in his day chosen by lot.[7]

It used to be thought that the secretary of the Boule and the secretary *kata prytaneian* were two distinct officials, primarily because both titles are mentioned within a few lines of one another in the Chalkotheke Decree of 353/2; the secretary *kata prytaneian* is ordered to make copies of an inventory of the Chalkotheke while the secretary of the Boule is given responsibility for publishing it on stone.[8] An inscription of circa 350 refers to this inscribed inventory as the stele that "Philokleides set up"; hence, Philokleides should be the secretary of the Boule. But Philokleides' name is also restored with near absolute certainty in the prescripts of two decrees of 353/2.[9] Since the secretary named in prescripts may be identified as the secretary *kata prytaneian* according to a list of Boule officials dating from 343/2, it seems that the secretary of the Boule and the secretary *kata prytaneian* must be different titles for the same official. The new title was perhaps instituted when the office became annual sometime between 368 and 363, and it was probably at that time that the post became sortitive. But the old title persisted alongside the new one for nearly half a century, before going out of use entirely around 315.[10]

Why the Athenians reformed the post of the secretary, from one elected each prytany to an annual position chosen by lot, is nowhere explained. Aristotle says that before the position became sortitive the names of "the most distinguished and trustworthy men" were inscribed as secretaries on stelai bearing alliances, proxeny decrees, and grants of citizenship.[11] What Aristotle meant by this statement is unclear; the names of secretaries known from before the reform are not those of men who played leading roles in public affairs at Athens as we know them from literary sources. It may be that individual *bouleutai* coveted the office and that the reform sought to reduce excessive competition for the simple prestige attached to the frequent display of the secretary's name in the prescripts of inscribed documents. Most Athenian magistracies were already sortitive by the 360s, so the shift in selection from ballot to lot may simply reflect an attempt to bring the position of state secretary into line with the mode of appointment employed for other state offices. But the reform may also point to a desire to bring greater efficiency to Athenian public records in general.[12] The selection of ten different secretaries each year must have led to some instability, and the creation of an annual office will at least have brought some consistency to the records produced in individual years. But what specific factors will have contributed to such a desire we cannot say, and it may be that the reform was motivated by causes wholly unknown to us.

Whatever the reasons for the reform, Aristotle spells out the duties of the state secretary in his account of the secretaries of the Athenian state:

"They also allot a secretary called the secretary *kata prytaneian*, who is responsible for the records and preserves decrees that are being enacted and has copied all the other documents and attends meetings of the Boule."[13] These responsibilities are well illustrated by references to the secretary in fourth-century inscriptions and literary sources. The secretary is named in the prescripts of decrees because he was present at sessions of the Ekklesia and kept copies of decrees from the time they were submitted for consideration, and he is charged with their publication because inscribed texts were copied from these records. The same duties also explain why the secretary is sometimes ordered to have the inscribed copies of decrees destroyed. We might suppose that the stelai inscribed with copies of decrees were considered part of the secretary's records regardless of their location, but it may be the case that the secretary is called on to have inscriptions removed because he maintained copies of all Athenian decrees within his archives. When an order to remove a stele went out, the secretary could ascertain from these records where inscribed copies of decrees were located and then have these stelai torn down.[14]

The chief secretary also worked with other types of records. A decree of 363/2 orders the generals of the city of Ioulis who were in Athens on an embassy to make a list of citizens of Ioulis who had led the city's revolt from the Second Athenian League and to deliver it to the secretary of the Boule.[15] The Chalkotheke Decree instructs the secretary *kata prytaneian* to make a copy of an inventory of the Chalkotheke conducted by the public slave Eukles, and then to make copies of the same building's contents from several inscribed stelai.[16] Still another decree of 347/6 orders envoys sent from the Bosporos to make a list of naval specialists whom they recruit at Athens and to give it to the secretary of the Boule.[17] The secretary *kata prytaneian* also received copies of their year-end accounts from magistrates, if I have interpreted a passage of Aeschines correctly.[18] We are not told what the secretary did with any of these documents, but it seems a reasonable supposition that he filed them with other records of a similar nature in the Metroon or updated earlier documents he already possessed from the newer ones he received.

Assisting the chief secretary were several minor secretaries. The Chalkotheke Decree refers to a group of secretaries called the secretaries *epi tois dēmosiois grammasi*, "in charge of the public records." With the secretary *kata prytaneian* they were to make copies of the inventory of the Chalkotheke prescribed by the decree.[19] Other sources mention secretaries with more specialized titles. One was the secretary *epi tous nomous*, the secretary "for the laws," mentioned in the *Athēnaiōn Politeia*, whose title implies that he was concerned with the city's *nomoi* or laws. This secretary was appointed by lot, and Aristotle said that "he attends meetings of the Boule and has texts of laws copied down."[20] At first glance, this duty seems odd: laws were enacted by *nomothetai*, not the Boule, during the fourth century. But both the Boule and the Ekklesia played some role in the enactment process, and texts of *nomoi* were kept in the Metroon, so Aristotle's description is probably not inaccurate.[21] Aristotle does, however, describe the secretary *epi tous nomous* as if he and the secretary *kata prytaneian* were parallel officials. This is probably incorrect. It is the secretary of the Boule who is usually assigned the task of publishing *nomoi* on stone, and to whom Diokles' law gives responsibility for their upkeep; the secretary *epi tous nomous* probably worked under the chief secretary's supervision.[22] Still another secretary was the secretary *epi ta psēphismata*, the secretary "in charge of decrees." Some scholars used to think that this secretary was identical with the secretary *kata prytaneian*, but several prytany catalogs mention both offices with the names of their respective holders: the two offices are therefore distinct.[23] This secretary presumably did for decrees what the secretary *epi tous nomous* did for laws. The inscriptions in which he appears, however, add nothing further, and we can only suppose that he assisted the chief secretary in the recording, copying, and distribution of texts of decrees for whatever purposes were deemed necessary.

Lists of officials of the Boule published on stone preserve the titles of a few other officials who were possibly associated with the records housed in the Metroon, including an *antigrapheus*, "copier," and an *anagrapheus*, "recorder."[24] Their duties, however, are nowhere specifically explained. Aeschines refers in his speech *Against Ktesiphon* to an *antigrapheus* who in an earlier period had played some role in reckoning and keeping track of state income, but these duties seem to have been transferred to the commissioner of the Theoric fund when his office was created, and the *antigrapheus* of the Boule was probably a different official.[25] Presumably, the official mentioned in bouleutic inscriptions was involved in the copying of several types of documents, a duty that may have occupied much of the time of the Metroon's staff.[26] The duties of the *anagrapheus* are similarly poorly attested. The title had been used by the board of officials who revised and updated Athens' law code in the late fifth century, and in two brief periods of oligarchic government in the late fourth and early third centuries an *anagrapheus* served as the chief secretary of the Athenian state.[27] Whatever activities the *anagra-*

pheus carried out under the democracy, it is probably noteworthy that they were deemed important enough for one holder of the office to receive honors by a decree of the Ekklesia.[28]

These officials are attested in fourth-century inscriptions that list members of the Boule and the bouleutic officials of individual years. Not every official, however, is listed in every list. So, for example, a list of officials from the year 343/2 names the secretary *kata prytaneian*, a secretary *epi ta psēphismata*, and an *antigrapheus*, but not a secretary *epi tous nomous* or an *anagrapheus*. Another list from the year 324/3 names the secretary *kata prytaneian*, the secretary *epi tous nomous*, and an *anagrapheus*, and all five secretaries are named together only in a list of councillors from the year 305/4.[29] What we should make of the absence of certain officials from the lists of individual years is unclear. The bouleutic lists are honorary inscriptions, so the absence of some officials from certain years may indicate only that the holder of an office was not honored in a given year.[30] But it is equally possible that some officials, like the *anagrapheus* and secretary *epi tous nomous* were not appointed every year, but only when the duties they carried out were specifically needed.[31]

None of these secretaries is explicitly connected with the Metroon and its archives, and the only fourth-century official for whom such a connection is made was not even an Athenian citizen but a *dēmosios*, a public slave. The Athenians employed public slaves in many areas of public life, and since most state officials served for only a single year, these slaves provided a degree of expertise and professionalism that the officials they served otherwise lacked.[32] Demosthenes says that a public slave oversaw the public records housed in the Metroon, and the same slave is referred to in fourth-century and Hellenistic inscriptions that call upon a *dēmosios* to deposit new documents or retrieve old ones from the building's archives.[33] A public slave is also referred to in conjunction with other state documents, where, however, the Metroon is not named. The Chalkotheke Decree orders a public slave to conduct an inventory of the Chalkotheke and to make a record of his results, and Aristotle also describes a public slave who fetched records of payments owed on state contracts and handed them over to the *apodektai* when payments fell due.[34] Although neither of these public slaves is tied directly to the Metroon, the documents each deals with are closely connected with the activities of the Boule, and it is difficult to avoid the conclusion that their public slave is the same one mentioned by Demosthenes.

How the Metroon's public slave worked with the state secretaries who are associated with Athenian laws, decrees, and other state documents is not known. Since, however, the slave alone is identified with the Metroon, it can be conjectured that the slave was responsible for filing and retrieving from the Metroon the documents that various secretaries had drawn up and copied. Such a separation of duties is hinted at by Aristotle's description (*Ath. Pol.* 47.2–5) of the documents used by the *pōlētai*. The *pōlētai* recorded the names of individual contractors, wrote up payment tablets according to the dates when payments were due, and then handed these texts over to the public slave, who filed and later retrieved them. A similar procedure may underlie a feature of Aristotle's description of the duties of the secretary *kata prytaneian*. Aristotle states that this secretary watched over "the decrees that are coming into being," or "that were being enacted."[35] He uses the present participle (*gignomena*) to describe the decrees handled by the secretary, a usage that suggests that the secretary dealt with the texts of decrees as they passed through the ratification process until they were approved. Once ratified, we might then imagine that texts of decrees were delivered to the public slave in the Metroon who filed them among its archives, just as he did with the documents composed by the *pōlētai*. The secretary of the Boule (or *kata prytaneian*) retained authority over many of the city's public records, but their actual deposition in and retrieval from the Metroon's archives was the duty of the public slave.

Although we cannot define their duties precisely, the number of officials devoted to the keeping of laws, decrees, and other state documents surely reflects a broader concern on the part of the Athenians for their public records in the second half of the fourth century. The city's documents were not handled by a single secretary and public slave,[36] but were administered by a small staff, not all of whom may be attested by name in our sources. Apart from the public slaves, these secretaries rotated out of office each year, but that too is not a sign of neglect: it was a practice typical of most Athenian magistracies. Evidence for specific secretaries with specialized duties dates from after 350 and a few decades after the chief secretary's office had been reformed, and so it may tempting to see in the relatively late date of this evidence a newfound concern on the part of the Athenians for the condition of their public records. But we should resist that temptation. The Chalkotheke Decree mentions an unspecified number of secretaries of the public records, none of whom is given a specific title, and this college may be much older in date and may have included other officials about whom no further evidence exists. Even before the late 350s secretaries other than the secretary of the Boule are known to have existed and worked with state documents. Demosthenes claimed that as a young man Aeschines had worked as an undersecretary (*hypogrammateus*), and some of his duties seem to have brought him into contact with the Boule and Ekklesia.[37] Still earlier, the speaker of Lysias's *Against Nikomachos* claimed in 400/399 that the Athenians had previously chosen Nikomachos and others to serve as undersecretaries, without specifying for what boards or officials.[38] Both Demosthenes and the prosecutor of Nikomachos use the title *hypogrammateus* in a pejorative sense in an attempt to blacken the social standings of their opponents, but for our purposes their statements suffice to show that Athenian officials were employing undersecretaries long before secretaries with more specific titles are attested. Cosecretaries and undersecretaries are also found in the service of several Athenian officials during the fifth century, and although none of these is explicitly associated with the Boule or Ekklesia, it is not unreasonable to suppose that the secretary of the Boule was assisted by a small staff from the middle of the fifth century: the various undersecretaries first mentioned by name in the 340s are very likely successors of more anonymous positions dating back to the fifth century. The appearance of secretaries with specific titles in the latter half of the fourth century reflects not so much a new concern for keeping archival records as a growing specialization in the duties assigned to some officials, a phenomenon not without parallel in other areas of Athenian government.[39]

In the same way, the reform of the post of the chief state secretary in the 360s may not signal a drastic change in Athenian attitudes toward state documents. The shift from an office that rotated every prytany to one held for an entire year certainly could have brought greater efficiency to the keeping of records of the Boule's and Ekklesia's business, and it probably reflects some desire to bring more order on them. But decrees on stone, the one place where we might expect to see traces of this increased efficiency, show no significant changes in the layout or structure of their contents in the 360s or 350s, and we have no grounds for believing that the manner in which secretaries drew up and preserved state documents changed in that period—except that a single secretary now oversaw the recording of decrees for an entire year. Broader shifts in attitudes toward writing and the value of documents in society may have played some role in this reform, but it may be preferable to see the change in tenure of the chief state secretary as resulting from developments in Athenian government and administration. Consider the frequency of meetings of the Ekklesia. At the time the *Athēnaiōn Politeia* was composed, the Ekklesia met four times each prytany or forty times a year. When the four meetings per prytany rule was instituted is not certain, but Hansen has suggested that in the late 350s the Ekklesia was restricted to three meetings a prytany or thirty meetings a year. Hansen also argues that the rule of three meetings per prytany was instituted around 355, when the Ekklesia was deprived of some of its judicial powers, and that prior to 355, there were no restrictions on the number of times the *prytaneis* might convene the Ekklesia each prytany.[40] The correctness of this reconstruction need not concern us here,[41] but possible changes in the duties of the Ekklesia or the frequency with which it met are potentially significant because of the effect institutional reforms may have had on the records produced by the Ekklesia and the secretaries who kept them. More frequent meetings will have meant an increase in the number of documents produced each prytany, and more records meant a greater strain on the chief secretary and his staff. In addition, an event such as the creation of the Second Athenian League in 378/7 undoubtedly had some impact on the volume of business handled by both the Boule and Ekklesia and therefore on the officials who kept their records. An increasing volume of records may have highlighted the weaknesses of a secretarial staff whose chief officer changed ten times each year. The Athenians addressed this weakness not because they had only started to realize the value of documents and archives in the fourth century, but because the institutional needs of their system of government demanded that changes should be made.

ii. Organization

Hansen has estimated that in the fourth century the Athenians enacted some three to four hundred decrees a year. It is more difficult to estimate how many laws were regularly enacted each year, but whatever their number, it seems likely that the Metroon was receiving a large number of laws and decrees annually, so that new documents were being added to an even larger number already housed within the archives.[42] Since the Athenians devoted a building and several officials to the administration of their state documents, it also seems reasonable to suppose that they applied some effort to the arrangement and organization of these records. Let us begin with the question of materials. *Pōlētai* documents, some of which were deposited in the Metroon, were written on wooden tablets. This makes some sense, as wooden tablets were frequently used for documents that were displayed temporarily or whose contents were frequently updated.[43] But wooden tablets were also used for more permanent types of records in the archival establishments of other Greek cities, and a similar use cannot be ruled out inside the Metroon.[44] Papyrus, however, was also available, and Athenian officials were familiar with its use. A decree of 403 orders the secretary of the Boule to hand over to the Samian Poses a *biblion*, a papyrus copy, of the decree in his honor; the secretary clearly had papyrus at his disposal. The Erechtheion accounts of the last decade of the fifth century also record the purchase of several rolls of papyrus onto which the *epistatai* supervising the temple's construction are said to have made copies of their accounts, copies that may have been destined for the *logistai* or even the secretary of the Boule himself.[45] With so little evidence we can only offer conjectures, but there seems little reason to doubt that many of the more permanent texts deposited in the Metroon were routinely recorded on papyrus.

We are also poorly informed about the physical means by which documents were stored in the Metroon. Nothing survives of the fourth-century Metroon above the foundation level, and little can be said about how its archives were physically stored inside the building. But shelving was used for storing objects in the Parthenon, where individual shelves were numbered and objects on shelves sometimes labeled. Boxes and chests were also used to store documents at Athens and in the archives of other ancient cities; it is not overly rash to assume that similar methods were used for the storage of archival documents in the Metroon.[46] That the Athenians took some steps to address the ways in which documents were kept is indicated by Aristotle's account of the *pōlētai*. Aristotle notes that when payments on state contracts fell due, a public slave removed the payment tablets from objects called *epistylia*.[47] The term *epistylion* is often used to refer to the architrave of a Greek temple, but more generally it can refer to any beam or rafter set on top of a column.[48] Since the contracts let out by the *pōlētai* constituted one of the chief sources of income of the Athenians in the fourth century, the Athenians might have displayed the names of individuals holding these contracts and the due dates of their payments, so that *epistylia* mentioned by Aristotle could refer to rafters or beams above the interior columns of the Metroon or of its porch.[49] But most scholars believe that the *epistylia* from which the *pōlētai*'s tablets were retrieved were some sort of pigeonholes or slots into which the tablets were inserted.[50] If this interpretation is correct, the existence of such an apparatus shows the Athenians devoting some attention to the systematic storage of one type of document, and if they took such steps for one class of documents, we may surely suppose that they did so for others.

Inscriptions were also set up in and near the Metroon, but their presence should not be thought to have had any bearing on the archives housed inside the building or their organization.[51] The fourth-century Metroon had served as a Bouleuterion during the fifth century, and it

PERSONNEL AND ORGANIZATION

stood immediately adjacent to the New Bouleuterion, where the Boule met, and the Tholos, where the *prytaneis* dined. This location, at the heart of the administrative center of Athenian government, made it a natural spot for the placement of stelai bearing texts related to the Boule and to the citizen body at large. Thus, a law of 353/2 concerning the administration of the Eleusinian Mysteries prescribes that its text was to be inscribed near a stele preserving an earlier law on the same subject and standing in front of the Metroon.[52] The date of the earlier law is unknown, but since the Boule was involved in the administration of the Mysteries, the placement of a stele bearing a law dealing with its responsibilities in front of the Metroon is sensible. Similarly, a monument recording honors voted to the heroes from Phyle, who helped restore the democracy in 403/2, also stood in or near the Metroon.[53] According to Aeschines, the Boule had been responsible for conducting a scrutiny of those individuals eligible for these honors, and it is this role that explains the presence of this inscription in the Metroon. Inscriptions were set up in many places around ancient Athens but most often where their texts had some relevance. These locations, however, have no bearing on the archival texts of decrees that were preserved in the Metroon.[54]

Within the Metroon itself, the building's archives were probably not without some semblance of order and organization. Aristotle's account of the *pōlētai* shows that their documents were drawn up and stored in an orderly fashion, and it is not unreasonable to suppose that similar measures were applied to the preservation of other types of state documents. The chief result of the revision of the Athenian law code at the end of the fifth century was a formal distinction between laws (*nomoi*) and decrees (*psēphismata*); laws were rules of permanent validity with general applicability that were passed by *nomothetai*, whereas decrees specified more immediate action with limited validity and were enacted by the Ekklesia. This distinction presumably carried over into the texts of laws that were housed in the Metroon. Indeed, the law code itself could be divided into four categories. Demosthenes cites in his speech *Against Timokrates* a law on *nomothesia* that stipulated that on the eleventh day of the first prytany of each year the Ekklesia was to vote on a review, section by section, of Athens' laws. First, the Athenians were to consider the laws concerning the Boule, then those concerning "common" matters, followed by those dealing with the nine archons, and finally those laws related to other magistrates.[55] Demosthenes does not elaborate on this fourfold division, but scholars have generally and rightly assumed that the broad categories mentioned in the law are a reflection of the manner in which the laws were physically arranged and organized. Since the physical texts of laws were preserved in the Metroon, this division should also reflect their arrangement in its archives.

The system, such as it was, was based broadly on Athens' magistrates and the laws concerning them and their duties. Thus, the bouleutic laws were those laws that governed the powers, duties, and responsibilities of the Boule; all these were arranged together in a single group, and the same was true for the laws on the nine archons and other magistrates.[56] Within these broad categories, laws could be subdivided even further. Thus, we hear of a law of the king archon and a law concerning the arbitrators, and other laws too were probably grouped around the chief archon, the polemarch, and other state magistrates.[57] Individual laws could also be identified by their content, so that we also hear of laws on *eisangelia* and treason.[58] But this does not conflict with a magisterial arrangement. Since Athenian magistrates had jurisdiction over particular areas of law, the identification of a law by its contents was virtually the same as calling it by the name of the official who administered it.

An arrangement of Athenian laws by magisterial authority is reflected in the second half of the *Athēnaiōn Politeia*.[59] There, Aristotle outlines the Athenian democracy as it functioned in his own day, and his analysis is organized along lines similar to those suggested by the law on *nomothesia*, namely, according to magistrates. Thus, sections 43–49 concern the Boule and should derive from the bouleutic laws; sections 50–54 and 60–61 deal with other officials and probably derive from the section of the code on "other magistrates"; sections 55–59 deal with the nine archons and should derive from the laws related to their powers. The second half of the *Athēnaiōn Politeia* makes numerous references to individual laws, and comparison of specific passages with the texts of laws quoted in the orators shows that Aristotle relied heavily on their texts when he composed the work.[60]

The Athenians also dated their laws. We have already discussed the law of Diokles, whose text is preserved in Demosthenes' speech *Against Timokrates* and which required that laws were to be valid from the date of their ratification.[61] The inscribed copies of some fourth-century laws do include the date on which they were passed, but others do not. We might assume that secretaries ignored the instructions of Diokles' law, but it seems more likely that the dates required by the law were recorded in archival texts and not copies on stone.[62] It is difficult to know what role, if any, the dating of laws played in their arrangement, but it is possible that precise dating was thought necessary not only to provide the effective date for the laws, but also to ensure that only the most recent law on a particular topic was considered valid.

But if the Athenians simply discarded the texts of old laws once new ones on the same subject were enacted, precise dating would not have been necessary, because only one law on any subject will have existed. Provisions for *nomothesia* actually take the annulment of old laws into consideration and require proposers of new laws to repeal existing laws on the same subject that were in conflict with the proposal.[63] Some evidence, however, suggests that even in the fourth century laws were revised more by means of amendment than annulment, a method that would have left the texts of older laws intact.

The law on the Eleusinian Mysteries of 353/2 revised an earlier law, proposed by a certain Chairemonides, on the same subject. The new law, however, frames itself not as replacing Chairemonides' law but only as adding to it. It does not call for destruction of the old law's text but specifies that its text should be inscribed near the stele carrying the earlier law.[64] How the new law was added to the old one in the Metroon's archives cannot be established, but the more recent law, with its enactment date, may simply have been amended to the text of the earlier one within the proper category. Another possible example of the enactment of new laws as supplements to and not replacements of older laws is provided by Demosthenes' discussion of *nomothesia* in his speech *Against Leptines*. Demosthenes complains that the correct procedure has been ignored, and he refers to an old law on *nomothesia* as if its provisions were still valid but largely ignored, a situation that is understandable if we assume that provisions of the original law had been amended piecemeal and not revoked by later supplements.[65] Demosthenes also suggests in that speech that the Athenians found it necessary to elect special commissions to sort through the laws for contradictory enactments, a procedure that would have been unnecessary if old laws were routinely erased or discarded.[66] That the texts of older laws were preserved is further suggested by references to the fourth-century Athenian constitution in the second half of the *Athēnaiōn Politeia*, where Aristotle several times compares current practices with those no longer in use.[67] Since Aristotle's analysis almost certainly derives from a direct consultation of the Athenian law code itself, these references are readily explained on the assumption that texts of older laws remained available for study and scrutiny and were not discarded, because their provisions were not actually rescinded but only revised or amended. In such a system, precise dates would prove valuable in determining what law was currently valid on a given subject.

While laws formed a separate category as a result of the late fifth-century revision of the law code and were arranged according to their own system, the same reform should not have affected the archival arrangement of decrees. That is, fourth-century decrees should have been organized according to a system similar to the one in place during the fifth century. Fifth-century Athenian documents on stone are generally organized according to the names of the officials, especially the secretaries, who created them, and we met in Chapter 3 some evidence that the archival texts of decrees were filed in a similar fashion, in prytany batches under the name of the secretary of the Boule in office and in annual groups under the name of the first secretary of the bouleutic year. We also saw that the texts of some decrees included an indication of the date of their ratification, in spite of the fact that the prescripts of inscribed decrees do not include similar chronological precision until well into the fourth century.[68] Although it is impossible to ascertain completely the degree to which these features carried over into the archives of the Boule or how systematically decrees were arranged in these archives, the fact that secretaries did not always include all the information at their disposal in the texts they had inscribed on stone should warn against minimizing the content and organization of the Boule's archives on the basis of what is found in inscribed prescripts alone.

Developments within decree prescripts over the course of the fourth century offer further clues about the types of information contained in the minutes of meetings of the Ekklesia kept by Boule secretaries, and possibly further insights into how records of these meetings, in the form of decrees, were organized. From the end of the fifth century, the names of archons begin to appear more regularly; this development coincides with a reform of the bouleutic and archontic calendars, by which the years of both became coterminous, so that they both started on 1 Hekatombaion.[69] As a result, an archon's name alone could serve as an indicator of the year by both calendars, and references to the first secretary of the Boule disappear. Archival copies of decrees presumably employed archon dating from the same time, if they had not done so before.[70] From the 390s, the tribe in prytany that is named in the prescripts of decrees is qualified by an ordinal numeral indicating which prytany of the year that tribe held; it seems reasonable to conclude that the secretary's records included similar notations. From the 360s, decree prescripts also start to include the specific day within the prytany on which their decrees were ratified, while from the late 340s prescripts begin to name the specific day and month on which their decrees were enacted according to the lunar, archontic calendar.[71] These details too were presumably part of the archival records drawn up by secretaries of the meetings of the Ekklesia at which decrees were ratified.

The growing chronological precision of fourth-century prescripts is generally taken as a sign that the archival records were also becoming more detailed. Rhodes associated the increasing number of chronological details found in prescripts with the reform of the chief secretaryship in the 360s and saw both as signs that the Athenians were paying closer attention to their public records in the fourth century.[72] Thomas looks at the growing precision somewhat differently. She notes the increasing degree of precision in the prescripts of decrees during the fourth century but calls attention to the omission of certain items and the latitude enjoyed by secretaries in framing the content and format of prescripts. These inconsistencies, she argues, reflect the generally undeveloped nature of Athenian record keeping, while the added details of the fourth century reflect a gradual process of development.[73]

The growing number of details in decree prescripts surely denotes some desire to provide more precise dates for inscribed documents. But we should not conclude that the same developments represent a new awareness of the value of precise dates or that previously no one had recognized that dates were important components of the texts of documents. The difficulty with views that derive the contents and organization of archival texts from the prescripts of inscribed decrees is their assumption that prescripts were mirror images of the records of meetings of the Ekklesia kept by secretaries and deposited in the Metroon. We often cannot determine how many details beyond those found in prescripts secretaries may have recorded in their minutes, but each of the details first found in fourth-century prescripts is found in documents of much earlier date. Numbered prytanies first appear in the prescripts of inscribed decrees in the 390s, but some documents were assigning ordinal numbers to prytanies already in the 430s.[74] The specific prytany date on which decrees were enacted may not appear in the prescripts of inscribed decrees until the 360s, but prytany dates were used in some documents, including decrees, already in the fifth century.[75] Dates by the lunar, archontic calendar were also not included in prescripts until the 340s, but dating by this method is attested in fifth-century documents.[76] Most of the fifth-century documents in which these dating formulae appear are financial in nature, but numbered prytanies and prytany dates are features of the bouleutic calendar; it would be odd if the Boule itself and its secretary did not make use of similar methods in their own records. If many inscribed documents were extracted from fuller, archival texts, as I have argued in Chapter 3, we must allow the possibility that more precise dates were routinely kept in the archival texts of decrees but frequently omitted from texts inscribed on stone. On this view, the increasing chronological precision evident in the prescripts of fourth-century decrees need not reflect a similar development in the archival texts of decrees; instead, it exhibits a desire to make the inscribed copies of documents represent more fully and accurately the archival texts from which they derive. The omission of particular details from the prescripts of decrees likewise need not betoken an absence of the same details from the archival texts of decrees; omissions may simply illustrate the latitude enjoyed by secretaries when they drew up the prescripts of individual decrees for publication.

That documents housed in the Metroon contained more detailed information, including precise dating formulae, than their counterparts on stone has been amply demonstrated by W. West. West points out that Aeschines cites in his speeches *On the Embassy* and *Against Ktesiphon* the dates of documents enacted in 346 according to the archontic calendar. Aeschines has read out the decree of the Boule dispatching the second embassy to Philip together with its date, which is given in terms of month and day according to the archontic calendar.[77] Similarly, in his speech *Against Ktesiphon*, Aeschines refers to Demosthenes' chairmanship of a meeting of the Ekklesia on 25 Elaphebolion in 346, at which peace terms with Philip were concluded and ratified. Aeschines has this decree, moved by Philokrates, and the name of Demosthenes, who as the chairman of the Ekklesia on that day put the decree to a vote, read out to the jury. He also reminds the dikasts how important the accurate preservation of public records is for judging the conduct of politicians.[78] Aeschines does not state that he obtained the date of Philokrates' decree and Demosthenes' chairmanship of the Ekklesia from the public archives, but this is surely to be assumed from his argument.

What makes these specific dates given by month and day in terms of the archontic calendar especially significant is that similar dating formulae do not begin to appear in the prescripts of inscribed decrees until 341/0, several years after the events Aeschines related. Prior to 341/0, inscribed decrees give their enactment dates only in terms of the bouleutic calendar by specifying the particular day within the prytany on which they were enacted. Aeschines does not suggest that his ability to supply dates in terms of the archon's calendar was unusual or innovative. Nor does Demosthenes challenge any of the dates offered by Aeschines, so there is no reason to suppose that Aeschines' use of these dates reflects anything new or specific to the particular documents he cites.[79] How then can we explain the discrepancy between the dates supplied by Aeschines and their absence in contemporary inscriptions? Since Aeschines insists throughout his speeches that the documents he cites were taken from the *dēmosia grammata*, the public records that were housed in the Metroon, we should probably conclude that the Metroon's archives were more detailed and included more specific dating formulae than contemporary inscriptions. When secretaries prepared texts of decrees to be published on stone before 341/0 (and even after that year), they simply omitted the archontic dates of those documents, even though these were available to them in their records.

Henry concluded his study of the prescripts of Athenian decrees with the important observation that secretaries were "never bound to include all the items" that were available to them in decree prescripts. But Henry's further conclusion that secretaries enjoyed wide latitude in the way they framed the minutes of meetings of the Ekklesia may not be entirely accurate. The contents of the prescripts of inscribed decrees are indicative only of what individual secretaries saw fit to include in the inscribed copies of decrees; they do not represent all the details that secretaries recorded and preserved in the minutes of meetings that they eventually deposited in the Metroon. Secretaries may have exercised some latitude in framing the minutes of a meeting, just as they did with inscribed texts, but those minutes, which provided the basis of the archival texts of decrees, were more detailed and more complex than the prescripts of inscribed decrees. How much more so we cannot say, but we must allow, on the basis of the evidence available to us, that at any particular date the city's archives contained more information than inscriptions of the same date indicate.

That the archival texts of decrees in the Metroon preserved more complete information about those decrees, including their dates by both the bouleutic and archontic calendars, should not occasion great surprise. The bouleutic calendar was the official calendar of the Athenian state, and many events related to the duties of the Boule and Ekklesia were expressed in dates by this system. One of the laws on *nomothesia* required the Athenians to vote on their law code, section by section, at the first meeting of the Ekklesia on the tenth day of the first prytany each year, and to decide whether revisions were thought necessary.[80] In addition, four meetings of the Ekklesia were held each prytany, with specific matters treated at some meetings.[81] But use of the bouleutic calendar may not have been immediately comprehensible to all Athenians. It was not the normal calendar of daily life, and the average Athenian dated events by month and day of the archontic calendar (which followed a lunar cycle); dates expressed in terms of the bouleutic year were probably meaningless to citizens who were not members of the Boule. So meetings of the Boule and Ekklesia were dated by both the bouleutic and archontic calendars to make their dates intelligible to ordinary Athenians.

That both systems were used is once again illustrated by events of the year 346. When Demosthenes proposed a decree in Elaphebolion of that year, calling for additional meetings of the Ekklesia to discuss peace terms with Philip, he did not suggest dates in terms of the prytany calendar, though he himself was a member of the Boule, but by the day and month of the archontic year.[82] Similarly, in an earlier speech of 353/2, Demosthenes refers to a decree of Timokrates enacted on 11 Hekatombaion of 354/3 and to a meeting of the *nomothetai* that was held on the following day. Demosthenes does not indicate how he knew these dates, which he provides in terms of the archontic calendar. But he does have the texts of the documents read out, so it is not unreasonable to suppose that archival texts of these documents offered some indication of their dates.[83]

West suggested that the dating of decrees by both the bouleutic and archontic calendars was instituted with the establishment of the Metroon at the end of the fifth century.[84] Since the prescripts of some fifth-century decrees include prytany dates but not reference to dates by the archontic calendar, this argument has some weight: decrees, we might imagine, were dated only by the Boule's calendar in the fifth century.[85] Moreover, the requirements of Diokles' law, which stated that laws were to be valid from the date of their enactment, might also suggest that specific dates according to the archontic calendar were not always recorded. But dates expressed by the archontic calendar did find some use in the archival texts of decrees even in the fifth century. Thucydides' texts of both the one-year truce enacted between Athens and Sparta in 423 and the Peace of Nikias of 421 include provisions specifying that they were to be valid from specific dates expressed in terms of the archontic calendar.[86] The inscribed copies of treaties and alliances do not include similar provisions specifying the dates of their implementation, but it is difficult to believe that such dates were not necessary in other cases. Thucydides' texts probably reflect copies taken from the archives, where specific dates were more frequently noted. Aristotle's account of the revolution of 411 and the accession of the Four Hundred may also be relevant. Aristotle says that the Boule of Five Hundred was dissolved on 14 Thargelion, that Aristomachos put the motion to a vote, and that the Four Hundred took office on 22 Thargelion, although the new council was not supposed to take over until 14 Skirophorion.[87] Aristotle's source for these dates is disputed, but they should derive ultimately from some type of documentary source.[88] If this is correct, it would provide strong evidence that even in the fifth century texts found in the archives included very precise indications of dates that were not routinely inscribed on stone until after the middle of the fourth century. It is surely noteworthy that Aristotle gives the date of the decree on which the Boule was dissolved (14 Thargelion) and the name of the person putting the motion to vote (Aristomachos), precisely those items that Aeschines (2.89) says were preserved in the archives "for all time."[89]

These observations about the preservation of specific dates of meetings of the Boule and the Ekklesia and the documents enacted at those meetings are not meant to suggest that the "filing" system in the Metroon was based on these dates; that is, a knowledge of the precise date, according to the archontic or bouleutic calendar, on which a decree was enacted may not have facilitated its retrieval from the archives.[90] The filing system was essentially an eponymous one, based on the names of officials who held different offices at the times that decrees were enacted. Armed with the name of the archon in whose year a decree was enacted (or, in the fifth century, the first secretary of the year), a search could be conducted among the decrees enacted in that year. With knowledge of the particular prytany in which a decree was enacted, the search could be narrowed more closely. And given the name of the person who presided over the meeting at which a decree was ratified, its location could be found most easily. With all of these items, retrieval should have been rather straightforward; with only one or two, locating a document may have been more difficult but probably was not impossible.

But however the filing system worked, the presence of the precise dates of decrees in their archival copies housed in the Metroon is important, for it reminds us that the archival copies contained more precise and detailed information than we find in inscriptions. It has been recognized for quite some time that Greek inscriptions often contain only extracts or abstracts of fuller texts that were stored in an archives. The prescripts and texts of inscribed decrees offer some insights into the nature of the archives' holdings, but we cannot rely on them entirely for our understanding of how the archives were arranged and organized.

III. Conclusion

It must be admitted that direct evidence for the system by which decrees and other documents were organized in the Metroon is quite thin, and the system I have outlined here depends largely on a priori considerations based on the ratification process of decrees and details found in their prescripts. But the system I have described does account for much of the available evidence; it explains the features of decree prescripts, which were derived from archival texts; and it indicates how documents other than decrees, such as election results, letters from Athenian generals, and *dogmata* enacted by Panhellenic bodies, were arranged in the Metroon: they too were stored under the meeting of the Boule and Ekklesia at which they were received. Such a system probably originated with the implementation of the bouleutic calendar in the late sixth or mid-fifth century, and although more chronological precision may have found its way into the archival texts of decrees over the course of the fourth century, as the prescripts of inscribed decrees suggest, we cannot exclude the possibility that fifth-century secretaries were including more detailed information in the records they kept of decrees. To attribute too high a degree of order and sophistication to the Metroon's archives would certainly be imprudent; documents were undoubtedly lost, misfiled, and perhaps inadvertently destroyed, and the Athenians could hardly have overcome the problems that sometimes plague even modern archival establishments. But we hear nothing of confusion, mishaps, or inadequacies, and although we must allow for potential shortcomings in any system, we should also avoid an excessive emphasis on possible but unattested weaknesses.

We shall examine questions of consultation of the Metroon's archives in the next chapter, but two points about the practical efficiency of its organization are relevant here. It might be objected that the system I have proposed was too complicated to be accessible to Athenian citizens, thus hindering consultation. But citizens may not have retrieved and consulted decrees and other documents on their own: locating, retrieving, and copying documents were duties performed by the secretaries or public slave associated with the Metroon. When payments fell due on state contracts, neither the *pōlētai* who drew up the contracts nor the *apodektai* who canceled them went to the Metroon and took out the payment tablets. This was the duty of a public slave.[91] The public slave also filed the *pōlētai* documents, and if this is the same public slave mentioned by Demosthenes as being set "over the public records" (Dem. 19.129), we might assume that he possessed a specialized knowledge of where and how individual records were located and stored. Another source also suggests that the archival staff conducted actual copying and distribution of documents. The prosecutor of Nikomachos claims that Nikomachos, when serving as *anagrapheus*, distributed copies of contradictory laws to the opposing parties in lawsuits.[92] We need not believe the charge leveled against Nikomachos, but the procedure underlying the charge may reflect actual practice. Litigants did not consult archival records of laws and other documents themselves but made requests to an official associated with the city's public records, who made and distributed copies to them. Athenian citizens certainly had access to the Metroon's archives, but it was unnecessary for them or others who wished to consult particular documents to understand the details of its filing system.

A second point emerges from a comment found in a speech of Demosthenes. Demosthenes (20.91) once refers to the appointment of special commissions whose task it was to remove contradictory laws from the Athenian law code.[93] The impression he conveys is that the city's laws had become terribly muddled by excessive legislation, and he suggests that the Athenians failed to respect the distinction between laws and decrees. But Demosthenes does not indicate that he had trouble finding texts of laws, and his complaint is directed at legislative procedure, not at the way that laws were stored or physically arranged. Demosthenes' silence about the retrieval of the laws, as opposed to the frequency and recklessness with which they were enacted, is indicative of Athenian speakers in general: we hear nothing of difficulties or problems in locating documents in the Metroon, and their frequent citation by orators and others seems to indicate that retrieving documents was not a difficult matter. Indeed, both Aeschines and Demosthenes cite documents that were decades old, and it was possible in the second century to retrieve documents from the Metroon dating back more than a century and a half.[94] Whatever shortcomings the archives of the Metroon may have possessed, we have no evidence that a lack of organization hindered consultation of its documents.

CHAPTER SEVEN

Consultation

Preceding chapters have examined several aspects of the Metroon's archives, from the types of documents they encompassed to possible methods by which they were arranged and organized. In this chapter we shall explore some of the ways in which those archives were used and consulted.[1]

1. Archival Documents and the Lawcourts

Athenians of the classical period were notoriously litigious. The fifth-century plays of Aristophanes poke fun at the Athenian infatuation with legal contests, and the speeches of the fourth-century Attic orators illustrate this characteristic of Athenian society in both their number and content. The Athenians possessed numerous lawcourts (*dikastēria*) in which disputes of a public and private nature were heard, and these met between 150 and 200 days each year.[2] The lawcourts themselves were manned by private citizens, who took on the roles of prosecutor, defendant, judge, and jury. Professional advocacy was prohibited, and although litigants sometimes enlisted the support of friends or relatives to speak on their behalf or hired speechwriters (*logographoi*) to compose their speeches, opposing parties were expected to deliver speeches in person in support of their cases. The role of judicial magistrates, themselves nonprofessionals who held office for a single year, was extremely limited. They conducted preliminary hearings and introduced suits to the courts over which they presided, but they had little discretion in legal matters and offered no interpretation of the relevant laws or explanation of the evidence. The final decision on virtually all matters was in the hands of jurors called dikasts, Athenian citizens over the age of thirty whose numbers in different courts ranged from several hundred to over a thousand. Dikasts acted as both judges and jurors: they heard the speeches delivered by the competing parties; weighed (without discussion) the evidence, which included both points of law and fact; issued a verdict; and fixed penalty when none was specified by law. Their decisions were not subject to appeal.[3]

Athenian dikasts swore to cast their verdicts according to the city's laws and decrees, but they relied on the litigants to explain relevant statutes to them.[4] Each party in a suit gathered together whatever evidence, including official documents, it felt might support its case, and presented these to the dikasts in the course of the speeches they delivered.[5] Texts of laws and decrees were available from any of several sources. Many were inscribed and publicly displayed on stone stelai around Athens, and texts of most, if not all, Athenian laws and decrees probably could be found in the city's archives, kept in the Metroon, from the end of the fifth century. But the sources from which litigants obtained the texts they cite are not always easy to determine. In the speeches that have survived, speakers routinely ask for laws and decrees to be read out by a courtroom clerk, but they seldom offer any indication of how they obtained these texts. A speaker will sometimes mention that a document was published on stone, and although he may not say that he copied the text from that stele, this usually seems a reasonable inference. Thus, Andokides cites in his speech *On the Mysteries* a decree proposed and carried by Demophantos that was set up on a stele in front of the Bouleuterion, and he calls upon the clerk of the court to read the text taken "from the stele."[6] Similarly, the speaker of Lysias 1, *Against Eratosthenes*, has read out a law that he describes as "from the stele on the Areopagos."[7] The practice of consulting stelai is well illustrated by a passage of the Demosthenic *Against Euergos and Mnesiboulos*. That speaker relates how, when a freedwoman died as a result of wounds inflicted by his opponents, he consulted the stele inscribed with Drakon's law on homicide in order to determine what legal recourse he might have.[8]

Consultation of the Metroon's archives, on the other hand, is somewhat more difficult to detect. That Athenian citizens had the right to enter the Metroon and did consult its records need not be doubted, and such consultation is clearly implied by a passage of the first Demosthenic speech *Against Aristogeiton*. The speaker concludes his speech by asking the jury of dikasts how, if they vote for Aristogeiton's acquittal, they will enter the Metroon if they should need something, commenting that "for surely each of you will not enter it individually to find valid laws, unless you all now leave having confirmed them together."[9] The speaker equates the validity of the laws housed in the Metroon with a vote for conviction, and he emphasizes this by envisioning individual dikasts entering the Metroon for the purpose of consulting the laws.[10] Only the laws housed in the Metroon are mentioned, but this may be due to the context, and citizens presumably enjoyed a similar right to consult other types of documents kept in the Metroon as well.

Several speeches supply indirect evidence that their speakers had consulted the archives of the Metroon in the way envisioned in the speech *Against Aristogeiton*. Demosthenes in his speech *On the Embassy* has read out a decree that appointed him and Aeschines to serve on the third embassy to Philip, and he states explicitly that its text was to be found in the Metroon; it seems reasonable to suppose that he obtained his text of the decree from its archives.[11] In the speeches *On the Embassy* and *Against Ktesiphon*, Aeschines refers to and has recited numerous documents related to the events leading up to the Peace of Philokrates in 346 and to the career of Demosthenes, and he emphasizes repeatedly that these were taken from the *dēmosia grammata*, the "public records."[12] These documents include decrees of the Boule and Ekklesia, records of elections, and letters from Athenian generals, as well as specific details related to these documents, such as their dates and proposers. We have already seen that many of the documents that Aeschines cites are otherwise attested as being stored in the Metroon, so the phrase *dēmosia grammata* is best understood as referring to that building's archives. In similar fashion, Demosthenes in the speech *On the Crown* claims that he will convict Aeschines on the basis of documents deposited *en tōi dēmos-iōi*.[13] Since that phrase is used to refer to central archival establishments in other city-states, and since many of the types of documents Demosthenes introduces in the speech were kept in the Metroon, his consultation of the Metroon's archives should not be doubted.

Other courtroom speakers do not refer to the Metroon or its archives in similar ways, but Aeschines' and Demosthenes' consultations of the building's records provide a satisfactory explanation for how other speakers, from Andokides (late fifth/early fourth century) to Deinarchos (late fourth century), acquired at least some of the laws and decrees they cite. Recently, however, some scholars have questioned the frequency with which Athenians went to the Metroon to obtain texts they wanted. Aeschines' consultation of archival documents, it is argued, represents a new and sudden realization of the value of archives, one that developed only in the second half of the fourth century. Earlier orators had referred to documents in their speeches, but they relied largely on inscriptions and cited documents for their paradigmatic value or simply for the texts they wanted to quote; sophisticated argumentation came later. Although the Metroon's archives existed from the end of the fifth century, it was not until the time of Aeschines in the middle of the fourth century that the Athenians recognized the value of those archives and put those records to use.[14]

Aeschines is certainly far more self-conscious in his use of state documents than the other orators, and the fact that he spent part of his early career as an undersecretary undoubtedly influenced his rhetorical methods and use of documents. But to call Aeschines the first to realize the significance of archival texts or to suppose that the Metroon's archives were ignored during the first fifty years of their existence is potentially misleading. Such arguments blur the fact that documents were cited in courtroom speeches from the early fourth century and that speakers sometimes attempted to build arguments on written, legal texts. Earlier orators do not refer to the Metroon by name, and they may not make the same types of arguments based on documents as does Aeschines. But laws and decrees played a role in legal rhetoric, and not all of their texts can be assumed to have been derived from inscriptions. A detailed study of laws and decrees and their use in the rhetoric of Athenian *dikastēria* cannot be undertaken here, but a brief survey of the speeches of several orators reveals some awareness of their value in courtroom oratory from the late fifth century. Aeschines and Demosthenes may cite state documents more frequently and in different ways than their predecessors, but their consultation of the Metroon's archives was neither new nor unique.

The speeches of Antiphon, who died in 411 and whose speeches are the earliest to have survived, do not call for a single law or decree to be read out. But it is not clear that Antiphon's speeches are typical of orators of his day. He was perhaps the first Athenian to compose speeches for delivery by others and to have speeches published. His three forensic speeches also emanate from homicide cases, and their features may not be fully representative of the ways in which litigants framed speeches in other types of cases.[15] But even if we allow that Antiphon is representative of forensic oratory of the late fifth century, his failure to cite specific laws or decrees should not be construed as ignorance of documents or a failure to consult them. He was certainly familiar with Athenian homicide law, and he was capable of making sophisticated arguments on the basis of written laws. In the speech *On the Murder of Herodes*, delivered around 420, the speaker Euxitheos claims that although his opponents accuse him of homicide, they have prosecuted him not with a suit of homicide but under the law against malefactors (*kakourgoi*), the provisions of which, he argues, do not apply to his case. Euxitheos does not have the laws on homicide or malefactors read out, but he does paraphrase them, noting, for example, that the law on malefactors explicitly concerned thieves and cloak snatchers and not killers, and that the homicide laws required the accused to keep away from specified places and trials to be held under the open sky, a provision his accusers have avoided.[16] Euxitheos offers no clue of how he or Antiphon knew the contents of these two laws, but his arguments depend on a familiarity with their wording. Inscriptions are not a likely source. Drakon's homicide law was published on stone only in 409/8, two years after Antiphon's death in 411, and we have no evidence that the law on *kakourgoi* was publicly displayed on stone. Although we cannot be certain, one possible scenario is that Antiphon or the speaker (or both) consulted, copied, and studied texts of these laws that magistrates had stored in their archives.[17] If litigants were conducting such consultation before the Metroon's foundation, there is no reason to doubt that they continued to do so afterward as well.

The oratory of Andokides, who was active in late fifth and early fourth century, also exhibits a knowledge of several state documents, some of which he may have obtained from archival texts. Unlike Antiphon, Andokides was not a professional speechwriter, so his rhetorical practices may be more typical of other Athenians of his day. In the speech *On His Return*, probably delivered around 410, Andokides mentions a decree whose terms had been revoked but which was still kept in the Bouleuterion, a passage that provides our best evidence that this building also housed texts of decrees before the Metroon's foundation.[18] In his speech *On the Mysteries*, delivered in 400/399, Andokides cites several more laws and decrees. Andokides had been charged with violating the terms of the decree of Isotimides, enacted in 415, which prohibited individuals guilty of sacrilege from entering sacred places. Andokides argued that the terms of that decree were no longer valid, and he produced several laws and decrees to support his position.[19] One of these was the decree of Demophantos, which Andokides mentions was inscribed on a stele; he may have copied its text from the stele itself.[20] But it is not clear that the other documents Andokides brought forward were also published on stone; Andokides, at any rate, does not say so. He first discusses the decree of Patrokleides, enacted in 405, which restored full rights to certain disenfranchised citizens, though perhaps not to Andokides himself. He also cites the decree of Teisamenos, which outlined the procedures for the enactment of additional laws after the restoration of the democracy in 403. He then discusses several other laws enacted after Teisamenos's decree, which defined more precisely that status of laws and legal administration after the revision of the law code.[21]

Scholars have noticed that the documents cited by Andokides do not necessarily support his case; by dwelling on them he is trying to create the impression, which may be false, that offenses committed prior to 403/2 were no longer punishable. But where did Andokides acquire these laws and decrees? The decrees of Patrokleides and Teisamenos, texts of which are preserved in Andokides' speech, do not contain publication clauses, and neither measure possesses the degree of permanency that is shared by many other Athenian documents on stone. We might assume that the supplementary laws discussed by Andokides were published in the stoa, perhaps the Royal Stoa, in which Andokides suggests that newly approved laws were published. But recent scholarship has made it far less certain that all Athenian laws were published in the Royal Stoa, and Andokides himself says that the supplementary laws were enacted after that publication took place.[22] Once again, absolute certainty of Andokides' sources for these documents is impossible, but it is not unreasonable to suggest that upon their enactment they had been deposited in the city's archives, perhaps located in the recently established Metroon, and that when Andokides found himself the subject of prosecution in 400/399, he sought out texts from those archives that he believed would support his defense, just as Aeschines would do more than fifty years later.

A speech of Lysias dating from the early 390s also uses documents to build its case, and some of these may have come from archival sources. The speaker of the speech *Against Agoratos* accused Agoratos of complicity in the death of a relative shortly before the installment of the Thirty in 404, and he has read out several documents that in his view support his accusations. These documents include decrees issued by the Boule calling for the arrest of Agoratos, and other decrees of the Ekklesia regarding information provided by him.[23] The speaker also has read out a decree of the Ekklesia granting immunity to a certain Menestratos for providing additional information about the conspirators, and a list of men who were put to death as a result of Agoratos's actions.[24] The speech also makes reference to a decree honoring the assassins of Phrynichos, a member of the Four Hundred, into whose text the speaker claims Agoratos had conspired to have his name included. That decree was inscribed on stone, so the speaker's knowledge of its text may have come from the inscription itself.[25] But stelai are not mentioned in conjunction with any of the other documents cited in the speech, and some of them, such as decrees of the Boule and decrees granting immunity, are not types of documents that were regularly published on stone during the fifth and fourth centuries. Decrees of both the Boule and Ekklesia were, however, preserved in the Metroon's archives, so it can be considered a strong possibility that the speaker obtained copies from that building's archives.[26] The speaker's methods are also noteworthy. Although he does not cite the date of any document, he cites their texts to support his arguments, just as Aeschines and Demosthenes would do later in the century.

Texts of laws are cited in the speeches of Isaios, which span the first half of the fourth century. Isaios's works are all concerned with inheritance disputes, so the documents appearing in them are laws on inheritance.[27] Solon had treated inheritance in his laws, and their texts might have been found on the *axones* and possibly *kyrbeis* on which Solon's laws were recorded. But probably inheritance had been the subject of legislation after Solon, and inheritance laws were almost certainly included in the revision of Athenian laws at the end of the fifth century. If we could be certain that all Athenian laws were displayed on a wall of stelai in or near the Stoa Basileios as a result of this revision, we could well imagine that the inheritance laws read out in the speeches of Isaios derived ultimately from the consultation of such an inscription. But the existence of a centrally inscribed law code is not certain, and laws on inheritance are not found in the extant body of fourth-century laws on stone. Isaios's references too may depend on archival consultation.

Other types of documents are cited in the speeches of Isokrates. In the speech *Trapezitikos* (c. 395) the speaker mentions and has read out a letter written by Satyros, the king of Bosporos, to the Athenians.[28] How he obtained a copy of this letter is not clear; letters from foreign rulers were not regularly published on stone, so the speaker may have possessed his own copy or found a text in the official archives kept in the Metroon. In the speech *Against Kallimachos* (c. 400), the speaker begins by describing a law of Archinos that established a new procedure called *paragraphē*, the type of case for which the speech was delivered, and he later discusses the agreements (*synthēkai*) that ended the civil war, restored the democracy, and proclaimed an amnesty in 403, and which, he claims, his opponent had violated.[29] The speaker does not say how he knew of these measures, and since the speech was delivered soon after they were ratified, his narrative may rely on his general knowledge of these events. But the text of the reconciliation agreement is read out to the court. We might assume that these agreements were published on stone so that their terms would be known to all citizens, but neither this speaker nor other sources that discuss the restoration of the democracy in 403 mention stelai in connection with the reconciliation agreement or amnesty.[30] Certainty, as always, is impossible, but here too reliance on texts obtained from the Metroon's archives cannot be ruled out.

Now it might be objected that many of these speeches are works of *logographoi*, professional speechwriters, and that their practices cannot be taken as representative of the habits of ordinary Athenians. Isaios, for example, might have had a personal collection of Athenian inheritance laws, so that the appearance of documents in speeches written by him could reflect not consultation of the Metroon's archives but simply his knowledge of Athenian inheritance law or, at most, his consultation of these laws and not that of Athenian litigants in general. Against such an argument it should be kept in mind that the Athenians disapproved of professionalism in the *dikastēria*, and speechwriters sought to remove from their speeches the appearance that they were composed by anyone other than the speaker himself.[31] That is, speechwriters took pains to make their speeches appear as if they were works of ordinary Athenians. If documents were accessible to or used by only elite speakers, we should probably not expect to find them cited frequently, if at all. Since laws and decrees do appear with some frequency, their use and consultation of them may be regarded as a practice shared by even nonelite citizens.

The procedures of public arbitration may also suggest that the consultation of laws for use in litigation, even by ordinary Athenians, was common.[32] In the fourth century, some types of private suits fell under the jurisdiction of officials known as the Forty. If the claims involved sums of less than ten drachmas, the Forty adjudicated the cases themselves, but if the value of the claim was greater, the case was submitted to a public arbitrator. The arbitrator listened to the opposing sides and tried to reach a compromise, but if this failed he issued a judgment. If one of the litigants was dissatisfied with the decision, he could appeal it to a *dikastērion*. In that case, all the documents that had been introduced at the hearing, oaths, testimony of witnesses, and laws, were placed in a jar called an *echinos*, which was sealed. The case was sent back to the Forty, who introduced it to a *dikastērion*, where the litigants were allowed to discuss only that evidence that had been produced before the arbitrator and was found in the jar.

Public arbitration of private disputes was first introduced around the year 400, and the requirement that evidence be submitted in writing may have been in place as early as 389.[33] Among the written evidence submitted at arbitrators' hearings were texts of laws. These hearings took place before cases went to a *dikastērion* and, therefore, before speeches were composed for delivery in front of a courtroom. The presentation of laws to arbitrators thus shows that Athenians consulted laws even before cases went to court, and before some litigants resorted to speechwriters. We obviously cannot know how frequently laws were cited at arbitrators' hearings, nor can we ascertain from where litigants obtained the texts of laws they brought with them. But the role of laws in arbitration proceedings indicates that their consultation was not a practice restricted to speeches composed by logographers. So too consultation of the Metroon, where texts of laws were kept, need not have been limited to those who relied on the logographer's craft.

It is the public speeches of Aeschines and Demosthenes, however, that provide the most frequent references to laws, decrees, and other state documents. Aeschines in particular emphasizes that the documents he produces in the speeches *On the Embassy* and *On the Crown* were taken from the public records, and the documents cited by Demosthenes in speeches delivered for the same cases probably came from a similar source. Demosthenes also made use of laws and decrees in his speeches *Against Leptines*, *Against Meidias*, *Against Aristokrates*, and *Against Timokrates*, all of which date from the 350s. Some of these documents, such as the honorary decrees cited in the speech *Against Leptines*, may have come from copies set up on stone stelai. But this need not be true of all the documents he refers to, and in composing these speeches too Demosthenes may have consulted the appropriate texts in the Metroon.[34]

The frequency with which documents are cited in the speeches of Aeschines and Demosthenes certainly conveys an impression of increasing comfort and familiarity with written records by Athenian orators in their rhetoric. But their practices probably grew out of ones already recognized by speakers before their time, and before drawing broader conclusions about possible changes in archival consultation based on the rhetoric of Aeschines and Demosthenes, we should keep in mind that a speaker's use of documents within a speech may have been dictated by the details of a particular case and the type of suit for which a speech was composed. Aeschines delivered the speech *On the False Embassy* in response to charges of misconduct for his actions while serving on the second embassy to Philip. Demosthenes accused Aeschines of giving false reports, misleading the Athenians, and of having been bribed and corrupted by Philip, and he produced several documents from the events of 346 to support these charges. More specifically, Demosthenes accused Aeschines of delaying the departure of the embassy, a delay that allegedly led to the fall of Athens' ally Kersebleptes to Philip.[35] Aeschines answered these charges point by point by focusing on many of the same documents cited by Demosthenes in order to discredit his case; his use of documents is a reaction to the specific charges brought by Demosthenes.

Since speeches from similar types of cases do not survive we cannot determine how innovative Aeschines' use of documents was in this speech. But trials of ambassadors and other Athenian officials are attested much earlier in the fourth century, and we cannot rule out the possibility that decrees and other official documents regularly played a role in such cases and that individuals defended their actions based on decrees and other state documents connected to their conduct, just as Aeschines did in the 340s.[36]

In similar fashion, Aeschines' citation of documents in his speech *Against Ktesiphon* was not the result of a sudden realization of the value of public archives but of the circumstances of the case in which those records were cited. The speech *Against Ktesiphon* was delivered in a *graphē paranomōn*, an indictment against an allegedly unconstitutional decree, brought by Aeschines against Ktesiphon and his motion to award Demosthenes a crown for his (Demosthenes') public services.[37] Aeschines cites several laws and decrees to support his case that Ktesiphon's motion was not only illegal but also untrue, and it is for this latter reason that he has so many documents read out relating to the career of Demosthenes, emphasizing that these were taken from the city's archives. This use of documents in a *graphē paranomōn* is hardly extraordinary. Demosthenes cites and has read out several laws and decrees in his speech *Against Leptines*, the provisions of which, he claims, Leptines had contravened or whose contents would be nullified by the passage of Leptines' law.[38] In the speech *Against Timokrates*, Demosthenes asks the court clerk to read out several laws on *nomothesia*, which he claims Timokrates had overlooked or violated in proposing a law on state festivals; he then adduces a series of other laws contradicted by Timokrates' proposal.[39] In the speech *Against Aristokrates*, Demosthenes runs through extracts from Athens' homicide laws whose provisions would be violated by passage of Aristokrates' decree,[40] and he presents several other decrees and official letters in an attempt to show that the decree was not only illegal but also inexpedient.[41] Demosthenes does not tell his audience how he obtained any of these documents, though references to stelai may suggest that some were obtained from inscriptions.[42] But this was almost certainly not true of the letters he cites in the speech *Against Aristokrates*, and it is reasonable to conjecture that these and perhaps other documents for which he names no source were obtained by consultation of the archives in the Metroon.

The earliest attested case of a *graphē paranomōn* occurred in 415, and nearly forty cases of this type are attested over the course of the next century.[43] Apart from those delivered by Aeschines and Demosthenes, speeches from other cases do not survive, but the citation of laws and decrees by Aeschines and Demosthenes can hardly have been unique or innovative.[44] It was natural in suits that challenged the validity and expediency of a proposed law or decree for speakers to cite other laws and decrees that the proposed measure contravened. The laws governing procedure in the *graphai paranomōn* and the similar procedure, *graphai nomon mē epitēdeion theinai* (against unconstitutional laws) may have required prosecutors to list in their indictments those laws and decrees whose contents were contravened by the allegedly illegal measure.[45] If this was the case, investigation and study of laws and decrees may have been a regular feature of such *graphai* from the time these procedures were created.

That speakers in *graphai paranomōn* were accustomed to cite laws and decrees as early as the fifth century may be deduced from a debate that decided the fate of several Athenian generals in 406. The generals had been recalled to Athens for their failure to rescue shipwrecked Athenian sailors after the battle at Arginusai, and when a certain Kallixenos introduced a *probouleuma* calling for a single trial for the all generals before the Ekklesia, Euryptolemos indicted this motion as unconstitutional but was shouted down in the Ekklesia and forced to withdraw his summons. Euryptolemos then offered another proposal to counter that of Kallixenos, according to which the generals would be tried under the terms of the decree of Kannonos; in the speech supporting his motion, Xenophon reports that Euryptolemos also suggested that the generals be tried under the laws on treason and temple robbery.[46] Although Euryptolemos's summons against the motion of Kallixenos never came to trial, and the alternative proposal he offered failed to be carried, the speech he delivered in support of his motion may illustrate the line of attack he would have followed had the case gone to court. Euryptolemos cited three different laws or decrees as alternatives to the motion presented by Kallixenos, and since he delivered this speech spontaneously, he presumably had not consulted their texts beforehand. But if Euryptolemos referred to laws and decrees on the spur of the moment, should we not suppose that given the opportunity to prepare the case for a trial, he and others would have consulted the texts of relevant laws and decrees in the same or similar way as Aeschines and Demosthenes did a half century later?

11. Archival Documents and Legislation

Given the frequency with which Athenian lawcourts met and the number of cases they heard each year, requests for laws and decrees to be used in legal proceedings may have constituted the most common reason why Athenians sought out texts from the Metroon's archives. Other situations, however, also offered opportunities for consultation. When Telesias of Troizen sought to obtain Athenian citizenship in the second century B.C., an Athenian by the name of Onasos produced a decree, whose text was filed in the Metroon, granting citizenship to one of his ancestors.[47] This earlier decree was moved by Stratokles of Diomeia, a politician active in the late fourth century, and it was therefore over 150 years old at the time that Onasos found and retrieved its text. Onasos seems not to have been the proposer of the decree. He was probably an Athenian friend or acquaintance of Telesias, who, when Telesias made a petition for Athenian citizenship, saw that the appropriate document, in this case a citizenship decree moved by Stratokles on behalf of Telesias's distant ancestor, was acquired from the Metroon.

Telesias's citizenship decree and its reference to an earlier document shows how speakers in the Ekklesia and proposers of decrees could consult the Metroon's holdings to find documents supporting motions currently under consideration. The decree, however, dates from the second century, and the extent to which the retrieval of decrees for similar reasons was a current practice in the fourth century deserves closer attention; we cannot automatically assume that practices of the Hellenistic period were already in use from the moment of the Metroon's foundation. When we turn to the fourth-century evidence, explicit parallels for the consultation indicated by the second-century decree for Telesias are surprisingly wanting. The political speeches of Demosthenes do not name the Metroon or cite documents with any frequency, and inscribed decrees of the fourth century do not include references to the Metroon similar to the one appearing in Telesias's citizenship decree.[48]

But some decrees do contain clauses recalling past awards and honors to their recipients or their ancestors. In the late 340s the Athenians reaffirmed for Arybbas of Mollosos a grant of citizenship made to his father and grandfather. How the proposer knew of these earlier grants is not stated, but the reaffirmation of an older citizenship grant resembles the one for Telesias two centuries later; consultation of the earlier decrees, housed in the Metroon, for Arybbas is certainly possible.[49] In 335, the Ekklesia voted a series of honors for a certain Phyleus, who had served as an official of the Boule in the previous year.[50] But the decree instructs the secretary to have not only its own text inscribed on stone, but also those of two other decrees, one of the Boule and another of the Ekklesia, enacted in the previous year. The time between the passage of all three decrees is very short, but it does not seem unlikely that the earlier two decrees played some role in the vote of the final award to Phyleus, and the texts of both almost certainly had to be retrieved, perhaps from the Metroon, for publication. In 325/4, Demosthenes of Lamptreus proposed and carried a decree honoring a certain Herakleides of Salamis for his goodwill and services and especially his previous contributions of grain to Athens.[51] Demosthenes also moved that in addition to the present decree the secretary *kata prytaneian* should have inscribed on stone earlier praises awarded to Herakleides, and below this decree there follow four more decrees enacted in earlier years in recognition of Herakleides' services to Athens.[52] Demosthenes was evidently familiar with the earlier decrees for Herakleides when he made his proposal, and although he does not describe how he knew their texts, the procedure underlying Telesias's citizenship decree, in which an older decree was retrieved from the Metroon in support of a current motion, offers a possible explanation.

The Metroon and its archives are admittedly not mentioned in these inscriptions, but they all date from the second half of the fourth century, a period in which the Metroon's archives were used by litigants and when the citation of documents in debates before the Ekklesia may have been becoming more common. Demosthenes, for example, tells us that Aeschines had read out the decrees of Miltiades and Themistokles and the Ephebic Oath at a meeting of the Ekklesia in 348 in an attempt to encourage support for a decree in favor of forming a Panhellenic coalition against Philip. Demosthenes himself referred to the fifth-century decree against Arthmios of Zeleia for similar reasons later in the 340s.[53] That is not to say that Aeschines and Demosthenes obtained these documents from the city's archives—Demosthenes refers explicitly to a bronze stele on the Acropolis on which the Arthmios decree was inscribed—or that the texts they read out were authentic fifth-century texts. But their use of documents in the Ekklesia may represent a growing awareness of the value that written records could have in deliberative oratory, and in such a context it is not difficult to imagine that other speakers and proposers of decrees consulted the Metroon to find decrees related to motions they themselves had proposed or favored.

But inscriptions of the first half of the fourth century also publish older decrees alongside more recent ones, and this practice may point to consultation of the Metroon's archives and use of documents to support or oppose current proposals from an earlier date. In 368/7, the Athenians passed a decree honoring the Mytileneans and a Mytilenean ambassador named Hieroitas for their services to them.[54] The decree calls for both its own publication and that of a decree passed a year before in response to an embassy on which Hieroitas and other Mytileneans served. This earlier decree is inscribed below the former one on the same stone and expresses Athenian gratitude for Mytilenean loyalty in an unspecified war.[55] Here too reference to the earlier decree in the text of the later one suggests that it was discussed when the later one was passed, and there is little reason to doubt that a text was available for consultation in the Metroon. Another decree, dating from 394/3, grants Athenian citizenship to Sthorys of Thasos.[56] The decree mentions that Sthorys's ancestors had been *proxenoi*, and it refers to earlier decrees in honor of Sthorys himself, but it too fails to relate how its proposer knew of these earlier decrees or the *proxenia* of Sthorys's ancestors. The decree for Sthorys was to be published near earlier awards made in his honor, so the proposer may have learned of them and the awards to his ancestors from an inscription.[57]

Another inscription of the early fourth century may actually preserve a decree enacted in the fifth century. The stone records a decree honoring a certain Herakleides of Klazomenai and making him a *proxenos* for his services to Athens, and although the inscription was probably published in the early 390s, many scholars believe that decree was actually ratified in the 420s.[58] Herakleides is known to have acquired Athenian citizenship, and it is possible that the earlier decree was republished along with decree of the 390s that made Herakleides an Athenian citizen. If so, Herakleides' earlier services and the decree that recognized them presumably played a role in the debate surrounding the later citizenship grant. The original decree was supposed to have been published on stone, but its republication could suggest that that stele was no longer standing. How a proposer of the 390s would have known of the earlier decree for Herakleides we cannot say for certain, but consultation and retrieval of its text from an archival collection is at least a possibility.

More direct reference to an older document occurs in a speech delivered by Andokides before the Ekklesia in 391. Andokides had just returned from Sparta and he and his fellow ambassadors had brought with them the terms of a treaty that would end the Corinthian War between Sparta and Athens and their respective allies. In the course of a speech arguing for ratification of the terms, Andokides quotes from the treaty that concluded the Peloponnesian War between Athens and Sparta more than ten years earlier and whose text was inscribed on stone. He contrasts that earlier treaty, in which the Athenians were severely punished, with the present peace proposal, in which the Athenians fared much better.[59] Unlike Aeschines and Demosthenes, who later cited fifth-century texts because their contents embodied values they hoped their audiences would emulate, Andokides refers to the Peloponnesian War treaty because its contents cast his own proposal in a much more favorable light. But like Aeschines and Demosthenes, Andokides viewed the older text as paradigmatic, except that its example was one to be avoided.

Andokides' citation of an older treaty in the 390s betrays some recognition of the value of documents in political debate, and it encourages us to consider whether Athenians were citing documents, inscribed or archival, in similar debates before the Boule or Ekklesia even earlier. Some speeches in Thucydides' history of the Peloponnesian War suggest that older documents were taken into consideration when new measures were proposed. Both Athenian and non-Athenian speakers refer to specific terms of the Thirty Years' Peace concluded between Athens and Sparta and their allies in 446 in speeches delivered just before the outbreak of the Peloponnesian War, and the Megarian Decree also seems to have been subject of some discussion.[60] Whatever one thinks of the historicity of these speeches, there is little reason to doubt that these texts were the subject of consultation and debate in the period before the outbreak of the war, as the Thucydidean speeches suggest. Later in the war, Thucydides relates how, when the Spartans sent a garrison by sea to Epidauros in 418, the Argives complained to the Athenians that this action constituted a violation of what was written in the Peace of Nikias of 421. As a result, Alkibiades persuaded the Athenians to append a statement to the stele recording that peace's terms, stating that the Spartans had failed to abide by their oaths.[61] Thucydides, who was absent from Athens at the time, offers no further information about the debate that arose after the Argive complaint or about the arguments used by Alkibiades or others to convince the Athenians to append the inscribed text of the Peace of Nikias. But his words indicate that the Argive grievance arose from a specific written provision of Nikias's Peace, and the fact that the Athenians chose to append the text of the stele suggests that its inscribed provisions were the object of some scrutiny and discussion. This seems confirmed by a passage of Aristophanes' Lysistrata. Lysistrata tells how the women of Athens tolerated the political miscalculations of their husbands for some time, and she mentions a particular occasion when Athenian wives questioned their husbands about what the Ekklesia had decided to write about the nullification of certain provisions on a stele.[62]

These documents are mentioned not as symbols or paradigms, but because their contents had significance to the events under discussion before the Ekklesia. But both the Peace of Nikias and the treaty ending the Peloponnesian War were inscribed on stelai, and it is not unlikely that the Thirty Years' Peace of 446 was also published on stone at Athens.[63] References, then, to these documents might imply that Athenians of the fifth century sometimes consulted inscriptions to prepare for debate in the Ekklesia and to promote or oppose motions they supported. If inscriptions preserved the only lasting texts of Athenian documents during the fifth century, we could then assume that consultation of documents during the fifth century was limited primarily to documents published on stone. But I have argued that the Athenians were keeping archives of documents already in the fifth century, and some of the evidence for those archives suggests that these records were also consulted when new measures came before the Ekklesia. The decree ordering the dispatch of a colony to Brea includes a provision requiring neighboring cities in Thrace to come to the aid of the colony if it is attacked, in accordance with an earlier set of agreements.[64] There is no reference to a stele or any other hint that these agreements were inscribed on stone, and the manner in which they are referred to, as ones drawn up while a person, whose name is lost, served as secretary, is unusual for inscribed documents. Their text may have been preserved only in archival form. Although we cannot prove that the proposer of the decree consulted these agreements when he made his motion, his reference to them is quite specific and suggests a precise knowledge of them. Similarly, an inscription of 423/2 preserves traces of four decrees concerning Athenian relations with the city Methone. The first three decrees on the stone date from the early 420s but they were not inscribed on stone until 423/2, when the last decree was enacted.[65] Certainty is impossible, but here too it seems reasonable to suppose that the three earlier decrees, their texts possibly acquired from the Boule's archives, played some role in discussions leading to the ratification of the fourth decree and the decision to publish all four decrees on stone.[66]

Consultation of archival texts is, admittedly, not mentioned explicitly in these inscriptions, and even in the fourth century the proposers of decrees do not mention visits to the Metroon or its archives. But decrees of the fifth and fourth centuries do show an awareness of earlier documents, and this suggests that speakers and proposers of decrees sometimes consulted older measures when new proposals on similar topics came before the Ekklesia. Certainly they often consulted laws or decrees inscribed on stone. This was probably true in the case of Andokides' quotation from the stele inscribed with the treaty ending the Peloponnesian War, and similar consultation probably lies behind the reaffirmation of a citizenship decree for two Akarnanians in 338/7. That decree mentions an earlier grant of citizenship to their grandfather and says that its text was published on the Acropolis.[67]

But not every reference to an older document mentions an inscription, and it is not safe to assume that decrees were always available on stone. Honorands and other persons named in decrees may have received and retained copies of measures concerning them, and privately held copies could also have supplied Athenians with a knowledge of older measures.[68] But such a hypothesis also assumes that Athenians would accept private copies of decrees as valid and binding on them, and that they would not attempt to verify past awards in the archival records of decrees that they themselves maintained. That is certainly possible, but it was a secretary of the Athenian state who was directed to see to the publication of older decrees alongside more recent ones, and it was the same secretary in whose records texts of decrees were regularly kept. The Metroon was located immediately adjacent to the Bouleuterion, the meeting place of the Boule, the body in which many decrees were first introduced and debated, and consultation of its archives could not have been difficult if and when questions arose, as they certainly must have, about the past services of an individual or city whose relations with Athens was on a meeting's agenda. It does not strain credulity to suggest that when embassies arrived in Athens from foreign cities, when foreigners sought honors for their services to Athens, or when new legislation came up for discussion, interested Athenians or members of the Boule itself sometimes sought out earlier decrees, preserved in the city's archives, on similar topics. That seems to be what took place in the case of Telesias of Troizen in the second century B.C., and a similar explanation accounts for references to earlier measures in decrees of the fifth and fourth centuries.[69]

III. Archives and Historians

One of the chief concerns of modern archival institutions is to preserve written records and to make them available for wider use, including scholarly research. But however accessible the Metroon may have been, ancient historians did not share their modern counterparts' interest in archival research. Greek historical writing had its origins in Ionian *historia*, "research" or "investigation," but investigation entailed discussions with living individuals, visits to foreign places, and observations of strange customs, not the consultation of written records. From the time of Herodotus, the first Greek historian, the focus of Greek historiography fell on the memorable words and deeds of men, especially in war and politics, and this focus remained central to virtually all subsequent writers of history. Research was a defining characteristic of the genre and consisted primarily of personal observation of events and the gathering of oral testimony from eyewitnesses and other well-informed sources.[70] Writers relied heavily on the oral traditions of families and cities for their knowledge of past events, but they also took into account written works left by earlier writers, in both prose and poetry. Consultation of the works of earlier historians is best represented by later authors such as Diodorus Siculus, who wrote in the first century and whose universal history drew on a wide range of earlier written sources. But already in the fifth century, Herodotus and Thucydides show their familiarity with the works of earlier poets and prose writers. Both knew their Homer, and Herodotus critiqued the earlier writings of Hekataios, who had written on geography and genealogy. Thucydides had read Hellanikos's history of Athens, which probably appeared late in the fifth century and whose treatment of the Pentakontaetia, the fifty-year period preceding the outbreak of the Peloponnesian War in 431, he criticized.[71] Orally transmitted information was a chief source for the ancient Greek historian, but written evidence supplied by literary works was not overlooked.

Historians also took some, albeit limited, interest in written records and documents. Herodotus does not reproduce any documentary texts in his history of the Persian Wars, but he does cite several inscriptions to illustrate points of his narrative, and he sometimes uses their texts to draw further conclusions about events he discusses.[72] Thucydides was familiar enough with an inscription on the Acropolis, one that recorded a sentence of exile against the tyrant Hippias and his family, to refer to its contents in support of his arguments about power relations among the sons of Peisistratos.[73] He also included full, verbatim texts of several truces and treaties in books 4, 5, and 8 of his history of the Peloponnesian War. The presence of these texts and their relationship to their surrounding narrative have been much discussed by scholars, and we cannot detail here the numerous issues they raise, especially in terms of the composition of Thucydides' work. But they do invite brief comment. Scholars have sometimes taken these treaties as a sign of the incompleteness of Thucydides' History, especially books 5 and 8. Had Thucydides lived to finish his work, it is argued, he would have removed the full texts of the treaties and replaced them with a speech or straight narrative. We have already noted that some of the speeches in book 1 of Thucydides' History show a familiarity with the terms of the Thirty Years' Peace and the Megarian Decree, and other passages also suggest a knowledge of documents, so this hypothesis is not unreasonable.[74] But if that was Thucydides' intention, it would highlight an important aspect of the methods of the Greek historians and their use of documents. Thucydides evidently gathered the texts of some documents, especially treaties, that were relevant to his subject matter, but his practice in many instances may have been to blend them into his narrative so as to leave few explicit traces of consultation. But even if Thucydides intended to leave the full texts of documents in his completed work, their presence would still be significant. Connor has suggested that the documents of books 4 and 5 possess a literary function: their contents illustrate the discrepancy between what was anticipated to happen and what actually transpired.[75] If Thucydides inserted these texts in his narrative for this reason, his decision to do so would betoken a rather sophisticated recognition of the value of documents in historical writing by one of the genre's first practitioners.

The loss of many historical works of the fourth century makes it impossible to know the extent to which later historians followed Thucydides by including and using documents in similar ways or for similar reasons in their narratives.[76] Historical writing certainly never became documentary in focus, and I am not suggesting that Thucydides or others conducted systematic searches for documents in the Metroon. But we should not imagine that historians neglected documents entirely, and official, written records may have attracted more attention from one class of writers who emerged in the classical period. Dionysios of Halikarnassos describes certain historians whose goal it was to bring to "common knowledge of all people whatever records and traditions were to be found among the natives of the individual nationalities or states, whether recorded in places sacred or profane."[77] Dionysios is referring to local historians or horographers, who composed histories of individual cities and peoples beginning in the late fifth century. Of interest is Dionysios's statement that these writers utilized written records (*graphai*) when composing their works. Jacoby questioned whether these *graphai* were documentary in nature.[78] His denial, however, derived largely from his desire to disprove the existence of official, preliterate chronicles reaching back to the earliest times, one of which Wilamowitz claimed was the chief source for the local historians of Athens. That chronicles did not exist in the form Wilamowitz believed is undoubtedly true, but Jacoby did not pay equal attention to the existence of other types of state documents, and we cannot dismiss the possibility that Dionysios's *graphai* refer to official documents that local historians sometimes utilized. At Athens alone, the laws of Drakon and Solon survived from the late seventh and sixth centuries into the fifth century, and other records were being published in inscriptions and kept in archives throughout the fifth century. Dionysios may not refer exclusively to public documents, but written records of many types were certainly available when historical writing turned its attention to local history in the late fifth century.[79]

The difficulty with assessing the amount of documentary research, into archives or inscriptions, undertaken by the historians of individual cities stems largely from the fact that their works survive only in fragments. At Athens, the city's history was recorded by several writers known as Atthidographers, whose lost works are called *Atthides* (sing. *Atthis*).[80] The earliest Atthidographer was Hellanikos of Lesbos, active in the late fifth century, but the heyday of Atthidography began in the fourth century, continued into the third, and was represented by such authors as Kleidemos, Androtion, and Philochoros, whose works are now lost. Each Atthidographer seems to have recorded the history of Athens from mythical times, when Athens was ruled by kings, down to his own day, although each differed in the emphasis devoted to different periods. Each also utilized a wide range of sources. The importance of oral traditions for both mythical and historical times cannot be underestimated, but written documents also played a role. This is demonstrated by the dating of some measures by archons and the arrangement of their works in an annalistic framework according to archon years.[81] Jacoby believed that this system went back to Hellanikos, in whose time a copy of the Athenian archon list was published on stone. But only two fragments of Hellanikos actually mention archon dates, both coming from the very end of the fifth century, and this has led some scholars to doubt Hellanikos's use of archon dating for events before the end of the fifth century.[82] The fragments of Hellanikos's work are probably too exiguous to reach a firm decision one way or another, but later *Atthides* did employ an annalistic framework based on archons, and consultation of the archon list by Hellanikos or one of his immediate successors must be assumed.

How far beyond the archon list the Atthidographers searched for or investigated documents, whether old or contemporary, is extremely difficult to establish, given the haphazard survival of their works. The fragments of Hellanikos deal predominantly with the mythical period when Athens was ruled by kings, and the few that are dated to historical times do not point to intensive study of public records. Those of Kleidemos, who wrote in the first half of the fourth century, are similarly slanted toward the mythical period, but Kleidemos did devote two of the four books of his *Atthis* to the fifth century, and one fragment concerns the reform by Kleisthenes of groups called naukraries. What Kleidemos said and how he obtained his information is unknown, but consultation of documents from the time of Kleisthenes cannot be ruled out.[83]

The fragments of Androtion, whose work appeared in the 330s, are more informative. Androtion dealt with the origin of ostracism and named Hipparchos, son of Charmos, as the institution's first victim. The actual text of Androtion is a matter of some controversy as is the date that he gave to the origin of ostracism, but we cannot exclude that he relied on the original law and records of those ostracized.[84] Androtion also discussed the duties of officials known as *kōlakretai*, who were responsible for disbursing state moneys for public business. The *kōlakretai* were no longer in existence in Androtion's time, so his account implies research of some sort. Wilamowitz suggested a law of Solon and this suggestion was accepted by Jacoby.[85] Androtion also credited Kleisthenes with the creation of officials called *apodektai*, the "receivers" of state income, who he seems to say replaced the *kōlakretai*. This is problematic for several reasons, but since we know Androtion's comments only through an intermediary source, it is not impossible that his original account was misunderstood, or that he himself mistook what he found in his source, which may have been documentary.[86] Androtion discussed the revolt of the Samians from the Athenian Empire in the late 440s, and he preserved a list of Athenian generals who served on that campaign; that list is almost universally believed to have derived from authentic documents.[87] He also gave thirty as the number of *syngrapheis* or commissioners who were elected to bring forth proposals on the eve of the oligarchic revolution at Athens in the year 411.[88] That number contradicts the one given by Thucydides but is corroborated by the decree of Pythodoros quoted in Aristotle's account in the *Athēnaiōn Politeia*. The wording of Androtion and Aristotle is not identical, so we cannot be certain that Aristotle drew on Androtion or that Androtion obtained his number of *syngrapheis* from Pythodoros's decree, but nor can the latter possibility be entirely rejected.

From his own time, Androtion also recorded a dispute of the late 350s between Megara and Athens over a piece of sacred land.[89] His account narrated the details of the settlement, named several of the officials involved, and mentioned a decree of Philokrates that played a role in the events. The brevity of the fragment does not admit any definitive conclusions concerning how Androtion came by these details, but reference to a decree indicates that he knew of at least one document related to the incident. Androtion also provided an account of a revision (*diapsēphisis*) of Athens' citizen rolls that occurred in the year 346/5.[90] This fragment too is extremely terse, but Harpokration calls Androtion's treatment of the revision "most complete." We learn from another, late source that the *diapsēphisis* was the result of a decree moved by a certain Demophilos, and although certainty, as always, is impossible, we cannot rule out that Androtion based his account in part on the original decree and was the source of its proposer's name.[91]

That Androtion was familiar with the use of documents to support a position is implied by a decree, whose text is preserved on stone, proposed by him in 347/6. It grants honors to Spartokos, Pairisades, and Apollonios, rulers of the Bosporos, and refers to earlier grants to their father and grandfather, Leukon and Satyros. Androtion moved that the two should receive the same gifts as their ancestors, and that they should receive crowns "in accordance with what was previously decreed for Leukon."[92] The specificity of the reference all but proves that Androtion had consulted this older decree and considered its contents when he made the current motion. He may have consulted a text of the decree in the Metroon, but his proposal for Spartokos and Pairisades also prescribed that it should be published near an inscription that recorded honors for Leukon and Satyros. Since Androtion was aware of this inscription's existence, it seems more likely that his citation of the earlier measures for Leukon and Satyros also depended on a knowledge of that text. But whatever Androtion's source, his citation of older documents indicates an awareness of their existence and that they could be used to support motions currently under consideration. How far the same method carried over into his historical writing cannot be determined, but the inscription's references to earlier decrees at least suggest that Androtion was capable of acquiring information from investigation of older documents.

Later Atthidographers, especially Philochoros, may also have utilized documents in the composition of their works, but a full treatment of their works is here unnecessary. The fragmentary state of the *Atthides* means that their sources are seldom self-evident, but documents seem to lie behind some fragments, and this makes plausible the guess that more were used in portions now lost. How they used documents in framing their narratives proves even more difficult to establish. To judge from Androtion's account of the Megarian-Athenian dispute and several fragments of Philochoros, the Atthidographers supplied the names of the proposers of some decrees and a summary of their contents but did not quote texts at length.[93] Their purpose in doing so may have been simply to provide background information on the events of the particular years with which those documents were associated. Whether they tried to draw further inferences about political events or the policies of individual Athenians cannot be ascertained, but there is no evidence in the surviving fragments that cited documents to provide moral exempla or for patriotic purposes, in a manner similar to that of some fourth-century orators.[94]

State documents were of course available from any number of sources in fourth-century Athens, so that even if one accepts that Kleidemos or Androtion consulted some state documents when writing their histories, it would be rash to argue that these had to come from the Metroon's archives—although this possibility cannot be altogether excluded. More intensive study of official records, however, including ones housed in the Metroon, can be assumed with more confidence for Aristotle and members of his school. Aristotle's works on the dramatic contests at the Lenaia and Dionysia were almost certainly based on written records related to those festivals going back well into the fifth century, and his work on the victors at the Pythian Games at Delphi, put together with his nephew Kallisthenes, illustrates similar research outside of Athens.[95] Among the other projects of Aristotle's school was the collection of laws from several Greek states, the study of which formed the basis of several historical and philosophical works.[96] Aristotle's description of the fourth-century Athenian democracy in the second half of the *Athēnaiōn Politeia* is a good example of their use. The organization of these sections, their numerous references to laws, and comparison of them with the texts of Athenian laws found in other sources all indicate that this part of the work drew on direct consultation of the Athenian law code.[97] It is perhaps conceivable that Aristotle and his students retrieved the texts of laws from a variety of sources: stone stelai, the offices of magistrates, or even private copies of individual measures. But we have no evidence that all Athenian laws were inscribed on stone or that they were readily available in magisterial archives or private collections. The Metroon, on the other hand, is identified by sources contemporary with the *Athēnaiōn Politeia* as the location in which the laws of Athens were kept. Investigation of its archives seems a reasonable enough hypothesis for the source of the analysis of the fourth-century Athenian democracy that encompasses the second half of that work.

Other works emanating from Aristotle's school, all now lost, most probably also drew on the same collection of laws drawn from the Metroon's archives. Theophrastos's *Nomoi* entailed a comparative study of the laws of many Greek states, including ones from Athens. The extant fragments include references to, excerpts from, and discussion of Athenian laws on such topics as *eisangeliai*, *nomothesia*, and ostracism.[98] Demetrios of Phaleron was also the author of a work *On Nomothesia at Athens*, which seems to have given a parallel but more detailed account of the workings of the Athenian constitution than that found in the second half of the *Athēnaiōn Politeia*;[99] it too presumably drew on the texts of laws. Demetrios also published a work entitled *On the Constitutions at Athens*; no identifiable fragments of this work survive, but its title suggests that study of laws may have lain behind its composition.[100]

Decrees were also the subject of study. In the late fourth or early third century, Krateros compiled a work entitled *Collection of Athenian Decrees*, perhaps, as Jacoby noted, as part of the same project for which Athenian laws were collected and used in such works as Aristotle's *Athēnaiōn Politeia*, Theophrastos's *Nomoi*, and Demetrios's works on Athenian legislation.[101] Its form is not entirely clear. The collection appears to have offered complete texts of decrees with a brief commentary, but we do not know how individual decrees were connected. Some of the decrees apparently derived from consultation of inscriptions. One fragment names a certain Andron as the author of the decree condemning the orator Antiphon for his role in the oligarchic coup of 411, and we learn elsewhere that this measure was engraved on a bronze stele. Other fragments mention fifth-century decrees against Arthmios, Diagoras, and Phrynichos, all of which were also displayed on bronze stelai, and the Peace of Kallias, whose text was visible on a stele in the fourth century, was also included in his work.[102] But other fragments deal with matters for which epigraphical texts may not have been available. Several relate to tribute assessments of the allies of Athens' fifth-century empire during the 450s or 440s. The earliest inscriptions recording tribute assessments, however, date from the 420s. Another fragment concerns a fifth-century decree dealing with the *nautodikai* and individuals falsely enrolled in phratries, a type of enactment for which there are no clear parallels in the corpus of fifth-century Athenian inscriptions.[103] We can never be sure that a certain type of document was not published on stone or bronze, but neither can we assume that the fifth-century democracy published all its decrees on either material. Krateros's collection of decrees encompassed at least nine books and spanned the entire fifth century. Inscriptions supplied some of the texts, but the surviving inscriptions on stone will not account for all decrees attested to have been in his collection. His study of archival texts housed in the Metroon, the successor of the fifth-century archives of the Boule, seems very likely.

The large-scale, documentary research underlying this and other works of Aristotle and his followers is unparalleled in earlier historical works, and it is difficult not to associate it with a growing acceptance of the written word that is evident in many areas of Athenian and Greek society over the course of the fourth century. The keeping of a large, centralized body of written records in the Metroon may have facilitated scholarly study of Athenian laws and decrees, and its consultation by litigants and possibly political orators will not have passed unnoticed in other areas, including historical writing. But I would caution against placing too much emphasis on the relatively late date at which writers began to compile and study documents systematically, or drawing the further inference that this development was related to a sudden discovery of archives in the second half of the fourth century.[104] Litigants and politicians were already citing and using laws and decrees in the late fifth century, the period when sources relevant to such practices first appear in large numbers, and although the Metroon is not mentioned by name, some individuals were consulting its archives from the time of its foundation. In historical works, Thucydides' citation of the full texts of treaties shows that documents were not unknown or ignored by historians, and the loss of so many historical works between his time and the late fourth century means that we cannot trace later developments as fully as we would like. Moreover, the more peculiar documentary interests of Aristotle were themselves connected to philosophical and historical developments reaching back into the fifth century. Plato had advocated the comparative study of legislation in his *Laws*, and references in that work suggest that he and his students had already begun to study and even compile Athenian laws before the middle of the fourth century.[105]

Even earlier, some documentary research may have informed the lost works of several writers.[106] Although Hellanikos's consultation of the Athenian archon list for his history of Athens cannot be demonstrated with absolute certainty, he was also the author of a work entitled *Priestesses of Hera at Argos*, which synchronized many events, both mythical and historical, with the priesthoods of individual Argive priestesses. No official records will have existed for the time of the Trojan War, but Hellanikos's work probably went down to the fifth century, when lists of Hera's priestesses at Argos may have been available. Also late in the fifth century, Hippias of Elis compiled a list of Olympic victors based on local records at Olympia. Plutarch criticized the early parts of that list for their unreliability, but we do not know the basis of his criticism.[107] Neither Hippias's nor Hellanikos's work was a systematic collection of documents on the scale of Theophrastos's *Nomoi* or Krateros's *Collection of Decrees*, but they do illustrate attempts to impose order on the past in part through documentary material. When Aristotle and his students turned to Athens' laws and decrees in the latter half of the fourth century, their study was not so much an innovation as the culmination of the growing use of writing that reached back a century or more.

At the same time, Aristotle's research into Athenian records presupposes the existence and availability of a large number of documents and records, some of them of much earlier date and at least some of them archivally preserved. Documentary research into past and present affairs was possible because documents existed, had been used, and were kept for quite some time. This is well illustrated in the second half of the *Athēnaiōn Politeia*. Aristotle not only provides an account of the democracy in his day, but he also compares current laws with obsolete ones on the same subjects. Formerly there had been thirty deme judges who traveled from deme to deme and adjudicated disputes between citizens, but in Aristotle's time these judges were forty, their numbers having been increased after the reign of the Thirty Tyrants.[108] Previously the secretary *kata prytaneian* had been an elected magistrate but in Aristotle's day he was selected by lot.[109] Generals were once elected one from each of the ten Athenian tribes but were now chosen from the entire citizenry.[110] Aristotle's knowledge of every earlier practice need not have arisen from investigation into older laws, but intense, scholarly study of Athenian laws is unattested before his day, and it is difficult to discern what other sources Aristotle could have relied on apart from his own research. Aristotle could carry out such research not because the keeping of documents and archives was a recent phenomenon but because it had been well established in Athens for a much longer period of time.

iv. Conclusion

The Metroon is not mentioned as an archives building until the second half of the fourth century, and its archival functions are attested to explicitly by only a few sources. But neither the relatively late date of these references nor the paucity of their numbers should be construed as evidence against the Metroon's regular use. It goes without saying that Athenians consulted texts in the Metroon primarily when they had some need to do so, but some practices of Athenian society may have made consultation a regular, though not necessary, feature in several areas of public and private life. Texts of laws and decrees are frequently quoted or referred to in the forensic speeches of the Attic orators, and although speakers seldom indicate the sources of the measures they cite, there is no reason to suppose that texts, some of which may not have been available from other sources, were frequently obtained from the Metroon's holdings. The Metroon could also provide texts to be cited in debates on measures coming before the Ekklesia. The evidence for this practice is less abundant, and consultation for this reason may not have been widespread, but inscriptions show that the Athenians did not enact laws and decrees entirely in ignorance of earlier documents on similar subjects, and the Metroon was one possible source for earlier texts. Historical research in the Metroon is nowhere explicitly attested and was certainly practiced by only a few writers, but Greek historical writers did not neglect documents entirely, and Aristotle and his students engaged in systematic study of Athenian laws and decrees, for which the Metroon served as the most accessible source.

We cannot assume, however, that such occasions provide anywhere near a complete picture of the reasons for which Athenians consulted the Metroon's archives or the frequency with which they did so. Other administrative needs may also have required consultation of the city's public records. Aeschines relates how at a meeting at Pella of the Athenian ambassadors who served on the second embassy to Philip, the ambassadors read the decree by which they had been appointed and reviewed what it was they were expected to do; that is, the ambassadors possessed a physical copy of the decree. That their possession of such a text was not unusual for an Athenian official is indicated by the *episkopos* of Aristophanes' *Birds*, who also carried with him a copy of the decree that authorized his appointment or outlined his duties.[111] The business of the Athenian state was routinely conducted by decrees of the Boule and Ekklesia, and it is quite possible that the distribution of decrees to generals, envoys, and other state officials was one of the principal ways in which the Metroon's documents were used. But even private citizens might need texts of state documents. The speaker of the Demosthenic speech *Against Euergos and Mnesiboulos* relates how, when he had been appointed to serve as a trierarch, Theophemos, one of his predecessors, refused to hand over his equipment. The speaker and other trierarchs approached the Boule and obtained a decree authorizing them to recover the equipment as best they could. Eventually, the speaker showed up at Theophemos's house, decree in hand, and demanded back the equipment.[112] Possession of a decree by a private citizen is also depicted in a scene of Aristophanes' *Assemblywomen*. An old woman confronts a young man and demands that he follow her home; when he resists she shows a decree enacted by the women's assembly that required young men to attend to the sexual needs of older women.[113] Aristophanes' purposes are comic, but the possession of the physical text of a decree by a citizen is not unparalleled, as the preceding example shows. Athenians with some frequency may have sought from the Metroon texts of state documents by which they pursued or protected their interests.

Kahrstedt suggested in his brief survey of Athenian archives that the establishment of the Metroon as Athens' archives building at the end of the century brought about a change in rhetorical practice. In the fifth century, orators seldom referred to documents and, when they did, they normally referred only to stelai. In the fourth century, however, documents were cited more frequently but their sources were seldom provided, probably because the Metroon was taken for granted.[114] Thomas, however, has pointed out that stelai continued to be cited into the fourth century, but she too seems to see a sharp divide between fifth- and fourth-century practice in terms of the use of archival documents.[115] The fourth century undoubtedly saw an increase in the use of documents in many areas of Athenian life, and the establishment of the Metroon and the collection of all valid Athenian laws under one roof may have facilitated consultation and thereby brought about an increase in the degree to which Athenians relied on documents in various contexts. But our evidence for the fourth century is far too different in kind from that of the fifth century to know how fifth-century orators dealt with laws and decrees in the lawcourts or before the Ekklesia. Antiphon, Andokides, and Lysias were each cognizant of ways in which laws and decrees could be cited to support a case or manipulated to enhance an argument, and although the sources of the texts they cite are not always transparent, some of them at least are almost certain to have come from the city's archives.

A charge leveled at Nikomachos in Lysias's speech *Against Nikomachos* is instructive. According to the speaker, Nikomachos provided contradictory laws to opposing parties in lawsuits, and he produced the law under which the politician Kleophon was condemned.[116] Nikomachos was one of the *anagrapheis* involved in drawing up the revised law code of the late fifth century when these alleged offenses occurred, and his distribution of copies of laws was probably in connection with his duties as an *anagrapheus*. But the activities that Lysias attributes to Nikomachos, his distribution of documents, need not have been unusual. After the revision of the laws was completed, litigants could have obtained texts of laws from the inscribed code in the Royal Stoa, if it existed, or from individual stelai. But there is little reason to doubt that some Athenians also requested copies of laws from an official by whom copies of all laws were kept. The law of Diokles shows that the secretary of the Boule had supervision over the Athenian law code by the year 403/2, and it is not impossible that Athenians regularly requested texts of laws from him from that time, just as others had sought them from Nikomachos a few years earlier.

This study has focused largely on Athenian record keeping during the classical period, but the history of the Metroon and its archives did not end in the fourth century. The Athenians experienced several constitutional upheavals in the late fourth century, but we do not know if or how these affected the administration of their archives. References to the Metroon are sparse in sources of the last quarter of the fourth century, but there seems little reason to believe that its archives were destroyed or that the deposition of documents ceased. A decree enacted upon the restoration of the democracy in 307/6 calls for the deposition of some type of document, perhaps a state contract for rebuilding the city walls, in the Metroon, and around the same time, another decree awarded Athenian citizenship to a man from Troizen. It too was kept in the Metroon, as we learn from its retrieval a century and a half later.[1] In the early third century, a *dogma* and letter of the Delphic Amphictyony concerning the rights of the *technitai* of Dionysos were deposited in the Metroon, judging from their later retrieval and inscription in the second century.[2] Throughout the third and second centuries, scattered references attest to the submission of accounts and other documents to the Metroon by individual magistrates and special commissions, a practice, however, that almost certainly dates back to the fourth century.[3] The philosopher Epikouros also deposited a special bequest in the Metroon before his death in 270, which may indicate that the Metroon's archives were expanding to include copies of documents of a more private nature. That practice is fairly well attested in other Greek cities during the Hellenistic period, but the unique character of the testimony makes it difficult to assess how frequently the Metroon received other documents similar in nature.[4]

Around the middle of the second century, the building identified as the Metroon, which had originally served as the Athenian council house in the fifth century, was torn down to make way for a larger and more elaborate shrine to the Mother of the Gods; this identification is assured by Pausanias. The new building had four adjacent rooms fronted on the east by an Ionic porch, and it may have possessed a second story, but the building's remains offer no clear clues as to where or how its archives were arranged or stored.[5] Construction, however, seems to have had little impact on the archives themselves or the ability of individuals to find and retrieve texts. For it was in 140/39 that a certain Onasos retrieved the late fourth-century citizenship decree for a remote ancestor of Telesias of Troizen, and it was a decade later that the *technitai* of Dionysos obtained from the Metroon the *dogma* and letter of the Delphic Amphictyons that had granted them special rights and privileges almost a century and a half earlier.[6]

We hear nothing of other consultations of the Metroon's archives by historians or ancient scholars during the Hellenistic period, but in the early first century, some evidence suggests that its documents did attract antiquarian interest, to their detriment. Athenaios, citing Poseidonios, relates that the Apellikon of Teos, better known for his purchase of the library of Aristotle and Theophrastos, surreptitiously made off with the original copies of the decrees housed in the Metroon.[7] How Apellikon achieved this feat is not indicated, but his association with Athens merits brief comment. Apellikon's theft is placed shortly before his association with the Athenian tyrant Athenion, under whose leadership the Athenians joined Mithridates in his war against Rome in 88, and Apellikon himself served as general in that war. In 86, the Athenians paid the price for their defiance of the Romans, and the city fell to Sulla, whose troops sacked the city. A connection may be suggested: although no damage to the Metroon is reported and none is indicated in the archaeological remains, the building's archives may have fallen a victim to the ravages of Sulla's troops, while blame later fell more conveniently on Apellikon.[8] Whatever the case, the alleged theft of the Metroon's decrees may suggest that its archives were depleted during the first century B.C.

But these events did not bring an end to the Metroon's use as an archives building. In A.D. 61/2, we have evidence for the deposition of a list of ephebes in the Metroon, and in the following century, Favorinus saw a document purporting to be the indictment brought against Socrates by his accusers.[9] The authenticity of that text is uncertain, and its presence in the Metroon in the second century after Christ may suggest that the building's character had changed from a working archives to a museum-like structure where old texts of antiquarian interest were displayed. The final blow, however, came with the Herulian sack of Athens in A.D. 267. The Metroon was among the buildings destroyed in the Herulian raid, and parts of it were found in the post-Herulian wall; it was not rebuilt in the same form, and later building activity shows no sign of continuity. When Julian refers to the Metroon in the fourth century A.D. its archival character was a thing of the past.[10]

From the first mention of the Metroon as an archive in 343 B.C. to Favorinus's reference to the indictment against Socrates in the second century of our era, the Metroon enjoyed a history of five hundred years as a repository for state documents. But the tradition of keeping written records of public business began much earlier than the Metroon's first attestation and reached back to the legislation of Drakon and Solon. With their acceptance of the written laws of these two lawgivers, the Athenians decided that some of the rules that governed the life of their community required preservation in writing. We do not see these early laws in operation, but we have no reason for doubting that Athenian magistrates and citizens used them in the administration of their legal and to some extent political institutions. The mention of officials called secretaries in inscriptions of the middle of the sixth century shows that by that time, if not before, the public functions of writing had expanded into other areas. Our sources for such uses are sparse and generally uninformative, and there is no reason to assume that written documents were a feature of every aspect of public life or used by all magistrates. But the use of writing by Athenian magistrates marks a departure from the earlier, limited use of writing to record and preserve the texts of laws, and it illustrates the recognition that writing could be used to preserve evidence of an official's conduct while in office.

Developments of the late sixth century were especially significant. From the end of that century we have some evidence suggesting the use of writing in the administration of the City Dionysia. But documents were not only used, they were also preserved, and records of the City Dionysia from the late sixth and early fifth centuries survived long enough to be inscribed on stone after the middle of the fourth century. Permanence together with ephemerality characterized the archives of some state officials, and this invites speculation about the long-term preservation of other types of written records, especially ones made of decisions of the Ekklesia. The laws of Drakon and Solon had been set down in writing in the late seventh and early sixth century, and although questions persist about their survival, there are good reasons for believing that they were available for study as late as the fourth century. We know too little about the Ekklesia during the sixth century and the procedures by which it enacted legislation to know how often it enacted new measures or kept similar written records of its decisions, but evidence from the late sixth century suggests both increased legislative activity and the preservation of some measures in writing. Especially significant is an inscription of the late fifth century that preserves the text of an oath, possibly the one first sworn by the new Boule of Kleisthenes in the final years of the sixth century, and a series of provisions concerning the relative powers of the Boule and the Ekklesia, which also date back to the late sixth and early fifth centuries.[11] In what form these were preserved before their publication on stone is unknown. The survival of records from the City Dionysia from the same period indicates that some magistrates were keeping archives of activities they oversaw, and this allows the suggestion that the Bouleutic Oath and other measures about the Boule were preserved in a similar type of archive. The Boule itself is the most likely body to have kept such records. But the Boule functioned primarily as a standing committee of the Ekklesia, so its archives should also have included records of that body as well. The Boule's archives, therefore, were the state's archives, preserving records of its central decision-making body.

Scholars have sometimes argued that the Athenians did not maintain archives during the fifth century, and that the primary documents of the Athenian state were those inscribed on stone. But the practice of publishing documents on stone may have been exceptional, and it was certainly a late development at Athens. The use of other materials for recording and preserving public records, on the other hand, enjoyed a more ancient heritage. The laws of Drakon and Solon had been recorded on wooden tablets, and state documents begin to appear on stone stelai in large numbers only around the middle of the fifth century, long after the Athenians had begun to use writing in public affairs. The inscribed decrees that do survive are disproportionately concerned with sacred business, honorary grants, and the administration of Athens' overseas empire, and their contents suggest that publication on stone was originally limited to documents of certain types. Laws and decrees dealing with nonsacred, internal matters certainly were written down by the secretary of the Boule, who kept records of business conducted at meetings of the Boule and Ekklesia. But the secretary did not publish all his records on stone, and future studies of ancient literacy and writing must come to terms with the fact that even as early as the fifth century most Athenian documents were recorded and preserved not on stone stelai but on less durable materials that were housed in some type of archives.

The number of records kept by the secretary of the Boule in the Boule's archives was undoubtedly small in the opening years of the fifth century, but it began to grow significantly as the amount of business handled by the Boule and Ekklesia increased, first, because of Athens' leading role in the Delian League and, second, as a result of the democratic reforms carried by Ephialtes. Decrees of the Boule and Ekklesia formed the bulk of these archives, but the Boule's supervisory duties over tribute payment, the Athenian navy, and the Eleusinian Mysteries may have dictated that it receive records related to these areas. We do not know how the Boule's archives were organized, but there is some evidence that archival documents were dated more precisely than their stone counterparts, and an arrangement under individual secretaries and in annual groups would not be unparalleled. By the late fifth century, the number of records had increased to such an extent that the archives required their own building; this structure came to be known as the Metroon, the sanctuary of the Mother of the Gods, by the early fourth century. At the same time, the great mass of legislation also led the Athenians to reorganize their laws, not all of which were found in the state archives of the Boule. It is no longer certain that the Athenians publicly displayed the revised code on stone when the revision and reorganization was completed, but there can be little doubt that the city's laws were deposited in the archives of the Boule, now housed in the Metroon, where they formed a separate and distinct part of its holdings.

Some scholars also posit a sharp change in Athenian and Greek attitudes toward writing around the end of the fifth century, and they count the establishment of the Metroon as one sign of these changes. Development there certainly was, but attitudes did not change overnight, and as far as Athenian documents and records are concerned, practices evolved over a long period of time and in a more gradual process that extended back well into the sixth century: the Athenians did not suddenly become "document-minded" in the fourth century. The Metroon itself probably functioned along similar lines as the Boule's archives had in the fifth century. Although laws and decrees were enacted by separate bodies during the fourth century, both continued to be preserved, as they had in the fifth century. Other types of documents made their way into the Metroon, from *pōlētai* contracts, accounts of magistrates, and letters sent by Athenian generals. The deposition of some of these may reflect fourth-century innovations, so that the Metroon came to serve as a sort of central archive for many of Athens' public records. But our sources for fifth-century practices are too inadequate to exclude the submission of many of the same types of documents to the Boule already in the fifth century, so changes in practice should not be overestimated. At the same time, not all Athenian public records were housed in the Metroon. Athenian magistrates continued to keep their own records of business they oversaw, and although copies of some of these may have been transferred to the Metroon, not all were, and the Metroon's character as a central archive was limited.

What mostly distinguished the archives found in the fourth-century Metroon from those of Boule in the fifth century was probably the volume of records that it received. Nearly five hundred inscribed decrees survive from the fourth century, while those of the fifth century come to less than half that amount. The increase in numbers should indicate not only that the Athenians were inscribing more decrees on stone but also that they were enacting more decrees in general, and any increase in the number of decrees produced will have increased the amount of records making their way into the Metroon. In addition, some magistrates had started to use writing in ways their predecessors had not. Thucydides portrays the general Nikias's decision to write a letter to the Athenians as an unusual undertaking; by the fourth century, generals and others were writing to the Boule and Athenians with greater frequency.[12] As such correspondence reached the Boule and Ekklesia, records were kept as part of the routine record keeping of the Boule's and Ekklesia's business. Writing was being used more widely in the fourth century, and this had an effect on the city's archives. But the preservation and upkeep of archival records, not published on stone, was not an innovation of the fourth century.

The Athenians addressed the growing volume of records by reforming the position of their chief state secretary and by assigning more specialized tasks to his assistants. We do not know how well or poorly these changes affected the arrangement and organization of the archives themselves. Some organization there was, though we catch only fleeting glimpses of it. It would be easy to exaggerate the efficiency of the archives by reconstructing a theoretically neat, orderly, and organized system. Certainly, not every document that should have been kept was so preserved; not every document that was preserved was put in its proper place. Records were undoubtedly lost and misfiled, or sometimes never reached their proper place. Modern archival establishments suffer from damage by fire, water, vermin, and pests. Although we do not hear of such nuisances, Athens' public records were hardly less susceptible to such dangers than their modern counterparts, and undoubtedly more so. Mantitheos suggests in a speech of Lysias that some records from the time of the Thirty had been subject to manipulation and fraud, and although these were not kept by the Boule, its own archives conceivably could have fallen victim to similar abuse, although Lykourgos portrays tampering with a text of a law in the Metroon as an offense worthy of death.[13] Moreover, in a system that was run essentially by nonprofessionals and whose supervising official rotated out of office ten times a year, inefficiency, oversight, and some degree of confusion are to be expected. The prescripts of inscribed decrees suggest that secretaries enjoyed some freedom in deciding what details they chose to include in the texts they had inscribed on stone; they may have exercised a similar freedom when they recorded the minutes of the meetings they attended. But the evidence also indicates that the prescripts of decrees do not tell the full story. The archives contained more detailed information, and we cannot take the omissions and inconsistencies of inscriptions as fully indicative of archival practice. It is perhaps significant that, although we have over a hundred speeches composed for delivery in Athenian courtrooms in which laws and decrees are frequently read out, we never hear of problems finding or locating documents, inscribed, archival, or otherwise.

Any inefficiencies or failings that we may feel compelled to hypothesize must be balanced with recognition of an equally important characteristic of Athenian record keeping and archival practice. The Athenians routinely preserved old records, especially of laws and decrees, even after their contents had become obsolete. This, however, has not always been the view of all scholars. Hignett, writing about the sources available to the fourth-century Atthidographers, questioned whether much documentary material was available to them from the earliest times. He believed that the Athenians were not in the habit of keeping the texts of old and obsolete laws, and that it was difficult if not impossible for the Atthidographers to differentiate between earlier and later enactments.[14] More recently, the work of Thomas on the complex interaction of literacy and orality in Athens and ancient Greece has held that the making and keeping of records was haphazard and unsystematic. Many documents were destroyed as soon as they had outlived their usefulness, while those that were kept were simply not used.[15]

The ancient evidence fails to sustain these negative conclusions. Certainly, some types of documents were erased or destroyed as soon as their usefulness had expired; this practice is evident above all in the *pōlētai* documents to whose recording, filing, and erasing Aristotle devotes considerable attention. But it is a characteristic even of modern archives to preserve only those records with enduring value (and even then often without success); it is unreasonable to expect more of the ancient Athenians. The *pōlētai* and other ephemeral documents are hardly representative of all Athenian records, and the preservation of laws and decrees was far more regular than an analogy based on *pōlētai* documents suggests. Skeptics will remain, but the laws of Drakon and Solon seem to have been preserved substantially intact for centuries, while an archon list was being kept up probably from the early seventh century. Inscriptions of the fourth and third centuries show that extremely detailed but uninscribed records, dating back to at least circa 500, were made and preserved of performances at the City Dionysia.[16] The Methone Decrees of the 430s and 420s illustrate that although decrees upon enactment were not automatically inscribed on stone, their texts were preserved in the Boule's archives whence they could be summoned at a later time.[17] Around 410 Andokides emphasized that a decree granting him immunity was still preserved, though its provisions had been nullified.[18] Indeed, the late fifth-century revision of the Athenian law code is comprehensible only on the assumption that texts of old measures were routinely kept and preserved in spite of their revocation by later enactments.

But it was not only types of documents that possessed a clear degree of permanent validity, such as laws, treaties, and alliances, that the Athenians preserved. The speaker of Lysias 13 cites several decrees of the Boule that had called for specific, immediate action but whose texts were still available several years after those actions were completed. He does not cite his source for these decrees, but the Metroon is a reasonable suggestion. Aeschines and Demosthenes similarly cite decrees of the Boule ordering the departure of embassies in their speeches *On the False Embassy*.[19] Those decrees too were purely ephemeral enactments with no enduring value once their instructions had been fulfilled. Still, their texts were kept in the belief, perhaps, that business conducted by the Boule and Ekklesia required preservation in writing in order to have evidence of past decisions of the people and a means by which to assess the conduct of state officials. Such preservation does not mean we can trust every Athenian document referred to, cited, or quoted in an ancient source as authentic. Nor does it guarantee that the Athenians succeeded in maintaining a text of every item of business ratified by the Boule and Ekklesia. But it is the task of the historian to recognize not only defects and inconsistencies but also general rules and practices. When in 343 Aeschines reminds his audience of dikasts that they, the Athenian people, kept records of decrees and other public business "for all time" he does not describe a new, innovative, or isolated practice. He calls attention to a custom well recognized for centuries.[20]

In the following notes, works of Greek and Latin authors are generally cited according to the abbreviations found in the *Oxford Classical Dictionary* (2nd ed.), though some works are called by their English titles (e.g., Aristophanes' *Clouds*). References to modern works are given by their author's last name and an abbreviated form of the title. Full citations will be found in the bibliography that follows the notes. Attention should also be paid to the following special abbreviations appearing in the notes.

Agora, 14	H. A. Thompson and R. E. Wycherley. *The Athenian Agora*. Vol. 14, *The Agora of Athens*. Princeton, 1972.
Agora, 15	B. D. Meritt and J. S. Traill. *The Athenian Agora*. Vol. 15, *Inscriptions: The Councillors*. Princeton, 1974.
Agora, 19	G. V. Lalonde, M. K. Langdon, and M. B. Walbank. *The Athenian Agora*. Vol. 19, *Inscriptions: Horoi, Poletai Records, Leases of Public Lands*. Princeton, 1991.
ATL	B. D. Meritt, H. T. Wade-Gery, and M. F. McGregor. *The Athenian Tribute Lists*. 4 vols. Cambridge, Mass., 1939–53.
Bonner-Smith	R. J. Bonner and G. Smith. *The Administration of Justice from Homer to Aristotle*. 2 vols. Chicago, 1930–38.
Busolt-Swoboda	G. Busolt and H. Swoboda. *Griechische Staatskunde*. 2 vols. Handbuch der Altertumswissenschaft, no. 4.1.1. Munich, 1920–26.
FGrHist	F. Jacoby. *Die Fragmente der griechischen Historiker*. 3 parts in 15 vols. Berlin and Leiden, 1923–58.
GG	*Griechische Geschichte*.
Harrison, *LA*	A. R. W. Harrison. *The Law of Athens*. 2 vols. Oxford, 1968–71.
HCT	A. W. Gomme, A. Andrewes, and K. J. Dover. *A Historical Commentary on Thucydides*. 5 vols. Oxford, 1945–81.
Hignett, *HAC*	C. Hignett. *A History of the Athenian Constitution to the End of the Fifth Century B.C.* Oxford, 1952.
IG	*Inscriptiones Graecae*.
IPriene	F. Hiller von Gaertingen, ed. *Inschriften von Priene*. Berlin, 1906.
Jeffery, *LSAG*	L. H. Jeffery. *The Local Scripts of Archaic Greece*. Rev. ed. with supplement by A. Johnston. Oxford, 1990.
Lipsius, *AR*	J. H. Lipsius. *Das attische Recht und Rechtsverfahren*. 3 vols. Leipzig, 1905–15.
LSJ	H. G. Liddell and R. Scott. *A Greek-English Lexicon*. 9th ed., revised by H. Stuart Jones and R. McKenzie. Oxford, 1940.

MacDowell, *LCA* D. M. MacDowell. *The Law in Classical Athens*. Ithaca, 1978.

Meiggs-Lewis R. Meiggs and D. M. Lewis. *A Selection of Greek Historical In-scriptions to the End of the Fifth Century BC*. Rev. ed. Oxford, 1988.

Rhodes, *CAAP* P. J. Rhodes. *A Commentary on the Aristotelian Athenaion Po-liteia*. Oxford, 1981.

Ruschenbusch, E. Ruschenbusch. ΣΟΛΟΝΟΣ ΝΟΜΟΙ. *Die Fragmente des Solo-*
SN *nischen Gesetzeswerkes mit einer Text- und Überlieferungs-geschichte*. Historia Einzelschriften 9. Wiesbaden, 1966.

SEG *Supplementum Epigraphicum Graecum.*

SIG W. Dittenberger. *Sylloge inscriptionum Graecarum*. 3rd ed. Leipzig, 1915–24.

Tod M. Tod. *A Selection of Greek Historical Inscriptions*. 2 vols. Ox-ford, 1948.

Wycherley R. E. Wycherley. *The Athenian Agora*. Vol. 3, *Literary and Epi-graphical Testimonia*. Princeton, 1957.

Introduction

1. Aeschin. 3.75. All dates are B.C. unless otherwise noted.

2. Modern scholarship dealing with Athenian documents and record keeping is scattered among works on diverse topics and is too voluminous to be reviewed in detail here. Important contributions on individual topics will be discussed in the text and notes.

3. See Posner, *Archives*, pp. 1–11, esp. 4–6; cf. also Thomas, *Oral Tradition*, p. 73, and *Literacy*, pp. 132–36, where the dangers of anachronism are emphasized, though perhaps excessively.

4. For discussion of modern archives and a definition, see Bradsher, "Introduc-tion," pp. 3–4.

5. So, e.g., the records of federal agencies in the United States become archival only when they are received by the National Archives, but in France, records are consid-ered archives from the moment they are created or received: see Bradsher, "Introduc-tion," pp. 3–4; Posner, *Archives*, pp. 4–5.

Chapter One

1. For a survey of early Attic texts, see Immerwahr, *Attic Script*, pp. 7–19; see also Jeffery, *LSAG*, pp. 66–78. Sacred laws concerning the Mysteries: *IG* I³ 231, 232; Salamis decree: *IG* I³ 1. All three inscriptions are dated to the late sixth century. A fourth sixth-century inscription, *IG* I³ 230, is also labeled a *lex sacra*, but its text is too fragmentary to define its contents more precisely.

2. For the appearance of topoi in literary traditions about Greek lawgivers, see Szegedy-Maszak, "Legends of the Greek Law-Givers"; Hölkeskamp, "Written Law in Archaic Greece," pp. 87–89; the creation of first "inventors" is the subject of Keingün-ther, *Protos Euretes*. References to Solonian laws in the fourth-century orators are discussed by Hansen, "Solonian Democracy"; cf. also Schreiner, *De Corpore Iuris*, pp. 12–60; Hignett, *HAC*, pp. 17–27.

3. The classic exposition of this view remains that of Hignett, *HAC*, pp. 12–27;

similar skepticism informs the work of R. Sealey: see esp. *Athenian Republic*, pp. 115–19, 140–45.

4. For this view applied to the legislation of Drakon and Solon, see Robb, *Literacy and Paideia*, pp. 125–56, esp. 126–34. An evolutionary model for the development of written law in ancient Greece is advocated especially by Hölkeskamp, "Written Law in Archaic Greece," and Thomas, "Written in Stone?"; see also Sealey, *Justice*, pp. 25–58. Both Hölkeskamp and Thomas, however, seem to me to exaggerate the degree to which ancient writers and modern scholars attribute "comprehensive" codes, covering every conceivable situation, to early Greek lawgivers, and neither treats the lawgiving of Solon in any detail. Hölkeskamp elsewhere ("Arbitrators, Lawgivers and the 'Codification of Law,'" pp. 56–57) declares that Solon's legislation must be considered exceptional. No justification for this assessment is offered.

5. *Ath. Pol.* 3.4: ὅπως ἀναγράψαντες τὰ θέσμια φυλάττωσι πρὸς τὴν τῶν ἀμφι[σ]βητο[ύ]ντων κρίσιν. I call Aristotle the author of the *Athēnaiōn Politeia* throughout this study, although I recognize that authorship probably involved collaboration with others. See Keaney, *Composition of Aristotle's Athenaion Politeia*, pp. 3–19.

6. Gagarin, "Thesmothetai," p. 71; Gagarin, *Early Greek Law*, pp. 55–56; Stroud, "State Documents," p. 20. So Gomme, *CR* 40 (1926): 161; Bonner-Smith, 1:85–88; Ostwald, *Nomos*, pp. 174–75. On the duties of the thesmothetai in the fourth century, see *Ath. Pol.* 59.1–6, and Lipsius, *AR*, pp. 68–74; Harrison, *LA*, 2:12–17; and MacDowell, *LCA*, pp. 25–27.

7. The date at which the archonship became an annual office is discussed by Jacoby, *Atthis*, pp. 169–76, and Cadoux, "Athenian Archons," p. 79. On the date of the legislation of Drakon, see Stroud, *Drakon's Law*, pp. 66–70.

8. See the works cited in n. 6.

9. See Ostwald, *Nomos*, pp. 12–19, for discussion of the terms *thesmos* and *thesmion*; also Quass, *Nomos und Psephisma*, pp. 11–14; Hirzel, *Themis*, pp. 320–58.

10. That is, thesmothetai should be "those who make laws." That Aristotle's account of them is based on inference and etymology is suggested by Rhodes, *CAAP*, pp. 102–3; Chambers, *Staat*, pp. 151–52; Sealey, *Justice*, p. 29. See also Hignett, *HAC*, pp. 76–77; Ledl, *Studien*, pp. 269–72. Humphreys, "Evolution of Legal Process," pp. 233–35, suggests that the first thesmothetai were assessors to the three chief archons; the view is attractive but is not supported by their title or other ancient testimony.

11. *Ath. Pol.* 41.2: μετὰ δὲ ταύτην ἡ ἐπὶ Δράκοντος, ἐν ᾗ καὶ νόμους ἀνέγραψαν πρῶτον.

12. For discussion of the problem, see Rhodes, *CAAP*, pp. 84–88, 485; Chambers, *Staat*, pp. 324–26.

13. Apart from *Ath. Pol.* 41.2 only Aulus Gellius (*NA* 11.18.3: *is Draco leges, quibus Athenienses uterentur, primus tulit*) makes Drakon the first to write down laws.

14. *Ath. Pol.* 16.10: νόμος γὰρ αὐτοῖς ὅδε· θέσμια τάδε Ἀθηναίων ἐστὶ καὶ πάτρια· ἐάν τινες {τυραννεῖν} ἐπανιστῶνται ἐπὶ τυραννίδι ἢ συγκαθιστῇ τὴν τυραννίδα, ἄτιμον εἶναι καὶ αὐτὸν καὶ γένος. Textual problems are summarized by Rhodes, *CAAP*, pp. 220–23; also Carawan, "Tyranny and Outlawry," pp. 305–20.

15. The preface also uses the plural pronoun τάδε, "the following," in reference to *thesmia*. This too could point to the existence of more than a single provision or a provision of greater length: see Gagarin, "Thesmothetai," p. 72 n. 7.

16. Ostwald, "Athenian Legislation against Tyranny," pp. 106–9; Gagarin, "Thes-

mothetai," pp. 72–77. J. K. Davies (CR 23 [1973]: 225–26) suggested that the tyranny law could have been enacted on several other occasions but was probably reenacted in the fifth century, when the term *patria* was current; but see the comments of Rhodes, *CAAP*, pp. 222–23.

17. *IG* I³ 7. The decree is found at lines 1–9, followed by an oracle of Apollo (lines 10–12). For further discussion, see Ostwald, *Popular Sovereignty*, pp. 144–46.

18. Stroud, "State Documents," p. 22, suggested that a law of Drakon or Solon could have included a provision calling for the thesmothetai to continue publishing their *thesmia*. But Stroud also took *thesmia* to mean "judicial decisions," a meaning which is otherwise unattested, and we do not hear of the thesmothetai keeping records of judicial decisions in later times, although we might expect to find such a reference if a law of Solon had given them this right or duty. An alternative possibility is that a law, of Drakon or Solon or of later date, reaffirmed *thesmia* that the thesmothetai had published and used before.

19. Thomas, "Written in Stone?," pp. 26–27, offers the attractive suggestion that some early laws were inscribed on stone to fix types of enactments not universally recognized. We cannot know what materials the putative *thesmia* of the thesmothetai were written on, but Thomas's suggestion could apply just as well to laws displayed on wood or some other material.

20. Sealey, *Justice*, p. 50, believes that Solon incorporated earlier written laws into his legislation.

21. For the date of Aristaichmos's archonship, see Stroud, *Drakon's Law*, pp. 66–71; Cadoux, "Athenian Archons," p. 92. For Drakon's laws on homicide: *IG* I³ 104 (discussed further in the text); Andok. 1.81, 83; Dem. 23.22–60, 47.73; on theft: Xen., *Oik.* 14.4; Gel. *NA* 11.18.3; Plut. *Sol.* 17; on idleness: Lys. fr. 17 Thalheim; *Lex Rhet. Cantab.* 665.19, s.v. ἀργίας δίκη; Diog. L. 1.55; on sacrilege: Plut. *Sol.* 17. For discussion of the nonhomicide laws attributed to Drakon, see Stroud, *Drakon's Law*, pp. 75–83. On the severity of Drakon's laws, see Arist. *Rhet.* 1400b20–23; Arist. *Pol.* 1274b16; Lyk. 1.65; Plut. *Sol.* 17. Repeal of the nonhomicide laws by Solon is mentioned at *Ath. Pol.* 7.1; see also Plut. *Sol.* 17. On the conservative nature of Athenian homicide law, see Antiph. 5.14 (= 6.2); Dem. 20.158; 23.51, 66; 24.210.

22. Sealey, *Athenian Republic*, pp. 115–16 (see also *Justice*, p. 43). The view that the name Drakon referred to a sacred snake was first suggested by Beloch, *GG*, 1.2:358–62.

23. For discussion of Kylon's failed coup, see Rhodes, *CAAP*, pp. 79–84; Andrewes, "Growth of the Athenian State," pp. 368–70; also Busolt, *GG*, 2:223–24; Stroud, *Drakon's Law*, pp. 70–74; Gagarin, *Drakon*, pp. 20–21.

24. Gagarin, *Early Greek Law*, pp. 58–59.

25. On the position of Drakon, see Stroud, *Drakon's Law*, pp. 74–75. For his possible service as a *thesmothetēs*, see Paus. 9.36.8 (Δράκοντος Ἀθηναίοις θεσμοθετήσαντος); this may mean simply that he issued *thesmoi*: see Rhodes, *CAAP*, p. 112.

26. For discussion of the "Drakonian Constitution" and references to earlier bibliography, see Rhodes, *CAAP*, pp. 84–88; Chambers, *Staat*, pp. 154–55.

27. Stroud, *Drakon's Law*, p. 81 n. 63, calls the ascription "of dubious value."

28. Diog. L. 1.55; *Lex. Rhet. Cantab.* 665.19, s.v. ἀργίας δίκη. Herodotus (2.177.2) mentions a similar law and says that Solon had copied it from Amasis and the Egyptians. Plutarch (*Sol.* 31.2) cites Theophrastos against Solonian authorship and in favor of Peisistratos. For a recent discussion of the measure, see Wallace, *Areopagos*, pp. 62–64.

29. Poll. 9.61 mentions a fine of twenty oxen; for the tradition that death was the offense for all crimes, see Prodikos ap. Arist. *Rhet.* 1400b19–23; Arist. *Pol.* 1274b15–18; Demades ap. Pl. *Sol.* 17.3.

30. Antiph. 5.14 (= 6.2); see, however, the qualification of Gagarin, *Drakon*, pp. 22–23.

31. For the text, translation, and epigraphical commentary, see Stroud, *Drakon's Law*, pp. 1–19; Gagarin, *Drakon*, pp. xiv–xvii.

32. This meaning was first suggested by Wolff, "Origin of Judicial Litigation," pp. 71–78; see also Stroud, *Drakon's Law*, p. 44; Gagarin, *Drakon*, pp. 47–48.

33. For Solon's use of the term *thesmos* to describe his laws, see Solon fr. 36 West, lines 18–20. On border markets, see Stroud, *Drakon's Law*, pp. 63–64.

34. Stroud, *Drakon's Law*, pp. 31–32. On the rubrics used by the *anagrapheis* in their revised calendar of sacrifices, see Dow, "Law Codes"; on rubrics in Athenian inscriptions in general, see Sickinger, "Inscriptions and Archives," pp. 290–92.

35. The first *axon* of Solon included a measure prohibiting export of certain agricultural products (Plut. *Sol.* 24.1 = fr. 65 Ruschenbusch), and there is no room for this law in the inscribed copy of Drakon's law: see Stroud, *Drakon's Law*, pp. 31–34. Figueira, "Draco," p. 292, cites Stroud for the view that these rubrics show that the law "belonged either to Solon's law code or to a later redaction claiming Solonian authority." That is not my reading of Stroud's conclusions.

36. So Stroud, *Drakon's Law*, p. 31.

37. For the calculations, see ibid., pp. 58–60. Ruschenbusch, *SN*, p. 25, working without knowledge of the heading "Second Axon" on the inscription, reached a slightly lower estimate for the size of an individual Solonian *axon*.

38. For doubts about the inscribed law's authenticity, see Hignett, *HAC*, pp. 308–11; Sealey, *Athenian Republic*, pp. 115–16; MacDowell, *LCA*, pp. 42–43; Figueira, "Draco," pp. 291–95. Todd, *Shape of Athenian Law*, p. 33 n. 6, suggests that the inscribed text of Drakon's law is "evidence only for what Athenians in 409/8 made of Drakon."

39. According to Humphreys, "Historical Approach," p. 36, later regulations on homicide are likely to have been added to Drakon's *axones* in the late seventh and sixth centuries. But she does not cite any evidence for such additions or suggest particular occasions when they might have occurred.

40. *IG* II² 140. See also my discussion of the law in Chapter 6, Section II.

41. For the attribution, see Dem. 23.51: ὁ μὲν νόμος ἐστὶν οὗτος Δράκοντος, ὦ ἄνδρες Ἀθηναῖοι, καὶ οἱ ἄλλοι δὲ ὅσους ἐκ τῶν φονικῶν νόμων παρεγραψάμην.

42. For these and other non-Drakontian features of the law cited by Demosthenes, see Stroud, *Drakon's Law*, pp. 54–56; see also Gagarin, *Drakon*, pp. 22–26. Solon's creation of the Heliaia is attested at Arist. *Pol.* 1273b35–1274a5; see Hansen, "The Athenian Heliaia," pp. 27–39, for discussion of this tradition. On the right of prosecution by "anyone who wishes," see *Ath. Pol.* 9.1, with Ruschenbusch, *Untersuchungen*, pp. 47–53.

43. Stroud, *Drakon's Law*, pp. 54–56; see also Gagarin, *Drakon*, p. 61.

44. So Stroud, *Drakon's Law*, 54–56. *Pace* Stroud, however, the homicide law cited by Demosthenes shows only that this one provision was changed by modification and supplementation. It does not preclude the wholesale replacement of other provisions that originally stood in Drakon's laws.

45. This or a similar view has been propounded by Busolt, *GG*, 2:139 n. 1; Lipsius,

AR, p. 125; Latte, "Mord," col. 281; Latte, "Φονικά," col. 526; Ruschenbusch, "ΦΟΝΟΣ," pp. 130–31, 145; Rhodes, *CAAP*, pp. 112–23. See most recently Wallace, *Areopagos*, pp. 17–19.

46. For a survey of alternative views, see Gagarin, *Drakon*, pp. 64–79.

47. Ibid., pp. 96–110.

48. For a summary of these and other objections to Gagarin's hypothesis, see Wallace, *Areopagos*, pp. 16–19, with references to earlier reviews of Gagarin's work.

49. Stroud, *Drakon's Law*, pp. 34–40.

50. Rhodes, *CAAP*, p. 131, refers to the later Athenian practice of destroying the documents when they became obsolete, and he therefore doubts that obsolete laws of Drakon could have survived for hundreds of years. But the evidence he cites may not be representative; see my discussions of the question in Chapters 3 and 6.

51. This, I take it, is the process envisioned by MacDowell, *LCA*, pp. 42–43, and Humphreys, "Historical Approach," p. 36.

52. Hignett, *HAC*, pp. 307–8, mentions this possibility only to reject it, but his reasoning puts too much reliance on the fourth-century ascription of all homicide legislation to Drakon.

53. The chief difficulty with Plutarch's collection of Drakontian laws, as Plutarch himself saw, was that its omission of Areopagites was contradicted by Solon's amnesty law, which referred to individuals condemned by the Areopagos. The contradiction is removed, however, if the Areopagos previously tried only cases of attempted tyranny and not homicide (so Ruschenbusch, "ΦΟΝΟΣ," pp. 132–35), or if the *ephetai* heard homicide cases on the Areopagos (Wallace, *Areopagos*, pp. 7–28) or were themselves chosen from the Areopagos (MacDowell, *Athenian Homicide Law*, pp. 52–56).

54. The *basileis* of Drakon's law (*IG* I³ 104, line 12) are usually identified with the king archon and the tribal kings of the four old Attic tribes, though Sealey, *Justice*, pp. 116–19, makes them private but powerful men in the community. On the law's retroactive clause (*IG* I³ 104, lines 19–20), see Stroud, *Drakon's Law*, pp. 50–51.

55. For discussions of Solon and his reforms, see the older discussions of Busolt, *GG*, 2:254–95, and Linforth, *Solon the Athenian*, 3–102, and, more recently, Rhodes, *CAAP*, pp. 118–20; Andrewes, "Growth of the Athenian State," pp. 375–91; Murray, *Early Greece*, pp. 181–200; Osborne, *Greece in the Making*, pp. 220–25. I have accepted dating of Solon's economic and legislative activity to his archonship, although this connection is not crucial to the extent or preservation of his laws, which are my central concern. The strongest alternative to this, the traditional view, is that proposed by Hammond, "Chronological Basis," pp. 145–69. Working from apparent chronological distinctions between Solon's *seisachtheia* and *nomothesia* in Plutarch and the *Ath. Pol.*, he sets the *seisachtheia* and other economic reforms in Solon's archonship, and the legislation in 592/1, a date that finds some support from the dating of Peisistratos's first attempt at tyranny at *Ath. Pol.* 14.1. Chambers, *Staat*, pp. 161–62, revives the view of Hignett (*HAC*, pp. 316–21), and separates Solon's archonship from his legislative activity, putting the latter in the 570s. For a recent, thorough defense of the traditional view, see Wallace, "Date of Solon's Reforms," pp. 81–95. The date of Solon's legislation should not affect its survival or organization.

56. On the problems of reconstructing Solon's work from these traditions, see, in addition to the works cited in the previous note, Chambers, *Staat*, pp. 159–60; Rhodes, *CAAP*, pp. 118–20. On topoi in traditions about Greek lawgivers, see Szegedy-Maszak, "Legends of the Greek Law-Givers." For the false attribution of

constitutional laws to Solon, see Hansen, "Solonian Democracy," pp. 71–99, esp. 82–87, who draws on Schreiner, *De Corpore Iuris*, pp. 12–60, for the view that by "laws of Solon" fourth-century orators meant only the revised law code of the late fifth century. On fourth-century *nomothesia*, see MacDowell, "Law-Making at Athens"; Rhodes, "*Nomothesia* in Fourth-Century Athens"; Hansen, "Athenian *Nomothesia*."

57. On this issue, see the summary of Wallace, *Areopagos*, pp. 48–52.

58. A minimalist view of Solon's laws is advocated by Robb, *Literacy and Paideia*, pp. 130–32. See also Hignett, *HAC*, p. 15, who, speaking of the constitutional laws of Kleisthenes and Solon, states that "careful conservation of such epoch-making documents even when they had become politically obsolete . . . was surely alien to the realism of the fifth-century Athenians."

59. According to Herodotus (1.29.2), the Athenians swore to use and not change Solon's laws for ten years. Aristotle (*Ath. Pol.* 7.2) and Plutarch (*Sol.* 25.1) put the figure at a hundred; see also Dio Chrys. *Or.* 80.6, Gell. *NA* 2.12.1 (= Solon fr. 93a, b Ruschenbusch). A prohibition against alteration of a *thesmos* is cited by Demosthenes (23.62 = Solon fr. 22 Ruschenbusch).

60. Ruschenbusch, *SN*, pp. 14–24; Jeffery, *LSAG*, pp. 51–52; Andrewes, "Survival," pp. 21–22; Stroud, *Axones*, p. 41; see also Rhodes, *CAAP*, pp. 132–33; Chambers, *Staat*, p. 167.

61. Ruschenbusch, *SN*, pp. 14–25; Andrewes, "Survival," pp. 21–28; see also Rhodes, *CAAP*, p. 132.

62. See esp. Stroud, *Axones*, pp. 41–44. His and other reconstructions are conveniently summarized by Chambers, *Staat*, pp. 167–69. Connor, "'Sacred' and 'Secular,'" pp. 185–88, has recently revived the view that the *axones* held secular laws and the *kyrbeis* regulations on sacred affairs. Connor bases his argument partly on the observation that the Athenians used bronze stelai for sacral texts, and stone and wood for more mundane matters. But that distinction is not wholly valid: see, among many others, *IG* I³ 230–32, for stone inscriptions recording sacred regulations. In addition, the *axones* are explicitly associated with texts on sacred matters: Plutarch (*Sol.* 23.4 = fr. 81 Ruschenbusch) says that the sixteenth *axon* included prices for sacrificial victims; see also frr. 83, 84 Ruschenbusch.

63. Ruschenbusch, *SN*, pp. 1–13; Andrewes, "Survival," pp. 21–28; Stroud, *Axones*; and Stroud, "State Documents," pp. 21–28. Continued doubts about the survival of the Solonian *axones* are expressed by Sealey, *Athenian Republic*, pp. 140–45.

64. Fr. 274 Kock. For discussion, see Stroud, *Axones*, pp. 3–4.

65. *Hesperia* 7 (1938): 1–76, no. 1, line 87.

66. On the work, mentioned in a list of Aristotelian works found in Hesychius, see Rose, *Aristotelis*, p. 16; Moraux, *Les listes anciennes*, pp. 250–51; Weil, *Aristote et l'histoire*, pp. 125–27; Ruschenbusch, *SN*, pp. 40–42. For Aristotle's collection and study of documents, see Bloch, "Studies in Historical Literature," pp. 303–76. See also the comments of Jacoby, *Atthis*, pp. 196–215, esp. 209–13. Chambers, *Staat*, p. 89, citing a suggestion of Moraux (*Les listes anciennes*, p. 251) refers to the possibility that Aristotle's work did not fill five books but was devoted only to five *axones* of Solon. But this interpretation is at odds with the method of book numbering used for other works in the same list: see Stroud, "Aristotle and Athenian Homicide," p. 218 n. 34.

67. For discussion of Hellenistic and Roman works on the *axones*, see Stroud, *Axones*, pp. 18–33; Ruschenbusch, *SN*, pp. 14–22, 39–52; see also Andrewes, "Survival," p. 21; Rhodes, *CAAP*, p. 132.

68. Ruschenbusch, *SN*, pp. 37–38, believes that the *axones* survived well into the Hellenistic period, but the evidence of the Hellenistic works he cites is too fragmentary to be sure. Stroud, *Axones*, p. 44, suggests that Aristotle may have studied the contents of Solon's *axones* from *kyrbeis*. Sealey, *Athenian Republic*, p. 141, points out that Polemon's and Eratosthenes' debate over the form of the *axones* should indicate that the *axones* "were so poorly preserved that their shape was open to dispute." Since we know of these works only through later references to them, extreme optimism or pessimism about the physical state of the *axones* in the Hellenistic period seems unwarranted.

69. See Ruschenbusch, *SN*, p. 11.

70. First *axon*: Plut. *Sol.* 24.1 (= Solon T5 Ruschenbusch); thirteenth *axon*: Plut. *Sol.* 19.3 (= Solon T7 Ruschenbusch); sixteenth *axon*: Plut. *Sol.* 23.4 (= Solon T8 Ruschenbusch); fifth *axon*: Schol. to Hom. *Il.* 21.282 (= Solon T6a Ruschenbusch). A twenty-first *axon* is generally assumed on the basis of Harpok., s.v. ὅτι οἱ ποιητοί (= Solon T9 Ruschenbusch). Although the note actually says the law came from the "twenty-first of the laws of Solon," Solon's *axones* are probably meant.

71. Another possibility is that the *axones* themselves did not survive, but that their contents could be reconstructed from texts of Solon's laws written on more durable objects like *kyrbeis*, or from texts possessed by Athenian magistrates that preserved source rubrics, like the ones found in the inscribed copy of Drakon's homicide law, which indicated the origin of specific laws on the *axones*.

72. By the same token, no attribution of a law to Solon can be rejected on the grounds that authentic information was unavailable.

73. On the limitations of the laws of Solon and documentary evidence for historical enquiry, see esp. the comments of Jacoby, *Atthis*, pp. 155, 333 n. 21.

74. Ruschenbusch, *SN*, pp. 8–10, cites Cicero (*De Leg.* 2.64), who may have obtained his information from a work of Demetrios of Phaleron (late fourth century), where Solonian funerary measures are distinguished from later funerary laws dating from the late sixth century. See also Ruschenbusch, *SN*, pp. 36–37.

75. Osborne, *Greece in the Making*, p. 222, claims that mention of a fine expressed in drachmas in a law standing on the first *axon* (Plut. *Sol.* 24.1 = Solon fr. 65 Ruschenbusch) casts doubts on the law's authenticity, since coinage was unknown in mainland Greece in Solon's day. But even before the introduction of coinage standardized weights of precious metals probably served as items of exchange. On the question of coinage, weights, and measures in Solon's reforms, see the balanced treatment of Rhodes, "Solon and the Numismatists," pp. 1–7; for comparison of the fines in Solon's laws to those of later times, see Ruschenbusch, *SN*, pp. 36–37.

76. For references to specific *axones*, see n. 70. For a fuller discussion of topics covered by Solon's laws, see Ruschenbusch, *SN*, pp. 25–26.

77. An arrangement by magistrates was first suggested by Schöll, "Über attische Gesetzgebung," pp. 83–139, and has been widely accepted since: see Busolt-Swoboda, p. 833 with n. 1. Ruschenbusch, *SN*, pp. 27–31, rejects the evidence for such an arrangement but his arguments are convincingly refuted by Stroud, *Drakon's Law*, p. 32 n. 11. Solonian law on treasurers: *Ath. Pol.* 8.1. Laws administered by the archon on the first *axon*: Plut. *Sol.* 24.1 (= Solon fr. 65 Ruschenbusch); Harpok., s.v. σῖτος (with the reading of Dindorf, and not that of Ruschenbusch, *SN*, p. 64 [T10]: see Stroud, *Drakon's Law*, p. 32 n. 10, for discussion of the correct reading).

78. Stroud, *Drakon's Law*, p. 31, notes the possibility that numbering of individual

axones was the work of the *anagrapheis* charged with publishing Drakon's law on homicide. At *Axones*, p. 7, he expresses more confidence that the *anagrapheis* found numbered *axones* in the records they studied.

79. Meiggs-Lewis, no. 20 (= *IG* IX² 1.3.718).

80. Bouleuterion and Agora: Anaximenes, *FGrHist* 72 F13 (= T18a Ruschenbusch). Prytaneion: Plut. *Sol.* 25.1 (= Solon T22 Ruschenbusch); Polemon ap. Harpok., s.v. ἄξονι (= T20 Ruschenbusch); Poll. 8.128 (= T18b Ruschenbusch); see also Paus. 1.18.3 (= Solon T21 Ruschenbusch). Stoa Basileios: *Ath. Pol.* 8.1; Acropolis: Anaximenes, *FGrHist* 72 F13; Poll. 8.128. For discussion, see Ruschenbusch, *SN*, pp. 31–32; Stroud, *Axones*, pp. 41–44. Robertson, "Solon's *Axones* and *Kyrbeis*," pp. 147–76, offers an ingenious but highly speculative reconstruction of the location of the *axones* and *kyrbeis* in the sixth century.

81. On the Bouleuterion and its building history, see Chapter 4, Section II. The remains of the Stoa Basileios have not received their final publication, but Shear, "Persian Destruction," pp. 427–29, discusses strong evidence pointing to a date c. 500; for references to other suggested dates, see Rhodes, *CAAP*, pp. 135–36. Robertson, "Solon's *Axones* and *Kyrbeis*," pp. 168–76, credits Peisistratos with constructing the Stoa Basileios and publishing Solon's laws there on *kyrbeis*.

82. *Ath. Pol.* 3.5, with Rhodes, *CAAP*, p. 105; on the location of the Athenian Prytaneion, see S. Miller, *Prytaneion*, pp. 38–54.

83. Anaximenes, *FGrHist* 72 F13: τοὺς ἄξονας καὶ τοὺς κύρβεις ἄνωθεν ἐκ τῆς ἀκροπόλεως εἰς τὸ βουλευτήριον καὶ τὴν ἀγορὰν μετέστησεν Ἐφιάλτης.

84. Wilamowitz, *Aristoteles*, 1:45 n. 7.

85. Poll. 8.128 (= T18b Ruschenbusch): ἀπέκειντο δὲ οἵ τε κύρβεις καὶ οἱ ἄξονες ἐν ἀκροπόλει πάλαι· αὖθις δ' ἵνα πᾶσιν ἐξῆι ἐντυγχάνειν, εἰς τὸ πρυτανεῖον καὶ τὴν ἀγορὰν μετεκομίσθησαν. For discussion of these passages, see Stroud, *Axones*, pp. 11–13.

86. Anaximenes, *FGrHist* 72 F44 (fr. 144b Ruschenbusch). For doubts about the Solonian origin of the funeral oration, see Jacoby, "Patrios Nomos," p. 39 n. 8.

87. *Ath. Pol.* 7.1, 55.5; see E. Will, *RPh* 42 (1968): 134–35. Robertson, "Solon's *Axones* and *Kyrbeis*," p. 157, rejects the Acropolis as the original location for the *axones* because "it would be very odd to place a lawcode inside a temple." But see my discussion in the text and the works cited in the following note.

88. See esp. Detienne, "L'espace de la publicité," pp. 29–81; also Hölkeskamp, "Written Law," pp. 89–102; Thomas, "Written in Stone?," pp. 28–29. Steiner, *Tyrant's Writ*, pp. 67–68, refers specifically to the *kyrbeis*, calling them "symbolic objects."

89. *Ath. Pol.* 7.1, 55.5. On the oath itself, see Rhodes, *CAAP*, pp. 100–101. When Aristotle describes the original duties of the first thesmothetai, he also says that they kept the *thesmia* for the judgment of disputes. He envisioned that written *thesmia* were used in administering justice.

90. The specific details of magisterial accountability before the fifth century are obscure. But there is wide agreement among scholars that procedures existed from the earliest times, and the Areopagos is widely thought to have heard complaints against magistrates; see, e.g., Sealey, "Ephialtes," pp. 18–20; Ostwald, *Popular Sovereignty*, pp. 12–13; but see also Wallace, *Areopagos*, pp. 53–55, who argues for popular jurisdiction.

91. Thomas, "Written in Stone?," pp. 25–31, esp. pp. 26–27. For a similar view, see Robb, *Literacy and Paideia*, pp. 85–87, 99–124.

92. On the impact of some of Solon's laws on existing practices, see Sealey, *Justice*, pp. 120–25. Earlier (p. 50), Sealey suggests that Solon may have incorporated earlier written rules, perhaps ones of the thesmothetai, into his laws. Sealey has also argued elsewhere ("Regionalism," p. 162; *Athenian Republic*, pp. 115–19) that Solon's main contribution was not changing laws but writing them down, but his arguments seem to me to rely too much on the absence of references to specific measures in the fragments of Solon's poetry.

93. On this point, see the excellent discussions of Thomas, *Oral Tradition*, pp. 15–34, *Literacy*, pp. 15–28, drawing on extensive, earlier literature.

94. For two recent but differing views of the impact of Solon's work, see Andrewes, "Growth of the Athenian State," pp. 275–91; Osborne, *Greece in the Making*, pp. 220–25.

95. On early law codes, see the excellent discussion of Sealey, *Justice*, pp. 25–58, esp. 55; see also Hölkeskamp, "Written Law in Archaic Greece," and Thomas, "Written in Stone?"

Chapter Two

1. Diod. 1.77; Hdt. 2.177 (= fr. 78a, b Ruschenbusch). This law is often identified with Solon's law on idleness; see Wallace, *Areopagos*, pp. 62–64, for a recent discussion (although Wallace does not consider the passage of Diodorus). On the Athenian legal procedure called *apographē*, see Harrison, *LA*, 2:211–17. That Solon undertook some sort of written, land census, a "cadastral survey," is suggested by Frost, "Attic Literacy," pp. 55–57. But that probably goes far beyond what can be assumed about Athenian literacy for the period. For a different view of the functioning of the Solonian census classes, see Connor, "Tribes, Festivals, and Processions," pp. 47–49.

2. Stroud, "State Documents," pp. 20–42, presents the most detailed survey of sixth-century Athenian documents; see also Rhodes, "Alles eitel Gold?"; Stahl, *Aristokraten*, pp. 6–53; and Raaflaub, "Athenische Geschichte," pp. 197–225. That most traditions about sixth-century Athens were oral in nature was established by Jacoby, *Atthis*, pp. 169–225; see also Thomas, *Oral Tradition*, esp. pp. 238–82, for important refinements of Jacoby's conclusions. An excellent but necessarily general survey of sixth-century literacy in the Greek world is offered in W. Harris, *Ancient Literacy*, pp. 45–64.

3. The texts and restorations are discussed by Raubitschek, *Dedications*, nos. 326, 327, 328. See also Jeffery, *LSAG*, p. 72, and W. Harris, *Ancient Literacy*, p. 50, who notes the significance of these secretaries but does not explore their activities in detail.

4. *IG* I³ 507. Raubitschek, *Dedications*, p. 353, points out the possibility that this Kinesias may have served as secretary for the officials listed on the opposite side.

5. *IG* I³ 508, lines 4–5: [. . . ί]ας ἐ/γρα[μάτευε . . .].

6. *IG* I³ 509, line 3–4: ἐγ]γραμάτε/υε · Φαιδρί[ο - - -]. For possible restorations, see Raubitschek, *Dedications*, p. 357.

7. For the foundation date of the Greater Panathenaia, see Cadoux, "Athenian Archons," p. 104. For discussion of the contests and identification of the officials named in the inscriptions, see Raubitschek, *Dedications*, pp. 352, 355–56. Davison, "Notes on the Panathenaea," pp. 29–33, points out that the dedications may have been set up by officials known as *athlothetai*, who managed the Greater Panathenaia

by the late fifth century, and that one or more of the sixth-century inscriptions may commemorate the lesser, annual Panathenaic festival. But that does not affect the secretaries who served the officials.

8. On *mnēmones*, see especially Lambrinudakis and Wörrle, "Reformgesetz," pp. 333–41; see also Thomas, "Written in Stone?," pp. 19–25; W. Harris, *Ancient Literacy*, pp. 73–74. Busolt-Swoboda, 1:480, lists the ancient testimony in more detail. Rememberers as scribes who use writing in the fourth century: Arist. *Pol.* 1321b38–40.

9. On *hieromnēmones*, see Pritchett, *Greek Archives*, pp. 36–39. For the Athenian *hieromnēmones* who represented Athens at the Delphic Amphictyony, see Aeschin. 3.115–16, 126–27. Other Athenian *hieromnēmones* include: *IG* I³ 243, lines 31–32, 70, a *lex sacra* that includes a decree from the deme Melite; *IG* II² 1232, lines 18–19, an early fourth-century decree of the Salaminioi, an Athenian *genos*; *IG* II² 1247, line 19, a third-century decree of the Mesogeioi, an Athenian cult association; *IG* II² 1596, line 5, which mentions *hieromnēmones* for a cult of Herakles from Alopeke.

10. On the secretary of the Boule, see Chapter 3, Section II; Chapter 6, Section I. Secretaries to judicial magistrates: Ar. *Clouds* 769–72; Antiph. 6.35. Undersecretaries to the *pōlētai*, *praktores*, and *poristai*: Antiph. 6.49.

11. These secretaries and their activities are discussed in more detail in Chapter 3, Section II. Pritchett, *Greek Archives*, p. 19, notes that "*grammateus* and *grammateuo* are probably the commonest words in *IG* I³."

12. Auditors in the Quota Lists: *IG* I³ 259, line 2; see also *IG* I³ 52, lines 7–9. The Areopagos is generally credited with the power to scrutinize the conduct of magistrates at the end of their term in office, a right it lost by Ephialtes' reforms: see esp. Ostwald, *Popular Sovereignty*, pp. 12–13, 55–62; Hignett, *HAC*, pp. 203–5; Sealey, "Ephialtes," pp. 18–20. A passage of Aristotle's *Politics* (1274a15–17; cf. 1281b31–34), however, may indicate that popular courts enjoyed this right from the time of Solon: see Wallace, *Areopagos*, pp. 53–55. Whatever body heard complaints against magistrates, most scholars seem to agree that magisterial accountability was an ancient practice. A detailed examination of fifth- and fourth-century procedures is offered by Piérart, "Les EYΘYNOI Athéniens," pp. 526–73.

13. Payments to the *athlothetai* for the Greater Panathenaia are mentioned at *IG* I³ 370, lines 66–68; see also *IG* I³ 375, lines 5–6. Prizes in musical and athletic contests: *IG* II² 2311; *Ath. Pol.* 60. Athena's robe and prize amphoras: *Ath. Pol.* 61.2. Another fourth-century inscription (*IG* II² 334 with *Hesperia* 28 [1959]: 239–47) preserves regulations for the annual, lesser Panathenaia, including instructions for the procurement of cattle for sacrifice, distribution of sacrificial meat, and reference to the costs involved. An excellent overview of the festival is offered by Parke, *Festivals*, pp. 33–50; see also Tracy, "Panathenaic Festival and Games," for a thorough review of the epigraphical evidence from later periods.

14. On the treasurers of Athena, see now D. Harris, *Treasures*, 1–39. According to *Ath. Pol.* 8.1, there was a "law about the treasurers" among Solon's laws. For the inventorying of objects by treasurers already in the sixth century, see *IG* I³ 510, discussed shortly in the text.

15. The *naukraroi* and a naukraric fund are mentioned at *Ath. Pol.* 8.3. The several theories about the duties of these officials are reviewed by Gabrielsen, *Financing the Athenian Fleet*, pp. 19–24. Ostwald, "Public Expense," pp. 373–79, postulates that the *naukraroi* kept registers of citizens liable for various public services; on this possibility, see Section IV.

16. The *pōlētai* are listed among the officials for whom a property qualification existed under Solon's laws (*Ath. Pol.* 7.3); their antiquity is accepted by Langdon, *Agora*, 19:67–69. Sacred and public property is referred to by Solon fr. 4 West, lines 12–13; for the suggestion that these properties were leased out with sureties in Solon's time, see Rihll, "EKTHMOPOI," pp. 101–27. Leases are mentioned in the earliest preserved Attic decree, *IG* I³ 1, dating from the late sixth or early fifth century: see Walbank, *Agora*, 19:153. On public property in general, see Lewis, "Public Property," pp. 245–60.

17. On Solon's calendar, see now Parker, *Athenian Religion*, pp. 43–55.

18. *IG* I³ 510: ηοι ταμίαι · τάδε χαλκία · [- - c. 12–14 - -ανέθεσαν]/ συνλέχσαν-τες · Διὸς κρατερ[όφρονι παιδί · - - c. 8–10 - -]/ 'Αναχσίον καὶ Εὔδιϟος καὶ Σ[- - c. 9–10 καὶ - - c. 8 - -]/καὶ 'Ανδοκίδες καὶ Λυσίμαχ[ος καὶ - - c. 8 - - καὶ - - c. 8 - -].

19. So Ferguson, *Treasurers of Athena*, p. 6 n. 1; Jeffery, *LSAG*, p. 72; Immerwahr, *Attic Script*, p. 28. D. Harris, *Treasures*, p. 14, states, "Strictly speaking, the inscription is a dedicatory plaque, not an inventory list."

20. *IG* I³ 376. A possible connection between the two texts was noted by Wade-Gery, *Essays*, p. 172 n. 3.

21. On the use of τάδε, "these things," see the inventories of the Parthenon, *IG* I³ 343–62. For the possibility that another tablet was originally located above this one, see the commentary to *IG* I² 393, p. 190.

22. For the earliest, large-scale temple in stone on the Acropolis, see Shear, "Tyrants and Buildings," pp. 2–3; the accumulation of dedications in Greek temples already in the sixth century is noted by Davies, "Religion and the State," pp. 386–87.

23. For the statues, see Schrader, *Die archaischen Marmorbildwerke*, pp. 207–12, nos. 309–11; see also W. Harris, *Ancient Literacy*, p. 50 n. 23. The association of one of the statues with a treasurer of Athena is made by Raubitschek, *Dedications*, p. 12.

24. *IG* I³ 4, side B, lines 1–4. Jordan, *Servants*, pp. 53–54, suggests that the inscription's provisions reconfirm practices that were already in place in the sixth century.

25. See esp. Immerwahr, "Book Rolls," pp. 17–19, for the appearance of writing tablets on Attic vases in the late sixth century. For the use of wooden tablets (*pinakes, sanides, grammateia*) by Athenian magistrates during the fifth century, see, e.g., Ar. *Clouds* 769–72; *IG* I³ 34, lines 14–18; *IG* I³ 68, lines 18–21; *IG* I³ 78, lines 26–30; *IG* I³ 476, line 291.

26. This and other inscriptions related to dramatic performances at the Dionysia are discussed by Pickard-Cambridge, *Dramatic Festivals*, pp. 71–74, with texts at pp. 101–7; physical features of the inscription itself are described in detail by Wilhelm, *Urkunden*, pp. 1–33, with a new fragment by Capps, "Greek Inscriptions," pp. 1–11. Pritchett, *Greek Archives*, pp. 21–22, 38, is one of the few recent scholars to note the significance of these inscriptions for Athenian record keeping.

27. For the date, see Capps, "Greek Inscriptions," pp. 10–11. But see the qualifications of Pickard-Cambridge, *Dramatic Festivals*, pp. 102–3, who points out that an earlier date cannot be excluded.

28. The work is referred to in lists of Aristotle's works preserved in Diogenes Laertius and Hesychius; see Rose, *Fragmenta*, pp. 8, 15.

29. Reisch, "Didaskaliai," cols. 398–401, argued that the *Nikai* was Aristotle's source; this was denied by Körte, "Aristoteles' Νῖκαι Διονυσιακαί," pp. 391–98, who argued that Aristotle's *Victories* are more probably reflected in *IG* II² 2325, an inscribed list of victorious poets from the early third century; see Pickard-Cambridge,

Dramatic Festivals, p. 103 n. 3. Jaeger, Aristotle, pp. 326–27, dates these works to the last stage of Aristotle's career.

30. See IG I³ 957–59, 961–62, none of which preserve the name of an archon. An archon is mentioned in IG I³ 960, dating from 415/14. An epigram celebrating a dithyrambic victory of Simonides in the year 477/6 (Simonides fr. 77 Diehl) also records the names of archon, poet, chorēgos, and tribe, virtually the same information said to have been recorded on the dedicatory plaque of Themistokles. But the epigram is probably a composition of the Hellenistic period: see Page, Further Greek Epigrams, pp. 241–43, no. 28. A dithyrambic victory by Simonides in 477/6 need not be doubted, but the author of the epigram may have learned the archon date of the victory from a work of Aristotle, who in turn relied on didascalic records. Reference to an archon year in Themistokles' choregic dedication is therefore unique in early, fifth-century choregic dedications. Is it too, like the Simonidean epigram, a later composition?

31. The difficulties of attracting chorēgoi around the middle of the fourth century are well illustrated by events surrounding Demosthenes' dispute with Meidias: Dem. 21.13. For further evidence for difficulties in finding willing liturgists in the 350s, see Rhodes, "Problems," p. 13; Christ, "Liturgy Avoidance," pp. 147–69, deals more generally with this subject.

32. A documentary origin for the Fasti and other didascalic records is assumed by, among others, Pickard-Cambridge, Dramatic Festivals, pp. 70–71; Wilhelm, Urkunden, pp. 1–33; Reisch, "Didaskaliai," cols. 398–401; Körte, "Aristoteles' Νῖκαι Διονυσιακαί," pp. 391–98; Capps, "Greek Inscriptions," pp. 1–11; Lesky, Greek Tragic Poetry, p. 31. Pritchett, Greek Archives, pp. 21–22, suggests that they may have been kept by the archon, hieromnēmones, or a Dionysiac guild.

33. The date of Aeschylus's first victory is given by the Parian Marble, FGrHist 239 A50. For the date of comedy's introduction to the City Dionysia, see Capps, Introduction of Comedy, pp. 25–29; Pickard-Cambridge, Dramatic Festivals, p. 82.

34. Suda, s.v. Αἰσχύλος. On the preservation of names of nonwinning playwrights, see my subsequent discussion.

35. So Connor, "City Dionysia," arguing in part from his dating for the incorporation of Eleutherai into the Athenian state. But see Sourvinou-Inwood, "Something to Do with Athens," who discusses features of the City Dionysia that point to a pre-Kleisthenic origin.

36. The Olympiad dates for Phrynichos and Choirilos are given under the Suda's entries for each author. Introduction of men's dithyrambs: FGrHist 239 A46. For the date of Lysagoras, see Cadoux, "Athenian Archons," p. 113.

37. Connor, "City Dionysia," pp. 13–15.

38. M. West, "Early Chronology," pp. 251–54, questions the documentary origin of the Suda's dates for Thespis, Choirilos, and Phrynichos, and argues that they are the product of Hellenistic calculations and not archival research. West points out that the dates given for these poets are expressed in Olympiads and that they are spaced three Olympiads apart, and he conjectures that the three-Olympiad interval was devised by Eratosthenes or someone else using a similar reckoning method. Specific Olympiads for each poet were reached by calculating back from a contest held in the seventieth Olympiad (500/499–496/5), in which Aeschylus, Choirilos, and Pratinas competed (Suda, s.v. Αἰσχύλος), a date that West accepts as archival in origin. But the Suda's use of Olympiads as opposed to archon years for these early performances

is not unusual; it also reckons dates for Sophocles and Euripides by Olympiads, even though details of their lives could be fixed to archon years in the chronographic tradition. More important, the system detected by West is not consistent. The *Suda* dates a victory of Phrynichos, but only productions for Choirilos and Thespis. A proper system should calculate the same event in each poet's life, such as his first victory or first performance. The fact that the *Suda* mentions different types of events for each poet could then be evidence that the dates are based on some authentic material, not on Hellenistic calculations.

39. For documents related to dramatic performances at the Rural Dionysia, which was celebrated in individual demes, see Pickard-Cambridge, *Dramatic Festivals*, pp. 45–52, who notes that most of our evidence belongs to the fourth century.

40. For the display of the names of victors in athletic contests on *leukōmata*, whitened wooden boards, see *IG* XII.5 647, lines 40–41. For the use of whitened tablets to display a wide variety of documents in the Greek world, see Wilhelm, *Beiträge*, esp. pp. 249–57.

41. Mosshammer, *Chronicle*, p. 309, expresses doubts about the availability of documents attesting to the first presentations for playwrights as early as the 450s, as opposed to records of their first victories; but see the discussion in the text.

42. On the didascalic notice for Aeschylus's *Supplices*, see Garvie, *Aeschylus' Supplices*, pp. 1–28. For similar information, see the hypotheses of Aeschylus's *Agamemnon*, Euripides' *Alcestis* and *Medea*, and Aristophanes' *Clouds*. On Aristotle's *Didaskaliai*, see Reisch, "Didaskaliai," cols. 398–401; Pickard-Cambridge, *Dramatic Festivals*, p. 71; Pfeiffer, *History of Classical Scholarship*, pp. 81, 132. On the hypotheses of fifth-century plays, see Raddatz, "Hypotheseis," cols. 414–24, esp. 415–17.

43. For the calculations, see Davies, "Demosthenes on Liturgies," pp. 33–34.

44. Dem. 21.8–9; on the law and its date, see Pickard-Cambridge, *Dramatic Festivals*, pp. 68–69, with 69 n. 6, and MacDowell, *Demosthenes: Against Meidias*, pp. 226–29. For the importance attached to the archon's conduct, see the third-century inscription published in *Hesperia* 7 (1938): 100–109, no. 18 (cited at Pickard-Cambridge, *Dramatic Festivals*, p. 69).

45. On appointment of *chorēgoi*, see Pickard-Cambridge, *Dramatic Festivals*, pp. 75–76, 86–91. According to the *Ath. Pol.* 56.2–3, the archon appointed only the *chorēgoi* for tragedies, while individual tribes provided *chorēgoi* for other events; earlier, however, the archon had appointed the *chorēgoi* for comedies as well. Even in cases where the archon did not appoint *chorēgoi*, however, as in dithyrambic contests, he retained some supervisory duties; see esp. Dem. 21.13–18. On the selection of a leading actor or protagonist, see Pickard-Cambridge, *Dramatic Festivals*, pp. 93–95. On the influence of past success in the selection of poets, see *POxy* 2737, discussed at Pickard-Cambridge, *Dramatic Festivals*, p. 359; Csapo and Slater, *Context of Ancient Drama*, pp. 105, 135, no. 71.

46. On the exemptions applying to *chorēgoi*, see *Ath. Pol.* 56.3; for the existence of some exemptions in the fifth century, see Rhodes, "Problems," pp. 2–3. For fuller, general discussion of liturgic exemptions, see Gabrielsen, *Financing the Athenian Fleet*, pp. 85–87.

47. *IG* I³ 1031. On the list, see most conveniently Meiggs-Lewis, no. 6. One fragment was published by Meritt, "Greek Inscriptions" (1939), no. 21, pp. 59–65; three additional fragments were published, with a reconstruction of the original inscription, by Bradeen, "The Fifth-Century Archon List," pp. 187–208. For pre-Solonian

archons, see line 9, where the name of Philombrotos, archon in the year before Solon (Plut. *Sol.* 14), is restored. In addition, a space to the left of the first preserved column indicates that another column preceded it. If the name of Philombrotos is correctly restored, the inscribed list must have included names of seventh-century archons.

48. Mosshammer, *Chronicle*, pp. 88–92, calls the inscribed list (p. 88) "the first of its kind," although he believes it was constructed from authentic material; see also Samuel, *Greek and Roman Chronology*, pp. 195–97, who also doubts existence of a list in any form before the late fifth century. Plommer, "Tyranny," pp. 126–29, points to discrepancies in the date of Drakon as a sign of the list's unreliability, but see now Stroud, *Drakon's Law*, pp. 66–70. Others who favor a late date for the compilation of an archon list include M. Miller, "Earlier Persian Dates," pp. 49–52; M. Miller, "Accepted Date," pp. 64–65, 79–83. Thomas, *Oral Tradition*, pp. 287–88, allows the list's authenticity to the mid-sixth century but also suggests that earlier names were subject to "manipulation and imaginative 'reconstruction,'" without, however, offering any reasons for this conclusion.

49. Herodotus's failure to make use of the archon list is adduced as an argument against a list's existence by Samuel, *Greek and Roman Chronology*, pp. 195–97, and others. But see Stroud, "State Documents," p. 34. Greek historiography did not develop out of official documents or records, though these did exist; scientific investigation of documents was a relatively late phenomenon and belonged to different genres (or subgenres) of historical writing: see Jacoby, *Atthis*, pp. 196–215; Jacoby, "Über die Entwicklung," pp. 49–59; Fornara, *Nature of Historiography*, pp. 16–23.

50. For arguments in favor of the archon list's authenticity as an early document, see in general Jacoby, *Atthis*, pp. 169–76; Cadoux, "Athenian Archons," pp. 77–79; and Stroud, "State Documents," pp. 32–35.

51. *Ath. Pol.* 13.1–2; for the specific years and further discussion, see Rhodes, *CAAP*, pp. 180–84.

52. The year 404/3 was also labeled an *anarchia* (Xen. *Hell.* 2.3.1; Diod. 14.3.1), because its archon, whose name (Pythodoros) was known, had served under an oligarchic regime: see Rhodes, *CAAP*, pp. 436–37. An *anarchia* is also mentioned in a later archon list: *IG* II² 1713, line 12, for the year 88/7. On that year, see Habicht, "Zur Geschichte Athens."

53. Survival of an authentic list dating back to the early sixth century would not guarantee the accuracy of other features of Aristotle's discussion of Damasias and his tenure; Aristotle (or his source) may simply have made further deductions on the basis of what was probably a bare list of names.

54. The point is rightly stressed by Thomas, *Literacy*, p. 67. Her solution, however, that "if anyone should need to calculate the number of years since a certain man held office, the official would probably be alive still," is uncharacteristically feeble.

55. See Plommer, "Tyranny," pp. 127–28. Thomas, *Oral Tradition*, p. 288, also finds it "remarkable that it took so long for archon dates to be used consistently."

56. *IG* I³ 21, lines 61, 86. Fornara, "Date of the 'Regulations for Miletus,'" pp. 474–75, argues that reference to Euthynos's archonship is retroactive and that the decree belongs later in the 440s. Mattingly has long argued for a much later date of 426/5 for Euthynos's archonship (see most recently "Athenian Coinage Decree," pp. 69–71), but I am not fully convinced.

57. *IG* I³ 259, line 3.

58. *IG* I³ 4, side A, lines 14–15; side B, lines 26–27.

59. Pritchett, *Greek Archives*, p. 22, suggests that the Fasti may have served as a source for the archon list.

60. On the authenticity of the amnesty law, see Ruschenbusch, *SN*, pp. 5–8.

61. The law is cited at Dem. 46.14 (= Solon fr. 49a Ruschenbusch); on its authenticity, see Sealey, *Justice*, pp. 121–22.

62. Studies of oral traditions in non-Greek societies suggest that the keeping of lists is a practice of peoples who already know writing, which the Greeks of the seventh and sixth centuries did; see Goody, *Domestication of the Savage Mind*, pp. 74–111.

63. See Stroud, "State Documents," p. 32, for other possible uses.

64. *Ath. Pol.* 53.4–7. See Rhodes, *CAAP*, pp. 591–96.

65. *Dikastai* or jurors (*Ath. Pol.* 63.3) and *bouleutai* (Xen. *Mem.* 1.2.35; see also the hypothesis to Dem. 22) were required to be thirty years of age. Thirty years is assumed to be the minimum age for most other offices as well; see, in general, Hansen, *Athenian Democracy*, pp. 88–90, 227–28. Develin, "Age Qualifications," pp. 149–59, argues that in some cases age restrictions were not applied or observed; contra Hansen, "Seven Hundred *archai*," pp. 151–73.

66. Military service by age-classes in the fifth century: Thuc. 1.105.4. Fifth-century age qualifications: *IG* I³ 61, lines 13–15, a decree of the early 420s, sets a minimum age of fifty for ambassadors to the Macedonian king Perdikkas; *IG* I³ 21, line 5, regulations for Miletus of 450/49, limits appointment to a board to those over a certain age, probably fifty; *IG* I³ 3, lines 9–10, an inscription from Marathon of c. 490–480, sets thirty as the minimum age for a board of *athlothetai*. Seventh-century age qualifications may have existed for the *ephetai* who tried homicide cases (*Suda*, s.v. ἐφεταί).

67. Solon fr. 27 West.

68. The possibility of orally transmitted lists of great length is entertained by M. Miller, "Accepted Date," pp. 64–65. The memorization of a list of archons by Hippias, as depicted by Plato (*Hippias Maior* 285e), is sometimes cited as evidence for the oral transmission of a list of archons. But Plato credits Hippias with this feat after a written list was already available.

69. For seventh-century archons, see Cadoux, "Athenian Archons," pp. 88–92.

70. See my discussion in Chapter 1.

71. For the inadequacies of orally transmitted lists, see Vansina, *Oral Tradition*, pp. 178–85. Reference may also be made to the preface of Hekataios's *Genealogiai* (*FGrHist* 1 F1), which criticizes the "many" and "absurd" genealogies of the Greeks. Fornara, *Nature of Historiography*, pp. 4–7, points out that Hekataios's words suggest a desire not to rationalize Greek genealogies but to bring some degree of order to them. A similar desire to avoid the difficulties inherent in orally transmitted lists could have motivated the Athenians and other Greeks to maintain lists of their eponymous officials, albeit at a much earlier date than the work of Hekataios.

72. See Plut. *Sol.* 25.3, *Ath. Pol.* 7.1; Hdt. 1.29.2. The sources disagree on whether the oath was administered before or after the legislation was issued: see Rhodes, *CAAP*, p. 135.

73. For the archon as the presiding magistrate over the Ekklesia, see Hignett, *HAC*, pp. 126–28.

74. According to Thucydides (6.54.6) and Herodotus (1.59.6), the Peisistratids left the laws and institutions of Athens intact. Aristotle's claim (*Ath. Pol.* 22.1) that the laws of Solon disappeared under the tyranny is probably incorrect; earlier in the

same work (*Ath. Pol.* 16), it is stated that Peisistratos ruled κατὰ τοὺς νόμους, "in accordance with the laws."

75. *Ath. Pol.* 16.2–3.

76. Stroud, "State Documents," p. 27, points out that the possible publication of these measures cannot be excluded.

77. On the possibility of an epigraphic source for Peisistratos's first attempt at tyranny, see Stroud, "State Documents," p. 27. A documentary origin for dating Peisistratos's first exile to the archonship of Hegesias (*Ath. Pol.* 14.4) was suggested by Sumner, "Notes on Chronological Problems," pp. 46–47. Jacoby, *Atthis*, p. 364 n. 69, suggested that the dating of Peisistratos's death to the archonship of Philoneos (*Ath. Pol.* 17.1) could have originated in a decree renewing his father's privileges for Hippias. For doubts about the documentary origin of these dates, however, see Rhodes, "Pisistratid Chronology," pp. 228–29.

78. For the figures on the duration of the reigns of Peisistratos and his sons, see Hdt. 1.62.1; 5.55, 65.3. It should be noted that evidence for the survival of specific archon dates in oral traditions is quite weak. Thomas, *Oral Tradition*, pp. 112–13, argues that Athenian families did not retain memory of past archonships, and that the traditions of both families and the polis, as reflected in oratory, were chronologically vague and imprecise (see *Oral Tradition*, pp. 95–154, esp. 119–23, 143–44; see also 221–37); see also Jacoby, *Atthis*, pp. 188–96. The dating of specific events in the reign of Peisistratos and his sons presumably arose from a combination of calculations based on documentary material and oral traditions: see Rhodes, "Pisistratid Chronology."

79. *IG* I³ 220, 231; *IG* I³ 1. Another sacred law, *IG* I³ 232, is dated 510–480.

80. On the stele, see Dover, *HCT*, 4:324–25. In the classical period, treason and attempted tyranny were tried by a procedure known as *eisangelia* before the Boule, Ekklesia, or a lawcourt; see Hansen, *Eisangelia*, pp. 21–28. That the ban on the Peisistratids was enacted by the Ekklesia was suggested by Ostwald, "Athenian Legislation," pp. 108–9.

81. *Ath. Pol.* 13.5. Jacoby, *FGrHist* 3b suppl. 1:158–62, questioned the historicity of the *diaspēphismos*, but his doubts were answered by Fornara, "*Diapsephismos*," pp. 243–46, who, however, argues against documentary evidence for the *diapsēphismos*; see also Hignett, *HAC*, p. 132, and Rhodes, *CAAP*, p. 188. A documentary origin, in the form of a decree, is suggested by Wade-Gery, *Essays*, p. 148; Stroud, "State Documents," pp. 29–30, posits that the decree was inscribed on stone.

82. Andok. 1.43. See MacDowell, *Andokides*, pp. 92–93. For the date of Skamandrios's archonship, see Cadoux, "Athenian Archons," p. 113; Wade-Gery, *Essays*, p. 146 n. 1.

83. The principal ancient sources are Hdt. 5.66, 69–73; *Ath. Pol.* 20–22; for recent discussions, see Fornara and Samons, *Athens*, pp. 37–58; Ostwald, "Reform of the Athenian State," pp. 303–25.

84. For the *lēxiarchika grammateia* and the registration process, see Whitehead, *Demes*, pp. 97–104; Rhodes, *CAAP*, pp. 493–502; on the age at which young men were registered, see Golden, "Demosthenes," pp. 25–38.

85. The *lēxiarchika grammateia* are first attested in *IG* I³ 138, line 6, which is dated in the corpus to before 434; their creation as a result of Perikles' citizenship law is argued by Patterson, *Pericles' Citizenship Law*, pp. 13–28.

86. Rejected, e.g., by Whitehead, *Demes*, pp. 34–35 (with n. 130), 98.

87. In addition to demes, both clans (*genē*) and phratries, kinship groups which may have controlled citizenship before the institution of Kleisthenes' deme-based systems, also kept written registers of their members called *koina grammateia* (*IG* II² 1237, lines 97–98; Is. 7.1, 16–17; Harpok. and *Suda*, s.v. κοῖνον γραμματεῖον καὶ ληξιαρχικόν). Such registers are not attested until the fourth century, but we have so little evidence for the organization and practices of these groups at any period that their use of membership rolls in earlier times cannot be excluded. Wooden tablets begin to appear in Attic vase paintings in large numbers at the end of the sixth century: Immerwahr, "Book Rolls," pp. 17–18; see also Beck, *Album*, index, s.v. "Literary and Humane education—tools of learning."

88. On this vase (Bâle 133) and a similar one dating from the 470s (Berlin F 2296), see Bugh, *Horsemen*, pp. 14–18, with references to further scholarship.

89. See Andrewes, "Kleisthenes' Reform Bill," pp. 241–48, for a sensible discussion of the implementation of Kleisthenes' reforms, one that required lists and registers, presumably written.

90. *Ath. Pol.* 29.3: Κλειτοφῶν δὲ τὰ μὲν ἄλλα καθάπερ Πυθόδωρος εἶπεν, προσαναζητῆσαι δὲ τοὺς αἱρεθέντας ἔγραψεν τοὺς πατρίους νόμους οὓς Κλεισθένης ἔθηκεν ὅτε καθίστη τὴν δημοκρατίαν. A following clause, which describes Kleisthenes' laws as more democratic than Solon's, probably was not part of the original amendment but is Aristotle's interpretation of the Kleitophon's intention; see Jacoby, *Atthis*, p. 384 n. 30; Rhodes, *CAAP*, p. 377.

91. For doubts on Kleitophon's sincerity, see, e.g., Ledl, *Studien*, pp. 24–25; Hignett, *HAC*, pp. 15–16; Day and Chambers, *Aristotle's History*, pp. 102–3. Even the skeptical Hignett (*HAC*, p. 130) allows that Kleitophon's motion implies that Kleisthenes' laws "were still extant in the archives."

92. *IG* I³ 105. For the text and discussion, see esp. Rhodes, *Athenian Boule*, pp. 195–99; also Ostwald, *Popular Sovereignty*, pp. 31–35. Among older studies, Wade-Gery, "Studies," pp. 113–22, remains valuable. Recently, Ryan, "Original Date," pp. 120–34, has argued that many of the provisions in the inscription date back to the legislation of Solon. If Ryan's arguments are correct, they would lend additional support to the view that texts of early sixth-century date survived to the end of the fifth century.

93. An oath is suggested by the use of the first-person singular verb ἐπιφσηφίζω at lines 27 and 28; see esp. Wade-Gery, "Studies," pp. 113–22; Rhodes, *Athenian Boule*, p. 196. First use of the Bouleutic Oath in the archonship of Hermokreon: *Ath. Pol.* 22.2. The year of Hermokreon's archonship is unknown; see Cadoux, "Athenian Archons," pp. 116–17, who places it in 501/0. A slightly earlier date, however, may be preferred: see Fornara and Samons, *Athens*, pp. 168–70, who suggest 506/5.

94. For the formula, see line 34; for discussion, see Rhodes, *Athenian Boule*, pp. 195–99, who prefers to date these provisions somewhat later.

95. Immerwahr, *Attic Script*, pp. 121–22; on this point, see also Chapter 3, Section I.

96. One feature of the text deserves mention. Lewis, "A Note on *IG* i² 114," p. 132, noted three pairs of vertical dots in line 43 of the inscription and suggested that they reflected the word τοι that stood in the original text; apparently, the secretary who transcribed the text from its original found a damaged or uncertain word, and rather than restore it, he copied exactly what he saw. If this interpretation is correct, it suggests that the Athenians were exceedingly scrupulous and careful in the transcribing and copying of ancient documents, even to the point of obscurity.

97. *IG* I³ 1453 §10 (pp. 898–99) (see also Meiggs-Lewis, no. 45, §12): προσγράψαι δὲ πρὸς τὸν ὅρκον [τ]ὸν τῆς βουλῆς τὸν γραμματέα τὸν τῆς [βουλῆς - - ca. 10 - - τα]δί· ἐάν τις κόπτηι νόμισ[μα] ἀργυρίο ἐν τῆισι πό[λεσι] καὶ μὴ χρῆται νομ[ίσμ-ασιν τοῖς] Ἀθη[να]ίων ἢ σταθμοῖς ἢ μέτ[ροις ἀλλὰ ξενικοῖς νομίσμασι]ν καὶ σταθμοῖς καὶ μέτροις, [- - - c. 14 - - -]τ[- - c. 6 - - κατὰ τὸ πρότε]ρον ψήφισμα ὃ Κλέαρχ[ος εἶπεν. The Coinage Decree is traditionally dated to 450–446 (Meiggs-Lewis, pp. 113–17; Lewis, "Athenian Coinage Decree," pp. 53–64), but a date c. 420 is to be preferred: see now Fornara and Samons, *Athens*, pp. 98–102, and Mattingly, "Athenian Coinage Decree." For the addition of a further clause to the Bouleutic Oath in 410/9, see Philochoros, *FGrHist* 328 F140. The fact that Philochoros preserves a specific year for the addition of a clause could also suggest that changes to the oath's text were dated.

98. See Chapter 1, Section II.

99. *IG* II² 120 uses the verb *prosanagraphein* to denote the addition of a measure to a stone stele; for *prosgraphein* used in conjunction with a wooden board, see Dem. 46.11.

100. Jacoby, *Atthis*, pp. 206–7, 383 n. 27. Jacoby's point was challenged by Hignett, *HAC*, pp. 15–16, but the latter's arguments seem overly ingenious.

101. First attested in *IG* I³ 7, dated to c. 460. A secretary is restored in the prescript of *IG* I³ 5, line 1, dated to c. 500, but restoration of other officials is possible. On the activities of the fifth-century secretary of the Boule, see Chapter 3, Section II.

102. Rhodes, *Athenian Boule*, pp. 16–19, 211–12.

103. Hignett, *HAC*, pp. 125–26; see also Rhodes, *Athenian Boule*, p. 18.

104. Decree of Skamandrios: Andok. 1.43. Archon dates in the Hekatompedon Decrees: *IG* I³ 4, side A, lines 14–15; side B, lines 26–27. For the dating of fifth-century documents and the later appearance of archon names in decree prescripts, see Chapter 3, Section III.

105. Other pre-Ephialtic measures identified by their archon year include the reform of the mode of appointment of archons in 487/6 and the ostracisms of the 480s: see *Ath. Pol.* 22.3–8. That these dates are probably documentary in origin is accepted by Rhodes, "Alles eitel Gold?," p. 56.

Chapter Three

1. Robb, *Literacy and Paideia*, pp. 141–47; see also Thomas, *Oral Tradition*, pp. 38–45, 69–83. Hedrick, "Writing, Reading, and Democracy," p. 173, describes the foundation of the Metroon's archives in the following terms: "Their establishment marks a vaguely sinister watershed in the history of political reading and writing in Athens. No longer were *all* public texts kept in monumental format, preserved as a matter of course as a part of the urban environment, where any casual passer-by can see them, walk around them, or lean on them. The consolidation of texts in the Metroon may usefully serve to mark the beginnings of a new and particular way of using texts."

2. See, e.g., Ostwald, *Popular Sovereignty*, pp. 410–11; Boegehold, "Establishment," pp. 23–30, esp. 28–30; also Stroud, *Drakon's Law*, pp. 28–29; MacDowell, *LCA*, p. 46. For documents in the Bouleuterion and its use as an archives, see Thompson, "Buildings," pp. 215–17; Jacoby, *Atthis*, p. 383 n. 27; Bradeen, "Fifth-Century Archon List," p. 205 n. 88.

3. So Kahrstedt, "Untersuchungen," pp. 25–32; similar views are entertained or

accepted by Thomas, *Oral Tradition*, pp. 68–83, esp. 73–77; Hedrick, "Writing, Reading, and Democracy"; Todd, *Shape of Athenian Law*, p. 56; Todd, "Lysias against Nikomachos," p. 123; Hornblower, *Commentary*, 2:359.

4. For discussion of the relationship between the democracy and overseas empire and the growing number of inscriptions on stone, see esp. Schuller, "Wirkungen des Ersten Attischen Seebunds."

5. On the rationale for publication on stone, see esp. Meritt, *Epigraphica Attica*, pp. 89–93; on the relationship between inscriptions and archival documents, see Wilhelm, *Beiträge*, pp. 298–99; Larfeld, *Handbuch*, 2:601, 642–44; Klaffenbach, "Bemerkungen," pp. 33–36; Woodhead, *Study of Greek Inscriptions*, pp. 37–38.

6. Kahrstedt, "Untersuchungen," pp. 25–32. Kahrstedt recognized that Athenian documents were sometimes displayed on wooden tablets, but the evidence he adduced focused, with the exception of the Solonian *axones*, primarily on stone inscriptions.

7. Kahrstedt cites the following passages: Nepos *Alc.* 4.5, 6.5; *IG* I² 106, line 21 (= *IG* I³ 106, line 22); *Ath. Pol.* 35.2. On the destruction of stelai, see further discussion in the text.

8. See, e.g., Dem. 9.41–44, 19.271–72, 20.127.

9. For such views, see esp. Thomas, *Oral Tradition*, pp. 38–83; Thomas, *Literacy*, pp. 84–88, 132–50, esp. 85: "the image of the 'stone archives of the Greeks' is not inappropriate, at least for the archaic and classical centuries." Thomas concedes that inscriptions were read "if necessary," but she attributes to them a primarily symbolic force. According to Hedrick, "Writing, Reading, and Democracy," p. 173, "For the first hundred years of the democracy . . . texts were systematically made public only in monumental form, that is, by setting them up in the public space of the city." Hedrick also argues that inscriptions were mnemonic devices and visual prompts whose contents were not actually read. On inscriptions as "talismans," see Steiner, *The Tyrant's Writ*, pp. 64–71.

10. So Klaffenbach, *Griechische Epigraphik*, p. 47, who quotes earlier comments to the same effect by Wilhelm.

11. See esp. Klaffenbach, "Bemerkungen," pp. 26–42, which remains the definitive study of the question.

12. For a good example of the imposition of false, anachronistic assumptions on Athenian record keeping, see Thomas, *Literacy*, p. 135: "It is difficult to believe that the stone inscriptions could be official authoritative documents, yet, as we have seen, they clearly were. The modern observer finds it hard to imagine an original document that is not on paper and carefully stored away in an archive." But why should it be surprising or difficult to believe that laws, decrees, and other state documents set up and displayed by state officials and often by the express order of the Athenian people were cited and consulted by Athenians? Thomas herself grants that inscriptions were set up to grant their texts more publicity.

13. For the secretary of the Hellenotamiai, see the headings to *IG* I³ 259–90. Note that the Hellenotamiai also employed undersecretaries. One is mentioned in the tribute quota lists of 443/2 (*IG* I³ 269, line 36) and 442/1 (*IG* I³ 270, line 2). For the secretaries to the treasurers of Athena, see the annual inventories of the cellae of the Parthenon, *IG* I³ 292–358. For secretaries to the *epistatai* of several building projects, see, e.g., *IG* I³ 436–51 (Parthenon); *IG* I³ 462–66 (Propylaia); *IG* I³ 474–79 (Erechtheion). For sixth-century secretaries, see Chapter 2, Section I.

14. In *IG* I³ 32, dated to c. 449–447, one of the five members of a board of *epistatai*, established to oversee the Eleusinian sanctuary, was to be elected *grammateus* for the entire board. A certain Antikles served as secretary to the *epistatai* for the construction of the Parthenon from the 440s into the 430s; his name is first mentioned in *IG* I³ 446 (437/6) and appears or is restored in the accounts of later years (*IG* I³ 447 [436/5], 448 [435/4], 449 [434/3], and 450 [433/2]). Antikles is also restored as a *syngrammateus* (cosecretary) in *IG* I³ 440 (443/2).

15. Ar. *Clouds* 768–72.

16. Antiph. 6.49.

17. For the rule, see Aeschin. 3.22; see also Rhodes, *Athenian Boule*, pp. 110–13. Already in the sixth century, however, some officials may have been using written accounts for this reason, as I argued in the previous chapter. But a legal requirement that such accounts had to be submitted in writing probably appeared only later.

18. See *IG* I³ 476, lines 188–91, a building account of the Erechtheion for 408/7, where the purchases of *sanides*, or wooden tablets, to be used for recording accounts is noted; see also lines 291–92. The same inscription (lines 289–91) mentions the purchase of *biblia*, rolls of papyrus for making copies; the purpose of these copies is unknown.

19. In the fourth century, officials' accounts were examined once every prytany by *logistai* selected from the Boule (*Ath. Pol.* 48.3); Rhodes, *Athenian Boule*, p. 111, suggests that the practice of prytany audits was already in use during the fifth century.

20. So, already, Ed. Meyer, *Forschungen*, 2:115. See now Pritchett, *Greek Archives*, pp. 14–29, esp. 23–24.

21. *IG* I³ 259–72. For discussion, see Meiggs-Lewis, no. 39; see also the comments of Meiggs, *Athenian Empire*, p. 236.

22. If such records were displayed at all, they were probably displayed on wooden tablets. Thus, *IG* I³ 34, lines 43–46, as restored, calls for the display on a whitened tablet of the names of cities that have paid their assessment in full; see also lines 18–22. For discussion of other types of records kept by the Hellenotamiai for which no epigraphical evidence survives, see Meiggs, *Athenian Empire*, pp. 233–37.

23. Inscribed assessment decrees: *IG* I³ 71, 77; see Meiggs-Lewis, no. 69, for discussion. On earlier assessments, see Meiggs, *Athenian Empire*, 235–36. Some of these assessments seem to have survived into the late fourth and early third centuries: see Krateros, *FGrHist* 342 F1–3, with Jacoby's comments ad loc.

24. So Ferguson, *Treasurers of Athena*, pp. 16 n. 1, 98–99. See, more recently, Samons, "The 'Kallias Decrees,'" pp. 91–102, for a valuable discussion of the nature of the records kept and published by Athena's treasurers.

25. Parthenon: *IG* I³ 436–51; Propylaia: *IG* I³ 462–66; Erechtheion: *IG* I³ 474–79; Athena Promachos: *IG* I³ 435; Athena Parthenos: *IG* I³ 453–60.

26. Fifth-century secular public buildings include the Stoa of Zeus Eleutherios, the Odeion of Perikles, South Stoa I in the Agora, and the New Bouleuterion. For an overview of Athenian building activity, sacred and secular, in the second half of the fifth century, see Boersma, *Athenian Building Policy*, pp. 65–96. Boersma's discussion (pp. 4–10) of contracting and construction procedures is extremely valuable.

27. In this respect, the paucity of inscribed documents reflecting the work of the *pōlētai* is striking. See the comments of Walbank, *Agora*, 15:152–53, noting that the "absence of records on stone before this date (367) seems to be a result of practice,

rather than an accident of survival. Such lease records, if they existed, were evidently kept on more perishable material than inscribed stone stelai and have not survived."

28. *IG* I³ 436–51. For a discussion of these accounts, see Meiggs-Lewis, no. 59.

29. *IG* I³ 474–79; see esp. *IG* I³ 476 (408/7), which is the best preserved.

30. The keeping of more detailed accounts in the fifth century would have been all the more necessary if, as in the fourth century (*Ath. Pol.* 48.3), officials were subject to audits of their accounts by the *logistai* every prytany, as suggested by Rhodes, *Athenian Boule*, p. 111.

31. For discussion of the evidence, see Chapter 5, Section II.

32. Thomas, *Oral Tradition*, pp. 38–83, esp. her conclusion (p. 82): "Many records were not preserved at all. Certain types of documents were destroyed as soon as the transaction they signified was over. The keeping of accounts was rudimentary." See also her remarks at *Literacy*, pp. 137–40.

33. *Ath. Pol.* 47.2–48.2; on the passage, see Rhodes, *CAAP*, pp. 552–59; useful also is the discussion of Finley, *Ancient History*, pp. 32–33.

34. *IG* I³ 52. For the traditional date of 434/3, see Meiggs-Lewis, no. 58. A slightly later date of 431, however, is probably preferable: see Kallet-Marx, "Kallias Decree."

35. See ibid., esp. lines 9–13: ἀποδόντον /[δὲ τ]ὰ χρέματα hοι πρυτάνες μετὰ τὲς βολὲς καὶ ἐχσαλειφόντον ἐπει/[δὰν] ἀποδᾶσιν, ζετέσαντες τά τε πινάκια καὶ τὰ γραμματεῖα καὶ ἐάμ π[ο ἄλ]λοθι εῖ γεγραμμένα. ἀποφαινόντον δὲ τὰ γεγραμμένα hοί τε hιερ/[ὲς κ]αὶ hοι hιεροποιοὶ καὶ εἴ τις ἄλλος οἶδεν.

36. Compare as well the procedure outlined in *IG* I³ 94. There, the *basileus*, in conjunction with the *pōlētai*, leases out a *temenos* for twenty years. The contracts were to be written onto a whitened wall, with payments made in the ninth prytany.

37. Finley, *Ancient History*, pp. 32–33; Finley, *Studies in Land and Credit*, p. 206 n. 17.

38. So Thomas, *Oral Tradition*, p. 54 with n. 132, who claims: "Many of the purely administrative decisions which were not recorded on stone or which were for immediate and temporary use were probably simply thrown away when their content had been followed."

39. Thomas (ibid., p. 54 n. 128) notes the two sets of tablets, and states that "apparently there is an official record and a separate document made for each prytany, and all is canceled at the end." But we have no evidence for the fate of the "official record," and the inference merely assumes what needs to be proved.

40. So Fornara, "The Date of the Callias Decrees," p. 194 n. 25; Linders, *The Treasurers of the Other Gods*, pp. 40–41; Kallet-Marx, "Kallias Decree," p. 107 n. 65.

41. In the Hellenistic period, and probably as early as the fourth century, all officials deposited copies of their accounts in the Metroon: see Chapter 5, Section II. But since the Boule was already responsible for the city's finances in the fifth century (see Rhodes, *Athenian Boule*, pp. 88–113), this requirement may have been in force in that century as well. If this is the case, and I think that it is likely, then such records could have served as the sources from which the *logistai* made their calculations.

42. On the Fasti, see Chapter 2, Section II. Similar records of dramatic performances at the Lenaia started being kept from the 440s; see Pickard-Cambridge, *Dramatic Festivals*, pp. 40–42, 107–16. The Lenaia's records were not published on stone until the early third century.

43. *IG* I³ 436–51; publication of the accounts of the first five years at a single date is

noted by the editors in their introduction to the inscription's text (*IG* I³, p. 431); other examples of delayed publication are cited by Pritchett, *Greek Archives*, p. 19.

44. *IG* I³ 435; on a single publication date, see Meritt, "Greek Inscriptions" (1936): 373.

45. For long-term leases, see *Ath. Pol.* 47.2, and the discussion of Walbank, *Agora*, 15:162–63.

46. See Meiggs-Lewis, no. 72, pp. 205–17, for discussion and earlier bibliography.

47. IG I³ 369, lines 98–122.

48. So Kahrstedt, "Untersuchungen"; Thomas, *Oral Tradition*, pp. 38–83, esp. 68–75; see also Hedrick, "Writing, Reading, and Democracy," p. 173, who sees inscriptions as characteristic of fifth-century practice, and archives of the fourth century.

49. Woodhead, *Study of Greek Inscriptions*, pp. 27–28; Robertson, "Laws of Athens," pp. 43–44; Pritchett, *Greek Archives*, p. 26: "The vast majority of psephismata were never inscribed on stone." The point was made nearly a century ago, with respect to Athenian decrees by Ed. Meyer, *Forschungen*, 2:115. Wilhelm, *Beiträge*, pp. 229–99, esp. 249–50, remains the fundamental examination of the question.

50. Honorary decrees: *IG* I³ 17, 18, 19, 20, 23, 24, 27, etc. Foreign affairs: *IG* I³ 9, 10, 11, 12, 14, 15, 16, 21, etc. Religious matters, included financial affairs: *IG* I³ 4, 5, 6, 7, 8, 32, 35, 36, 50, etc. Walbank, *Athenian Proxenies*, pp. 7–8, suggests that publication on stone was an extra privilege awarded to only some *proxenoi*. Some early decrees were set up only at the expense of non-Athenian parties (*IG* I³ 10, 17, 18, 37, 40), a practice that may suggest that the Athenians did not put much importance on publication, unless someone else was willing to bear the cost.

51. As noted by Immerwahr, *Attic Script*, pp. 121–22. The following decrees found in the first fascicle of *IG* I³ seem to be concerned primarily with domestic, nonsacred matters: *IG* I³ 2(?), 45, 49, 104, 105. See also the figures of Hansen, *Athenian Ecclesia*, pp. 108–18, for inscribed laws and decrees of the fourth century.

52. The following laws are attested in the fifth century for which no comparable, contemporary epigraphical evidence exists: a law changing the mode of election of archons from election to sortition (*Ath. Pol.* 22.5); the law opening up the archonship to the *zeugitai* (*Ath. Pol.* 26.2); Perikles' citizenship law (*Ath. Pol.* 26.4); the law establishing jury pay (*Ath. Pol.* 27.3; Plut. *Per.* 9); a law or decree placing restrictions on comedy (Schol. Ar. *Acharn.* 67); the decree of Kannonos regulating procedures in high crimes against the state (Xen. *Hell.* 1.7.20, 34).

53. For destruction of a stele recording a proxeny decree by the Thirty Tyrants, see *IG* II² 6 (= Tod, no. 98) and n. 71 below. Aristotle (*Ath. Pol.* 35.2) says that the Thirty tore down the laws of the Areopagos from the Areopagos; he does not mention a stele specifically, but this seems to be implied: see Rhodes, *CAAP*, p. 440. A purge of documents, including those inscribed on stone, is also attested in the decree of Patrokleides of 405 (Andok. 1.77–79). But its focus is on documents recording the names of those owing money to the state, and only a few of these will have been inscribed on stone.

54. The secretary is first attested in *IG* I³ 7, dated to c. 460, but the title can be restored in the prescript of *IG* I³ 5, line 1, dated to c. 500.

55. Ferguson, *Athenian Secretaries*, pp. 1–12; see also Rhodes, *Athenian Boule*, pp. 133–35.

56. Assistants (*hyperetai*) to the Boule are attested in *IG* I³ 1390. Other undersecre-

taries (ὑπογραμματεῖς) are mentioned at Ar. *Frogs* 1084; see also Antiph. 6.49. According to the speaker of Lysias's *Against Nikomachos*, the defendant Nikomachos had served as an undersecretary before his selection as *anagrapheus* in 410 (Lys. 30.28). Note also the cosecretaries named at *IG* I³ 269, 270, 440, 441.

57. See the opening lines of *IG* I³ 7, 9, 10, 12, 17, 31, etc.

58. Thomas, *Literacy*, p. 86, asks, "why make a frail papyrus copy of the authoritative copy when you had the law on stone?" But laws and decrees were presumably written down on wood or papyrus before being transferred to stone; stone masons did not inscribe texts from dictation.

59. *Ath. Pol.* 45.4: οὐκ ἔξεστιν οὐδὲν ἀπροβούλευτον οὐδ' ὅ τι ἂν μὴ προγράψωσιν οἱ πρυτάνεις ψηφίσασθαι τ¨ δήμῳ. See Rhodes, *CAAP*, pp. 543–44; Hansen, *Athenian Democracy*, pp. 138–39; Rhodes, *Athenian Boule*, pp. 52–53.

60. For the procedure and terminology, as reflected in the texts of inscribed decrees, see Rhodes, *Athenian Boule*, pp. 52–58; more generally, Hansen, *Athenian Democracy*, pp. 138–49. The suggestion of Thomas, *Oral Tradition*, p. 69, that the "process of passing decrees involves written notices posted beneath the eponymous heroes, as is well known," is mistaken; the authorities she cites refer to the process of *nomothesia* (i.e., passing *nomoi* or laws), which differed from the process of enacting decrees, at least in the fourth century. Agendas of meetings of the Ekklesia were published (*Ath. Pol.* 43.3–4), probably four or five days in advance (Photios, s.v. πρόπεμπτα), but it is uncertain how detailed these texts were and what details about individual proposals they offered.

61. See, e.g., *IG* I³ 52, line 2 (= Meiggs-Lewis, no. 28).

62. See, e.g., Xen. *Hell.* 1.7.34 (where the phrase ἔγραψε γνώμην is used); Aeschin. 1.188; 2.18, 53; Dem. 3.14; 18.27, 75; 19.47, 154; 20.38; [Dem.] 7.19, 23; [Dem.] 59.4. See also O. Miller, *De decretis atticis quaestiones epigraphicae*, pp. 9–10.

63. Consider also the use of legislative boards of *syngrapheis*, "composers in writing," to write up and draft legislation, already attested c. 450 in *IG* I³ 21; see also *IG* I³ 78; Andok. 1.96; *Ath. Pol.* 30.1; Ostwald, *Popular Sovereignty*, pp. 415–16. See also Plut. *Per.* 37.3, where Plutarch, referring to Perikles' citizenship law, says that Perikles "wrote the law" (νόμον ἔγραψε).

64. Aeschin. 2.67–68: μαρτυρεῖ Ἀμύντωρ Αἰσχίνῃ... Δημοσθένην ἐπιδείξασθαι παρακαθήμενον ψήφισμα [γεγραμμένον] ἑαυτ¨, ἐφ' ᾧ ἐπεγέγραπτο ἰτὸῖ Δημοσθένους ὄνομα, καὶ ἀνακοινοῦσθαι αὐτὸν αὐτ¨, εἰ δ¨ τοῖς προέδροις ἐπιψηφίσαι....

65. Ar. *Thesm.* 431–32: ταῦτ' ἐγὼ φανερῶς λέγω, / τὰ δ' ἄλλα μετὰ τῆς γραμματέως συγγράψομαι. See Rhodes, *Athenian Boule*, 139.

66. See, e.g., Nepos *Alc.* 4.5; *IG* II² 43, lines 31–35; *IG* II² 116, lines 39–40; Philochoros, *FGrHist* 328 F135.

67. *IG* I³ 61; see Meiggs-Lewis, no. 65, for discussion.

68. The date of the first decree is debated; it is generally dated to c. 430 (so Meiggs-Lewis, no. 65; *ATL*, 3:133), but Mattingly, "Methone Decrees," pp. 154–65, argues for a date of 427/6 for the first decree on the basis of his redating of related tribute lists. The divergence is for our purposes not important. The second decree is dated to 426/5 on the basis of the name of the secretary, Megakleides, who is mentioned in a record of loans (*IG* I³ 369.5 = Meiggs-Lewis, no. 72) as secretary in the first prytany in the archonship of Euthynos (426/5).

69. See Chapter 2, Section IV.

70. *Ath. Pol.* 22.3–5.

71. *IG* II² 6; see Tod, no. 98, for discussion. See also *IG* I³ 229; *IG* II² 52, 66; *Hesperia* 17 (1948): 54–60, no. 65, for other decrees thought to have been torn down by the Thirty. Other suspected fourth-century republications of fifth-century decrees include *IG* I³ 227, 228; *IG* II² 13, 17, 32, 49, 63, 77, 95; in these, no reason is given for republication. For discussion, see Rhodes, *Athenian Boule*, pp. 82–85.

72. For the evidence, see my discussion in the text.

73. Kahrstedt, "Untersuchungen," pp. 30–31. See also Thomas, *Oral Tradition*, pp. 45–50, 73–75; Thomas, *Literacy*, pp. 84–86, where the epigraphists L. Robert and A. Wilhelm are criticized for anachronism in their discussions of ancient archives. For some illustrations of Thomas's misreading of epigraphical evidence, see Sickinger, "Inscriptions and Archives."

74. E.g., *IG* I³ 84, lines 26–28. For the phrase's use with respect to documents displayed on wooden boards, see *IG* I³ 133, lines 10–11; Andok. 1.84; Dem. 24.25.

75. See esp. Meritt, *Epigraphica Attica*, pp. 89–90; Hansen, *Athenian Democracy*, pp. 311–12. Thomas, *Oral Tradition*, pp. 60–61, translates σκοπεῖν to mean "to see" or "to look at," but the verb is more specific and conveys the sense of scrutinizing or examining: see LSJ, s.v. σκοπέω.

76. See also the comments of Boegehold, "Establishment," p. 24: "The document itself or a copy or abstract of the document is official and valid in whatever disposition it exists, no matter if form and phraseology in the original vary somewhat from that in copy or abstract. No one disposition makes a document *ipso facto* more valid or authoritative or authentic." See also Klaffenbach, "Bemerkungen," pp. 35–36; Klaffenbach, *Griechische Epigraphik*, pp. 52–55; and Robert, "Épigraphie," p. 459.

77. Kahrstedt, "Untersuchungen," pp. 30–31; Thomas, *Oral Tradition*, pp. 51–53.

78. Thomas, *Oral Tradition*, p. 53, claims that "archive copies are destroyed along with the public stelai," but she cites no evidence to support this; the only possibly relevant text is the decree of Patrokleides, which, as we have seen, was enacted under emergency circumstances. Its provisions may not reflect normal practices. For further discussion of the destruction of inscriptions, including possible evidence for the survival of archival texts after the removal of stelai, see Chapter 6, Section II.

79. See Aristotle's description of the fourth-century secretary, the secretary *kata prytaneian*, at *Ath. Pol.* 54.3 (discussed further in Chapter 6); similar duties may be assumed for the fifth-century secretary.

80. *IG* II² 1, lines 61–62 (= Tod, no. 97).

81. Ar. *Birds* 1024–25. See Meiggs, *Athenian Empire*, p. 586; Dunbar, *Aristophanes: Birds*, pp. 564–65.

82. For other *episkopoi*, see *IG* I³ 14, lines 13–14; *IG* I³ 34, line 7; see also the *archontes* mentioned in *IG* I³ 34, line 6; *IG* I³ 156, lines 5–7. According to Aristotle (*Ath. Pol.* 24.3), the Athenians employed over seven hundred magistrates at the height of the empire; the figure is often doubted, but the number of overseas officials was certainly high. See Hansen, "Seven Hundred *archai*"; Rhodes, *CAAP*, p. 305.

83. For clauses calling for publication in non-Athenian cities, see, e.g., *IG* I³ 16, lines 44–45; *IG* I³ 37, lines 40–43; *IG* I³ 40, 61–64. See also the text of the Coinage Decree (*IG* I³ 1453 = Meiggs-Lewis, no. 45), fragments of which have surfaced in seven cities; and *IG* I³ 1454, 1454bis, and 1454ter, fragments of other Athenian decrees also published elsewhere.

84. *IG* I³ 1453 §10 (= Meiggs-Lewis, no. 45 §12); for further discussion, see Chapter 2, Section IV.

85. *IG* I³ 98, lines 12–15. See Meiggs-Lewis, no. 80, pp. 247–50, for discussion.

86. *IG* I³ 118, lines 38–42.

87. *IG* I³ 127, lines 27–30. On the implications of this decree for the foundation of the Metroon, see Chapter 4.

88. On the Boule's role in naval matters, see *Ath. Pol.* 46.1; Rhodes, *Athenian Boule*, pp. 113–21. The generals, however, were responsible for choosing trierarchs; see the Themistokles Decree (Meiggs-Lewis, no. 23, lines 18–23); Schol. Ar. *Knights* 912; Dem. 35.48; 39.8; *Ath. Pol.* 61.1. Their role, however, does not exclude the possibility that the Boule kept its own list of trierarchs. In *IG* II² 1623, lines 209–12, a trierarch is said to have received a trireme in accordance with a decree of the Boule.

89. *IG* I³ 78, lines 26–30. For the Boule's role in the administration of the Eleusinian Mysteries, see Rhodes, *Athenian Boule*, pp. 93–95, 127–29.

90. *IG* I³ 34, lines 5–10, 16–18; see also Ps.-Xen. *Ath. Pol.* 3.2; Rhodes, *Athenian Boule*, pp. 89–91.

91. For the Boule's role in assessing tribute, see *IG* I³ 71 (= Meiggs-Lewis, no. 69, with commentary), and *ATL*, 3:70–78.

92. *IG* I³ 68, lines 11–21 (as restored), requires the Hellenotamiai to report to the Ekklesia the names of those cities that have paid the tribute, those that have not, and those that have paid only in part; the names of defaulters are to be posted and displayed on wooden tablets.

93. Curtius, *Das Metroon*, pp. 4–5; Wachsmuth, *Die Stadt der Athens*, pp. 327–44. More recently, Francis, *Image and Idea*, pp. 112–20, argued that a central archive, called τὸ δημόσιον, existed from the time of Ephialtes in a small building just to the north of the Bouleuterion. For this building, commonly but probably mistakenly identified as an archaic shrine to the Mother of the Gods, see further discussion in the text. We hear nothing of Francis's putative archive before the last decade of the fifth century, when other factors suggest that the Bouleuterion was converted into the city's archives building and was itself called τὸ δημόσιον; see Chapter 4, Section II.

94. *IG* I³ 78, lines 26–30; Meiggs-Lewis, no. 73. The decree is dated c. 422.

95. *IG* I³ 68, lines 52–57, dated to 426; Meiggs-Lewis, no. 68. This list is distinct from the publication of the decree on a stone stele mentioned earlier in lines 25–26; presumably the list of collectors was written on a wooden tablet.

96. For a similar use of the Bouleuterion on Delos as an archives building, see Klaffenbach, "Bemerkungen," pp. 23–25.

97. The inscriptions, with their texts, are:

1. *IG* I³ 56, lines 4–8 (c. 440–425): ἀ/[ναγράψαι . . . .⁸.⁻.⁹. . . .]ιον ἐν τῶ/[ι βολευτηρίωι ἐν σαν]ίδ[ι] πρό/[ξενον καὶ εὐεργέτη]ν Ἀθηναί/[ων . . .].

2. *IG* I³ 155, lines 4–9 (c. 435–425): Κρίσονα [. . . . . . . .¹⁶ . . . .]/δελφος καὶ δεκ[. . . .⁷. . . γράφσαι πρ]/οχσένος καὶ εὐ[εργέτας ἐν στέλει λ]/ιθίνει ἐμ πόλει [καὶ ἐν τᾶι βολευτε]/ρίοι ἐς σανίδα τ[ὸν γραμματέα τὲς β]/ολὲς τέλεσι τ[οῖς . . .].

3. *IG* I³ 165, lines 6–11 (before 420): τὸ δὲ φσ]/έφισμα τ[όδε ἀναγρ]άφσα[το hο γραμματεὺς ὁ τ]/ὲς βολὲς [ἐν στέλε]ι λιθίνε[ι καὶ καταθέτο ἐμ] /πόλει ός [ἐν καλλί]στοι καὶ ΕΜ[. . .⁶. . . βολευτ]/[ε]ρίοι ἐ[ν σανιδί]οι ἵναπερ τὰ ἄλλ[α . . .

98. Thompson, "Buildings," pp. 215–17; Pritchett, *Dionysius of Halicarnassus*, p. 54; Pritchett, *Greek Archives*, pp. 26–27; Shear, "Bouleuterion," pp. 185–86.

99. Wilhelm, *Beiträge*, esp. pp. 229–38. Klaffenbach, "Bemerkungen," pp. 21–28, showed that in some of the cases discussed by Wilhelm archival deposition of some

documents, and not public display, was intended. But Klaffenbach's conclusions do not apply to all the examples examined by Wilhelm, and Klaffenbach notes (pp. 23–25) that, although council chambers served as archives buildings in several cities, they were also a place for the public display of important documents, as Wilhelm had argued.

100. See also Plut. *Per.* 30.1, where it is suggested that the Megarian Decree was displayed on a *pinax*, a wooden tablet; see also Schol. Ar. *Peace* 246.

101. Andok. 2.23: ἔτι γὰρ νῦν ἐγγέγραπται (sc. τὸ ψήφισμα) ἐν τ᾿᾿ Βουλευτηρίῳ. The significance of the passage for the keeping of archival records seems to have been recognized first by O. Miller, *De decretis atticis quaestiones epigraphicae.*

102. See *Ath. Pol.* 42.1 with Rhodes, *CAAP*, p. 497.

103. At *IG* I³ 476, lines 289–91, the verb ἐγγράφειν is used in association with writing on papyrus.

104. For the excavations and remains of the building, see Thompson, "Buildings," pp. 127–35; see also Thompson and Wycherley, *Agora*, 14:29–38; Camp, *Athenian Agora*, pp. 52–53, 90–91. Thompson originally dated the building to c. 500, but later changed this dating to c. 460, bringing the construction of the Bouleuterion in line with the reforms of Ephialtes (Thompson, "Athens Faces Adversity," pp. 345–46; Thompson, "The Pnyx in Models," pp. 136–37; Thompson, "Building for a More Democratic Society," pp. 198–204). An extensive review of the excavation records and remains by Shear, "Persian Destruction," pp. 418–24, places the Bouleuterion's construction squarely around 500. Shear also identifies traces of burning, ash, and debris associated with the building's destruction by the Persians in 479 and its subsequent rebuilding.

105. For the use of shelving for storage of objects housed in the Parthenon, see, e.g., *IG* II² 1443, lines 12–88; and D. Harris, *Treasures*, p. 1.

106. For the building, see Thompson, "Buildings," pp. 135–40; Thompson and Wycherley, *Agora*, 14:30–31; Camp, *Athenian Agora*, p. 93.

107. Shear, "Bouleuterion," pp. 171–78, reviews evidence for the cult of the Mother of the Gods in detail and finds no evidence for her public worship before the end of the fifth century. He suggests that the building identified as a Metroon by Thompson may have served as a public treasury. The identification of the building as a Metroon had been rejected already by Francis, *Image and Idea*, pp. 112–20; Francis's suggestion that it served as a public records office called τὸ δημόσιον is not supported by any ancient evidence. (I am grateful to Professor Shear for kindly examining the pottery from the old "Metroon" with me in 1992, for providing me with an offprint of his article, and for discussing with me several points related to the building history of the Bouleuterion.)

108. On the decentralized nature of Athenian archives before the late fifth century, see Stroud, *Drakon's Law*, pp. 28–29; see also Ostwald, *Popular Sovereignty*, p. 410; Boegehold, "Establishment," pp. 29–30. Drakon's law and the king archon: *IG* I³ 104, lines 5–7.

109. For the sake of convenience, I subsume the "headings" and "superscripts" of inscriptions under the rubric "prescript." On prescripts and their functions, see Henry, *Prescripts*, esp. pp. 10 n. 36, 104–5; see also Ferguson, *Athenian Secretaries*, pp. 27–31; Rhodes, *Athenian Boule*, p. 135; and, most recently, W. West, "Public Archives," pp. 530–31.

110. So, e.g., the proposal of Demosthenes seen by Amyntor had Demosthenes'

name on it, but apparently not the names of presiding officials (Aeschin. 2.67: see n. 64 above). These would be added by the secretary to a decree's text at the time of publication.

111. The archon's name is first securely attested in a prescript in *IG* I³ 80 of 421/0. On the date of the Segesta alliance, see now Chambers, Gallucci, and Spanos, "Athens' Alliance with Egesta." On archon dating and the 421 rule, see Mattingly, "Athens and Eleusis"; Henry, "Archon-Dating."

112. Thomas, *Oral Tradition*, pp. 78–79, argues for inadequacies of the system; see also Todd, "Lysias against Nikomachos," pp. 124–25, on the absence of archon dates.

113. For list of generals of 441/0, see Androtion, *FGrHist* 324 F38; on lists of officials in general, see Jacoby, *Atthis*, p. 174.

114. Ferguson, *Athenian Secretaries*, pp. 14–18. Of course, the names of all secretaries were presumably recorded when they were elected by the Boule.

115. The decree is conventionally dated to c. 445; see Meiggs-Lewis, no. 49, for discussion. For reference to the secretary, see lines 17–21: ἐὰν δέ τις ἐπιστρα[τεύει ἐπὶ τὲν γῆ]ν τὲν τᾶν ἀποίκον, βοεθὲν τὰ[ς πόλες h/ος ὀχσύ]τατα κατὰ τὰς χσυγγραφὰς ὀᾳ[ὶ ἐπὶ . ./ . . .6. . .]το γραμματεύοντος ἐγένον[το περὶ τ/ᾶν πόλε]ον τᾶν ἐπὶ Θράικες.

116. Other Athenian decrees cross-reference their provisions with texts inscribed on other stelai: see Tod, no. 118, lines 19–24; *IG* II² 40, lines 18–20.

117. In the second edition of *IG*, the lacuna of line 20 is partially restored (*IG* I² 45, line 16): πρό]το γραμματεύοντος, "when so-and-so was first secretary [sc. of the Boule]." This restoration is questioned by Meiggs-Lewis, because it leaves too little room for the name of the secretary. But see Ferguson, *Athenian Secretaries*, p. 30.

118. For a brief discussion of the Athenian calendars, see Rhodes, *Athenian Boule*, pp. 224–29, with references to earlier literature; and Chambers, *Staat*, pp. 339–48. Pritchett and Neugabauer, *Calendars of Athens*, remains a valuable introduction to calendric and epigraphical problems.

119. First mention of the first secretary of the year in a decree: *IG* I³ 53 (Meiggs-Lewis, no. 63); the date, however, at which the prescript was inscribed is disputed: see Meiggs-Lewis, pp. 178–80. The first unambiguous mention of the first Boule secretary in an inscribed decree is found in *IG* I³ 71, lines 55–57, of 425/4. Mention of the first secretary of the Boule appears or can be restored in *IG* I³ 436–51, the building accounts of the Parthenon, which date from 447/5 to 433/2.

120. So, e.g., in the Tribute Quota Lists (*IG* I³ 259–90), and the Parthenon building accounts (*IG* I³ 436–51).

121. The names of an archon and first Boule secretary are given in *IG* I³ 446, 447, 449, 450; both probably should be restored in *IG* I³ 448.

122. So, e.g., Perikles' citizenship law is dated to the archonship of Antidotos (451/0) (*Ath. Pol.* 26.4); a measure concerning restrictions on comic performances is dated to the archonships of Morychides (440/39), repealed in the archonship of Glaukos (437/6) (Schol. Ar. *Acharn.* 67). Treaty with Leontinoi: *IG* I³ 53 (Meiggs-Lewis, no. 63); assessment decree: *IG* I³ 71, lines 55–57.

123. On the nature of many inscribed documents as extracts, see Wilhelm, *Beiträge*, pp. 275–84; Boegehold, "Establishment," p. 24; and my comments on inscribed financial records earlier in Section II of this chapter.

124. Thomas, *Oral Tradition*, pp. 78–80.

125. *IG* I³ 369.

126. *IG* I³ 377, lines 4–5, 5–7, 8, etc. (dated 407/6 [?]); *IG* I³ 378, lines 9, 10, 11, 20 (dated 406/5 [?]). See also mention of prytany dates in the Erechtheion accounts: *IG* I³ 475, lines 91–92, 272–85.

127. *IG* I³ 430, lines 5–6, 10, 13.

128. Photios, s.v. πρόπεμπτα.

129. *IG* I³ 45, lines 7–14.

130. See, e.g., *IG* I³ 40, lines 12–14 (446/5), where members of the Boule and dikasts swear that ambassadors from Chalkis will be granted access to the Boule and Ekklesia within ten days of their arrival in Athens. In *IG* I³ 46, lines 33–34, a provision requires colonists to leave Athens within thirty days (presumably from the date of the decree's enactment); see also *IG* I³ 64, lines 6–7; *IG* I³ 85, lines 7–12; *IG* I³ 93, line 15; *IG* I³ 105, lines 38–39, 51, for other actions to be completed or undertaken within a set number of days.

131. On the composition question, see Andrewes and Dover, *HCT*, 5:384–444; on these documents and their relationship to Thucydides' narrative, see Gomme, *HCT*, 3:680–82; see also C. Meyer, *Urkunden*, pp. 13–35, with references to earlier scholarship.

132. Thuc. 4.118.11–12: Ἔδοξεν τ˙ δήμῳ. Ἀκαμαντὶς ἐπρυτάνευε, Φαίνιππος ἐγραμμάτευε, Νικιάδης ἐπεστάτει. Λάχης εἶπε, τύχῃ ἀγαθῇ τῇ Ἀθηναίων, ποιεῖσθαι τὴν ἐκεχειρίαν καθ᾿ ἃ ξυγχωροῦσι Λακεδαιμόνιοι καὶ οἱ ξύμμαχοι αὐτῶν καὶ ὡμολόγησαν ἐν τ˙ δήμῳ· τὴν ἰδῖ ἐκεχειρίαν εἶναι ἐνιαυτόν, ἄρχειν δὲ τήνδε τὴν ἡμέραν, τετράδα ἐπὶ δέκα τοῦ Ἐλαφηβολιῶνος μηνός.

133. Thuc. 5.19.1: ˙Ἄρχει δὲ τῶν σπονδῶν ἰὲν μὲν Λακεδαίμονῖ ἔφορος Πλει-στόλας Ἀρτεμισίου μηνὸς τετάρτῃ φθίνοντος, ἐν δὲ Ἀθήναις ἄρχων Ἀλκαῖος Ἐλαφηβολιῶνος μηνὸς ἕκτῃ φθίνοντος.

134. Hornblower, *Commentary*, 2:359, discusses the possibility that the decree ratifying the one-year truce existed only in a published copy on the Acropolis, citing with approval a view of Thomas (*Oral Tradition*, p. 76) that decrees on foreign relations were set up on the Acropolis. But neither Hornblower nor Thomas offers any parallels for publication on stone of a decree of such limited duration, and Hornblower himself expresses reservations. The peace treaty of 421, however, was to be published at Olympia, Isthmia, and Delphi, as well as at Athens and Sparta (Thuc. 5.18.10). Thucydides may have obtained a copy taken from these inscriptions, but for reasons outlined in the text I think this unlikely. I see no compelling objections to the preservation of these decrees in archives maintained by the Boule, which Thucydides could have consulted when he returned to Athens after the Peloponnesian War (so Kirchhoff, *Thukydides*, pp. 21–27). But it seems more likely that he obtained his texts much earlier from a copy that was distributed to a private citizen or one of the signatories. See Gomme, *HCT*, 3:605–7; Andrewes, *HCT*, 5:383. See also my discussion for the distribution of decrees by the secretary of the Boule in Section II.

135. In a sense, the omission of dates from inscribed copies of decrees makes some sense. Publication was not necessary to validate a decree, but publication of a decree on a stone stele may have implied that a decree's contents were valid. Hence, there was no need to record a specific enactment date, since any standing decree could be assumed to be valid, regardless of its date.

136. *SEG* 41 (1991): no. 9, lines 3–4: [ἐπὶ] Ἀλκαίο ἄρχοντος *vacat* / [ἐ]νάτηι καὶ δεκάτηι τῆς πρυτανείας. See also Hansen, "Was the Athenian Ekklesia Convened?," p. 103, who reaches a similar conclusion to the one discussed in the text. The decree

was at least the second on the stone; traces of another decree appear above the preserved text, and this decree, presumably later in date, will have ordered publication of the earlier text. See also the decree of the Boule of 411 indicting Antiphon, Archeptolemos, and Onomakles for treason ([Plut.] *Vit. X Or.* 833e–f); its prescript indicates that it was enacted on the twenty-first of the prytany (though the name of the tribe holding the prytany is not mentioned). This too may suggest that prytany dates were normally included in the records of the proceedings of the Boule during the fifth century, but not routinely inscribed on stone.

137. On archon dating, see n. 111.

138. Henry, *Prescripts*, pp. 104–5.

139. On Krateros, see Jacoby, *FGrHist* 342; Krech, *De Crateri*, esp. pp. 5–25.

140. For discussion of Krateros's collection of decrees and its sources, see Chapter 7, Section III.

Chapter Four

1. The main sources for the Four Hundred and the intermediate regime succeeding them are the eighth book of Thucydides' history of the Peloponnesian War and *Ath. Pol.* 29–33. For discussion of the events, see Hignett, *HAC*, pp. 268–80, 356–78; Sealey, *Essays*, pp. 111–32; Rhodes, "Five Thousand," pp. 115–27; Ostwald, *Popular Sovereignty*, pp. 337–411; on the sources, see Rhodes, *CAAP*, pp. 362–39; Andrewes, *HCT*, 5:184–256.

2. *Ath. Pol.* 29.2–3; for the suggestion that Pythodoros's motion called for a review of Solon's laws, see Walters, "Ancestral Constitution," pp. 135–37; on the proposals in general, see Ostwald, *Popular Sovereignty*, pp. 369–74; Andrewes, *HCT*, 5:213–15; Rhodes, *CAAP*, pp. 372–77. On Pythodoros's decree and Kleitophon's amendments, see also my discussion in Chapter 2, Section IV.

3. On these documents, see *Ath. Pol.* 30.2–31, with Rhodes, *CAAP*, pp. 387–89; Chambers, *Staat*, pp. 280–85; see also E. Harris, "Constitution of the Five Thousand."

4. So Harrison, "Law-Making," p. 31; Stroud, *Drakon's Law*, p. 24.

5. On the locations of the laws of Drakon and Solon, see Chapter 1.

6. For discussion, see Chapter 2, Section IV.

7. The keeping of laws related to their duties by individual magistrates may be inferred from the *basileus*'s possession of a text of Drakon's homicide law: *IG* I³ 104, lines 8–9. For the same reason, the secretary of the Boule may have had a text of the Bouleutic Oath (*IG* I³ 1453 §10 [= Meiggs-Lewis, no. 45 §12]).

8. So Harrison, "Law-Making," p. 31, noting difficulties arising from "accretions" to the laws of Drakon and Solon.

9. That fifth-century litigants consulted archival texts may be indicated by a charge leveled against Nikomachos in Lysias's speech *Against Nikomachos*, where the speaker claims (Lys. 30.3) that opposing litigants received contradictory laws from Nikomachos. On the limited publication of decrees on stone during the fifth century, see Immerwahr, *Attic Script*, pp. 121–22, and my discussion in Chapter 3, Section II. On the locations of inscriptions, see Sickinger, "Inscriptions and Archives," p. 293.

10. See Chapter 3, Section III.

11. On fourth-century procedures and the distinction between *nomoi* and *psēphismata*, see, e.g., Ostwald, *Nomos*, pp. 1–3; Quass, *Nomos*, pp. 23–44, 68–72; Hansen, *Athenian Ecclesia*, pp. 161–76, 179–206; Sealey, *Athenian Republic*, pp. 45–58.

12. On this point, see Hansen, "*Nomos,*" p. 316; Ostwald, *Nomos,* p. 2 with n. 2; and, most recently, Rhodes, "Athenian Code," pp. 91–92; Robertson, "Laws of Athens," p. 43.

13. For Solon's laws on inheritance, see *Ath. Pol.* 9.2; Solon frr. 49–52 Ruschen-busch; on Athenian inheritance law in general, Harrison, *LA,* 1:122–62.

14. For the keeping of magisterial archives, see n. 7.

15. In this respect, it would be useful to know when the *graphē paranomōn,* a procedure for indicting unconstitutional proposals, was instituted. The earliest attested use of the procedure occurred in 415 (Andok. 1.17), but its origins may be much earlier; proposed dates range from the time of Solon to the late fifth century. See Wolff, *Normenkontrolle,* pp. 18–19; Ostwald, *Popular Sovereignty,* p. 135 n. 158, for discussion and references to further literature.

16. Thucydides (8.97.2) mentions *nomothetai* who were appointed under the intermediate regime before the democracy was fully restored; *pace* Ostwald, *Popular Sovereignty,* pp. 406–10, I do not believe that their work was connected with those of the *anagrapheis*; for discussion of the various *syngrapheis* and *anagrapheis* of this period, see Stroud, *Drakon's Law,* pp. 20–28.

17. For recent discussions, see Sealey, *Justice,* pp. 44–50; Rhodes, "Athenian Code," pp. 87–100; Robertson, "Laws of Athens," pp. 43–75. Todd, "Lysias against Nikomachos," offers a good study of Lysias's speech and the background to it. Earlier discussions include: Harrison, "Law-Making," pp. 26–35; Dow, "Athenian Calendar," pp. 270–93; Dow, "Walls" pp. 58–73; Dow, "Law Codes," pp. 3–36; MacDowell, *Andokides,* pp. 194–99; Fingarette, "New Look," pp. 330–35; Clinton, "Nature," pp. 27–37; Ostwald, *Popular Sovereignty,* pp. 414–20, 511–24.

18. The chronology of the *anagrapheis'* terms is provided by Lys. 30.2–5; see Dow, "Athenian Calendar," pp. 271–72; Ostwald, *Popular Sovereignty,* p. 407; Rhodes, "Athenian Code," pp. 88–89.

19. Lys. 30.4: ἀναγράψαι τοὺς νόμους τοῦ Σολῶνος.

20. Clinton, "Nature," pp. 28–30, argues that the *anagrapheis* were concerned only with the laws of Solon still in use: they published those plus any revisions to them but omitted Solonian laws rendered obsolete by later legislation. At the same time, they did not publish sixth- and fifth-century laws on subjects not treated by Solon. Clinton also notes (pp. 32–33) in support of this view that a publication of the entire Athenian law code on stone probably could not have fit inside the Stoa Basileios. Clinton's view is attractive, but references to the "laws of Solon" in the orators included not only revisions of Solon's laws but also laws on subjects not addressed by Solon (e.g., Dem. 20.93 on *nomothesia*), and among the inscribed laws attributed to the *anagrapheis* is a law on naval matters (*IG* I³ 236), which is difficult to see as either a Solonian law or a revision of a Solonian law. Clinton's general conclusion, that the *anagrapheis* did not publish all Athenian laws, seems sound, but I think we must take the phrase, "the laws of Solon," in the duties of the *anagrapheis* in the broader sense of the fourth-century orators.

21. Lys. 30.2. Rhodes, "Athenian Code," p. 89, suggests that a term limit of four months was not expressly stated when the *anagrapheis* were appointed; Harrison, "Law-Making," p. 30, suggests the opposite. I see no way to decide the question.

22. So Robertson, "Laws of Athens," pp. 52–56; see also Rhodes, "Athenian Code," p. 92. Dow, however, took a much broader view of the duties and powers of the *anagrapheis* ("Law Codes").

23. We do hear, however, of *syngrapheis* during this period: Demophantos is named as a *syngrapheus* in a decree of 410/9 that deals with tyranny and draws on earlier measures on the same subject (Andok. 1.96–98), while *IG* I³ 99 preserves a *gnōmē* or "decision" of a board of *syngrapheis* concerning the repayment of moneys owed to Athena. Ostwald, *Popular Sovereignty*, pp. 407–11, 414–16, believes that *syngrapheis* operated continually from 410 to 404, and that they collected laws which the *anagrapheis* then prepared for publication. I do not believe that the evidence is sufficient to warrant this view, but I suppose that *syngrapheis* could have been appointed by the Ekklesia on a piecemeal or ad hoc basis to deal with specific laws or measures in cases where the *anagrapheis* were uncertain about which of the provisions they found were still valid.

24. See Lys. 30.2, for charges that Nikomachos "registered some laws and erased others."

25. On the Thirty, see Xen. *Hell.* 2.3.2; annulment of laws of Ephialtes (with destruction of stelai implied) and some of Solon's laws: *Ath. Pol.* 35.2 (see also Chapter 3 for destruction of other stelai); a scholiast to Aeschin. 1.39 states that the Thirty "maltreated" the laws of Drakon and Solon; what this consisted of is unclear. Fingarette, "New Look," pp. 330–35, argued that the Thirty were responsible for an erasure found on one side of the wall of joining stelai (see further discussion in the text), and this is accepted by Ostwald, *Popular Sovereignty*, pp. 479–80. Since we cannot know what originally stood in the erasure, certainty is impossible, but the scholium to Aeschines 1.39, not cited by Fingarette, lends her arguments additional support.

26. For Nikomachos's second term, see Lys. 30.17–21; Robertson, "Laws of Athens," pp. 65–66, argues that in their second term the *anagrapheis* also continued to compile secular laws. Although this is possible, I believe that their work with secular law was superseded by the appointment of the boards of *nomothetai* mentioned in the decree of Teisamenos (Andok. 1.83–84).

27. Andok. 1.80–91; for discussions of Andokides' account, see MacDowell, *Andokides*, pp. 194–99; Harrison, "Law-Making," pp. 32–33; and, most recently, Robertson, "Laws of Athens," pp. 60–65, and Rhodes, "Athenian Code," pp. 95–100.

28. Andok. 1.84: τοὺς δὲ κυρουμένους τῶν νόμων ἀναγράφειν εἰς τὸν τοῖχον, ἵνα περ πρότερον ἀνεγράφησαν, σκοπεῖν τ᾿᾿ βουλομένῳ. For discussion of publication, see my discussion in the text.

29. The Thirty are explicitly attested as destroying only stelai (see n. 25); we have no evidence that they conducted systematic purges of documents written on other media and found in the city's archives.

30. The boards of *nomothetai* named in Teisamenos's decree must have been created before the decree's enactment since the decree itself makes no provisions for their appointment. See Harrison, "Law-Making," p. 33; MacDowell, *Andokides*, pp. 194–99; Ostwald, *Popular Sovereignty*, pp. 510–14.

31. Andok. 1.85–87. Other sources attest to still further measures, not referred to by Andokides, enacted shortly after the restoration of the democracy; see Ostwald, *Popular Sovereignty*, pp. 497–509.

32. Andok. 1.85: ἀγράφῳ δὲ νόμῳ τὰς ἀρχὰς μὴ χρῆσθαι μηδὲ περὶ ἑνός. For discussion, see MacDowell, *Andokides*, pp. 125–26; Ostwald, "Was There a Concept of ἄγραφος νόμος?," pp. 91–92.

33. Andok. 1.87: τοῖς νόμοις χρῆσθαι ἀπ᾿ Εὐκλείδου ἄρχοντος. For discussion, see MacDowell, *Andokides*, pp. 128–29.

34. Andok. 1.87: ψήφισμα δὲ μηδὲν μήτε βουλῆς μήτε δήμου νόμου κυριώτερον εἶναι. For discussion, see MacDowell, *Andokides*, p. 127; Rhodes, "Athenian Code," pp. 96–97.

35. Dem. 24.42: τοὺς νόμους τοὺς πρὸ Εὐκλείδου τεθέντας ἐν δημοκρατίᾳ καὶ ὅσοι ἐπ᾽ Εὐκλείδου ἐτέθησαν καὶ εἰσὶν ἀναγεγραμμένοι, κυρίους εἶναι. For further discussion of Diokles' law and its relationship to the revision of the laws, see Hansen, "Diokles' Law."

36. It is also possible that the qualification refers to laws enacted under the Four Hundred in 411, since the events of that year could also be distinguished from events under the democracy; see Patrokleides' decree of 405 (Andok. 1.78). But it seems unlikely that any laws enacted in that year would have remained "on the books" after the restoration of the full democracy in 410.

37. One feature of the wording of Diokles' law requires comment. In literal terms, the law makes valid laws enacted under the democracy and prior to Eukleides' archonship, and laws enacted during Eukleides' archonship and "written up." Clinton, "Nature," p. 28, takes this distinction to mean that laws enacted before Eukleides' archonship did not have to be "written up," meaning published in the work of the *anagrapheis*, to be valid. But Clinton may take too limited a view of the duties of the *anagrapheis* in their first term; see n. 20 above. I take the phrase "and have been written up" to be a reference to the provisions of Teisamenos's decree. Under Teisamenos's decree laws were being enacted not by the Boule and Ekklesia, as they had been previously, but by *nomothetai*; therefore, it was necessary for newly enacted laws to be "written up" immediately, as Teisamenos's decree stipulates; laws approved but not yet written up during Eukleides' archonship were not to be valid. This requirement, however, has no bearing on the work of the *anagrapheis* in their first term or whether the laws compiled by them were also "written up." On the physical form of publication of the *anagrapheis'* work and the laws enacted by Teisamenos's decree, see the discussion in the text.

38. Ostwald, *Popular Sovereignty*, pp. 497–524; Sealey, *Athenian Republic*, pp. 146–48.

39. For the organization of laws in the Metroon, see Chapter 6, Section II.

40. For this view, see, e.g., Fingarette, "New Look," pp. 330–35; Clinton, "Nature," pp. 27–37; Rhodes, "Athenian Code," pp. 90–91, 100; MacDowell, *LCA*, pp. 46–48; Hansen, *Athenian Democracy*, pp. 162–64.

41. Lys. 30.4; for the use of *anagrapsai* to denote publication on stone, see, e.g., *IG* I³ 10, lines 22–27; *IG* I³ 40, lines 57–63; *IG* I³ 62, lines 7–11; Andok. 1.51; Aeschin. 3.70; [Dem.] 59.105; Lys. 30.20. But see n. 48 below.

42. *IG* I³ 104, 105.

43. For the wall of joining stelai, see esp. Dow, "Law Codes," pp. 3–36; Dow, "Athenian Calendar," pp. 270–93; Dow, "Walls," pp. 58–73. The erasure was identified and discussed by Dow, "Walls," pp. 58–73. The texts in the old Attic alphabet are published as *IG* I³ 236–41; the texts written in Ionic are: *IG* II² 1357; *Hesperia* 3 (1934): 46–47, no. 34; *Hesperia* 4 (1935): 5–32, no. 2; *Hesperia* 10 (1941): 31–37, no. 2.

44. The change in alphabet is mentioned by Theopompos, *FGrHist* 115 F155; see also Douris, *FGrHist* 76 F66. The erasure itself is attributed to the Thirty (Fingarette, "New Look," pp. 330–35) or the restored democracy of 403/2 (Clinton, "Nature," pp. 32, 35) or to the speaker of Lysias's *Against Nikomachos*, who was victorious in his prosecution of Nikomachos in the early 390s (Robertson, "Laws of Athens," pp. 65–75).

45. Andokides does not name the stoa in which, according to him, the Athenians published their laws, but because Drakon's homicide law was to be set up in front of the Stoa Basileios (*IG* I³ 104), and because Aristotle (*Ath. Pol.* 7.1) says that Solon's laws were set up in the same place, it is frequently inferred that copies of all of Athens's laws could be found there in the fourth century. See Ostwald, *Popular Sovereignty*, pp. 513 n. 60, 519; Rhodes, "Athenian Code," p. 99. But, as Hansen, "Diokles' Law," pp. 70–71, points out, we hear nothing of current Athenian laws in the Stoa Basileios after Andokides' speech.

46. See Dow *apud* Rhodes, *CAAP*, pp. 134–35, 441–42; Ostwald, *Popular Sovereignty*, pp. 519–20.

47. Robertson, "Laws of Athens," pp. 46–75, esp. 46–60. Rhodes, "Athenian Code," p. 99, accepts some of Robertson's conclusions but believes that the *anagrapheis* had published laws on stone in or near the Stoa Basileios; for further criticisms of Robertson's conclusions, see Sealey, *Justice*, pp. 45–49.

48. See, e.g., *IG* I³ 68, lines 19–20; *IG* I³ 78, lines 26–30; Andok. 1.83 (the decree of Teisamenos, discussed previously); Aeschin. 3.38; Dem. 24.23; *Ath. Pol.* 47.2–5.

49. Robertson, "Laws of Athens," pp. 55–60, noting the emphasis on public expenditure on the face inscribed in the old Attic alphabet.

50. Dow, "Law Codes," p. 9, noted that sacred laws were far more numerous than secular, but he also pointed out ("Walls," p. 67) that less than 10 percent of the original inscription survives; any deductions drawn from the surviving fragments of the joining stelai about their original content can only be regarded as tentative.

51. Hansen, *Athenian Democracy*, p. 164; Hansen, "Diokles' Law," pp. 63–71.

52. Dem. 24.42: τοὺς δὲ μετ' Εὐκλείδην τεθέντας καὶ τὸ λοιπὸν τιθεμένους κυρίους εἶναι ἀπὸ τῆς ἡμέρας ἧ ἕκαστος ἐτέθη, πλὴν εἴ τ῾̈ προσγέγραπται χρόνος ὅντινα δεῖ ἄρχειν. ἐπιγράψαι δὲ τοῖς μὲν νῦν κειμένοις τὸν γραμματέα τῆς βουλῆς τριάκοντα ἡμερῶν. τὸ δὲ λοιπόν, ὃς ἂν τυγχάνῃ γραμματεύων, προσγραφέτω παραχρῆμα τὸν νόμον κύριον εἶναι ἀπὸ τῆς ἡμέρας ἧς ἐτέθη.

53. The prescripts of some fourth-century laws do include the dates according to the bouleutic calendar on which they were enacted (*IG* II² 140, lines 2–3); other laws, however, fail to provide any specific dating formula in their prescripts: see *SEG* 26 (1976–77): no. 72. I suspect that the type of statement regarding the effective date of a law intended by Diokles' law is precisely like the one found in the one-year truce concluded between Athens and Sparta in 423 (Thuc. 4.118); see my discussion in Chapter 3, section III.

54. So, also, Hansen, "Was the Athenian Ekklesia Convened?," pp. 103–6. In the fourth century, the secretary of the Boule is given responsibility for the publication of *nomoi* as well as *psēphismata* in the fourth century, probably because his (or the Boule's) archives were the source of official copies of Athenian laws.

55. See Chapter 3, Section II.

56. The only other possible occasion for the establishment of the Metroon as an archives building that I can suggest is the reform of the office of the secretary of the Boule in the 360s B.C. But this seems too late for the archaeological evidence.

57. Andok. 2.24 (see Chapter 3); earliest explicit reference to a document housed in the Metroon: Dem. 19.129 (343 B.C.). Thompson, "Buildings," pp. 215–17, had suggested that a passage of Athenaios (9.72.407b–c), which describes Alkibiades erasing a document found in the Metroon, provided a terminus ante quem of 407, when

Alkibiades last left Athens, but the historicity of the event is subject to grave doubts: see Kahrstedt, "Untersuchungen," pp. 27, 31 n. 32, and my discussion in Chapter 5, Section IV.

58. Aeschin. 2.59, 92.

59. *IG* II² 140, lines 31–35.

60. *IG* II² 1445, line 24; see Woodward, "Treasure-Records," pp. 99–100; Wycherley, no. 507.

61. For the old and new Bouleuterion, see Thompson, "Buildings," pp. 115–224; see also Thompson and Wycherley, *Agora*, 14:29–38; Camp, *Athenian Agora*, pp. 90–94. Evidence for the date of construction of the new Bouleuterion has been reviewed by Shear, "Bouleuterion," pp. 178–84. The latest datable piece is a bolsal whose closest parallel dates to c. 400.

62. Theoph. *Characters* 21.11 (= Wycherley, no. 494); see also Dem. *Proem.* 54 (= Wycherley, no. 474).

63. *SEG* 26 (1976–77): no. 72, lines 10–13: ἐὰν δὲ ὑπ[όχαλκον] /ἢ ὑπομόλυβδον ἢ κίβδηλον διακοπτέτω πα[. . .6. . .]/α καὶ ἔστω ἱερὸν τῆς Μητρὸς τῶν θεῶγ καὶ κ[αταβαλ]/λέτω ἐς τὴμ βολήν. The requirement that counterfeit coins, sacred to the Mother of the Gods, be deposited with the Boule suggests that the coins were deposited in the Metroon itself. See also Aristotle's account of the *pōlētai*, where certain of their records are handed over to the Boule (*Ath. Pol.* 47.2, 4); but these records too seem to have been kept in the Metroon: see my discussion in Chapter 5.

64. Ps.-Plut. *Vit. X Orat.* 842f (= Wycherley, no. 491): μέλλων δὲ τελευτήσειν εἰς τὸ μητρ῭ον καὶ τὸ βουλευτήριον ἐκέλευσεν αὐτὸν κομισθῆναι, βουλόμενος εὐθύνας δοῦναι τῶν πεπολιτευμένων.

65. Photios and *Suda*, s.v. μητραγύρτης· ἐλθών τις εἰς τὴν Ἀττικὴν ἐμύει τὰς γυναῖκας τῇ μητρὶ τῶν θεῶν, ὡς ἐκεῖνοί φασιν. οἱ δὲ Ἀθηναῖοι ἀπέκτειναν αὐτὸν ἐμβαλόντες εἰς βάραθρον ἐπὶ κεφαλήν. λοιμοῦ δὲ γενομένου, ἔλαβον χρησμὸν ἱλάσασθαι τὸν πεφονευμένον. καὶ διὰ τοῦτο ᾠκοδόμησαν βουλευτήριον, ἐν ᾧ ἀνεῖλον τὸν μητραγύρτην, καὶ περιφράττοντες αὐτὸ καθιέρωσαν τῇ μητρὶ τῶν θεῶν, ἀναστήσαντες καὶ ἀνδριάντα τοῦ μητραγύρτου. ἐχρῶντο δὲ τ῭ Μητρῴῳ ἀρχείῳ καὶ νομοφυλακείῳ, καταχώσαντες καὶ τὸ βάραθρον. Wycherley, no. 487, notes that a scholium to Ar. *Plutus* 431, tells the same story without, however, referring to a Bouleuterion or Metroon, and that Apostolios 11.34 (fifteenth century A.D.), substitutes δικαστήριον for βουλευτήριον. On these legends, see now Parker, *Athenian Religion*, pp. 188–91.

66. Shear, "Bouleuterion," pp. 173, 177–78.

67. On plagues in foundation legends, see the myth associated with Artemis at Brauron (*Suda*, s.v. Ἄρκτος ἢ Βραυρωνίοις); there, a plague and oracle are connected with the origins of certain rituals associated with the cult of Artemis. Wilamowitz, "Galliamboi," p. 195 n. 3, points out that the story of the introduction of the cult of the Mother at Athens first appears in Julian, *Or.* 5.159a (fourth century A.D.), where, however, nothing is said of the murder of the *mētragyrtēs* or the Bouleuterion. Wilamowitz also suggests that the story as told by Photios lacks historical value.

68. On this goddess, see Burkert, *Greek Religion*, pp. 177–78; Parker, *Athenian Religion*, pp. 188–98.

69. Kratinos, frr. 62, 82 Kock; Eur. *Helen* 1301–68; Soph. *Phil.* 391–402; Ar. *Birds* 848–75; see Shear, "Bouleuterion," pp. 173–75.

70. On the introduction of foreign gods in the late fifth century, see Garland, *Introducing New Gods*; Dodds, "Maenadism," pp. 171–76; Parker, *Athenian Religion*, pp. 188–98.

71. Paus. 1.3.5; Pliny *Nat. Hist.* 36.17; see also Arrian *Periplous* 9. Date of Pheidias's exile: Philochoros, *FGrHist* 328 F141; see Ostwald, *Popular Sovereignty*, pp. 192–93. We have little evidence for the chronology of Agorakritos's career except for Pliny's statement that he was a student of Pheidias. This suggests little more than that Agorakritos was active in the second half of the fifth century; regarding his responsibility for the cult statue of the Mother of the Gods in the Metroon, it may be noteworthy that Alkamenes, another student of Pheidias, was active as late as 403/2 (see Paus. 9.11.6); the same should be true for Agorakritos as well.

72. Andok. 1.77–79; on the decree's provisions, see, most recently, Boegehold, "Andokides," pp. 149–162.

73. *IG* I³ 127, lines 25–32 (see n. 81 below).

74. Hdt. 1.14.2; Aeschin. 3.58, 273.

75. E.g., Dem. 24.123; 37.25; 39.14; 58.45; see Schulthess, "ὀφείλοντες τ῀ δημοσίῳ," cols. 627–29. A law quoted at Dem. 24.45 seems to differentiate between sacred debts owed to the gods (τοῖς θεοῖς) and secular debts owed to the public treasury (τ῀ δημοσίῳ).

76. Hdt. 6.52, 57, where *to dēmosion* seems to refer to a public hall or building. The terms of the Peace of Nikias (Thuc. 5.18) order the Athenians to return Spartan prisoners who are held *en tōi dēmosiōi* or simply *en dēmosiōi*; the wording suggests a contrast between a specific place *to dēmosion* and the more general public domain.

77. See Klaffenbach, "Bemerkungen," pp. 6–22, esp. 11–14; Boegehold, "Establishment," pp. 23–24. Earlier, Wilhelm, *Beiträge*, pp. 235–99, esp. 257–64, had argued that instructions for documents to be set up in the *dēmosion* or among the *dēmosia grammata* referred to their display on a whitened tablet in a public place; the examples cited by Klaffenbach, however, make this view unacceptable; see *SIG* 3 368; *IG* XII.7.67; *IPriene* 64.

78. Dem. 19.129: ἀλλ' ὑπὲρ μὲν τῆς ἐξωμοσίας ἐν τοῖς κοινοῖς τοῖς ὑμετέροις γράμμασιν ἐν τ῀ μητρῴῳ ταῦτ' ἐστίν, ἐφ' οἷς ὁ δημόσιος τέτακται, καὶ ψήφισμ' ἄντικρυς περὶ τούτου τοῦ ὀνόματος γέγραπται.

79. Dem. 18.142: Τί οὖν ταῦτ' ἐπήραμαι καὶ διετεινάμην οὑτωσὶ σφοδρῶς; ὅτι καὶ γράμματ' ἔχων ἐν τ῀ δημοσίῳ κείμενα, ἐξ ὧν ταῦτ' ἐπιδείξω σαφῶς, καὶ ὑμᾶς εἰδὼς τὰ πεπραγμένα μνημονεύοντας, ἐκεῖνο φοβοῦμαι, μὴ τῶν εἰργασμένων αὐτ῀ κακῶν οὗτος ἐλάττων ὑποληφθῇ. See also Dem. 18.55, 19.129.

80. Boegehold, "Establishment," pp. 21–30.

81. *IG* I³ 127, lines 25–32: ταῖς δὲ τριήρεσι /[ταῖς] ὅσαις ἐς Σάμωι χρῆσθαι αὐτοῖς δ]ᾶναι ἐπισκευασαμένοις καθότι ἂν αὐ/[τοῖς δ]οκῆι· τὰ δὲ ὀνόματα τῶν τριηράρχων, ὧν ἦσαν αὗται αἱ νῆες, ἀπογράψαι/ [τὸς πρέσ]βες τῶι γραμματεῖ τῆς βολῆς καὶ τοῖς στρατηγοῖς, καὶ τούτων εἴ πο/[......¹¹.....]α γεγραμμένον ἐν τῶι δημοσίωι ὡς παρειληφότων τὰς τριήρες,/ [ἅπαντα ἐξαλειψά]ντων οἱ νεωροὶ ἁπανταχόθεν, τὰ δὲ σκεύη τῶι δημοσίωι ἐσ/[πραξάντων ὡς τάχιστα κα]ὶ ...

82. It must nonetheless be noted that the decree does call for a list of trierarchs to be given to the secretary of the Boule. By the time of this decree, his and the Boule's archives evidently included more than the decrees alone.

83. Andok. 1.78–79; for recent discussion of the decree, see Boegehold, "Andokides."

84. Andok. 1.79: τὰ δὲ ἄλλα πάντα ἐξαλεῖψαι τοὺς πράκτορας καὶ τὴν βουλὴν κατὰ τὰ εἰρημένα πανταχόθεν, ὅπου τι ἔστιν ἐν τ᾽ δημοσίῳ, καὶ εἰ ἀντίγραφόν που ἔστι, παρέχειν τοὺς θεσμοθέτας καὶ τὰς ἄλλας ἀρχάς.

85. Andrewes, "Androtion," pp. 14–15, 24 n. 5, has objected to Boegehold's interpretation. He points out that the word πανταχόθεν ("from everywhere") in connection with *dēmosion* points to a scattered disposition of documents in the offices of different magistrates, not in a central archive. He further suggests that the Boule itself is not to search for documents but is to receive them from other magistrates, such as the thesmothetai mentioned in the decree. Against this view, it should be noted that the Boule is explicitly ordered to erase documents, and that the thesmothetai are mentioned in an additional cancellation clause that follows mention of the *dēmosion*; not only is the Boule, presumably through its secretary, to see to the destruction of documents, but other magistrates are to hand those over for erasure. The two clauses seem to draw a distinction between documents housed in the *dēmosion* and ones kept by other magistrates; see also Boegehold, "Andokides," p. 154 n. 10.

86. See also Aeschin. 2.59, 92, where documents otherwise attested in the Metroon are connected with the Bouleuterion; even at that time the original, old Bouleuterion might still be called after its original function. On the gradual shift in the nomenclature, see also Rhodes, *Athenian Boule*, p. 31.

87. A similar view was outlined by Wilamowitz, *Aus Kydathen*, pp. 205–6. Although Demosthenes (19.129) connects the public records with the Metroon already in 343, it is not until 323 (Dein. 1.86) that the archives are actually said to be under the care or tutelage of the Mother of the Gods.

88. On this practice, see Chapter 7.

89. Shear, "Bouleuterion," pp. 171–78, offers an excellent survey of evidence for Kybele's worship in the period, and identifies as Kybele the goddess whose cult was located in the Athenian Metroon. Francis, *Image and Idea*, pp. 112–20, argues for the establishment of the Metroon in the late fifth century as a result of the introduction of the cult of Kybele to Athens, and for a close relationship between the Asian Mother goddess and the keeping of public records; see also Curtius, *Das Metroon*, pp. 11–15.

90. A cult of the Mother existed in Agrai, site of the Lesser Mysteries, and this goddess was the recipient of public worship from the early fifth century (*IG* I³ 234, line 5; see also *IG* I³ 369, line 91; *IG* I³ 383, line 50). Although this is doubted by Shear ("Bouleuterion," p. 172), it is not unreasonable to associate this old, native goddess with the Mother in the Agora. It was to this old goddess, who had become assimilated with Kybele, to whom Agorakritos's statue was dedicated. On the possible antiquity of a cult Mother of the Gods, see now Parker, *Athenian Religion*, pp. 188–94.

91. Robertson, "Laws of Athens," pp. 52–60. See also Boegehold, "Establishment," p. 29, who suggests that the *anagrapheis* may have pointed out the need for a centralized archives building.

92. Another development of this period may also reflect a concern for bringing more order to the Boule's records. In the last decade of the fifth century, the Athenians made the bouleutic calendar coterminous with the archontic calendar. Since the Boule used its calendar for dating its (and the Ekklesia's) records, this reform may have facilitated both filing and consultation of the Boule's records. See Meritt, "Athenian Calendar Problems," pp. 201, 211, who dates the reform to 407/6; see also Rhodes, *Athenian Boule*, p. 224.

1. Jacoby, *Atthis*, p. 383 n. 27; see also Wilamowitz, *Aus Kydathen*, pp. 205–6. The archaeological remains of the Bouleuterion/Metroon complex, however, suggest that Jacoby's formulation should be modified in that the Boule and not its archives found a new home: see Chapter 4, Section II.

2. Curtius, *Das Metroon*, pp. 15–20; Kahrstedt, "Untersuchungen," pp. 25–27; Posner, *Archives*, pp. 108–10; Thompson and Wycherley, *Agora*, 14:36. An optimistic view of the Metroon's holding is best expressed by Hansen, *Athenian Democracy*, p. 11, who states: "The Athenians did have a state archive in the Metroön in the Agora, where a copy of every public document, written on papyrus, was available to any citizen on request."

3. Thomas, *Oral Tradition*, p. 38 n. 72, suggests that laws were deposited in the Metroon only in the late fourth century. She accounts for other types of documents attested in the Metroon as the result of a change in archival practice that occurred in the Hellenistic period. See also Georgoudi, "Manières d'archivage," p. 228: "le *Mètroon* semble avoir été principalement un dépôt de lois et décrets."

4. See Curtius, *Das Metroon*, pp. 15–17; Kahrstedt, "Untersuchungen," p. 26 with n. 4; Posner, *Archives*, p. 108.

5. On fourth-century legislative practice, see MacDowell, "Law-Making at Athens"; Rhodes, "*Nomothesia* in Fourth-Century Athens"; Hansen, "Athenian *Nomothesia*."

6. Libanios, *Declam.*, 23.36 (Wycherley, no. 485): μεστὸν γὰρ τὸ Μητρ ̈ον τῶν ἐμῶν ψηφισμάτων καὶ νόμων.

7. Harpok., Photios, and *Suda*, s.v. μητρ ̈ον (Wycherley, nos. 482, 488). Lykourgos's speech *Against Aristogeiton* is widely dated to 325/4; the date of Deinarchos's speech *Against Pytheas* is unknown.

8. Lyk. 1.68: φέρε γάρ, ὦ ἄνδρες, εἴ τις ἕνα νόμον εἰς τὸ Μητρ ̈ον ἐλθὼν ἐξαλείψειεν, εἶτ' ἀπολογοῖτο ὡς οὐδὲν παρὰ τοῦτον τῇ πόλει ἐστίν, ἆρ' οὐκ ἂν ἀπεκτείνατ' αὐτόν; ἐγὼ μὲν οἶμαι δικαίως, εἴπερ ἐμέλλετε καὶ τοὺς ἄλλους σώζειν. Posner, *Archives*, p. 114, suggests on the basis of this passage the existence of a law that forbade the bringing of false documents into the Metroon. This is not stated by Lykourgos, but such a law is mentioned in the second hypothesis to Demosthenes' speech *On the Crown* (§4), which forbade the introduction into the Metroon of false documents: κελεύει γὰρ μηδέποτε ψευδῆ γράμματα εἰς τὸ Μητρῷον εἰσάγειν, ἔνθα ἐστιν ὅλα τὰ δημόσια γράμματα. This statement is probably based on a text inserted into the speech (18.54–55), which purports to give the text of Aeschines' indictment. But this text is widely recognized as a forgery, and this particular passage is nothing but a misinterpretation of the charges made by Aeschines in his speech *Against Ktesiphon* (3.50); see Lipsius, *AR*, p. 392; Gwatkin, "Legal Arguments," p. 130. That is not to say that the Athenians tolerated the deposition of forged documents into the Metroon. Evidence for such a law, however, is wanting.

9. [Dem.] 25.90 (Wycherley, no. 477): τί οὖν ἐρεῖτ', ὦ ἄνδρες Ἀθηναῖοι, εἰ προέμενοι τοὺς νόμους ἔξιτε; ποίοις προσώποις ἢ τίσιν ὀφθαλμοῖς πρὸς ἕκαστον τούτων ἀντιβλέψεσθε; πῶς δ' εἰς τὸ μητρ ̈ον βαδιεῖσθ', ἄν τι βούλησθε; οὐ γὰρ δήπου καθ' ἕν' ὑμῶν ἕκαστος ὡς ἐπὶ κυρίους τοὺς νόμους πορεύσεται, εἰ νῦν μὴ βεβαιώσαντες αὐτοὺς ἔξιθ' ἅπαντες κοινῇ; For the implications of this passage on the consultation of the Metroon's holdings, see Chapter 7, Section I.

10. Thomas, *Oral Tradition*, p. 38 n. 72; see also Hansen, *Athenian Democracy*, p. 164, who suggests, however, that laws came to be deposited in the Metroon shortly after its foundation.

11. For Diokles' law, see Chapter 4, Section II.

12. On the role of the Boule and Ekklesia in fourth-century *nomothesia*, see the law quoted at Dem. 24.20–23, where the Ekklesia (and, by necessity, the Boule) is deeply involved in *nomothesia*. For other aspects of the Boule's involvement, see Hansen, *Athenian Democracy*, pp. 168–69.

13. For the secretary's involvement in the publication of *nomoi*, see *SEG* 26 (1976–77): no. 72, lines 47–48 (375/4), where the secretary announces the contract for the stele to the *pōlētai*; see also *IG* II² 140, lines 31–36.

14. Curtius, *Das Metroon*, p. 15; Kahrstedt, "Untersuchungen," p. 26; Posner, *Archives*, p. 108. Aeschines in his speech *Against Ktesiphon* (3.187) refers to honors decreed for the heroes of Phyle in 403/2, and he says that this grant, in the form of a decree, was still to be seen "in the Metroon." Scholars have sometimes taken this reference as evidence for the archival deposition of decrees in the Metroon (Kahrstedt, "Untersuchungen," p. 29). But Aeschines has been discussing a series of publicly displayed monuments, including inscriptions, honoring heroes from Athens' past, and the same should be true of his reference to the decree honoring the Phyle heroes: he refers to an inscribed stele for the Phyle heroes, not an archival text. An inscription with the text of this decree was discovered in the excavations of the Metroon: see Raubitschek, "Heroes of Phyle," pp. 284–95. But the inscription itself is not to be counted as part of the archives. The Boule was given discretionary powers in examining those who claimed to have participated in the resistance to the Thirty at Phyle (Aeschin. 3.187), and the decree honoring them was erected at the Metroon because of that building's former function as a Bouleuterion and its proximity to the new Bouleuterion. A record of the decree was probably also preserved inside the Metroon's archives, but that is not the text to which Aeschines refers.

15. Dem. 19.121–34. For discussion, see E. Harris, *Aeschines*, pp. 167–68.

16. Dem. 19.129 (Wycherley, no. 476): καὶ ταῦτ᾽ οὐκ ἔνεστιν ἐμοὶ μὲν οὕτω, τούτῳ δ᾽ ἄλλως πως εἰπεῖν· ἀλλ᾽ ὑπὲρ μὲν τῆς ἐξωμοσίας ἐν τοῖς κοινοῖς τοῖς ὑμετέροις γράμμασιν ἐν τῷ μητρῴῳ ταῦτ᾽ ἐστίν, ἐφ᾽ οἷς ὁ δημόσιος τέτακται, καὶ ψήφισμα ἄντικρυς περὶ τούτου τοῦ ὀνόματος γέγραπται.

17. Aeschines, of course, provides a different version of these events: see Aeschin. 2.94–96. Demosthenes later contradicts his outline of events presented here when he describes an election of a fourth embassy at 19.172.

18. On the Harpalos affair see Worthington, "Chronology," pp. 63–76, with references to further literature.

19. On the decree, see Hyp. 5.2; Dein 1.4, 61; Plut. *Dem.* 26: ὁ δὲ Δημοσθένης εἰσήνεγκε ψήφισμα τὴν ἐξ Ἀρείου Πάγου βουλὴν ἐξετάσαι τὸ πρᾶγμα καὶ τοὺς ἐκείνῃ δόξαντας ἀδικεῖν δοῦναι δίκην.

20. Hyp. 5.2, 30; Dein. 1.1, 8, 61, and esp. 82–83, where two decrees are distinguished.

21. Dein. 1.86 (Wycherley, no. 473): ἔθετο συνθήκας μετὰ τοῦ δήμου, γράψας τὸ ψήφισμα καθ᾽ ἑαυτοῦ, παρὰ τὴν μητέρα τῶν θεῶν, ἣ πάντων ἐν τοῖς γράμμασι δικαίων φύλαξ τῇ πόλει καθέστηκε.

22. For the deposition of contracts with a third party, see [Dem.] 25.69, 33.15, 35.14, 48.11; Lyk. 1.23.4; see also Finley, *Studies in Land and Credit*, pp. 26–27, and Boegehold, "Establishment," p. 26.

23. *IG* II² 583, lines 4–9 (Wycherley, no. 497): δοκ/εῖ τῆι βουλῆι τὸ]ν δημόσιον τὸν ἐκ τ[οῦ Μητρώιου τὸ ψή/φισμα καθ᾽ ὅ ἐστιν] αὐτοῖς ἡ ἰσοτέλε[ια παραδοῦναι τῶ/ι γραμματεῖ· τὸν δὲ] γραμματέα παρα[λαβόντα ἀναγράψ/αι τὴν ἰσοτέλειαν] προσαναγράψαν[τα τὸ ψήφισμα τόδ/ε καὶ τὸ πρότερον γεν]όμενον αὐτοῖ[ς. For discussion of the restorations, see Wilhelm, *Beiträge*, p. 230.

24. *IG* II² 971 (Wycherley, no. 501), lines 11–24, esp. 19–24. For text and commentary, see recently M. Osborne, *Naturalization*, 1:213–16 (D102), 2:189–91, 3:85.

25. On Stratokles, see Dinsmoor, *Archons*, pp. 13–14; Ferguson, *Hellenistic Athens*, pp. 119–20; Fiehn, "Stratokles," pp. 269–71. For decrees moved by Stratokles, see Dinsmoor, *Archons*, p. 14; Habicht, "Athenischer Ehrendekret," p. 39 with n. 15; M. Osborne, *Naturalization*, 2:121 n. 495.

26. M. Osborne, *Naturalization*, 3:85, suggests a connection between Demetrios and Teleias's ancestor.

27. *IG* II² 1132 (Wycherley, no. 504). An inscription preserving the same decrees was found at Delphi: see *Fouille de Delphes*, 3.2, no. 68, pp. 71–74. At Delphi, however, only the two decrees were inscribed and in reverse order from the Athenian copy. See Kahrstedt, "Untersuchungen," p. 26 with n. 5; Posner, *Archives*, p. 107.

28. Ibid., lines 28–31: τοὺς γραμματεῖς ἀνα[γράψαι τὸ δόγμα]/ εἰστήλαν λιθίναν καὶ στῆσαι ἐν [Δελφοῖς· πέμψαι]/ δὲ καὶ ποτὶ Ἀθηναίους τοῦ δόγματο[ς τοῦδε ἀντίγρα]/φον ἐσφραγισμένον.

29. Ibid., lines 90–91: ἀναγράψαι δὲ τὸ δόγμα ἐ[ν Δ]ελφοῖς, ὁ/[μ]οίως δὲ καὶ διαποστείλασθαι τοῦ δόγματος τοῦδε ἀντί[γ]ραφον πρὸς/ τὸν δῆμον τὸν Ἀθηναίων.

30. Sickinger, "Inscriptions and Archives," pp. 289–92; see also Wilhelm, *Beiträge*, p. 239. Thomas, *Oral Tradition*, p. 77 with n. 200, puts the inscription in the Metroon and cites its presence there as indicative of the archives' disorder.

31. Aeschin. 2.32: συμμαχίας γὰρ Λακεδαιμονίων καὶ τῶν ἄλλων Ἑλλήνων συνελθούσης, εἷς ὢν τούτων Ἀμύντας ὁ Φιλίππου πατὴρ καὶ πέμπων σύνεδρον καὶ τῆς καθ᾽ αὑτὸν ψήφου κύριος ὤν, ἐψηφίσατο Ἀμφίπολιν τὴν Ἀθηναίων συνεξαιρεῖν μετὰ τῶν ἄλλων Ἑλλήνων Ἀθηναίοις. Καὶ τούτων τὸ κοινὸν δόγμα τῶν Ἑλλήνων καὶ τοὺς ψηφισαμένους ἐκ τῶν δημοσίων γραμμάτων μάρτυρας παρεσχόμην. The date of this congress is disputed, and suggested dates range from 376 to 369; for a summary of different views, see Ryder, *Koine Eirene*, pp. 127–30; Sealey, *History of the Greek City States*, pp. 429–30; Cargill, *Second Athenian League*, pp. 85–87.

32. Aeschin. 2.16–17, 45–46; Dem. 19.17–18, 31; see also *IG* II² 40, lines 4–6.

33. Aeschin. 3.123–25.

34. Aeschin. 2.89–93; see also 2.58–60.

35. Aeschin. 2.89; 3.73–75.

36. Aeschin. 3.24: καί μοι ἀνάγνωθι, ἐπὶ τίνος ἄρχοντος καὶ ποίου μηνὸς καὶ ἐν τίνι ἡμέρᾳ καὶ ἐν ποίᾳ ἐκκλησίᾳ ἐχειροτονήθη Δημοσθένης τὴν ἀρχὴν τὴν ἐπὶ τὸ θεωρικόν. ΔΙΑΛΟΓΙΣΜΟΣ ΤΩΝ ΗΜΕΡΩΝ. οὐκοῦν εἰ μηδὲν ἔτι περαιτέρω δείξαιμι, δικαίως ἂν ἁλίσκοιτο Κτησιφῶν· αἱρεῖ γὰρ αὐτὸν οὐχ ἡ κατηγορία ἐμή, ἀλλὰ τὰ δημόσια γράμματα. On Athenian elections, see Hansen, *Athenian Assembly*, pp. 120–23.

37. Aeschin. 2.58: τῶν γὰρ πρεσβειῶν, ἃς ἐξεπέμψατε εἰς τὴν Ἑλλάδα, ἔτι τοῦ πολέμου τοῦ πρὸς Φίλιππον ὑμῖν ἐνεστακότος, οἱ μὲν χρόνοι τῆς αἱρέσεως, ὅτε ἐξεπέμφθησαν, καὶ τὰ τῶν πρεσβευσάντων ὀνόματα ἐν τοῖς δημοσίοις ἀνα-

γέγραπται γράμμασι, τὰ δὲ σώματά ἐστιν αὐτῶν οὐκ ἐν Μακεδονίᾳ, ἀλλ᾽ Ἀθήνησι. The circumstances surrounding the departure and return of these ambassadors are disputed. For discussion and references to earlier literature, see E. Harris, *Aeschines*, pp. 158–61.

38. Aeschin. 2.89–90. Other letters from Athenian generals are also read out in speeches: Aeschin. 2.134; Dem. 23.151; see also the letters read at Dem. 23.159–62.

39. Curtius, *Das Metroon*, p. 20; Kahrstedt, "Untersuchungen," p. 26 n. 6; Posner, *Archives*, p. 111.

40. *IG* II² 1534 A and 1535. A more recent text, with commentary and discussion, is given by Aleshire, *Athenian Asklepieion*, pp. 249–336.

41. The document is restored as a *logos*, "account," at *IG* II² 1534 A, line 56; Aleshire, *Athenian Asklepieion*, p. 251, restores a special inventory, an *exetasmos*.

42. *Hesperia* suppl. 4 (1940): 144–47, line 17 (Wycherley, no. 608): καταβέβληνται δὲ καὶ λόγους εἰς τὸ Μητρῷον ἀκ[ολούθως τοῖς νόμοις - - -]. Wycherley, following Schweigert, dates the decree to 191/0 on the basis of the name of the archon Hippias. Hippias is now dated to 181/0: see Meritt, "Athenian Archons," p. 181.

43. *IG* II² 840, lines 18–28 (Wycherley, no. 498). An earlier decree of 221/0 orders an inventory of the same sanctuary, to be conducted by a commission of Areopagites, *bouleutai*, and others (*IG* II² 839). The commission is to submit an account for audit, but neither the *logistai* nor the Metroon are mentioned.

44. Note, however, that in line 41 of the inscription (*IG* II² 840) the weights of several objects in the list have not been engraved. Presumably, these weights were included in the official copy sent to the Metroon.

45. *IG* II² 1013. The text of lines 49–62 is supplemented by a second copy of the inscription, published as *Hesperia* 7 (1938): 127–46, no. 27. For discussion, see Ferguson, *Hellenistic Athens*, pp. 429–35.

46. *IG* II² 1013, lines 53–54 (Wycherley, nos. 503, 605): καταβαλλέσθωσαν δὲ καὶ χειρόγραφον ἐν τῶι Μητρῴωι ὧν ἂν παραλάβωσι καὶ παραδῶσιν · ἐὰν δὲ τοῦ/τὸ μὴ καταβάλλωνται μὴ ἐξέστω αὐτοῖς ἐλευθέραν λειτουργίαν θητωνεῖν.

47. Records of annual transfers, or *paradoseis*, are reflected in the inscribed, annual transfer of objects in Athenian sanctuaries from one board of treasurers to another; see, e.g., *IG* I³ 292–362; *IG* II² 1370–1492. For discussion, see Aleshire, *Athenian Asklepieion*, pp. 103–10.

48. *IG* II² 847 (Wycherley, no. 499).

49. Ibid., lines 27–30: καὶ περὶ τούτων ἁπάντων τούς τε λόγους ἀ/[π]ενηνόχασιν πρὸς τοὺς λογιστὰς καὶ εἰς [τὸ]/ μητρῷον καὶ τὰς εὐθύνας δεδώκασιν ἐν τῶι δικαστηρίωι κατὰ τοὺς νόμους.

50. E.g., *Hesperia* suppl. 4 (1940): 144–47, line 17 (Wycherley, no. 608); see n. 42.

51. *IG* II² 956. The inscriptions honoring the *agonothetai* probably emanate from a penteric festival, a Greater Theseia, perhaps instituted sometime in the second century. See Pélékidis, *Histoire*, pp. 229–30, 295–300.

52. *IG* II² 956, lines 20–22 (Wycherley, no. 500): καὶ περὶ ἁπάντων ὧν ᾠκονόμηκεν ἀπενήνοχεν λό/γους εἰς τὸ μητρῶιον καὶ πρὸς τοὺς λογιστὰς καὶ τὰς εὐθύνας ἔδωκεν.

53. *IG* II² 958, lines 16–18; see also the note under Wycherley, no. 500; on the date, see Meritt, "Athenian Archons," p. 182.

54. *IG* II² 957, lines 12–14.

55. Helly, *Gonnoi II*, no. 109, pp. 120–27, with references to earlier bibliography.

56. Ibid., lines 35–43: τοὺς δὲ/ σπονδοφόρους τοὺς ἐπαγγέλιλίον/τας τά τε Ἐλευσίνια καὶ τὰ Πα/ναθήναια καὶ τὰ Μυστήρια προσαπο/φέρειν εἰς τὸ Μητρῶιον ἐν τοῖς λό/γοις τὰ ὀνόματα τῶν θεωροδο/κούντων πατρόθεν ὅταν καὶ /τὰς πόλεις τὰς ἀποδεξαμένας [τ]ὰς σπονδὰς ἀποφέρωσιν. See also E. Harris, *Aeschines*, p. 213 n. 21.

57. *IG* II² 1672, lines 4, 106–7, 227. For a useful discussion of the dates on which *spondophoroi* set out from and reported back to Athens, see now E. Harris, *Aeschines*, pp. 162–64.

58. Curtius, *Das Metroon*, p. 20; Kahrstedt, "Untersuchungen," p. 26 n. 6.

59. Dziatzko, "Archive," col. 558, citing *IG* I² 374, lines 289–91 (= *IG* I³ 476, lines 289–91; cf. *IG* I³ 477, lines 1–2); see also Lewis, *Papyrus in Classical Antiquity*, p. 73. Shear, "Bouleuterion," pp. 188–89, cites the same inscriptions as evidence for the deposition of records in a central archive. D. Harris, *Treasures*, p. 17, likewise suggests that copies of the Parthenon inventories were being deposited in the Metroon from c. 408, citing Posner, *Archives*, pp. 108–9, 115–16, and Boegehold, "Establishment," p. 27, both of whom, however, give sources of Hellenistic date. Boegehold, "Establishment," p. 29, points out that the Hellenistic evidence need not serve as an accurate guide to practices of the classical period.

60. *SEG* 30 (1980): no. 61. On the law's date, see Clinton, "A Law in the City Eleusinion," pp. 272–75.

61. *SEG* 30 (1980): no. 61, line 22, restored as follows: οἱ δὲ σπονδοφόροι ἀπογ]ραφόντων τῶι γρα[μματεῖ τὰ ὀνόματα τῶν πόλεων. See Clinton, "A Law in the City Eleusinion," p. 277, who also draws a connection with the Hellenistic inscription from Gonnoi (see above nn. 55 and 56).

62. *IG* II² 120. For the date, see Schweigert, "Inscriptions," pp. 281–89. For a brief discussion of the decree, see also Rhodes, *Athenian Boule*, pp. 92–93.

63. Linders, *Studies*, p. 42 n. 58, concludes that the Boule did not have its own copies of earlier inventories, but that the treasurers did.

64. See *Ath. Pol.* 48.3–5, 54.2, with Rhodes, *CAAP*, pp. 560–62, 597–99; see also Piérart, "Les ΕΥΘΥΝΟΙ Athéniens," pp. 526–73.

65. Aeschin. 3.14–15: καὶ λόγον καὶ εὐθύνας ἐγγράφειν πρὸς τὸν γραμματέα καὶ τοὺς λογιστάς.

66. The relevance of the law cited by Aeschines to the Metroon was suggested by Harrison, *LA*, 2:29 n. 1; see also Piérart, "Les ΕΥΘΥΝΟΙ Athéniens," pp. 565–67.

67. For the differences between fifth- and fourth-century *euthynai* practices, see Rhodes, *Athenian Boule*, pp. 110–12; Piérart, "Les ΕΥΘΥΝΟΙ Athéniens," pp. 526–73.

68. On the Boule's role in state finances, see Rhodes, *Athenian Boule*, pp. 88–113.

69. Plut. *Per.* 32.3–4.

70. Frost, "Pericles and Dracontides," pp. 69–72, associates the decree of Drakontides with the attack on Pheidias in 438/7 and believes that Perikles was prosecuted while serving as *epistatēs* for one of the Acropolis building projects. Hansen, *Eisangelia*, pp. 71–73, however, follows an older view and puts the decree in 430/29 and ties it to Perikles' removal from the generalship in that year. See Ostwald, *Popular Sovereignty*, pp. 191–98, for discussion.

71. Details of the first of the Kallias Decrees are also suggestive. There, the Boule is given authority to oversee the *logistai*'s calculations of moneys owed to the Other Gods (*IG* I³ 52, line 9). As I have argued (Chapter 3, Section I), the *logistai* did not make calculations from records supplied by local officials associated with the Other

Gods (mentioned in lines 10–13), but from documents they already possessed. The *logistai* may have kept such records in the Logisterion (attested at Andok. 1.77), but given the supervisory powers of the Boule in the decree, it too may have had copies of the relevant documents.

72. Posner, *Archives*, p. 108; Rhodes, *CAAP*, p. 557; see also Curtius, *Das Metroon*, pp. 19–20.

73. *Ath. Pol.* 47.2–5. On the *pōlētai*, see Rhodes, *CAAP*, pp. 552–57; Langdon, *Agora*, 19:57–69.

74. *Ath. Pol.* 47.2: καὶ τὰ τέλη τὰ εἰς ἐνιαυτ[ὸ]ν πεπραμένα ἀναγράψαντες εἰς λελευκωμένα γραμματεῖα τόν τε πριάμεν[ο]ν καὶ ὅ[σ]α ἂν πρίηται τῆι βουλῆι παραδιδόασιν; *Ath. Pol.* 47.5: εἰσφέρεται μὲν οὖν εἰς τὴν βουλὴν τὰ γραμματεῖα κ[ατὰ] τὰς καταβολὰς ἀναγεγραμμένα, τηρεῖ δ' ὁ δημόσιος.

75. See also the deposition of counterfeit coins with the Boule in the fourth-century law on silver coinage (*SEG* 26 [1976–77]: no. 72, lines 10–13); although they were to be deposited with the Boule, they also were considered sacred to the Mother, a probable sign that they were to be kept in her sanctuary.

76. *IG* II² 463, line 28–29: . . . τοῦ τεί]χους κ[α]ὶ εἰς τὸ μ[ητ]ρῷον πρὸ[ς] τὸν δημ[όσ/ιον].

77. The connection between *IG* II² 463 and *Ath. Pol.* 47.5 was pointed out by Wilhelm, *Beiträge*, p. 232 n. 3. A public slave in the dockyards also deals with record keeping (*IG* II² 163, lines 194–99). On public slaves at Athens, see now Lewis, "Public Property," pp. 254–58.

78. On the Poleterion, see Langdon, *Agora*, 19:165–67.

79. For the Boule's role in finance, see [Xen.] *Ath. Pol.* 3.2. On the Boule's role in tax contracts, see, e.g., Aeschin. 1.119; Andok. 1.134; *Ath. Pol.* 47.2; Rhodes, *Athenian Boule*, pp. 89–113.

80. See Chapter 3, Section I.

81. The *pōlētai* are frequently mentioned in fifth-century decrees, where they are ordered to let out contracts for the erection of stelai. For their role in other contracts, see *IG* I³ 35, lines 8–9; *IG* I³ 45, lines 10–14; *IG* I³ 84, lines 5–6. Rhodes, *Athenian Boule*, p. 96, suggests that the Boule's supervision over the *pōlētai* dated back to the time of Ephialtes' reforms.

82. *IG* II² 1990, line 9 (Wycherley, no. 510): τούσδε παρέδωκεν ἐφήβους εἰς τὸ μητρ῀ον.

83. *Ath. Pol.* 53.4: οἱ δ' ἔφηβοι ἐγγραφόμενοι πρότερον μὲν εἰς λελευκωμένα γραμματεῖα ἐνεγράφοντο, καὶ ἐπεγράφοντο αὐτοῖς ὅ τ' ἄρχων ἐφ' οὗ ἐνεγρά-φησαν καὶ ὁ ἐπώνυμος ὁ τῶι προτέρωι ἔ[τ]ει δεδιαιτηκώς, νῦν δ' εἰς στήλην χαλκῆν ἀναγράφονται, καὶ ἵσταται ἡ στήλη πρὸ τοῦ βουλευ[τ]ηρίου παρὰ τοὺς ἐπωνύμους.

84. For the role of generals and taxiarchs in calling up citizens for campaigns, see Ar. *Peace* 1170–86; Lys. 13.79, 14.6, 15.5. For the interest of the Boule in military mobilizations in the fourth century, see, e.g., Dem. 50.6, 16.

85. On the parade, see *Ath. Pol.* 42.4; for the changed role of the Boule, see Rhodes, *Athenian Boule*, pp. 173–74.

86. Pélékidis, *Histoire*, pp. 71–79; Reinmuth, *Inscriptions*, pp. 123–38.

87. Harpok., s.v. στρατεία ἐν τοῖς ἐπωνύμοις.

88. For the availability of different editions of the *Ath. Pol.*, see Keaney, "Date," pp. 326–36; Rhodes, *CAAP*, pp. 51–58. Both Keaney and Rhodes take the change in

ephebic registration, from whitened tablets to bronze stelai, as reflecting the reform of the *ephebeia* in the 330s, and use this as evidence that the *Ath. Pol.* was composed after that reform. Although I agree with their conclusions concerning the date of the *Ath. Pol.*, I am not convinced that the publication of names of ephebes on bronze stelai must have been an immediate result of that reform. Neither Rhodes nor Keaney puts any emphasis on the slight variation in Harpokration's text.

89. For a similar case in which documents deposited with the Boule may have been stored in the Metroon, see my discussion of *pōlētai* documents in Section II.

90. Curtius, *Das Metroon*, p. 19; Posner, *Archives*, p. 108; Lipsius, *AR*, p. 821; see also Harrison, *LA*, 2:91, Thompson and Wycherley, *Agora*, 14:36. See, however, the doubts of Kahrstedt, "Untersuchungen," pp. 26–27.

91. Ath. 9.72.407b–c: καθ᾽ ὃν δὲ χρόνον θαλασσοκρατοῦντες Ἀθηναῖοι ἀνῆγον εἰς ἄστυ τὰς νησιωτικὰς δίκας γραψάμενός τις καὶ τὸν Ἡγήμονα δίκην ἤγαγεν εἰς τὰς Ἀθήνας. ὃ δὲ παραγενόμενος καὶ συναγαγὼν τοὺς περὶ τὸν Διόνυσον τεχνίτας προσῆλθε μετ᾽ αὐτῶν Ἀλκιβιάδῃ βοηθεῖν ἀξιῶν. ὃ δὲ θαρρεῖν παρακελευσάμενος εἰπών τε πᾶσιν ἕπεσθαι ἧκεν εἰς τὸ Μητρ῀ον, ὅπου τῶν δικῶν ἦσαν αἱ γραφαί, καὶ βρέξας τὸν δάκτυλον ἐκ τοῦ στόματος διήλειψε τὴν δίκην τοῦ Ἡγήμονος. ἀγανακτοῦντες δ᾽ ὅ τε γραμματεὺς καὶ ὁ ἄρχων τὰς ἡσυχίας ἤγαγον δι᾽ Ἀλκιβιάδην, φυγόντος δι᾽ εὐλάβειαν καὶ τοῦ τὴν δίκην γραψαμένου.

92. Wehrli, "Chamaileon."

93. Ar. *Clouds* 769–72. On Hegemon, see Körte, "Hegemon," cols. 2595–96.

94. Pickard-Cambridge, *Dramatic Festivals*, pp. 275–309.

95. Diog. L. 2.40 (Wycherley, no. 478): ἡ ἀντωμοσία τῆς δίκης τοῦτον εἶχε τὸν τρόπον· ἀνάκειται γὰρ ἔτι καὶ νῦν, φησὶ Φαβωρῖνος, ἐν τ῀ Μητρῴῳ. *Antōmosia* was the general term for the oaths sworn by parties at the preliminary hearing, affirming or denying the validity of the charges; see Harrison, *LA*, 2:99–100.

96. On Favorinus, see Schmid, "Favorinus," cols. 2078–84.

97. The results of certain types of judicial procedures were sometimes published on stone: see Boegehold, *Agora*, 28: no. 148, p. 117, with references to other examples. Such published records presumably reflect more detailed ones kept by individual magistrates.

98. For a possible parallel to this practice, consider the archaizing revival of the *agōgē* at Sparta in Roman times: Kennel, *Gymnasium of Virtue*, pp. 70–97, esp. 94–97.

99. Thus, Kahrstedt, "Untersuchungen," p. 27, suggested that the indictment erased by Alkibiades involved a trial before the Boule itself.

100. On the Boule's judicial authority, see Rhodes, *Athenian Boule*, pp. 147–71; for that of the Ekklesia, Hansen, *Athenian Assembly*, pp. 118–20. For records of judicial proceedings before both the Boule and Ekklesia, see Lys. 13.22, 28, 33, 35, 38, 50. A *krisis* ("verdict") of the Boule is cited at Lys. 13.50; see also the indictment against Themistokles, which was commented on by Krateros (*FGrHist* 342 F11). The fact that a record of the charge brought against Themistokles was included in Krateros's collection of decrees suggests that the indictment took the form of a decree, perhaps issued by the Boule; for a similar case, compare the indictment for treason against Antiphon, Archeptolemos, and Onomakles (*FGrHist* 342 F5). We do not know in what form the indictment of Themistokles survived; it may have been inscribed on a stele, like that of Antiphon, but the presence of the demotic and patronymic of Themistokles' accuser, Leobotes, may suggest an archival source: similar features do not appear in inscribed Attic decrees until the late fifth century.

101. Diog. L. 10.16 (Wycherley, no. 480): κατὰ τάδε δίδωμι τὰ ἐμαυτοῦ πάντα Ἀμυνομάχῳ Ξιλοκράτους Βατῆθεν καὶ Τιμοκράτει Δημητρίου Ποταμίῳ κατὰ τὴν ἐν τ΅ Μητρῴῳ ἀναγεγραμμένην ἑκατέρῳ δόσιν.

102. Clay, "Epicurus," p. 22, identifies the grant with the will itself, but see Finley, *Studies in Land and Credit*, p. 218 n. 70.

103. Harpok., s.v. δόσις.

104. Is. 1.3, 14, 18, 21, 22; one of the officials in question is identified as an *astynomos* at 1.15, but see the reservations of Finley, *Studies in Land and Credit*, p. 218 n. 77, who also questions whether the document deposited by Kleonymos was a will. On the speech, see Wyse, *Speeches of Isaeus*, pp. 175–79. It cannot be dated precisely.

105. So Finley, *Studies in Land and Credit*, pp. 26–27.

106. Ferguson, "Laws of Demetrius," pp. 265–76.

107. The deposition of documents of a private nature into the archives of Hellenistic city-states is well illustrated by second-century law on archival practice from Paros: Lambrinudakis and Wörrle, "Reformgesetz." See also W. Harris, *Ancient Literacy*, pp. 120–21, with references to further literature.

108. [Plut.] *Vit. X orat.* 841–42: τὸν δέ, ὡς χαλκᾶς εἰκόνας ἀναθεῖναι τῶν ποιητῶν, Αἰσχύλου Σοφοκλέους Εὐριπίδου, καὶ τὰς τραγῳδίας αὐτῶν ἐν κοιν΅ γραψαμένους φυλάττειν καὶ τὸν τῆς πόλεως γραμματέα παραναγινώσκειν τοῖς ὑποκρινομένοις· οὐκ ἐξεῖναι γὰρ ἰπαρ῏ αὐτὰς ὑποκρίνεσθαι.

109. Curtius, *Das Metroon*, p. 21; Kahrstedt, "Untersuchungen," p. 27; Posner, *Archives*, p. 108. Thompson and Wycherley, *Agora*, 14:36, are more cautious; see also Thomas, *Oral Tradition*, pp. 48–49.

110. On the factors contributing to the law's enactment, see Page, *Actors' Interpolations*, pp. 1–2.

111. The authenticity of the law and the creation of official copies of the tragedies of Aeschylus, Sophocles, and Euripides seem to be confirmed by a story found in Galen (*Comm. in Hipp. Epidem. 3*, 2.4, quoted in Fraser, *Ptolemaic Alexandria*, 2:147 n. 2). According to the story, Ptolemy III borrowed texts of the plays of the three fifth-century tragedians from the Athenians, leaving a deposit of fifteen talents. Later, however, he returned only the copies made from the originals while keeping the original for the Library at Alexandria; see Pfeiffer, *History of Classical Scholarship*, p. 82.

112. For the enrollment of new citizens, see *Ath. Pol.* 42.1–2 with Rhodes, *CAAP*, pp. 493–505. On the failure of the Athenians to keep records of certain types of documents, see Thomas, *Oral Tradition*, pp. 82–83.

113. *Ath. Pol.* 49.1–2.

114. On the location of the Hipparcheion, see Bugh, *Horsemen*, pp. 219–20; for the "Cavalry Archives," see Kroll, "Archive," pp. 83–140; Braun, "Dipylon-Brunnen," pp. 197–269.

115. Dem. 19.197, 21.52; Dein. 1.78, 98.

116. For consultation of the Delphic oracle, see *IG* II² 204, lines 42–54, where a special commission brings back *manteia*, oracles, from Delphi that are read to the Ekklesia. For other oracles mentioned in Athenian inscriptions, see *IG* I³ 7; *IG* I³ 78, lines 4–5, 25–26, 33–34; *IG* II² 137, line 6.

117. For letters of Philip of Macedon, see Aeschin. 2.128; Dem. 18.39, 77, 221; 19.38, 51, 161, 187. [Dem.] 12 purports to be a letter sent by Philip to Athens in 340, but its authenticity is questioned: see Griffith, *History of Macedonia*, 2:714–16. A letter from the Thracian king Kotys is read out at Dem. 23.115; cf. Dem. 23.174, 178.

118. *IG* I³ 127, lines 25–32; see Chapter 4, Section II, for discussion.

119. *IG* II² 212, lines 58–65. Tod, no. 167, p. 197, suggests that those recruited, the *hypēresia*, were rowers; see also Jordan, *Athenian Navy*, pp. 257–58, who interprets *hypēresia* as slave-rowers. But the term *hypēresia* probably refers to specialists and officers: see Gabrielsen, *Financing the Athenian Fleet*, pp. 106–7, with references to earlier literature.

120. On the Boule's role in naval affairs, see Rhodes, *Athenian Boule*, pp. 113–21. In the fourth century, naval matters were the immediate responsibility of the *epimelētai*, who published some of their records on stone. See Gabrielsen, *Financing the Athenian Fleet*, esp. p. 14.

121. For the Boule's fifth-century archives, see Chapter 3, Section II.

122. On the survival of the laws of Drakon and Solon, see Chapter 1. On the Bouleutic Oath, see Chapter 2, Section IV.

123. See, e.g., the deposition in the Bouleuterion of a list of demes and cities making firstfruit offerings to Demeter and Kore: *IG* I³ 78, lines 26–30.

124. Thuc. 7.8.2; see Dover, *HCT*, 4:385; W. Harris, *Ancient Literacy*, p. 78. For the preservation of letters from generals among the *dēmosia grammata*, see n. 38 above. On the growing use of writing in the fourth century, see W. Harris, *Ancient Literacy*, pp. 66–93; Thomas, *Oral Tradition*, pp. 68–94; Thomas, *Literacy*, pp. 132–44.

Chapter Six

1. For a positive assessment of the organization of the Metroon's archives, see Curtius, *Das Metroon*, pp. 23–24, whose conclusions are followed by Posner, *Archives*, pp. 112–14. A more pessimistic view is offered by Thomas, *Oral Tradition*, pp. 72–83.

2. According to Aristotle, *Ath. Pol.* 44.1, one of the *prytaneis* was chosen by lot to serve as *epistatēs* or chairman for a single day and night, during which time he had charge of the keys of the sanctuaries in which the city's treasures and documents were preserved. I assume that the Metroon with its archives was included among these sanctuaries, but since the *epistatēs* did not actually produce or keep records, his role in their administration was minimal and is not discussed here. It should be noted, however, that if the Metroon is included among these sanctuaries (which seems likely), the Athenians must have valued their public records enough to keep them under lock and key.

3. For the secretary of the Boule in the fifth century, see Chapter 3, Section II; on his responsibility for the revised law code, see Chapter 4, Section II.

4. For a discussion of these changes, see Rhodes, *Athenian Boule*, pp. 134–43; Alessandrì, "Alcune osservazioni," pp. 7–70.

5. *IG* II² 104 (Tod, no. 134) of 368/7 names Mnesiboulos as secretary in one prytany, while *IG* II² 106 (Tod, no. 135) and 107, also of 368/7, name Moschos as secretary in another. In three decrees of 363/2, *IG* II² 109, 110, 111 (Tod, no. 142), however, each belonging to a different prytany, Nikostratos is named as secretary, suggesting that by this year the office of secretary had been made annual. Ferguson, "Introduction of the Secretary-Cycle," pp. 393–97, dated the change to 366/5 and hypothesized that for the first ten years after the change, the tribe of the secretary was chosen from different tribes determined by lot. From 356/5, however, secretaries were chosen from the ten tribes in the reverse of their official order. See now Alessandrì, "Alcune osservazioni," pp. 7–70.

6. The title secretary *kata prytaneian* is first attested in *IG* II² 120, line 20 (353/2). The identification of the secretary mentioned in the prescript with the secretary *kata prytaneian* is deduced from *IG* II² 223 C (= *Agora*, 15: no. 34, line 1) of 343/2, where in a list of officers of the Boule Kleostratos is named secretary *kata prytaneian*; in the prescripts of *IG* II² 224 and 225, both dating from the same year, Kleostratos is also named as secretary (ἐγραμμάτευε). Hence, the secretary *kata prytaneian* and the secretary named in the heading of decrees were identical and the titles alternative names for the same office.

7. *Ath. Pol.* 53.3–4. That this secretary was not a member of the Boule is demonstrated by *IG* II² 1749, a prytany list of the tribe Antiochis for 341/0. From *IG* II² 228 and 229 we know that Onesippos of the deme Araphne and the tribe Antiochis was secretary for 341/0. But in lines 63–65 of *IG* II² 1749, where the demesmen of Araphne of Antiochis are listed, his name is not mentioned.

8. See Schulthess, "Γραμματεῖς," col. 1722, on the basis of *IG* II² 120, lines 13–19: καὶ ἐπειδὰν τὸ οἴκημα ἀ/[νοι]χθεῖ ἐξετάζεν κατὰ ἔθνος ἕκαστα καὶ ἐπιγράφεν τ/[ὸν] ἀριθμόν, ἀντιγράφεσθαι δὲ τὸγ γραμματέα τὸγ κατὰ/ [πρ]υτανείαν καὶ τοὺς ἄλλους γραμματιτεῖεας τοὺς ἐπὶ τοῖ/[ς δ]ημοσίοις γράμμασιν· ἐπειδὰν δὲ ἐξετασθῆι πάντα κ/[αὶ] ἀναγραφῆι, τὸγ γραμματέα τῆς βουλῆς ἀναγράψαντα/ [ἐν] στήληι λιθίνηι στῆσαι ἔμπροσθεν τῆς χαλκοθήκη[ς].

9. Reference to the stele set up by Philokleides: *SEG* 19 (1962): no. 129, lines 13–14. The fragment is to be added to *IG* II² 1438; Philokleides restored as secretary of 353/2: *IG* II² 138, 139.

10. Both Ferguson, *Athenian Secretaries*, pp. 8–11, and Brillant, *Les secrétaires athéniens*, pp. 27–51, esp. 34–49 (where earlier scholarship is reviewed), had suggested that the two secretaries were identical before the publication of the fragment identifying Philokleides. Most recently, Alessandrì, "Alcune osservazioni," pp. 13–32, has argued that the secretary *kata prytaneian* and the secretary of the Boule were two distinct officials who coexisted; I remain unconvinced. The latest surviving mention of the secretary of the Boule occurs in *IG* II² 448 of 318/17; for the secretary *kata prytaneian* publishing decrees, see, e.g., *IG* II² 222, 223 (both of 343/2), 235 (340/39), 240 (337/6), 338 (333/2), etc.

11. *Ath. Pol.* 54.3: πρότερον μὲν οὖν οὗτος ἦν χειροτονητός, καὶ τοὺς ἐνδο-ξοτάτους καὶ πιστοτάτους ἐχ[ει]ροτόνουν· καὶ γὰρ ἐν ταῖς στήλαις πρὸς ταῖς συμμαχίαις καὶ προξενί[αι]ς καὶ πολιτείαις οὗτος ἀναγράφεται.

12. Rhodes, *Athenian Boule*, pp. 137–38; see also Henry, *Prescripts*, pp. 20–23, 34–37, and Rhodes, *CAAP*, pp. 602–3.

13. *Ath. Pol.* 54.3: κληροῦσι δὲ καὶ γραμματέα τὸν κατὰ πρυτανεῖαν καλού-μενον, ὃς τῶν γραμμάτων ἐστὶ κύριος καὶ τὰ ψηφίσματα τὰ γιγνόμενα φυλάττει καὶ τἆλλα πάντα ἀντιγράφεται καὶ παρακάθηται τῆι βουλῆι. On the secretary *kata prytaneian*, see the discussions of Rhodes, *CAAP*, pp. 599–603; Alessandrì, "Alcune osservazioni," pp. 13–32; Schulthess, "Γραμματεῖς," cols. 1711–21; Brillant, *Les secrétaires athéniens*, pp. 27–51; Ferguson, *Athenian Secretaries*, pp. 9–11.

14. Destruction of stelai: *SEG* 26 (1976–77): no. 72, lines 55–56: εἰ δὲ τι ψήφισμα γέγραπταί πο ἐστήληι πα[ρὰ τ]/όνδε τὸν νόμον, καθελέτω ὁ γραμματεὺς τῆς βολ[ῆς]; see also *IG* II² 43, lines 31–35, where the secretary of the Boule is instructed to see to the destruction of stelai. *IG* II² 116, lines 39–40, however, assigns the task of destroying an earlier inscription to the treasurer of the people. From this it is possible to infer that the destruction of individual stelai was assigned to officials in whose care

those stelai were, while the destruction of numerous stelai was assigned to the Boule's secretary so that he could determine where these were located and then inform the appropriate official to see to the stele's removal. Philochoros, *FGrHist* 328 F55a, b, records the destruction of the stele preserving the terms of the Peace of Philokrates, though no official is explicitly associated with its removal.

15. *IG* II² 111, lines 42–45: ἀπογράψαι δ/ὲ αὐτῶν τὰ ὀνόματα αὐτί[κα μά]λα ἐναντίον τοῦ δήμου τῶι γ/ραμματεῖ τοὺς στρατηγοὺ[ς τ]οὺ[ς] Ἰουλιητῶν τοὺς ἐπιδημοῦν/τας Ἀθήνησι.

16. *IG* II² 120, lines 15–16 (see n. 8 above).

17. *IG* II² 212, lines 59–63. Compare also the list of trierarchs delivered to the secretary in *IG* I³ 127, lines 27–28, and Chapter 3, Section II.

18. Aeschin. 3.15; see Chapter 5, Section II.

19. *IG* II² 120, lines 15–17 (see n. 8 above).

20. *Ath. Pol.* 54.4: κληροῦσι δὲ καὶ ἐπὶ τοὺς ν[ό]μους ἕτερον ὃς παρακάθηται τῆι βουλῆι, καὶ ἀντιγράφεται καὶ οὗτος πάντας. Other texts mentioning this secretary include: *Agora*, 15: no. 53, line 19; no. 58, line 78; no. 62, line 235; see Rhodes, *CAAP*, pp. 603–4; Alessandrì, "Alcune osservazioni," pp. 32–36; Ferguson, *Athenian Secretaries*, p. 66; Brillant, *Les secrétaires athéniens*, pp. 97–108; Schulthess, "Γραμματεῖς," cols. 1722–23.

21. For the Boule's role in *nomothesia*, see Hansen, *Athenian Democracy*, pp. 168–69.

22. Publication of *nomoi* by the secretary of the Boule: *IG* II² 140, lines 31–35; *SEG* 12 (1953): no. 87, lines 22–27; *SEG* 38 (1988): no. 72, lines 47–48. On Diokles' law, see Chapter 4, Section II.

23. Brillant, *Les secrétaires athéniens*, pp. 97–108, identified the two. Both officials are named or restored in *Agora*, 15: nos. 34 (= *IG* II² 223C), 58, 62; see Rhodes, *Athenian Boule*, p. 138 n. 5, for earlier scholarship.

24. The *anagrapheus* is attested at *Agora*, 15: nos. 43, line 215; 53, line 13; 58, line 84; 62, line 231; see Brillant, *Les secrétaires athéniens*, pp. 77–92, and Schulthess, "Γραμματεῖς," col. 1724, for earlier discussions. The *antigrapheus* is attested in *Agora*, 15: nos. 12, lines 66–67; 43, line 231; 58, lines 80–81; 62, lines 233–34. See Brillant, *Les secrétaires athéniens*, pp. 127–34, and Schulthess, "Γραμματεῖς," cols. 1726–28, for earlier discussions.

25. The other *antigrapheus* is mentioned at Dem. 23.38, 70; Aeschin. 3.25; Harpok., s.v. ἀντιγραφεύς. For discussion of his duties, see Rhodes, *Athenian Boule*, pp. 237–39.

26. An *antigrapheus* is mentioned, in direct connection with the Metroon, in an ephebic inscription of 128/7, where he is named alongside the secretary *kata prytaneian* in the prescripts of two decrees; presumably, he was responsible for having the texts of the decrees copied from the Metroon. For the text, see *Hesperia* 24 (1955): 220–39, lines 104–5, 117–18 (= Wycherley, no. 519). For discussion of the *antigrapheus*, see Meritt, "Greek Inscriptions" (1946), pp. 211–12.

27. On the late fifth-century *anagrapheis*, see Chapter 4. On the late fourth- and early third-century *anagrapheus*, see Ferguson, *Hellenistic Athens*, pp. 19–26, 136–38; Dow, "Athenian Anagrapheis," pp. 40–41; Schulthess, "Γραμματεῖς," col. 1726.

28. *IG* II² 415.

29. *Agora*, 15: nos. 53, lines 13–21; 59, lines 76–85.

30. So Meritt and Traill, *Agora*, 15:8.

31. Rhodes, *CAAP*, p. 603, suggests that the post of secretary *epi tous nomous* was a recent creation at the time of its appearance in the *Athēnaiōn Politeia*.

32. See Jacob, *Les esclaves publics*; Busolt-Swoboda, 2:979–81.

33. Dem. 19.129: ἐν τοῖς κοινοῖς τοῖς ὑμετέροις γράμμασιν ἐν τῷ μητρῴῳ ταῦτ' ἐστίν, ἐφ' οἷς ὁ δημόσιος τέτακται; see also *IG* II² 583; 839, lines 42–45; 840, lines 10–11 (discussed in Chapter 5, Section II).

34. *IG* II² 120, lines 11–15 (n. 8 above); *Ath. Pol.* 47.4.

35. *Ath. Pol.* 54.3 (see n. 13 above).

36. This is implied by Thomas, *Oral Tradition*, p. 81.

37. Dem. 19.237, 18.261. Aeschines' service as a secretary should belong to the 360s and 350s. On Aeschines' early career, see E. Harris, *Aeschines*, pp. 29–30. Harris suggests that Aeschines was the secretary who read documents to the Boule and Ekklesia, who is mentioned by Aristotle (*Ath. Pol.* 54.4) and in several bouleutic inscriptions. An undersecretary to the Boule is honored in Hellenistic inscriptions: *IG* II² 913, lines 31–35; 914, line 4; 915, lines 31–35.

38. Undersecretaries: Lys. 30.28. The same speaker also indicates that it was illegal for a man to serve as an undersecretary for the same official or board more than twice: Lys. 30.29 (ὑπογραμματεῦσαι μὲν οὐκ ἔξεστι δὶς τὸν αὐτὸν τῇ ἀρχῇ τῇ αὐτῇ). Rhodes, *Athenian Boule*, p. 139 n. 3, questions whether this rule was in force earlier in the fifth century. For fifth-century undersecretaries to other officials, see Ant. 6.35; *IG* I³ 476, lines 62, 268, and Chapter 3, Section I.

39. For fifth-century assistants to the Boule, see *IG* I³ 1390. For growing specialization in the duties of state magistrates, compare the assignment of specific areas of responsibility to members of the board 1 of Athenian generals, a practice first attested in the late 350s: see *Ath. Pol.* 61.1, with Rhodes, *CAAP*, pp. 678–82; Chambers, *Staat*, p. 408.

40. Hansen, *Athenian Assembly*, pp. 20–24.

41. Hansen's views have been challenged in a number of valuable articles by E. Harris: see "How Often Did the Athenian Assembly Meet?"; "When Did the Athenian Assembly Meet?"

42. For Hansen's estimate of the number of decrees, see *Athenian Assembly*, p. 108; see also Hansen, "Number of *Rhetores*," pp. 128–31.

43. *Ath. Pol.* 47.2–5; see Chapter 5, Section III. For other uses of wooden tablets, compare the *pinax* on which the cavalry register was recorded (*Ath. Pol.* 48.2); the display of proposed or revised laws on *sanides* (Andok. 1.83; Aeschin. 3.38–39); and the use of writing tablets in the *dikastēria* (Ar. *Clouds* 768–72; [Dem.] 46.11).

44. Klaffenbach, "Bemerkungen," pp. 21–22.

45. Papyrus copy to Poses: *IG* II² 1, lines 61–62; papyrus text of decree carried by an *episkopos*: Ar. *Birds* 1078; purchase of papyrus for copies in Erechtheion accounts: *IG* I³ 476, lines 289–91; 477, lines 1–2. Thomas, *Oral Tradition*, pp. 75–83, takes the possible use of different materials as a sign of confusion and disorder. But even modern archives are characterized by records preserved on different media: see Bradsher, "Introduction," p. 12.

46. Numbered shelves are attested in the Opisthodomos (*IG* II² 1445, lines 31–34) and in the Hekatompedon (*IG* II² 1371, lines 6–11; 1393, lines 6–11; 1424a, lines 5–21; 1443, lines 12–88). On shelves and letter labels in the Parthenon, see D. Harris, *Treasures*, pp. 23–24. On the use of boxes or chests (κιβωτοί) to store documents, see Ar. *Knights* 1000; [Dem.] 25.61; *IG* II² 1174, lines 4–13. Posner, *Archives*, p. 112, and

Thomas, *Oral Tradition*, p. 80, also call attention to the use of *echinoi* for the storage of legal documents in Athens (*Ath. Pol.* 53.2), suggest that they may also have been used in the Metroon, and take them as a sign of the archives' disorder. Evidence for the use of storage vessels is sought in the story that Diogenes the Cynic made his home in a *pithos* in the Metroon (Diog. L. 6.2.23 [Wycherley, no. 479]). But anecdotal stories about the living quarters of Hellenistic philosophers are probably not reliable guides for the Metroon's archives, and even if we allow that documents were stored in clay vessels, that does not necessitate disorganization. For the storage of documents in the archival establishments of other ancient societies, see Posner, *Archives*, index, s.v. "Archival Equipment," "Archival Functions."

47. *Ath. Pol.* 47.5: ὅταν δ' ἦ χρημάτ[ων κ]αταβολή, παραδίδωσι τοῖς ἀποδέκταις αὐτὰ ταῦτα καθελὼν ἀπὸ [τῶν] ἐπιστυλίων ὧν ἐν ταύτηι τῆι ἡμέραι δεῖ τὰ χρήματα καταβληθ[ῆ]ναι [καὶ] ἀπαλειφθῆναι.

48. LSJ, s.v. ἐπιστύλιον; Plut. *Per.* 13.7; Vitruvius 4.3.4; see also *IG* II² 1627, lines 334–35; 1628, line 516; 1629, line 991; and 1631, lines 224–25, where *epistylion* refers to some crossbeam or component of a catapult.

49. For other whitened wooden tablets used to display public announcements, often at the monument of the Eponymous Heroes, see, e.g., Aeschin. 3.39; Andok. 1.78; Hesychius, s.v. σανίς.

50. Sandys, *Aristotle's Constitution of Athens*, p. 186. Earlier, Kaibel, *Stil und Text*, p. 38, had suggested that *epistylia* represented some types of niches; see also Wilhelm, *Beiträge*, p. 248; Posner, *Archives*, p. 112; Rhodes, *CAAP*, p. 572; Thomas, *Oral Tradition*, p. 80.

51. As does Thomas, *Oral Tradition*, pp. 77–78.

52. *IG* II² 140, lines 31–35: τὸν δὲ γραμμα[τέα τῆς βουλῆς]/ προσαναγράψαι τ[ὸν νόμον τόνδε]/ πρὸς τὸν πρότερο[ν τὸν Χαιρημον]/ίδου εἰς τὴν στήλ[ην τὴν ἔμ-προσθ]/εν τοῦ Μητρώιου.

53. Aeschin. 3.187. As argued in Chapter 5, Section I, this passage probably refers to the stele inscribed with the text of the decree honoring the heroes from Phyle, not an archival text housed within the Metroon.

54. Sickinger, "Inscriptions and Archives," pp. 292–96. See also Wilhelm, *Beiträge*, p. 298: "Die Verewigung von Urkunden an öffentlichen oder heiligem Orte hat mit dem Archivwesen im eigentlichen Sinne des Wortes nichts zu tun."

55. Dem. 24.20: ἐπὶ δὲ τῆς πρώτης πρυτανείας τῇ ἐνδεκάτῃ ἐν τ‥ δήμῳ. ἐπειδὰν εὔξηται ὁ κῆρυξ, ἐπιχειροτονίαν ποιεῖν τῶν νόμων, πρῶτον μὲν περὶ τῶν βουλευ-τικῶν, δεύτερον δὲ τῶν κοινῶν, εἶτα οἳ κεῖνται τοῖς ἐννέα ἄρχουσιν, εἶτα τῶν ἄλλων ἀρχῶν.

56. The exception is the "common laws," whose content is unclear. Ruschenbusch, *SN*, pp. 27–31, argues forcefully that the "common" laws were those which applied to all citizens. MacDowell, "Law-Making at Athens," p. 67, however, maintains that they were laws affecting all magistrates.

57. Law of the king archon: Ath. 6.27.235b; law on the arbitrators: Lys. fr. 16 Thalheim; *IG* II² 179, line 9; Dem. 20.94.

58. The law on *eisangelia* is referred to by Hyp. 4.3. The law on treason is mentioned at [Plut.] *Vit. X Orat.* 837d; Xen. *Hell.* 1.7.22.

59. For discussions of Aristotle's sources in the second part of the *Athenaion Politeia*, see Bursy, *Aristotelis*, pp. 1–8; Rhodes, *CAAP*, pp. 33–35; and Chambers, *Staat*, p. 84, who notes: "Der deskriptive Teil, der die Verfassung zur Zeit des Aristo-

teles betrachtet, fußt wahrscheinlich auf den authenischen Gestzen selbst und auf Aristoteles' Beobachtung ihrer Wirkung."

60. References to laws: *Ath. Pol.* 43.6; 45.1; 48.1; 49.4; 51.1, 3; 53.5, 6; 57.4; 60.2; 67.1. To Aristotle's account of the duties of the chief archon (*Ath. Pol.* 56.7), compare the law quoted at [Dem.] 43.75. To Aristotle's account of the duties of the *basileus*, compare the laws quoted at Dem. 23.22, 53. For further discussion, see Rhodes, *CAAP*, pp. 33–35.

61. Dem. 24.42; on this law, see also Chapter 4, Section II.

62. Dates are given in the prescripts of the law on the Mysteries: *IG* II² 140, lines 1–3; and the laws on sacred matters: *IG* II² 333, line 13. Neither the law on silver coinage (*SEG* 38 [1988]: no. 72) nor the law on attempted tyranny (*SEG* 12 [1953]: no. 87) includes a precise date in its prescript. It is noteworthy that Demosthenes' citation of Diokles' law occurs a half century after the law was enacted, but we have no reason to assume that its provisions had been revoked.

63. Dem. 20.93; 24.20, 33; Aeschin. 3.38–40. See Rhodes, "*Nomothesia* in Fourth-Century Athens," pp. 55–60.

64. *IG* II² 140, lines 31–35.

65. Dem. 20.89–99. On the old law mentioned by Demosthenes and its relationship to other laws, see Rhodes, "*Nomothesia* in Fourth-Century Athens," pp. 55–60; for different views, see Hansen, "Athenian *Nomothesia*," pp. 346–52; MacDowell, "Law-Making at Athens," pp. 62–74. On fourth-century *nomothesia* in general, see Hansen, *Athenian Democracy*, pp. 165–77.

66. Dem. 20.91. *Pace* Hansen, "Athenian *Nomothesia*," pp. 355–56, who takes these commissions to be ones appointed under the "Inspection Law" discussed at Aeschin. 3.38–40, I follow Rhodes, "*Nomothesia* in Fourth-Century Athens," p. 60, and MacDowell, "Law-Making at Athens," p. 72, and believe that Demosthenes refers to specially appointed commissions.

67. *Ath. Pol.* 45.3; 49.3; 51.3; 53.4; 54.3, 7; 55.2, 4; 56.3; 60.2; 61.1; 62.1; 67.4–5. In at least one of these cases (e.g., *Ath. Pol.* 45.3), Aristotle's knowledge of earlier practice probably does not derive from the text of an earlier law. The same, however, is not true in other cases: see Rhodes, *CAAP*, pp. 34–35, and his commentary on the preceding passages.

68. See Chapter 3, Section III.

69. On the date of the calendar change, see Meritt, "Athenian Calendar Problems," pp. 201, 211, who dates it to 407/6; see Rhodes, *Athenian Boule*, p. 224. On the increasing prominence of archon names in the prescripts of inscribed decrees, see Henry, *Prescripts*, pp. 19–24.

70. Cross-referencing between the first Boule secretary and archons had been used in some documents from the 440s: see Chapter 3, Section III.

71. First instance of numbered prytany: *IG* II² 18 (Tod, no. 108; 394/3); first instance of date within prytany: *IG* II² 105 + 323 (Tod no. 136; 368/7); first instance of date according to archontic calendar: *IG* II² 229 with p. 659 (341/0). See Henry, *Prescripts*, pp. 24–27, 37–38; W. West, "Public Archives," p. 534 with n. 10.

72. Rhodes, *Athenian Boule*, pp. 137–38.

73. Thomas, *Oral Tradition*, pp. 79–80.

74. See, e.g., *IG* I³ 364, lines 10–11, 21–22; *IG* I³ 365, lines 4–5; *IG* I³ 368, line 3; *IG* I³ 369.

75. *SEG* 41 (1991): no. 9; [Plut.] *Vit. X Or.* 833e–f; for prytany dates in financial

documents, see *IG* I³ 369, 370, 377, 378. See also my discussion of these texts in Chapter 3, Section III.

76. *IG* I³ 377, lines 4–5, 5–7, 8, etc. (dated 407/6 [?]).

77. Aeschin. 2.90.

78. Aeschin. 3.73–75.

79. See also the precise dates given by Demosthenes in 343 for events of 346 (Dem. 19.57–58), though he does not state that these were taken from the archives.

80. Dem. 24.20.

81. *Ath. Pol.* 43.3–6; see also *Ath. Pol.* 44.4, where the dates of elections are specified in terms of the bouleutic calendar.

82. Aeschin. 2.61, 3.68; see also *IG* II² 212, lines 53–57, a decree of 347/6 that calls for a meeting of the Ekklesia to be held on 18 Elaphebolion.

83. Dem. 24.26; see also [Dem.] 50.4, where the speaker refers to a decree of 362/1 dated by the archontic calendar to 24 Metageitnion; here too we do not know where the speaker learned the date, but since the decree is read out, I assume that the date was attached to the original copy obtained from the archives.

84. W. West, "Public Archives," p. 536.

85. For the importance of the bouleutic calendar in dating documents, see Henry, *Prescripts*, p. 20, and Hansen, "Was the Athenian Ekklesia Convened?"

86. Thuc. 4.118.11–12; 5.19.1; see Chapter 3, Section III, for further discussion.

87. *Ath. Pol.* 32.1: ἐπικυρωθέντων δὲ τούτων ὑπὸ τοῦ πλήθους, ἐπιψηφίσαντος Ἀριστομάχου, ἡ μὲν βουλὴ ἰῂ ἐπὶ Καλλίου πρὶν διαβουλεῦσαι κατελύθη μηνὸς Θαργηλιῶνος τετράδι ἐπὶ δέκα, οἱ δὲ τετρακόσιοι εἰσήιεσαν ἐνάτῃ φθίνοντος Θαργηλιῶνος. ἔδει δὲ τὴν εἰληχυῖαν τῶι κυάμωι βουλὴν εἰσιέναι δ ἐπὶ δέκα Σκιροφοριῶνος.

88. For two recent discussions of Aristotle's use of these dates, see Rhodes, *CAAP*, pp. 362–68, 385–89, 404–6; Andrewes, *HCT*, 5:234–36. Compare also the synchronization of bouleutic and archontic dates in fifth-century financial records, e.g., *IG* I³ 369, line 79.

89. Andrewes, "Androtion," pp. 22–23, however, suggests that the dates may have come from a speech. Also relevant to the discussion is the ongoing debate between E. Harris, "When Did the Athenian Assembly Meet?," and Hansen, "Was the Athenian Ekklesia Convened?," on whether the Ekklesia met according to the bouleutic or archontic calendar. My own view is that the records of meetings of the Ekklesia expressed dates in both calendars from the middle of the fifth century.

90. *Pace* W. West, "Public Archives," pp. 539–40, who suggests that "ideally, one would have to know the day on which a decree was passed in order to retrieve it easily."

91. *Ath. Pol.* 47.5–48.1.

92. Lys. 30.3.

93. Dem. 20.91.

94. See esp. *IG* II² 971, 1132. Compare also the *dogma* referred to by Aeschines in 346 that had been enacted more than twenty years before (Aeschin. 2.32), and the decrees of 346 cited by Aeschines in 330 (Aeschin. 3.75).

Chapter Seven

1. For earlier discussions of consultation of the Metroon, see Curtius, *Das Metroon*, pp. 21–22; Posner, *Archives*, 113–14; Thomas, *Oral Tradition*, pp. 68–73.

2. For a recent account of the various courts, their development, and some of their features, see Boegehold, *Agora*, 28:3–50; cf. also MacDowell, *LCA*, pp. 24–40; Harrison, *LA*, 2:1–60.

3. This overview is necessarily brief and not intended to provide a full account of the operation of the *dikastēria*. In addition to the authorities cited in the previous note, see also the excellent survey of Todd, *Shape of Athenian Law*, esp. pp. 77–97, which focuses on the personnel of the courts and the reliance on amateurs at all levels.

4. On the dikastic oath, see Harrison, *LA*, 2:48; see also the recent discussions of Sealey, *Justice*, p. 51; Todd, *Shape of Athenian Law*, pp. 54–55.

5. For the gathering of evidence, see Harrison, *LA*, 2:133–54, esp. 134–35, on laws and decrees.

6. Andok. 1.95: καί μοι ἀνάγνωθι τὸν νόμον τὸν ἐκ τῆς στήλης. Andokides himself calls the measure Solonian, but its text, which is included in Andokides' speech, indicates that it was proposed in 410/9 by a certain Demophantos. See MacDowell, *Andokides*, pp. 134–35.

7. Lys. 1.30: ἀνάγνωθι δέ μοι καὶ τοῦτον τὸν νόμον ἰτὸνῖ ἐκ τῆς στήλης τῆς ἐξ Ἀρείου πάγου.

8. Dem. 48.73. Other references to stelai in forensic speeches include: Dem 19.270–72; 20.36, 64, 127, 159; [Dem.] 58.56; 59.105; Dein. 2.24; Lyk. 1.118, 125–26.

9. [Dem.] 25.99: πῶς δ᾽ εἰς τὸ μητρ¨ον βαδιεῖσθ᾽, ἄν τι βούλησθε; οὐ γὰρ δήπου καθ᾽ ἕν᾽ ὑμῶν ἕκαστος ὡς ἐπὶ κυρίους τοὺς νόμους πορεύσεται, εἰ νῦν μὴ βεβαιώσαντες αὐτοὺς ἔξιθ᾽ ἅπαντες κοινῇ.

10. Thomas, *Oral Tradition*, p. 69, dismisses this passage as evidence for the consultation of documents in the Metroon, suggesting that the speaker's words denote not the consultation of documents but a visit to the Metroon in a "symbolic and semi-religious light." But the dikasts are imagined visiting the Metroon if they want something (ἄν τι βούλησθε), and since the Metroon housed the city's laws, it is difficult to see what else they would want when visiting this building (we know virtually nothing about cult activity in the building). Thomas misinterprets the critical phrase ὡς ἐπὶ κυρίους τοὺς νόμους πορεύσεται, claiming that ἐπί in this passage can mean "in the presence of," so that the dikasts would simply enter the Metroon to be "in the presence of laws which were still valid." But according to the standard lexica (LSJ, s.v. ἐπί), when ἐπί has the meaning "in the presence of," it usually takes a noun in the genitive case, while ἐπί plus the accusative after verbs of motion often implies "the object or purpose for which one goes." The speaker's use of ὡς before ἐπί should also denote purpose: see LSJ, s.v. ὡς, c.iii. Hence, my translation "to find valid laws"—that is, to consult or look up laws that are still valid. Thomas's interpretation, however, is cited with apparent approval by Todd, *Shape of Athenian Law*, p. 58 n. 11.

11. Dem. 19.129; on the phrase, see Chapter 4, Section II. See also Deinarchos's reference (1.86) to a decree moved by Demosthenes that was under the care of the Mother of the Gods; its text too was presumably acquired from the Metroon's archives.

12. Aeschin. 2.58–69, 89–92; 3.24, 75; see Chapter 5, Section I.

13. Dem. 18.142; on the phrase, see Chapter 4, Section II.

14. See Thomas, *Oral Tradition*, pp. 68–73, who calls Aeschines (p. 69) "the first to exploit the public records as part of his demagogic rhetoric." She later concludes (p.

81) that "it was not until the mid-fourth century that the value of its [the Metroon's] records seems to have been properly realized." Todd, *Shape of Athenian Law*, p. 58 n. 11, questions whether the Metroon was the primary source for the texts of laws cited by the orators and points out that stelai are cited more frequently.

15. Antiphon's role as the first to publish and compose written speeches is mentioned at Plut. *Mor.* 832d. His three speeches are *On the Stepmother* (Antiph. 1), *On the Murder of Herodes* (Antiph. 5), and *On the Chorus Boy* (Antiph. 6); speeches 2–4, the *Tetralogies*, are rhetorical compositions, not intended for delivery in actual cases.

16. Antiph. 5.8–19; on Euxitheos's arguments, see Gagarin, *Murder of Heroides*, pp. 17–29. Euxitheos also states (5.17) that his opponents refused to let him offer sureties for his release while awaiting trial, although this was possible under the law. For references to provisions of Athenian homicide in other speeches by Antiphon, see Antiph. 6.4, 6, 36.

17. Close study of laws is also implied in Lysias's speech *Against Theomnestos* (Lys. 10.6–20), which attempts to build an argument based on the precise, but obscure, wording of a Solonian law.

18. Andok. 2.23; see Chapter 3, Section II, for discussion.

19. The decree is mentioned at Andok. 1.8, 71; cf. Lys. 6.9, 24. For discussion of Andokides' arguments about its validity, see MacDowell, *Andokides*, pp. 199–203.

20. Andok. 1.95–98: καί μοι ἀνάγνωθι τὸν νόμον τὸν ἐκ τῆς στήλης.

21. Andok. 1.73–87. On these documents and their relevance to Andokides' case in 400/399, see MacDowell, *Andokides*, pp. 200–203. Robertson, "Laws of Athens," pp. 60–64, takes an especially sinister view of Andokides' motives.

22. Andok. 1.86. For the location of the stoa in which the revised laws were set up, see Robertson, "Laws of Athens," pp. 64–65; Rhodes, "Athenian Code," pp. 98–99. See also Chapter 4, Section I.

23. Lysias 13.23, 28, 33, 35, 59. A heading ΨΗΦΙΣΜΑΤΑ at section 51 suggests that one or more decrees were read out there also, but the speaker's words speak of a verdict issued by the Boule that sat under the regime of the Thirty; this was presumably cast in the form of a decree.

24. Lys. 13.38, 55.

25. Lys. 13.71–73.

26. Agoratos too may have cited documents in his own speech to support his own claims. The speaker points out (Lys. 13.71) that Agoratos was not responsible for the assassination of Phrynichos and that he was not made a citizen by the same decree that bestowed citizenship on Thrasyboulos. Instead, Agoratos had bribed the mover of the decree to have his name added as a "benefactor" (see Meiggs-Lewis, no. 85, lines 26–27). It seems likely that Agoratos also referred to this inscription in his own speech, as evidence of his goodwill to the Athenians. Compare also Lysias 10 (*Against Theomnestos*) of 384/3, where the speaker makes detailed arguments about the specific wording of individual laws.

27. Laws governing inheritance cases are cited at Is. 2.16; 3.38, 42, 53; 6.8; 7.2; 8.34; 10.10; 11.1, 4, 11.

28. Isok. 17.52.

29. Isok. 18.2–3, 18, 19, 20.

30. Accounts of the reconciliation agreement and amnesty are given at *Ath. Pol.* 39; Xen. *Hell.* 2.4.38–43; other references include Andok. 1.90; Lys. 6.39; 13.80; for discussion of the terms, see Loening, *Reconciliation Agreement*, pp. 19–58. Loening con-

cludes (p. 30) only that the agreements "were recorded and available in some form to interested parties for consultation." See also Krentz, *Thirty*, pp. 102–8.

31. Todd, *Shape of Athenian Law*, pp. 94–95.

32. An account of arbitration is provided by *Ath. Pol.* 53; see Rhodes, *CAAP*, pp. 587–96; Chambers, *Staat*, pp. 378–80.

33. On the date of the institution of public arbitrators see MacDowell, "Chronology of Athenian Speeches," pp. 269–71; for the date from which testimony was submitted in writing, see Ruschenbusch, "Drei Beiträge," pp. 34–35. Others date the change to the 370s, following Calhoun, "Oral and Written Pleadings."

34. E.g., letters such as those read out in the speech *Against Aristokrates* (Dem. 23.116, 151, 159–62) were not routinely inscribed on stone.

35. For discussion of the charges, see E. Harris, *Aeschines*, p. 116.

36. More than 130 prosecutions of Athenian magistrates for corruption, treason, and other charges are cataloged by Hansen, *Eisangelia*, pp. 66–120. Speeches survive from only a small minority of cases, many of which could have provided some opportunity for the citation of documents. See esp. Dem. 19.276–90, where Demosthenes compares the present cases against Aeschines with the prosecution and condemnation of Epikrates in 392/1; among the charges against Epikrates was that he acted in violation of his instructions (παρὰ τὰ γράμματα) and gave false reports to the Boule. A speech of Lysias (Lys. 28, *Against Ergokles*) was delivered by a speaker for the prosecution at the trial of the general Ergokles; no documents are cited, but the speech was not the only one delivered, as its opening sentence indicates (Lys. 28.1).

37. On the case, see Gwatkin, "Legal Arguments," pp. 129–41; E. Harris, *Aeschines*, pp. 138–48; Wankel, *Demosthenes*, pp. 8–41.

38. Decrees: Dem. 20.36, 44, 54, 60, 70, 86; laws: Dem. 20.27, 90–93. Unlike Aeschines' speech *Against Ktesiphon*, this speech is a *graphē nomon mē epitēdeion theinai*, an indictment against an unconstitutional law. Procedure in the two types of cases, however, was closely related.

39. Dem. 24.20–23, 33, 42–65. This speech too was delivered in a *graphē nomon mē epitēdeion theinai*.

40. Homicide laws: Dem. 23.22–62; other laws and decrees: Dem. 23.86–89.

41. Dem. 23.115, 159–62, 174–78, 183.

42. E.g., the decree honoring Leukon (Dem. 20.33–34) and the decree honoring certain Thasian supporters of Athens (Dem. 20.59–63).

43. For a catalog, see Hansen, *Sovereignty of the People's Court*.

44. Lysias 32, found in Dion. Hal. *Lys.*, preserves a portion of a speech from a *graphē paranomōn*.

45. See Aeschin. 3.200; Dem. 18.111; 22.34; 23.51, 63, 215.

46. Xen. *Hell.* 1.7.1–34. For its relationship to *graphai paranomōn* proceedings, see Wolff, *Normenkontrolle*, pp. 48–50.

47. *IG* II² 971, lines 23–24: ἐπέδειξεν δὲ ['Ονασος τὸ ψήφισμα τοῦ δήμου] / ἐν τῶι Μητρώιωιῖ κατ[ακεχωρισμένον τὸ περὶ αὐτοῦ]. See also Chapter 5, Section I.

48. [Dem.] 7.33, however, does refer to a letter from Philip, although its text is not read out. See also *IG* II² 583, lines 4–9 (Wycherley, no. 497; see also Chapter 5, Section I), a decree that calls for the publication of an earlier grant of *isotelia* from the Metroon.

49. *IG* II² 226, lines 1–5. See M. Osborne, *Naturalization*, 2:81–83, for discussion of the dates and occasions of the earlier grants.

50. *IG* II² 330.

51. *IG* II² 360, lines 1–27.

52. Ibid., lines 28–78. The four decrees consist of two decrees of the Ekklesia and two preliminary decrees of the Boule; see Rhodes, *Athenian Boule*, pp. 66–67, for discussion of their relationship.

53. Aeschines reads out decrees: Dem. 19.303; Demosthenes and the decree of Arthmios: Dem. 9.41–46. For discussion, see Thomas, *Oral Tradition*, pp. 83–87.

54. *IG* II² 107 (= Tod no. 131), lines 1–34.

55. Ibid., lines 35–end. For discussion of the context, see Tod, pp. 96–98.

56. *IG* II² 17. See M. Osborne, *Naturalization*, 1:43–45 (D8) for a new text, which I follow. The inscription actually preserves two decrees, the first (lines 1–12) of the Boule, the second (lines 13–40) of the Ekklesia. Since Aristokrates served as secretary when both decrees were enacted (lines 1–2, 13), both were enacted in the same prytany. The first decree may be a *probouleuma*, a preliminary decree of the Boule, that was ratified by the following decree of the Ekklesia, and the secretary has inadvertently had both texts inscribed on stone. For discussion of similar decrees of the Boule, see Rhodes, *Athenian Boule*, pp. 82–85.

57. Publication is ordered in lines 9–10 and again in lines 33–37.

58. *IG* I³ 227 with addenda, p. 955; see also Meiggs-Lewis, no. 70, with addenda, p. 313, for discussion.

59. Andok. 3.12. On the embassy and the terms brought back by Andokides and his colleagues, see Hamilton, *Sparta's Bitter Victories*, pp. 233–59, with references to earlier literature. On the relationship between this embassy and the one reported by Philochoros (*FGrHist* 328 F140a), see Badian, "King's Peace."

60. Thirty Years' Peace: Thuc. 1.140.2, 1.145; cf. also 1.35.2, 40.2, 67.2, 78.4. Megarian Decree: 1.139.1.

61. Thuc. 5.56.2–3. On the incident, see Andrewes, *HCT*, 4:77.

62. Ar. *Lys.* 510–14. Henderson, *Lysistrata*, p. 135, takes the passage to be a reference to Alkibiades' actions in 418, as reported by Thucydides; see also Andrewes, *HCT*, 4:77–78. Wilamowitz, *Lysistrate*, however, took Lysistrata's mention of a stele more generally, as a reflection of a common practice. Although I am inclined to follow Henderson and to take Lysistrata's allusion to a stele more specifically, acceptance of Wilamowitz's view would lend my hypothesis further support by its implication that speakers in the Ekklesia discussed written texts with some frequency.

63. The treaty was inscribed on a bronze plaque at Olympia: Paus. 5.23.4. Other fifth-century treaties that were inscribed and publicly displayed at Athens include the Peace of Nikias, set up on the Acropolis (Thucydides 5.18.10; cf. 5.56.2); and the treaty ending the Peloponnesian War, discussed by Andokides (Andok. 3.12).

64. *IG* I³ 46, lines 17–21; see Chapter 3, Section II, for text and discussion.

65. *IG* I³ 61; see Chapter 3, Section II, for text and discussion.

66. For other fifth-century decrees referring to earlier decisions of the Ekklesia, see *IG* I³ 40, line 49; *IG* I³ 52, lines 2–6, and a reference in the Coinage Decree (*IG* I³ 1453 §10) to an earlier measure proposed by Klearchos.

67. *IG* II² 237; the earlier grant is referred to at lines 15–21.

68. For the distribution of copies to honorands, see *IG* II² 1, lines 61–62 (= Tod, no. 97), discussed in Chapter 3, Section II.

69. A complaint of Isokrates in his work *Antidosis* (15.79–83) may also be signifi-

cant, where he faults certain Athenians who investigate the texts of laws in prepara-
tion for making new ones. Was such study a regular phenomenon?

70. See in particular the discussion of Fornara, *Nature of Historiography*, pp. 47–52.

71. On Herodotus's use of earlier written sources, see Lateiner, *Historical Method*,
pp. 91–108. On Thucydides' knowledge of earlier written sources, esp. Hellanikos, see
Hornblower, *Thucydides*, pp. 83–88.

72. On Herodotus's use of inscriptions, see now Pritchett, *Liar School*, pp. 144–491.

73. The texts are the one-year truce concluded between Athens and Sparta (4.118–
19), the Peace of Nikias (5.18–19), an Athenian-Spartan alliance (5.23–24), an alliance
between the Athenians, Argives, Mantineans, and Eleans (5.47), an Argive-Spartan
truce and treaty (5.77, 79), and three Spartan-Persian treaties (8.18, 37, 58). We do not
know Thucydides's sources for these treaties, but neither the one-year truce of 423
nor the Spartan-Persian treaties include publication clauses, so nonepigraphical
sources may be assumed. According to Thomas, *Oral Tradition*, p. 90, historians
"used documents infrequently, if at all." But she also says that "Thucydides cited
contemporary documents only in Book V."

74. For the Thirty Years' Peace and Megarian Decrees, see n. 60 above. Documents
possibly underlying other passages: 2.24.1; 3.114.3; 4.16.1–2; 6.6.3, 8.2, 26.1. For discussion of Thucydides' use of documents, see esp. C. Meyer, *Die Urkunden*. On the
incomplete nature of books 5 and 8, see Andrewes, *HCT*, 5:361–83. Andrewes (p. 383)
favors the view that the documents of books 4, 5, and 8 "might in the final version
have been replaced by shorter summaries."

75. Connor, *Thucydides*, pp. 144–47. See also Hornblower, *Commentary*, 2:113–19,
for other possible explanations.

76. Xenophon paraphrases the terms of the treaty ending the Peloponnesian War
(*Hell.* 2.2.20), provides an abbreviated text of the King's Peace of 387 (5.1.31), and
discusses treaties and treaty negotiations in several other passages (6.2.1; 6.3.1–19;
7.1.1; 7.1.36–40). Theopompos, a fourth-century historian who composed several
historical works, argued from the letter forms of an inscription carrying the terms of
the fifth-century Peace of Kallias between Athens and Persia that its text was a
forgery; see *FGrHist* 115 F153 and F154, with Jacoby, *FGrHist* 2b.1:380, and the comments of Connor, *Theopompos*, pp. 77–98.

77. Dion. Hal. *De Thuc.* 5 (translated by Pritchett, *Dionysios*, p. 3). Dionysios,
however, is probably wrong about the date of these writers: see Fornara, *Nature of
Historiography*, pp. 16–23.

78. Jacoby, *Atthis*, p. 178.

79. For further discussion of this passage, see Pritchett, *Dionysios*, p. 54. On the
actual date of the local historians to whom Dionysius refers, see Fornara, *Nature of
Historiography*, pp. 16–23.

80. The fundamental work on the Atthidographers remains Jacoby, *Atthis*. An
excellent overview of their works can be found in Harding, *Androtion*, pp. 1–52.

81. See Jacoby, *Atthis*, pp. 86–99.

82. Hellanikos, *FGrHist* 323a F25, F26, both dating to 407/6; for Hellanikos's use of
archon dating, see Jacoby, *FGrHist* 3b suppl. 1:14–21. Pritchett, *Greek Archives*, pp.
42–48, however, has recently questioned the strength of Jacoby's arguments.

83. Jacoby (*FGrHist* 323a) dates only eight of the twenty-six fragments that can be
reasonably assigned to Hellanikos's *Atthis* to the sixth century or later. On Kleidemos,

see Jacoby, *FGrHist* 3b suppl. 1:57–61, who states (p. 60): "We cannot appraise the whole of K[leidemos]'s achievement because we do not know how much work in archives and elsewhere he put into it. . . . Certainly the amount of work put into it was considerable." See also Harding, *Androtion*, pp. 10–13. Kleidemos's account of the naukraries is found at *FGrHist* 323 F8. Jacoby, *FGrHist* 3b suppl. 1:66–67, withheld judgments on its foundation.

84. *FGrHist* 324 F6. See Harding, *Androtion*, pp. 94–99, for discussion of Androtion's account and its relation to Aristotle's description at *Ath. Pol.* 22.4.

85. *FGrHist* 324 F36. See Harding, *Androtion*, pp. 134–38. For the possibility of a documentary origin for the fragment, see Wilamowitz, *Aristoteles*, 1:52, and Jacoby, *FGrHist* 3b suppl. 1:147, who suggests that Androtion quotes the law verbatim.

86. *FGrHist* 324 F5. See Jacoby, *FGrHist* 3b suppl. 1:117–20, and Harding, *Androtion*, pp. 90–94, for discussion of the problems and possible solutions.

87. *FGrHist* 324 F38; Jacoby, *FGrHist* 3b suppl. 1:148–50; Harding, *Androtion*, pp. 143–48.

88. *FGrHist* 324 F43; Jacoby, *FGrHist* 3b suppl. 1:151–52; Harding, *Androtion*, pp. 161–62.

89. *FGrHist* 324 F30; Jacoby, *FGrHist* 3b suppl. 1:142–43; Harding, *Androtion*, pp. 37–38, 125–27.

90. *FGrHist* 324 F52; Jacoby, *FGrHist* 3b suppl. 1:157–62; Harding, *Androtion*, pp. 174–78. For discussion of the revision, see Whitehead, *Demes*, pp. 106–9.

91. Demophilos's name is given by a scholiast to Aeschin. 1.77. Other fragments of Androtion may suggest that he consulted documentary sources: F34 on Solon's *seisachtheia* (though Androtion's explanation need not be accepted, he may have tried to explain the cancellation of debts on the basis of other material found in Solon's laws); F44, on a Spartan embassy to Athens in 408; F54 on a Persian embassy to Athens in 344/3 and the Athenian reply. For Androtion's use of documents, see, in general, Harding, *Androtion*, pp. 36–38, 43–47. Andrewes, "Androtion," pp. 16–17, suggests that Androtion is likely to have consulted documents, but he also suggests that Androtion may have received some texts through private transmission.

92. *IG* II² 212, lines 20–33.

93. So, already, Jacoby, *Atthis*, pp. 204–5, but see the modifications of Jacoby's view by Harding, *Androtion*, pp. 36–38. For fragments of Philochoros suggesting a study of older documents, see *FGrHist* 328 F49–51, F53–56, F64.

94. So Harding, *Androtion*, p. 44, against Thomas, *Oral Tradition*, pp. 90–91, who asserts, "Their aims do not seem so remote from those of the orators who cited exemplary decrees simply to illustrate broad and accepted patriotic beliefs of the past."

95. For Aristotle's works on Athenian drama, see Pickard-Cambridge, *Dramatic Festivals*, p. 71. See also my discussion in Chapter 2, Section II. On the Delphic victor list, see Tod, no. 187.

96. See Bloch, "Studies in Historical Literature," pp. 303–76, esp. 355–76. Bloch does not mention the Metroon by name, but he suggests that the laws gathered by Aristotle and his students must have been come from archival sources.

97. For references, see Chapter 6, Section II. Wilamowitz, *Aristoteles*, 1:214–16, argued that Aristotle's analysis of contemporary Athenian democracy was, like his historical account of its development, largely dependent on an earlier analysis of the constitution, written by an anonymous Atthidographer around the year 380. These

arguments were laid to rest by Bursy, *De Aristotelis*, pp. 8–51; see also Busolt-Swoboda, p. 96 with n. 1; Rhodes, *CAAP*, pp. 33–34; Chambers, *Staat*, p. 84.

98. On Theophrastos's *Nomoi*, see Szegedy-Maszak, *Nomoi of Theophrastus*, which includes references to earlier literature. Theophrastos's discussion of *eisangeliai* is represented in fr. 2; of *nomothesia* in fr. 1 (as part of the duties of the thesmothetai); and ostracism in fr. 18a, b.

99. On this work, see *FGrHist* 228 F4–7, with Jacoby's brief discussion *FGrHist* 2b *Komm.*, pp. 646–47.

100. On this work, see *FGrHist* 228 T1, 10. Demetrios also drew up an *Anagraphē Archontōn* (*FGrHist* 228 F1–3), which too may have entailed investigation into old records.

101. *FGrHist* 342. See Jacoby, *FGrHist* 3b *Komm.*, pp. 94–99; Krech, *De Crateri*.

102. *FGrHist* 342 F12 (Antiphon), 14 (Arthmios), 16 (Diagoras), 17 (Phrynichos). The Peace of Kallias is mentioned in F13; its publication on a stele in the fourth century is known from Isokrates' *Panegyrikos* (4.120) and Theopompos (*FGrHist* 115 F154).

103. *FGrHist* 342 F1–3 (tribute assessment), F4 (*nautodikai*). The earliest tribute assessment decree on stone dates from the 420s (*IG* I³ 71); earlier ones may have been kept only in the archives of the Boule, which oversaw tribute collection: see Chapter 3, Section II. The decree on the *nautodikai* (F4) is not the same as Perikles' citizenship law: see Jacoby, *FGrHist* 3b *Komm.*, pp. 101–2.

104. So Thomas, *Oral Tradition*, pp. 83–94.

105. See Plato *Laws* 951a–952d. For Plato's use of Athenian laws, see Morrow, *Plato's Cretan City*, pp. 10–12, and index, s.v. "Athenian Laws."

106. See Fornara, *Nature of Historiography*, pp. 16–23, esp. 21–22, for Hellanikos's use of documentary material and the tradition within which this is set.

107. *FGrHist* 6 F2 (= Plut. *Numa* 1). Since Plutarch is not specific in his criticism, not much can be made of it. We do not know, for instance, if he was referring to an early part of the Olympic victor list that took it back into mythical times. See Jacoby's comments (*FGrHist* 1a 1:477) on the passage.

108. *Ath. Pol.* 53.1.

109. *Ath. Pol.* 54.3.

110. *Ath. Pol.* 61.1. Other cases where Aristotle contrasts current with past practice can be found at 45.3, 49.3, 51.3, 53.4, 54.7, 55.2, 55.4, 56.3, 60.2, 61.1, 62.1, 67.4–5.

111. Ar. *Birds* 1024–25; see Chapter 3, Section II.

112. [Dem.] 47.20–42.

113. Ar. *Ekkl.* 1011–20.

114. Kahrstedt, "Untersuchungen," p. 31.

115. Thomas, *Oral Tradition*, pp. 68–83.

116. Lys. 30.3, 11. Lysias also claims that "when the magistrates were imposing fines and introducing cases into the courts, he did not wish to hand over the law." Robertson, "Laws of Athens," p. 34 n. 36, suggests that the sentence refers to Nikomachos's failure to give texts of laws to magistrates who administered justice. Magistrates may have sought texts from Nikomachos because the law code was in a state of transition at the time, but it is equally possible that magistrates had routinely retrieved copies of old or new measures related to their duties from the chief secretary, for whom Nikomachos and the other *anagrapheis* substituted while the laws were being revised.

Conclusion

1. *IG* II² 971, lines 23–24. For text and discussion, see Chapter 5, Section I.

2. *IG* II² 1132. For text and discussion, see Chapter 5, Section I.

3. *IG* II² 840, lines 25–28; 847, lines 27–30; 956, lines 20–22; 1013. For texts and discussion, see Chapter 5, Section II.

4. Diog. L. 10.16. For text and discussion, see Chapter 5, Section IV.

5. Thompson and Wycherley, *Agora*, 14:36–38; Camp, *Athenian Agora*, p. 179.

6. *IG* II² 971, 1132; see Chapter 5, Section I.

7. Ath. 5.214d–e (Wycherley, no. 469). The text is given at *FGrHist* 87 F36, and as F253 in Edelstein and Kidd, *Posidonius*. For discussion and further bibliography, see Kidd, *Posidonius*, 2:863–87, esp. 882–83.

8. For Sulla's sack, see Plut. *Sulla* 14; Paus. 1.20.3. On damage to the Agora, see Thompson and Wycherley, *Agora*, 14:23 and index, s.v. "Sulla." Pausanias (10.21.6) reports the theft of objects from the Stoa of Zeus Eleutherios.

9. *IG* II² 1990, line 9; Diog. L. 2.40; for texts and discussion, see Chapter 5, Section IV.

10. On the Herulian destruction, see Thompson and Wycherley, *Agora*, 14:208–10. Julian (*Or.* 5.159a) describes the Metroon as the place where "the records of the Athenians used to be kept."

11. *IG* II² 105.

12. Thuc. 7.8.2; cf. the variety of letters in Dem. 23.113–83; Aeschin. 2.90.

13. Lys. 16.6–7; Lyk. 1.67.

14. Hignett, *HAC*, pp. 12–27, esp. 14–17.

15. Thomas, *Oral Tradition*, pp. 38–83.

16. *IG* II² 2318–25; see Chapter 2, Section II.

17. *IG* I³ 61.

18. Andok. 2.23.

19. Lys. 13.23, 28; Dem. 19.154; Aeschin. 2.92.

20. Aeschin. 2.89.

Aleshire, S. *The Athenian Asklepieion.* Amsterdam, 1989.

Alessandrì, S. "Alcune osservazioni sui segretari ateniesi nel IV sec. A.C." *ASNP* 12 (1982): 7–70.

Andrewes, A. "The Survival of Solon's Axones." In ΦΟΡΟΣ: *Tribute to B. D. Meritt*, edited by D. W. Bradeen and M. F. McGregor, pp. 21–28. Locust Valley, N.Y., 1974.

——. "Androtion and the Four Hundred." *PCPhS*, 2nd ser., 22 (1976): 14–25.

——. "Kleisthenes' Reform Bill." *CQ*, n.s., 27 (1977): 241–48.

——. "The Growth of the Athenian State." *CAH²* 3.3 (1982): 360–91.

——. "The Tyranny of Peisistratos." *CAH²* 3.3 (1982): 392–416.

Badian, E. "The King's Peace." In *Georgica: Greek Studies in Honour of George Cawkwell*, edited by M. A. Flower and M. Toher, pp. 25–48. University of London, Institute of Classical Studies, bulletin suppl. 58. London, 1991.

Beck, F. A. G. *Album of Greek Education.* Sydney, 1975.

Beloch, K. J. *Griechische Geschichte.* 2nd ed. 4 vols. in 8. Strasbourg and Berlin, 1912–27.

Bloch, H. "Studies in Historical Literature of the Fourth Century B.C." *HSCP* suppl. 1 (1940): 303–76.

Boegehold, A. L. "The Establishment of a Central Archive at Athens." *AJA* 76 (1971): 21–30.

——. "Andokides and the Decree of Patrokleides." *Historia* 39 (1990): 149–62.

——. *The Athenian Agora.* Vol. 28, *The Lawcourts at Athens.* Princeton, 1995.

Boersma, J. S. *Athenian Building Policy from 561/0 to 405/4 B.C.* Groningen, 1970.

Bonner, R. J. *Evidence in Athenian Courts.* Chicago, 1905.

Bradeen, D. W. "The Fifth-Century Archon List." *Hesperia* 32 (1963): 187–208.

Bradsher, J. G. "An Introduction to Archives." In *Managing Archives and Archival Institutions*, edited by J. G. Bradsher, pp. 1–17. Chicago, 1988.

Braun, K. "Der Dipylon-Brunnen B1: Die Funde." *AM* 85 (1970): 197–269.

Brillant, M. *Les secrétaires athéniens.* Paris, 1911.

Bugh, G. *The Horsemen of Athens.* Princeton, 1988.

Burkert, W. *Greek Religion.* Translated by J. Raffan. Cambridge, Mass., 1985.

Bursy, B. *De Aristotelis* Πολιτείας 'Αθηναίων *partis alterius fonte et auctoritate.* Dorpat, 1897.

Busolt, G. *Griechische Geschichte.* 2nd ed. 3 vols. in 4. Gotha, 1893–1904.

Cadoux, T. J. "The Athenian Archons from Kreon to Hypsichides." *JHS* 68 (1948): 70–123.

Calhoun, G. M. "Oral and Written Pleadings in Athenian Courts." *TAPA* 50 (1919): 177–93.

Camp, J. M. *The Athenian Agora.* London, 1986.

Capps, E. *The Introduction of Comedy into the City Dionysia.* Chicago, 1903.

———. "Greek Inscriptions: A New Fragment of the List of Victors at the City Dionysia." *Hesperia* 12 (1943): 1–11.

Carawan, E. "Tyranny and Outlawry: *Athenaion Politeia* 16.10." In *Nomodeiktes: Greek Studies in Honor of Martin Ostwald,* edited by R. M. Rosen and J. Farrel, pp. 305–20. Ann Arbor, 1993.

Cargill, J. *The Second Athenian League.* Berkeley, 1981.

Chambers, M. *Aristoteles. Der Staat der Athener.* Berlin, 1990.

Chambers, M., R. Gallucci, and M. Spanos. "Athens' Alliance with Egesta in the Year of Antiphon." *ZPE* 83 (1990): 38–60.

Christ, M. "Liturgy Avoidance and Antidosis in Classical Athens." *TAPA* 120 (1990): 147–69.

Clay, D. "Epicurus in the Archives of Athens." *Hesperia* suppl. 19 (1982): 17–26.

Clinton, K. "A Law in the City Eleusinion concerning the Mysteries." *Hesperia* 49 (1980): 258–88.

———. "The Nature of the Late Fifth-Century Revision of the Athenian Law Code." *Hesperia* suppl. 19 (1982): 27–37.

Connor, W. R. *Theopompos and Fifth Century Athenian Politics.* Washington, D.C., 1968.

———. *Thucydides.* Princeton, 1984.

———. "Tribes, Festivals and Processions: Civic, Ceremonial and Political Manipulation in Archaic Greece." *JHS* 107 (1987): 40–50.

———. " 'Sacred' and 'Secular': Ἱερα καὶ ὅσια and the Classical Athenian Concept of the State." *Ancient Society* 19 (1988): 161–88.

———. "City Dionysia and Athenian Democracy." In *Aspects of Athenian Democracy,* pp. 7–32. *Classica et Mediaevalia.* Dissertationes 11. Copenhagen, 1990.

Csapo, I., and W. J. Slater. *The Context of Ancient Drama.* Ann Arbor, 1995.

Curtius, C. *Das Metroon in Athen als Staatsarchiv.* Berlin, 1868.

Davies, J. K. "Demosthenes on Liturgies: A Note." *JHS* 87 (1967): 33–40.

———. "Religion and the State." *CAH*² 4 (1988): 368–88.

Davison, J. A. "Notes on the Panathenaea." *JHS* 78 (1958): 23–42.

Day, J., and M. Chambers. *Aristotle's History of Athenian Democracy.* Berkeley, 1962.

Detienne, M. "L'espace de la publicité, ses opérateurs intellectuels dans la cité." In *Les savoirs de l'écriture. En Grèce ancienne,* edited by M. Detienne, pp. 29–81. 2nd ed. Lille, 1992.

Develin, R. "Age Qualifications for Athenian Magistrates." *ZPE* 61 (1985): 149–59.

Dinsmoor, W. B. *The Archons of Athens in the Hellenistic Age.* Cambridge, Mass., 1931.

Dodds, E. R. "Maenadism in the *Bacchae*." *HThR* 33 (1940): 155–76.

Dow, S. "The Law Codes of Athens." *Proceedings of the Massachusetts Historical Society* 71 (1953–57): 3–36.

———. "The Athenian Calendar of Sacrifices: The Chronology of Nikomakhos' Second Term." *Historia* 9 (1960): 270–93.

———. "The Walls Inscribed with Nikomakhos' Law Code." *Hesperia* 30 (1961): 58–73.

———. "The Athenian Anagrapheis." *HSCP* 67 (1963): 37–54.

Dunbar, N. *Aristophanes: Birds.* Oxford, 1995.

Dziatzko, K. "Archive." *RE* 2.1 (1896): 553–64.

Edelstein, L., and I. G. Kidd, eds. *Posidonius.* Vol. 1, *The Fragments.* Cambridge, 1972.

Ferguson, W. S. *The Athenian Secretaries*. Cornell Studies in Classical Philology no. 7. New York, 1898.

——. *Hellenistic Athens*. London, 1911.

——. "The Laws of Demetrius of Phalerum and Their Guardians." *Klio* 11 (1911): 265–76.

——. "The Introduction of the Secretary-Cycle." *Klio* 14 (1914–15): 393–97.

——. *The Treasurers of Athena*. Cambridge, Mass., 1932.

Fiehn, [K.]. "Stratokles." *RE* 5A.1 (1931): 269–71.

Figueira, T. "The Strange Death of Draco on Aegina." In *Nomodeiktes: Greek Studies in Honor of M. Ostwald*, edited by R. M. Rosen and J. Farrel, pp. 287–304. Ann Arbor, 1993.

Fingarette, A. "A New Look at the Wall of Nikomakhos." *Hesperia* 40 (1971): 330–35.

Finley, M. *Studies in Land and Credit in Ancient Athens, 500–200 B.C.: The Horos Inscriptions*. New Brunswick, N.J., 1952.

——. *Ancient History: Evidence and Models*. London, 1985.

Fornara, C. W. "The Date of the Callias Decrees." *GRBS* 11 (1970): 185–96.

——. "The *Diapsephismos* of *Ath. Pol.* 13.5." *CP* 65 (1970): 243–36.

——. "The Date of the 'Regulations for Miletus.'" *AJP* 92 (1971): 473–75.

——. *The Nature of Historiography in Ancient Greece and Rome*. Berkeley, 1983.

Fornara, C. W., and L. J. Samons. *Athens from Cleisthenes to Pericles*. Berkeley, 1991.

Francis, E. D. *Image and Idea in Fifth-Century Greece*. London, 1990.

Fraser, P. M. *Ptolemaic Alexandria*. 3 vols. Oxford, 1972.

Frost, F. J. "Pericles and Dracontides." *JHS* 84 (1964): 69–72.

——. "Attic Literacy and the Solonian *Seisachtheia*." *Ancient World* 15 (1987): 51–58.

Gabrielsen, V. *Financing the Athenian Fleet*. Baltimore, 1994.

Gagarin, M. *Drakon and Early Athenian Homicide Law*. New Haven, 1981.

——. "The Thesmothetai and the Earliest Athenian Tyranny Law." *TAPA* 111 (1981): 71–77.

——. *Early Greek Law*. Berkeley, 1986.

——. *The Murder of Herodes. A Study of Antiphon 5*. Frankfurt, 1989.

Garland, R. *Introducing New Gods: The Politics of Athenian Religion*. Ithaca, N.Y., 1992.

Garvie, A. F. *Aeschylus' Supplices: Play and Trilogy*. Cambridge, 1967.

Georgoudi, S. "Manières d'archivage et archives de cités." In *Les savoirs de l'écriture. En Grèce ancienne*, edited by M. Detienne, pp. 221–47. 2nd ed. Lille, 1992.

Golden, M. "Demosthenes and the Age of Majority at Athens." *Phoenix* 33 (1979): 25–38.

Goody, J. *The Domestication of the Savage Mind*. Cambridge, 1977.

Griffith, G. T. *A History of Macedonia*. Vol. 2. Oxford, 1979.

Gwatkin, W. E. "The Legal Arguments in Aeschines' *Against Ctesiphon* and Demosthenes' *On the Crown*." *Hesperia* 26 (1957): 129–41.

Habicht, C. "Zur Geschichte Athens in der Zeit Mithridates' VI." *Chiron* 6 (1976): 127–42 (= *Athen in Hellenistischer Zeit*, pp. 216–30. Munich, 1994).

——. "Athenischer Ehrendekret vom Jahre des Koroibos (306/05) für einen königlichen Offizier." *AJAH* 2 (1977): 37–39 (= *Athen in Hellenistischer Zeit*, pp. 337–39. Munich, 1994).

Hamilton, C. D. *Sparta's Bitter Victories: Politics and Diplomacy in the Corinthian War*. Ithaca, N.Y., 1979.

Hammond, N. G. L. "The Chronological Basis of Solon's Reforms." In *Studies in Greek History*, pp. 145–69. Oxford, 1973.

Hansen, M. H. *The Sovereignty of the People's Court in Athens in the Fourth Century BC and the Public Action against Unconstitutional Proposals*. Odense, 1974.

——. *Eisangelia: The Sovereignty of the People's Court in Athens in the Fourth Century BC and the Impeachment of Generals and Politicians*. Odense, 1975.

——. "*Nomos* and *Psephisma* in Fourth-Century Athens." *GRBS* 19 (1979): 315–30.

——. "Seven Hundred *archai* in Classical Athens." *GRBS* 21 (1980): 151–73.

——. "The Athenian Heliaia from Solon to Aristotle." *ClMed* 40 (1981–82): 9–47.

——. *The Athenian Ecclesia: A Collection of Articles, 1976–83*. Copenhagen, 1983.

——. "The Number of *Rhetores* in the Athenian *Ecclesia*." *GRBS* 25 (1984): 123–55.

——. "Athenian *Nomothesia*." *GRBS* 26 (1985): 345–71.

——. *The Athenian Assembly in the Age of Demosthenes*. Oxford, 1987.

——. "Diokles' Law (Dem. 24.42) and the Revision of the Athenian Corpus of Law in the Archonship of Eukleides." *C&M* 41 (1990): 63–71.

——. "Solonian Democracy in Fourth-Century Athens." In *Aspects of Athenian Democracy*, pp. 71–99. *Classica et Mediaevalia*. Dissertationes 11. Copenhagen, 1990.

——. *The Athenian Democracy in the Age of Demosthenes*. Oxford, 1991.

——. "Was the Athenian Ekklesia Convened according to the Festival Calendar or Bouleutic Calendar?" *AJP* 114 (1993): 99–113.

Harding, P. *Androtion and the Atthis*. Oxford, 1994.

Harris, D. *The Treasures of the Parthenon and Erechtheion*. Oxford, 1995.

Harris, E. "The Constitution of the Five Thousand." *HSCP* 93 (1990): 243–88.

——. "When Did the Athenian Assembly Meet?" *AJP* 112 (1991): 325–41.

——. *Aeschines and Athenian Politics*. Oxford, 1995.

Harris, W. V. *Ancient Literacy*. Cambridge, Mass., 1989.

Harrison, A. R. W. "Law-Making at Athens at the End of the Fifth Century B.C." *JHS* 75 (1955): 26–38.

Hedrick, C. "Writing, Reading, and Democracy." In *Ritual, Finance, Politics: Athenian Democratic Accounts Presented to David Lewis*, edited by R. Osborne and S. Hornblower, pp. 157–74. Oxford, 1994.

Helly, B. *Gonnoi*. Vol. 2, *Les Inscriptions*. Amsterdam, 1973.

Henderson, J., ed. *Aristophanes: Lysistrata*. Oxford, 1987.

Henry, A. S. *The Prescripts of Athenian Decrees*. Mnemosyne suppl. 49. Leiden, 1977.

——. "Archon-Dating in Fifth Century Attic Decrees: The 421 Rule." *Chiron* 9 (1979): 23–30.

Hirzel, R. *Themis, Dike und Verwandtes*. Leipzig, 1907.

Hölkeskamp, K.-J. "Arbitrators, Lawgivers and the 'Codification of Law' in Archaic Greece." *Metis* 7 (1992): 49–81.

——. "Written Law in Archaic Greece." *PCPhS* (1992): 87–117.

Hornblower, S. *Thucydides*. London, 1987.

——. *A Commentary on Thucydides*. Vol. 2. Oxford, 1996.

Humphreys, S. "The Evolution of Legal Process in Ancient Athens." In *Tria Corda. Scritti in onore de Arnaldo Momigliano*, edited by E. Gabba, pp. 229–51. Como, 1983.

——. "A Historical Approach to Drakon's Law on Homicide." In *Symposion 1990. Vorträge zur griechischen und hellenistischen Rechtsgeschichte*, edited by M. Gagarin, pp. 17–45. Vienna, 1991.

Immerwahr, H. "Book Rolls on Attic Vases." In *Classical, Medieval, and Renaissance Studies in Honor of Berthold Louis Ullman*, edited by C. Henderson Jr., 1:17–48. Rome, 1964.

———. *Attic Script*. Oxford, 1990.

Jacob, O. *Les esclaves publics à Athènes*. Paris, 1928.

Jacoby, F. "Über die Entwicklung der griechischen Historiographie und den Plan einer neuen Sammlung der griechischen Historikerfragmente." *Klio* 9 (1909): 80–123 (= *Abhandlung zur griechischen Geschichtsschreibung*, edited by H. Bloch, pp. 16–64. Leiden, 1956).

———. "Patrios Nomos: State Burial in Athens and the Public Ceremony in the Kerameikos." *JHS* 64 (1944): 37–66 (= *Abhandlungen zur griechischen Geschichtsschreibung*, edited by H. Bloch, pp. 260–315. Leiden, 1956).

———. *Atthis*. Oxford, 1949.

Jaeger, W. *Aristotle. Fundamentals of the History of His Development*. 2nd ed. Translated by R. Robinson. Oxford, 1948.

Jordan, B. *The Athenian Navy in the Classical Period*. University of California Publications. Classical Studies 13. Berkeley, 1975.

———. *Servants of the Gods: A Study in the Religion, History and Literature of Fifth-Century Athens*. Hypomnemata 55. Göttingen, 1979.

Kahrstedt, U. "Untersuchungen zur athenischen Behörden. II. Die Nomotheten und die legislative in Athen." *Klio* 37 (1938): 1–32.

Kaibel, G. *Stil und Text der Politeia Athenaion des Aristoteles*. Berlin, 1893.

Kallet-Marx, L. "The Kallias Decree, Thucydides, and the Outbreak of the Peloponnesian War." *CQ*, n.s., 39 (1989): 94–113.

Keaney, J. J. "The Date of Aristotle's *Athenaion Politeia*." *Historia* 19 (1970): 323–36.

———. *The Composition of Aristotle's Athenaion Politeia: Observation and Explanation*. New York, 1992.

Keingünther, A. *Protos Euretes. Untersuchungen zur Geschichte einer Fragestellung*. *Philologos* suppl. 26 (1933).

Kennel, N. M. *The Gymnasium of Virtue*. Chapel Hill, 1995.

Kidd, I. G. *Posidonius*. Vol. 2, *The Commentary*. Cambridge, 1988.

Kirchhoff, A. *Thukydides und sein Urkundenmaterial. Ein Beitrag zur Entstehungsgeschichte seines Werkes*. Darmstadt, 1968.

Klaffenbach, G. "Bemerkungen zum griechischen Urkundenwesen." *Sitzb. Berlin* 6 (1960): 5–42.

———. *Griechische Epigraphik*. 2nd ed. Göttingen, 1966.

Körte, A. "Aristoteles' Νῖκαι Διονυσιακαί." *CP* 1 (1906): 391–98.

———. "Hegemon." *RE* 7.2 (1912): 2595–96.

Krech, P. *De Crateri ΨΗΦΙΣΜΑΤΩΝ ΣΥΝΑΓΩΓΗΙ et de locis aliquot plutarchi ex ea petitis*. Berlin, 1888.

Krentz, P. *The Thirty at Athens*. Ithaca, N.Y., 1982.

Kroll, J. H. "An Archive of the Athenian Cavalry." *Hesperia* 46 (1977): 83–140.

Lambrinudakis, W., and M. Wörrle. "Ein hellenistische Reformgesetz über das öffentliche Urkundenwesen von Paron." *Chiron* 13 (1983): 283–368.

Larfeld, W. *Handbuch der griechischen Inschriften*. Vol. 2. Leipzig, 1902.

Lateiner, D. *The Historical Method of Herodotus*. Phoenix suppl. vol. 23. Toronto, 1989.

Latte, K. "Mord." *RE* 16.1 (1933): 278–89.

——. "Φονικά." *RE* 20.1 (1941): 526.

Ledl, A. *Studien zur älteren athenischen Verfassungsgeschichte.* Heidelberg, 1914.

Lesky, A. *Greek Tragic Poetry.* Translated by M. Dillon. New Haven, 1983.

Lewis, D. M. "A Note on *IG* i² 114." *JHS* 87 (1967): 132.

——. "The Athenian Coinage Decree." In *Coinage and Administration in the Athenian and Persian Empires*, edited by I. Carradice, pp. 53–64. BAR International Series 343. Oxford, 1987.

——. "Public Property in the City." In *The Greek City: From Homer to Aristotle*, edited by O. Murray and S. Price, pp. 245–63. Oxford, 1990.

Lewis, N. *Papyrus in Classical Antiquity.* Oxford, 1974.

Linders, T. *Studies in the Treasure Records of Artemis Brauronia Found in Athens.* Stockholm, 1972.

——. *The Treasurers of the Other Gods and Their Functions.* Beiträge zur klassischen Philologie 62. Meisenheim am Glan, 1975.

Linforth, I. M. *Solon the Athenian.* Berkeley, 1919.

Loening, T. *The Reconciliation Agreement of 403/402 B.C. in Athens: Its Content and Application.* Hermes Einzelschriften 53. Stuttgart, 1987.

MacDowell, D. M. *Andokides: On the Mysteries.* Oxford, 1962.

——. *Athenian Homicide Law in the Age of the Orators.* Manchester, 1963.

——. "The Chronology of Athenian Speeches and Legal Innovations in 401–398 B.C." *RIDA* 18 (1971): 267–73.

——. "Law-Making at Athens in the Fourth Century B.C." *JHS* 95 (1975): 62–74.

——. *Demosthenes: Against Meidias.* Oxford, 1990.

Mattingly, H. B. "The Methone Decrees." *CQ*, n.s., 11 (1961): 154–65.

——. "Periclean Imperialism." In *Ancient Society and Institutions: Studies Presented to Victor Ehrenberg*, edited by E. Badian, pp. 193–223. London, 1966.

——. "Athens and Eleusis: Some New Ideas." In ΦΟΡΟΣ: *Tribute to B. D. Meritt*, edited by D. W. Bradeen and M. F. McGregor, pp. 90–103. Locust Valley, N.Y., 1974.

——. "The Athenian Coinage Decree and the Assertion of Empire." In *Coinage and Administration in the Athenian and Persian Empires*, edited by I. Carradice, pp. 65–71. BAR International Series 343. Oxford, 1987.

Meiggs, R. *The Athenian Empire.* Oxford, 1972.

Meritt, B. D. "Greek Inscriptions." *Hesperia* 5 (1936): 355–430.

——. "Greek Inscriptions." *Hesperia* 8 (1939): 48–90.

——. *Epigraphica Attica.* Cambridge, 1940.

——. "Greek Inscriptions." *Hesperia* 15 (1946): 138–264.

——. "Athenian Calendar Problems." *TAPA* 96 (1964): 200–260.

——. "Athenian Archons 347/6–48/7." *Historia* 26 (1977): 161–91.

Meyer, C. *Die Urkunden im Geschichtswerk des Thukydides.* 2nd ed. Zetemeta 10. Munich, 1970.

Meyer, Ed. *Forschungen zur alten Geschichte.* 2 vols. Halle, 1899.

Miller, M. "The Earlier Persian Dates in Herodotus." *Klio* 37 (1959): 29–52.

——. "The Accepted Date for Solon: Precise, but Wrong?" *Arethusa* 2 (1969): 62–86.

Miller, O. *De decretis atticis quaestiones epigraphicae.* Vratislava, 1885.

Miller, S. G. *The Prytaneion: Its Function and Architectural Form.* Berkeley, 1978.

Moraux, P. *Les listes anciennes des ouvrages d'Aristote.* Louvain, 1951.

Morrow, G. R. *Plato's Cretan City: A Historical Interpretation of the Laws.* Princeton, 1960.

Mosshammer, A. A. *The Chronicle of Eusebius and the Greek Chronographic Tradition*. Lewisburg, Pa., 1979.

Murray, O. *Early Greece*. 2nd ed. Cambridge, Mass., 1993.

Osborne, M. J. *Naturalization in Athens*. 4 vols. Brussels, 1981–83.

Osborne, R. *Greece in the Making, 1200–479 BC*. London, 1996.

Ostwald, M. "The Athenian Legislation against Subversion and Tyranny." *TAPA* 86 (1955): 104–28.

———. *Nomos and the Beginnings of Athenian Democracy*. Oxford, 1969.

———. "Was There a Concept of ἄγραφος νόμος in Classical Greece?" In *Exegesis and Argument: Studies in Greek Philosophy Presented to Gregory Vlastos*, edited by E. N. Lee, A. P. D. Mourelatos, and R. M. Morty, pp. 70–104. Assen, 1973.

———. *From Popular Sovereignty to the Sovereignty of Law*. Berkeley, 1986.

———. "The Reform of the Athenian State by Cleisthenes." *CAH²* 3.3 (1988): 303–46.

———. "Public Expense: Whose Obligation? Athens 600–450 B.C.E." *PAPhS* 139 (1995): 368–79.

Page, D. L. *Actors' Interpolations in Greek Tragedy*. Oxford, 1934.

———, ed. *Further Greek Epigrams*. Cambridge, 1981.

Parke, H. W. *Festivals of the Athenians*. Ithaca, N.Y., 1977.

Parker, R. *Athenian Religion: A History*. Oxford, 1996.

Patterson, C. *Pericles' Citizenship Law of 451–50 B.C.* New York, 1981.

Pélékidis, C. *Histoire de l'éphebie attique des origines à 31 avant Jésus-Christ*. Paris, 1962.

Pfeiffer, R. *History of Classical Scholarship from the Beginnings to the End of the Classical Age*. Oxford, 1968.

Pickard-Cambridge, A. *The Dramatic Festivals of Athens*. 2nd ed. Revised and edited by J. Gould and D. M. Lewis. Oxford, 1968.

Piérart, M. "Les ΕΥΘΥΝΟΙ Athéniens." *AC* 40 (1971): 526–73.

Plommer, W. H. "The Tyranny of the Archon List." *CR* (1969): 126–29.

Posner, E. *Archives in the Ancient World*. Cambridge, Mass., 1972.

Pritchett, W. K. *Dionysius of Halicarnassus: On Thucydides*. Berkeley, 1975.

———. *The Liar School of Herodotus*. Amsterdam, 1993.

———. *Greek Archives, Cults, and Topography*. Amsterdam, 1996.

Pritchett, W. K., and O. Neugabauer. *The Calendars of Athens*. Cambridge, Mass., 1947.

Quass, F. *Nomos und Psephisma. Untersuchungen zum griechischen Staatsrecht*. Zetemeta 55. Munich, 1971.

Raaflaub, K. "Athenische Geschichte und mündliche Überlieferung." In *Vergangenheit in mündlicher Überlieferung*, edited by J. von Ungern-Sternberg und H. Reinaupp, pp. 197–225. Stuttgart, 1988.

Raddatz, [G. W.]. "Hypotheseis." *RE* 9.1 (1914): 414–24.

Raubitschek, A. E. "The Heroes of Phyle." *Hesperia* 10 (1941): 284–95.

Raubitschek, A. E., with L. H. Jeffery. *Dedications from the Athenian Acropolis*. Cambridge, Mass., 1949.

Reisch, [E.]. "Didaskaliai." *RE* 5.1 (1903): 398–401.

Rhodes, P. J. *The Athenian Boule*. Oxford, 1972.

———. "The Five Thousand in the Athenian Revolutions of 411 B.C." *JHS* 92 (1972): 115–27.

———. "Solon and the Numismatists." *NC* 15 (1975): 1–11.

——. "Pisistratid Chronology Again." *Phoenix* 30 (1976): 219–33.

——. "Problems in Athenian Eisphora and Liturgies." *AJAH* 7 (1982): 1–19.

——. "*Nomothesia* in Fourth-Century Athens." *CQ*, n.s., 35 (1985): 55–60.

——. "The Athenian Code of Laws, 410–399 B.C." *JHS* 111 (1991): 87–100.

——. " 'Alles eitel Gold'? The Sixth and Fifth Centuries in Fourth Century Athens." In *Aristote et Athènes*, edited by M. Piérart, pp. 53–64. Paris, 1993.

Rihll, T. E. "EKTHMOPOI: Partners in Crime?" *JHS* 111 (1991): 101–27.

Robb, K. *Literacy and Paideia in Ancient Greece.* Oxford, 1994.

Robert, L. "Épigraphie." In *L'histoire et ses méthodes*, edited by Ch. Samaran, pp. 453–97. Paris, 1961.

Robertson, N. "Solon's *Axones* and *Kyrbeis*, and the Sixth-Century Background." *Historia* 35 (1986): 147–76.

——. "The Laws of Athens, 410–399 BC: The Evidence for Review and Publication." *JHS* 110 (1991): 43–75.

Rose, V. *Aristotelis qui ferebantur librorum fragmenta.* Stuttgart, 1966.

Ruschenbusch, E. "ΦΟΝΟΣ: Zum Recht Drakons und seiner Bedeutung für das Werden des athenischen Staates." *Historia* 9 (1960): 129–54.

——. *Untersuchungen zur Geschichte des athenischen Strafrechts.* Graezisitische Abhandlungen 4. Cologne and Graz, 1968.

——. "Drei Beiträge zur öffentlichen Diaita in Athen." In *Symposion 1982. Vorträge zur griechischen und hellenistischen Rechtsgeschichte*, edited by F. J. F. Nieto, pp. 31–40. Cologne, 1989.

Ryan, F. X. "The Original Date of the δῆμος πληθύων Provisions in *IG* I³ 105." *JHS* 114 (1994): 120–34.

Ryder, T. T. B. *Koine Eirene.* London, 1965.

Samons, L. J. "The 'Kallias Decrees' (IG i³ 52) and the Inventories of Athena's Treasure in the Parthenon." *CQ*, n.s., 46 (1996): 91–102.

Samuel, A. E. *Greek and Roman Chronology.* Handbuch der Altertumswissenschaft, no. 1.7. Munich, 1972.

Sandys, J. E. *Aristotle's Constitution of Athens.* 2nd ed. London, 1912.

Schmid, [W.]. "Favorinus." *RE* 6.2 (1909): 2078–84.

Schöll, R. "Über attische Gesetzgebung." *SB Munich* (1886): 83–139.

Schrader, H., ed. *Die archaischen Marmorbildwerke der Akropolis.* Frankfurt, 1939.

Schreiner, J. *De Corpore Iuris Atheniensium.* Bonn, 1913.

Schuller, W. "Wirkungen des Ersten Attischen Seebunds auf die Herausbildung der athenischen Demokratie." In *Studien zum Atthischen Seebund. Xenia* Konstanzer Althistorische Vorträge und Forschungen 8, edited by W. Schuller, pp. 87–101. Konstanz, 1984.

Schulthess, A. "Γραμματεῖς." *RE* 7.2 (1912): 1712–80.

Schweigert, E. "Inscriptions from the North Slope of the Acropolis." *Hesperia* 7 (1938): 281–89.

Sealey, R. "Regionalism in Archaic Athens." *Historia* 9 (1960): 155–80.

——. "Ephialtes." *CP* 59 (1964): 11–22.

——. *Essays in Greek Politics.* New York, 1967.

——. *A History of the Greek City States, 700–338 B.C.* Berkeley, 1976.

——. *The Athenian Republic.* University Park, Pa., 1987.

——. *The Justice of the Greeks.* Ann Arbor, 1994.

Shear, T. L., Jr. "Athenian Agora: Excavation of 1970." *Hesperia* 40 (1971): 241–79.

——. "Athenian Agora: Excavations of 1973–1974." *Hesperia* 44 (1975): 365–70.

——. "Tyrants and Buildings in Archaic Athens." In *Athens Comes of Age: From Solon to Salamis*, edited by W. Childs, pp. 1–15. Princeton, 1978.

——. "The Persian Destruction of Athens. Evidence from Agora Deposits." *Hesperia* 62 (1993): 383–482.

——. "Bouleuterion, Metroon and the Archives at Athens." In *Studies in the Ancient Greek Polis. Historia* Einzelschriften 95, edited by M. H. Hansen and K. Raaflaub, pp. 157–90. Stuttgart, 1995.

Sickinger, J. "Inscriptions and Archives in Classical Athens." *Historia* 43 (1994): 286–96.

Sourvinou-Inwood, C. "Something to Do with Athens: Tragedy and Ritual." In *Ritual, Finance, Politics. Athenian Democratic Accounts Presented to David Lewis*, edited by R. Osborne and S. Hornblower, pp. 269–90. Oxford, 1994.

Stahl, M. *Aristokraten und Tyrannen im archaischen Athen.* Stuttgart, 1987.

Steiner, D. *The Tyrant's Writ: Myths and Images of Writing in Ancient Greece.* Princeton, 1994.

Stroud, R. *Drakon's Law on Homicide.* University of California Publications. Classical Studies 3. Berkeley, 1968.

——. "An Athenian Law on Silver Coinage." *Hesperia* 43 (1974): 157–88.

——. "State Documents in Archaic Athens." In *Athens Comes of Age: From Solon to Salamis*, edited by W. Childs, pp. 20–42. Princeton, 1978.

——. *The Axones and Kyrbeis of Drakon and Solon.* University of California Publications. Classical Studies 19. Berkeley, 1979.

——. "Aristotle and Athenian Homicide." In *Aristote et Athènes*, edited by M. Piérart, pp. 203–21. Paris, 1993.

Sumner, G. V. "Notes on Chronological Problems in the Aristotelian ᾿Αθηναίων πολιτεία." *CR*, 2nd ser., 11 (1961): 31–54.

Szegedy-Maszak, A. "Legends of the Greek Law-Givers." *GRBS* 19 (1978): 199–209.

——. *The Nomoi of Theophrastus.* New York, 1981.

Thomas, R. *Oral Tradition and Written Record in Classical Athens.* Cambridge, 1989.

——. *Literacy and Orality in Ancient Greece.* Cambridge, 1992.

——. "Written in Stone? Equality, Orality and the Codification of Law." In *Greek Law in Its Political Setting: Justifications Not Justice*, edited by L. Foxhall and A. D. E. Lewis, pp. 9–31. Oxford, 1996.

Thompson, H. A. "Buildings along the West Side of the Agora." *Hesperia* 6 (1937): 1–226.

——. "Athens Faces Adversity." *Hesperia* 50 (1981): 343–55.

——. "The Pnyx in Models." In *Hesperia* suppl. 19 (1982): 130–47. Princeton, 1982.

——. "Building for a More Democratic Society." In Πρακτικά του XII Διεθνούς Συνέδριου Κλασικής Αρχαιολογίας, Αθήνα, 4–10 Σεπτεμβριου 1983, 4:198–204. Athens, 1988.

Todd, S. *The Shape of Athenian Law.* Oxford, 1993.

——. "Lysias against Nikomachos: The Fate of the Expert in Athenian Law." In *Greek Law in Its Political Setting: Justifications Not Justice*, edited by L. Foxhall and A. D. E. Lewis, pp. 101–31. Oxford, 1996.

Tracy, S. "The Panathenaic Festival and Games: An Epigraphic Inquiry." *Nikephoros* 4 (1991): 133–53.

Vansina, J. *Oral Tradition as History.* Madison, Wis., 1985.

Wachsmuth, C. *Die Stadt der Athens*. Berlin, 1888.

Wade-Gery, H. T. "Studies in Attic Inscriptions of the Fifth Century B.C., B. Charter of the Democracy, 410 B.C. = IG i² 114." *ABSA* 33 (1932–33): 113–52.

———. *Essays in Greek History*. Oxford, 1958.

Walbank, M. *Athenian Proxenies of the Fifth Century B.C.* Toronto, 1978.

Wallace, R. "The Date of Solon's Reforms." *AJAH* 8 (1983): 81–95.

———. *The Areopagos Council*. Baltimore, 1989.

———. "Aristotelian Politeiai and *Athenaion Politeia* 4." In *Nomodeiktes: Greek Studies in Honor of Martin Ostwald*, edited by R. M. Rosen and J. Farrel, pp. 269–86. Ann Arbor, 1993.

Walters, K. R. "The 'Ancestral Constitution' and Fourth-Century Historiography in Athens." *AJAH* 1 (1976): 129–44.

Wankel, H. *Demosthenes: Rede für Ktesiphon über den Kranz*. 2 vols. Heidelberg, 1976.

Wehrli, F. "Chamaileon." *RE* suppl. 11 (1968): 368–72.

Weil, R. *Aristote et l'histoire*. Paris, 1960.

West, M. L. "The Early Chronology of Attic Tragedy." *CQ*, n.s., 39 (1989): 251–54.

West, W. C. "Public Archives in Fourth Century Athens." *GRBS* 30 (1989): 529–43.

Whitehead, D. *The Demes of Attica*. Princeton, 1986.

Wilamowitz-Moellendorf, U. von. "Die Galliamboi des Kallimachos und Catullus." *Hermes* 14 (1878): 194–201.

———. *Aus Kydathen. Philologische Untersuchungen* 1. Berlin, 1880.

———. *Aristoteles und Athen*. 2 vols. Berlin, 1893.

———, ed. *Aristophanes: Lysistrate*. Berlin, 1927.

Wilhelm, A. *Urkunden dramatischer Aufführungen in Athen*. Vienna, 1906.

———. *Beiträge zur griechischen Inschriftenkunde*. Vienna, 1909.

Wolff, H. J. "The Origin of Judicial Litigation among the Greeks." *Traditio* 4 (1946): 31–87.

———. *"Normenkontrolle" und Gesitzsbegriff in der attischen Demokratie*. Heidelberg, 1970.

Woodhead, A. G. *The Study of Greek Inscriptions*. 2nd ed. Cambridge, 1981.

Woodward, A. M. "Treasure-Records from the Athenian Agora." *Hesperia* 25 (1956): 79–121.

Worthington, I. "The Chronology of the Harpalos Affair." *SO* 62 (1986): 63–76.

Wyse, W. *The Speeches of Isaeus*. Cambridge, 1904.

Accounts. *See* Financial documents; Inventories

Acropolis: as location of Solon's laws, 29–30; records kept on, 111

Aeschines: on Drakon, 16; sees written proposal of Demosthenes, 75; cites documents from *dēmosia grammata*, 109, 115, 120–22, 137, 154–55, 162; declines appointment to embassy, 118; cites documents on embassy to Philip, 120, 137, 186; cites law on magisterial accountability, 126, 142; cites letters, 136; on *antigrapheus*, 143; serves as undersecretary, 145–46, 163, 245 (n. 37); on decree for Phyle heroes, 149, 235 (n. 14); provides dates for documents, 154–55; cites older documents, 159, 195; use of documents in forensic speeches by, 162–63, 165, 166, 168–70; cites fifth-century documents, 172, 173–74

Aeschylus: date of first victory, 43; plays dated, 44, 45. *See also* Tragedies

Age qualifications, 50–51, 212 (nn. 65, 66)

Agorakritos, 108, 232 (n. 71)

Akarnanians: citizenship decree for, 175

Alkibiades: inscribed curses against destroyed, 79; proposes decree, 89; and Metroon, 131–32; emends inscription, 174

Ambassadors: deliver reports to Metroon, 120–21; names kept in Metroon: 121–22; receive written instructions, 186. See also *Spondophoroi*

Anagrapheis: republish homicide law of Drakon, 16–23, 84, 103, 105; and fifth-century revision of law code, 62, 97–

105, 113. *See also* Law Code, Athenian; Nikomachos

Anagrapheus, 143–44

Anaximenes, 30

Andokides: cites fifth-century law as Solonian, 24–25; and decree of Patrokleides, 76, 108–11, 115; and decree of Menippos, 77, 82, 106, 109, 137, 195; and revision of law code, 97, 99–104; use of documents in forensic speeches by, 161, 164–65; cites treaty ending Peloponnesian War, 173–74, 175. *See also* Law Code, Athenian; Teisamenos, decree of

Androtion: use of documents by, 179, 180–82, 254 (n. 91)

Antigrapheus, 143, 244 (n. 26)

Antiphon: use of documents by, 163–64; decree against, 183

Apellikon, 189

Arbitration proceedings: citation of documents at, 167–68

Archives: defined, 5–6, 198 (n. 5); more detailed than inscriptions, 87–91, 153–56, 194. *See also* Boule, archives of; Documents; Inscriptions; Magistrates: archives of; Metroon

Archon (eponymous), 14; keeps records, 43, 45–47, 57, 59–60, 95, 96, 134–35; presides over Ekklesia, 52. *See also* Archon dating

Archon dating: in didascalic records, 42–43, 45, 47; in decree prescripts, 49, 84–85, 87, 89–91, 152, 224 (n. 111); in early fifth and sixth centuries, 49–51, 53, 60, 87, 209 (n. 30); in Atthidographers, 179. *See also* Decrees: prescripts and dating of

Archon list: published on stone, 47–48, 59; antiquity and authenticity of, 48–49, 51, 61, 211 (nn. 48, 49); *anarchiai* in, 49, 211 (n. 52); used by Atthidographers, 179, 184; and Fasti, 212 (n. 59)

Archons: swear to uphold laws, 30, 31

Archonship: becomes annual, 10, 48

Archontic calendar: used to date documents, 86–90, 153–57, 233 (n. 92)

Areopagos Council: not mentioned in Drakon's laws, 16, 22–23, 202 (n. 53); oversees homicide cases in classical period, 20; and Solon's reforms, 32; in decree of Teisamenos, 99; and Harpalos affair, 118

Arginusai generals: trial of, 170

Aristophanes of Byzantion: source of hypotheses, 45

Aristophanes: refers to documents, 75, 79–80, 174, 186; on Kybele, 108

Aristotle: on thesmothetai, 10–14; and archaic law on tyranny, 12–13, 199 (n. 16); as author of work on Solon's *axones*, 28, 203 (n. 66); and *kyrbeis*, 30; mentions Solonian laws "not in use," 33–34; *Nikai Dionysiakai*, 42; as source of Fasti, 42–43; *Didaskaliai*, 45, 208 (n. 29); and archon list, 48–49; on *pōlētai*, 69, 127–29, 145, 148; cites fifth-century laws, 77; and cavalry records, 82, 135–36; and ephebic lists, 130–31; on secretary *kata prytaneian*, 140–42; on secretary *epi tous nomous*, 142–43; gives dates for Four Hundred, 156–57; researches documents, 182, 183, 184–85, 186; library of, 189. See also *Athēnaiōn Politeia*

Arthmios of Zeleia, 172, 183

Arybbas of Molossos: citizenship decree for, 171

Asklepieion: records in Metroon, 122

Athēnaiōn Politeia: relies on Athenian laws, 150, 182; compares current and obsolete practices, 151, 185. *See also* Aristotle

Athenaios: mentions Metroon, 131, 189

Athena Promachos statue: accounts of, 70–71

Athenian Empire: and record keeping, 61, 64, 72, 75, 92, 95, 192

Athenion, 189

Athlothetai, 38, 206–7 (n. 7)

Atthidographers: use of documents, 179–82, 194

Attic Stelae: dates in, 88

Axones: appearance of, 17, 26–27; numbered, 17–18, 27–29, 34, 204 (n. 70); size of text on, 17–18, 28–29, 201 (n. 37); of Drakon, 17–18, 95; ascribed only to Drakon and Solon, 18, 22, 201 (n. 39); contain secular measures, 26, 203 (n. 62); of Solon, 26–30, 33–34, 95; survive into Hellenistic period, 27, 204 (n. 68); location of, 29–31, 205 (nn. 80, 87). *See also* Drakon—homicide law of; *Kyrbeis*; Solon—laws of

Basileis (kings), 24

Basileus (king archon), 14; has copy of Drakon's homicide law, 16–17, 226 (n. 7)

Boule, archives of: and Kleisthenic reforms, 58–59, 95, 191; in fifth century, 73–83, 95–97, 127, 129, 175, 191–92; housed in Metroon, 114, 120–22, 128–29, 176; include judicial records, 133

Bouleuterion: as possible site of Solon's laws, 29–30; documents in, 77, 81–83; 105–6, 109, 128, 130, 161, 164; physical remains of, 82–83, 111, 223 (n. 104); converted into archives building, 106, 113, 148–49, 192; proximity to Metroon, 106–8, 176

Bouleutic calendar, 86–91, 127, 153–57, 158, 233 (n. 92)

Bouleutic Oath (*IG* I³ 105), 57–59, 80, 113, 137, 191, 214 (nn. 92–94), 215 (n. 97)

Boxes: for storing documents, 148, 245–46 (n. 46)

Brea Decree (*IG* I³ 46), 85–86, 175

Bronze: laws and decrees inscribed on, 18; *kyrbeis* made from, 26–27, 31; sixth-century plaque, 40, 41; durability of, 41; not attested for didascalic

records, 42; stelai of, 57, 172, 183, 203
(n. 62); ephebic lists on, 130–31

Cavalry records, 82; sixth-century, 56;
not in Metroon, 135–36
Chairemonides, law of, 19, 149, 151
Chalkotheke Decree, 125–26, 141, 142,
144, 145
Chamaileon of Herakleia, 131–32
Choirilos, 44, 209–10 (n. 38)
Chorēgoi: names of preserved, 42–43,
45–47, 209 (n. 30). *See also* Didascalic
records; Fasti
City Dionysia: foundation of, 44. *See
also* Didascalic records: from Di-
onysia
Coinage decree: mentions Bouleutic
Oath, 58–59, 80; published overseas,
221 (n. 83)
Comedy: introduced to City Dionysia,
43
Cosecretaries, 146, 217 (n. 14)

Damasias, 48–49, 211 (n. 53)
Decrees (*psēphismata*): relation to laws
(*nomoi*), 52–53, 96, 101, 116; not automatically inscribed on stone, 73–74,
75–77, 91–92, 119, 191, 219 (nn. 49, 52);
fifth-century preservation of, 74–78;
submitted in writing, 75; republication of, 77–78; prescripts and dating
of, 84–91, 142, 152–57, 158, 225–26
(n. 136); housed in Metroon, 118–22.
See also Documents
Deinarchos: mentions Metroon as archive, 116, 117, 118; cites oracles, 136
Delian League. *See* Athenian Empire
Demetrios of Phaleron, 134, 204 (n. 74);
consults documents, 182–83
Demophantos, 161
Dēmosia grammata: refers to "archival
records," 109, 115, 116, 120–22, 137,
162. *See also* Aeschines: cites documents from *dēmosia grammata*
Demosion: refers to "state archive," 108–
12, 115, 162, 222 (n. 93)
Demosthenes: and Aeschines, 1, 145–46,
195; cites homicide laws, 19, 169; at-

tributes later law to Solon, 25; cites
law on Dionysia, 46; submits written
proposal, 75; documents in forensic
speeches of, 109, 162–63, 168–70;
cites public records, 115; mentions
public slave in Metroon, 115, 119, 144,
158; mentions Metroon, 116, 117, 118,
119, 126; elected controller of Theoric
Fund, 121; cites oracles, 136; on
nomothesia, 149–50, 151, 159; gives
dates of documents, 156; speech
Against Euergos and Mnesiboulos, 161,
186; cites historical documents, 172,
173–74
Demosthenes of Lamptreus: cites older
decrees, 172
Diagoras, 183
Diapsēphisis (of 346/5): mentioned by
Androtion, 180–81
Diapsēphismos, 54, 213 (n. 81)
Didascalic records: from City Dionysia,
43–47, 57, 61, 66, 70, 72, 90, 182, 190,
210 (nn. 41, 42); from Lenaia, 70, 182,
218 (n. 42). *See also* Fasti
Dikastēria. *See* Lawcourts
Diodorus Siculus, 35, 177
Diogenes Laertius: on indictment of Socrates, 132; on will of Epikouros, 133
Diogenes the Cynic, 245–46 (n. 46)
Diokles, law of, 101–2, 105, 117, 150, 187,
229 (n. 37)
Dionysios of Halikarnassos, 178–79
Documents: as symbols, 3, 30–31, 65;
erasure of, 41–42, 68–71, 76, 79, 127–
28, 129, 194–95, 202 (n. 50); long-term
preservation of, 41–43, 70–72, 136–37,
190–91, 194–95; forged, 43; consultation of, 45–47; limited publication on
stone, 47, 63, 66–68. *See also* Archives; Decrees; Didascalic records;
Financial documents; Inscriptions;
Laws; Metroon
Drakon: laws of, 1, 8, 9, 10, 33, 39, 42, 95,
98, 137, 138, 178, 190, 191, 195; traditions about, 9, 15–16; date of legislation of, 10, 15; as first lawgiver, 11–12,
14–16; constitution of, 12, 16; not a
snake, 15; and earlier laws, 23–24

—homicide law of: republished by *anagrapheis*, 16–17, 84, 103, 105, 164; calls itself *thesmos*, 17; written on *axones*, 17–18; length and scope of, 17–18, 23, 34; authenticity of, 17–23; innovations in, 23–24; consulted, 161, 164. See also *Axones*

Drakontides, decree of, 127, 238 (n.70)

Ekklesia: sixth-century records of, 51–55, 56–60, 190–91; fifth-century records of, 73, 74–76, 192; minutes of meetings, 79, 122, 129, 153; records kept in Metroon, 114, 116–22; judicial records of, 135; decrees cited at meetings of, 171–76, 181, 185–86. See also Decrees; Laws

Elections: sixth-century records of, 52; records kept in Metroon, 121–22, 158

Eleusinian Mysteries: sacred laws concerning, 8, 53–54; Boule supervises, 81, 192; accounts deposited in Metroon, 123–4, 126. See also Chairemonides, law of

Envoys. See Ambassadors; *Spondophoroi*

Ephebic lists: kept in Metroon, 129–31, 135, 189

Ephebic oath: cited by Aeschines, 172

Ephetai: in Drakon's law, 20, 22; age qualifications, 212 (n.66)

Ephialtes: moves *axones* and *kyrbeis*, 30; and *euthynai*, 38; and record keeping, 59–60, 61, 64, 92, 96, 97, 192; reforms of, 94; Thirty destroy laws of, 99

Epikouros: will of, in Metroon, 133–34, 188

Epistylia, 148, 246 (n.50)

Eratosthenes: on *axones*, 27, 209–10 (n.38)

Erechtheion, accounts of building, 68, 125, 148

Euripides, 108. See also Tragedies

Euryptolemos, proposal of, 170

Euthynai, 38, 126–27, 205 (n.90), 207 (n.12), 217 (n.19); deposited in Metroon, 123–24, 125, 126–27

Fasti (*IG* II² 2318), 42–47, 59, 208 (n.26).

See also City Dionysia; Didascalic records

Favorinus: sees indictment of Socrates in Metroon, 132, 189, 190

Festival calendar. See Archontic calendar

Financial documents, 38–40, 66–72, 86–87, 90–91; deposited in Metroon, 68, 122–27, 188, 192. See also *Euythnai*

Four Hundred, 94–95, 111

Generals: lists of, 85, 180; records kept by, 91, 130

Graphai paranomōn: documents cited in, 1, 169–70; origin of, 227 (n.15)

Harpokration: uses variant text of *Athēnaiōn Politeia*, 130–31, 239–40 (n.88); cites Metroon as archive, 116; on *dosis*, 133; on *diapsēphisis* of 346/5, 180

Hekataios, 212 (n.71); and Herodotus, 177

Hekatompedon Decrees: require record keeping, 40–41, 43; archon dating in, 60

Hellanikos of Lesbos: and Thucydides, 177; *Atthis*, 179; *Priestesses of Hera*, 184

Hellenotamiai: employ secretaries, 66; records of, 66–67, 81; in Kallias Decrees, 69

Herakleides of Klazomenai: honorary decree for, 173

Herakleides of Salamis: honorary decree for, 172

Herodotus: on Solon, 35; and archon list, 48; and Greek historiography, 176, 177; attributes law on idleness to Solon, 200 (n.28)

Hieroitas: honorary decree for, 172–73

Hieromnēmones, 37, 207 (n.9)

Hieropoioi: employ secretaries, 37–39

Hipparchos, 180

Hippias (son of Peisisteratos), 12, 53–54

Hippias of Elis, 177, 184

Historiography, Greek, 176–77, 211 (n.49); and documents, 177–85

Hypodikos of Chalkis, 44

Inscriptions: as incomplete guide to Athenian record keeping, 4–5, 47, 59, 66–67, 73–74, 91–92, 157; differentiated from archival texts, 4–5, 64–72, 148–49; as less detailed than archival texts, 5, 44–45, 67–68, 87–90, 154–57; as symbols, 31, 65, 174–75; destruction of, 64, 73, 79, 142, 221 (n.78), 243–44 (n.14); consultation of, 64–65, 161–87 passim. *See also* Decrees; Documents; Laws; Thirty Tyrants: destroy documents

Inventories: 40–41, 64, 67, 68; deposited in Metroon, 122–23, 125–27, 142. *See also* Financial documents; Parthenon inventories

Isaios: and *dosis*, 133–34; use of documents by, 166

Isokrates: use of documents by, 166–67; on consultation of laws, 252–53 (n.69)

Judicial records, 11, 66; of thesmothetai, 10–14; in Metroon, 131–33; publication of, 240 (n.97)

Julian, 190

Kallias, Peace of, 183

Kallias Decrees: documents in, 69–70, 238–39 (n.71)

Kallixenos, 170

Kannonos, decree of, 170, 219 (n.52)

Kerkyra: accounts of expedition to, 87

Kleidemos, 179, 182

Kleisophos, decree of: mentions *to dēmosion*, 108–9, 110, 115. *See also* Trierarchic lists

Kleisthenes: and City Dionysia, 44, 209 (n.35); reforms of, 54–55, 62; establishes Boule and archives, 55, 74, 92, 95, 191; and *lēxiarchika grammateia*, 55–56; laws of, 56–59, 94; and naukraries, 179; and *kolakretai*, 180

Kleitophon: amends decree of Pythodoros, 56–57, 94, 214 (nn.90, 91)

Kleonymos, decree of, 81

Koina grammateia, 214 (n.87)

Krateros: collection of decrees, 92, 183–84, 240 (n.100)

Kratinos: on *kyrbeis*, 27; on Kybele, 108

Kreon: as first archon, 48

Kybele, 108, 112

Kylon, 15, 23

Kyrbeis, 95, 102, 166; relation to *axones*, 26–27; location of, 29–30; preserve sacred measures, 31, 203 (n.62)

Law code, Athenian: revision of, 62, 93–105, 113, 116, 117, 140, 195; published on stone, 103–4, 192; archivally preserved, 104–5, 192. See also *Anagrapheis*; Diokles, law of; Stoa Basileios

Law codes, 9, 34, 199 (n.4)

Lawcourts: documents cited in, 160–70, 184, 185, 194, 251 (n.36); litigants gather documents for use in, 161

Laws (*nomoi*): and *thesmia*, 12; revised by amendment, 18–19, 151; housed in Metroon, 50, 116–18, 122, 135, 137; relation to decrees, 52–53, 96, 101, 116; in fifth century, 73–74, 95–96, 219 (n.52); published on stone, 117–18; organization and dating of, 149–52, 230 (n.53), 247 (n.62). *See also* Documents; Drakon: laws of; Law code, Athenian; Solon—laws of

Legislative debate: documents in, 170–76

Leontinoi, Athenian treaty with, 87

Letters: kept in Metroon, 121, 135, 136, 138, 158, 192; cited in forensic speeches, 166, 169

Lēxiarchika grammateia, 82, 135; and Kleisthenic reforms, 55

Logistai, 38, 66, 69, 71, 123–25, 126, 148, 218 (n.30), 238–39 (n.71); accounts of, 71–72, 88

Logographoi. See Speechwriters

Lykourgos: and Metroon, 107, 116–17, 124, 193–94; law of, on tragedies, 134–35

Lysias: attributes law to Drakon, 16; speech *Against Nikomachos*, 27, 97–98, 102, 146, 187; speech *For Man-*

kles, 42, 209 (n. 30); on law of
Lykourgos, 134
Polemarch, 14, 91
Polemon: on *axones*, 27
Pōlētai: employ secretaries, 37, 66; keep
documents, 39, 71; erase documents,
68–70; let out publication contracts,
75; keep documents in Metroon, 127–
29, 135, 145, 147, 148, 149, 158, 192
Poristai: employ undersecretaries, 37
Poseidonios, 189
Poses, 79, 148
Praktores: employ undersecretaries, 37;
in decree of Patrokleides, 111
Praxiergidai inscription, 13
Proposers: names preserved in Me-
troon, 121; cite older decrees, 171–76,
181. *See also* Decrees
Propylaia: accounts of building, 67
Prytaneion: as location of Solonian *axones*, 27, 29–30, 95
Public slaves, 123; in Metroon, 64, 115,
118, 119, 144–45, 158; and *pōlētai* docu-
ments, 68–69, 127–28, 158; in Chal-
kotheke Decree, 125–26
Pythodoros, decree of, 56, 94, 180, 226
(n. 2)
Pythophanes: citizenship decree for, 80

Royal Stoa. *See* Stoa Basileios

Salamis Decree, 8, 54
Samos: accounts of expedition to, 87
Scribes: in sculpture, 40; in vase painting, 56
Secretaries (*grammateis*), 36–41, 66, 86–
87, 190, 216 (n. 13); *epi tois demosiois
grammasi*, 125, 142–43
Secretary *epi ta psēphismata*, 143, 144
Secretary *epi tous nomous*, 142, 143, 245
(n. 31)
Secretary *kata prytaneian*, 140–44, 145,
172, 185, 243 (nn. 6, 7)
Secretary of the Boule: and Drakon's
homicide law, 16, 105; records business of Boule and Ekklesia, 37, 74–78,
81–82, 90, 91–92, 114, 115–16, 122; up-
dates texts of documents, 58, 80; dis-

tributes copies of decrees, 79–80,
158–59, 187; receives documents, 80–
81, 110, 125, 126–27, 136, 142; adds prescripts, 84; name used for filing, 85–
87, 151–52, 157; keeps texts of laws,
104–5, 117–18; conducts inventory,
125; office of reformed, 140–41, 146–
47, 193, 242 (n. 5)
Selymbrian hostages: lists of, 80
Shelving, 148
Skamandrios: law from archonship of,
54, 60
Socrates, 132, 189, 190
Solon: repeals laws of Drakon, 8, 15, 24;
traditions concerning, 9, 24–26
—laws of: extent of, 9, 28–29, 34; called
thesmoi, 13, 201 (n. 33); date of, 24, 202
(n. 55); constitutional, 25, 32–33; survival of, 25–29, 33–34, 52–53, 137, 138,
178, 190, 191, 195; regarding amnesty,
28, 29, 32, 34, 50, 52–53; organized by
magistrates, 29, 204 (n. 77); location
of, 29–31; consultation of, 30–31; impact of, 31–33, 206 (n. 92); innovations in, 32–33; writing in, 35; and
calendar of sacrifices, 39; *naukraroi*
in, 39; treasurers in, 39; on inheritance, 50, 96; archon dates in, 50, 51;
and revision of law code, 94, 96–97,
98–99, 102; coinage in, 204 (n. 75).
See also Axones, Kyrbeis
Sophocles, 108. *See also* Tragedies
Spartokos, 136, 181
Speechwriters (*logographoi*), 160; use of
documents by, 167–68
Spondophoroi: deposit accounts in Metroon, 124, 125
Stelai. *See* Inscriptions
Sthorys of Thasos: honorary decree for,
173
Stoa Basileios: Drakon's homicide law
published at, 16–17; *kyrbeis* in, 29–
30, 95; revised law code published in,
103–4, 117, 165, 166, 187, 227 (n. 20),
230 (n. 45)
Stratokles of Diomeia, 119, 171. *See also*
Telesias
Suda: on dates of dramatic perfor-

CPSIA information can be obtained
at www.ICGtesting.com
Printed in the USA
LVHW05s1747070618
579966LV00002B/203/P